CHAINSAWS,
slackers,
AND
SPY
KIDS

# Thirty Years of Filmmaking in Austin, Texas

UNIVERSITY OF TEXAS PRESS ⩔ AUSTIN

# CHAINSAWS,
## slackers,
## AND
## SPY
## KIDS

ALISON **MACOR**

*The publication of this book was supported in part by the University of Texas Press Advisory Council.*

Copyright © 2010 by Alison Macor
All rights reserved
Printed in the United States of America
Second paperback printing, 2010

Requests for permission to reproduce material
from this work should be sent to:
   Permissions
   University of Texas Press
   P.O. Box 7819
   Austin, TX 78713-7819
   www.utexas.edu/utpress/about/bpermission.html

Library of Congress Cataloging-in-Publication Data

Macor, Alison, 1966–
   Chainsaws, slackers, and spy kids : thirty years of
filmmaking in Austin, Texas / Alison Macor.
         p. cm.
   Includes bibliographical references and index.
   ISBN 978-0-292-70605-7 (cloth : alk. paper) — ISBN 978-0-292-
72243-9 (pbk. : alk. paper)
   1. Motion picture industry—Texas—Austin—History. I. Title.
   PN1993.5.U78M33 2009
   791.4309764′31—dc22                         2009024364

FOR **PAUL**

# Contents

Acknowledgments | ix

**Introduction | 1**
The Hippies and the Cowboys All Looked Alike

**1  A Living Nightmare | 17**
Tobe Hooper and *The Texas Chainsaw Massacre*

**2  Eagle Pennell and the Rise of Regional Filmmaking | 48**

**3  Made in Austin | 64**
The *Austin Chronicle* and *Red Headed Stranger*

**4  *Slacker* | 87**
The Least Auteur Film Ever Made

**5  The *Mariachi* Kid | 115**
Robert Rodriguez and *El Mariachi*

**6  The Reluctant Quarterback | 150**
Richard Linklater and *Dazed and Confused*

**7  Winning the Battle, Losing the War | 188**
*The Newton Boys*

**8  The Company Man | 221**
Tim McCanlies and *Dancer, Texas Pop. 81*

**9** *Office Space* | 249
The Making of a Cult Classic

**10** Rebel With or Without a Crew | 273
Robert Rodriguez and *Spy Kids*

Conclusion | 304
Outside the System, Inside the System

Notes | 315
Selected Bibliography | 345
Index | 347

# Acknowledgments

**T**his book simply wouldn't exist without the generosity of others. I asked for a lot—interviews, phone numbers, photographs, more interviews—and received so much. I suspect that more than a few people made calls or sent e-mails on my behalf, and for that, I will always be grateful.

My greatest thanks go to the more than 150 individuals who agreed to be interviewed (in a few cases, multiple times) for this book. They shared their thoughts, opinions, memories, and, most important, their time. Not all of the interviews made it into the final manuscript, but I found every person's contribution to be helpful as I researched and wrote this history.

I want to thank all of the staff at the University of Texas Press, including Victoria Davis for cheerfully and efficiently shepherding the editing of the manuscript and Jim Burr for his editorial work, insights, and assistance. I am also indebted to the anonymous reviewer who read the first draft and provided invaluable suggestions about content and structure, and to Joe O'Connell, who read a later draft and gave very helpful feedback. I would especially like to thank Dave Hamrick, whose enthusiasm for this project brought it to the attention of the Press in the first place. Thanks also to Evan Smith, who made the introduction.

Special thanks to Steve Wilson and the staff of the Harry Ransom Center's Reading and Viewing Room; Connie Todd, Katie Salzmann, and the staff of the Southwestern Writers Collection at Texas State University-San Marcos;

Richard Linklater; Bud Shrake; Stephanie Friedman; Betty Layton; Sara Johnson Greene; Kirsten McMurray; Suzanne McCanlies; Chuck and René Pinnell; Wyatt McSpadden; Dan Winters; Marjorie Baumgarten; Andrew Long; Martin Chait; John Pierson; Precision Camera & Video; and Agnes Varnum, Chris Esquivel, and the Austin Film Society.

Many friends and colleagues offered their support and encouragement during the seven years it took to complete this book, and I will always be grateful for their friendship. In particular I would like to thank Amy Lowrey, Sue Murray, Chale Nafus, Judith Rhedin, and Amy Schapiro. Additionally I owe a tremendous debt to Teri Sperry, a close friend whose editorial expertise kept this project viable during a particularly difficult time.

My two families, the Macors and the Mitchells, supported me and this project in ways too numerous to list here. I can never thank them enough. My grandfather, Edgar Lehmann, did not live to see the publication of this book, but he rooted for its completion always.

My son Truman was born as I wrapped up this project. He is more entertaining than even the best movie. I am thankful that he was an easygoing infant who didn't seem too bothered by my occasional absences, both mental and physical.

I think Austin just became a magnet
for people who had a different take on
things. Out of that, a scene emerged.
MIKE SIMPSON

# Introduction

## The Hippies and the Cowboys All Looked Alike

A ustin's insular film community is a lot like the Texas high school Richard Linklater dramatized in *Dazed and Confused* (1993): it has its cliques, its hazing rituals, its small-scale dramas, and plenty of comedy. Nowhere was this more in evidence than at the first Texas Film Hall of Fame, which took place on March 8, 2001, on the eve of the annual South by Southwest Film Festival. Pulled together in less than six weeks, the spectacle was the brainchild of Louis Black and Evan Smith. Black is the editor of Austin's alternative weekly newspaper The *Austin Chronicle* and was at the time president of the Austin Film Society (AFS), a nonprofit film organization that Linklater and friends had created in 1985. Smith had recently been promoted to editor of *Texas Monthly* magazine and was a newly appointed AFS board member. The Texas Film Hall of Fame honored such Texans as actor Sissy Spacek and screenwriters Robert Benton and Bill Wittliff. Writer-director Quentin Tarantino, *Cookie's Fortune* screenwriter Anne Rapp, actor Rip Torn, and other celebrities were on hand to pass out the awards. The eclectic mix of honorees, while certainly deserving, also spoke to who was available on such short notice. As the AFS artistic director and a self-proclaimed film purist, Linklater had his doubts about the AFS-sponsored event. The Texas Film Hall of Fame seemed to be less about honoring the art of filmmaking and more about the spectacle of celebrity. Other naysayers worried that they'd quickly run out of deserving Texans.

The Texas Film Hall of Fame unfolded in Austin Studios, a multimedia complex housed in the former airport. Four months earlier, the AFS had finalized a deal with the city to convert part of the airport into much-needed production space for local and out-of-town film and television projects. The twenty-acre complex included a spacious office building and hangars that functioned as soundstages and prop warehouses. Some in the film industry questioned the nonprofit's ability to run a film studio, but on that March evening, Black, Smith, and other members of the film society's board of directors were eager to show off the new facilities. But one look at the chaotic scene hours before the ceremony revealed that the show was far from ready. The hangar stood half-empty as vendors delivered tables, chairs, and flowers. AFS Executive Director Rebecca Campbell barked orders into a walkie-talkie while volunteers scurried around her. And as invited guests and presenters such as former Texas governor Ann Richards entered the hangar later that evening, they could still smell the wet paint drying on the stage.

AFS board member Chale Nafus ran into the former governor a week later, and they chatted about the event. Richards chuckled and made a comment about the evening that could have easily summed up three tumultuous decades of Austin moviemaking. "That," she said in her inimitable drawl, "was an odd party."[1]

The "odd party" that is Austin's independent film production scene and filmgoing culture first took root in the late 1960s and early 1970s. Local filmmakers became energized by the movie industry revolution dubbed the New Hollywood. Films such as *Bonnie and Clyde* (1967), *The Graduate* (1967), and *Easy Rider* (1969) made them think about storytelling and characters in new ways, and emerging film school–educated directors like Martin Scorsese, Francis Ford Coppola, and Steven Spielberg made a career in movies seem almost tangible. "By the late '60s and early '70s," writes Peter Biskind in his chronicle of the period, "if you were young, ambitious, and talented, there was no better place on earth to be than Hollywood." Austin offered a pretty good alternative, however. In the early 1970s Austin was both a fairly conservative state capital and a thriving, progressive college town whose residents numbered 296,000. The city's growth in the preceding decade had mirrored the kind of population explosion typical of much larger Texas cities like Houston and Dallas, yet Austin maintained a laidback feel. The legislature met only every other year, and in the summers many of the university students left town, making the city feel even smaller.[2]

By 1970 nearly twenty movie theaters served the capital city. Two of these theaters, the Varsity and the Texas, were located just across the street from the University of Texas campus, where a handful of university-sponsored film programs screened foreign-language, experimental, and classical Hollywood films. These programs also brought in legendary directors like Fritz Lang and Jean-Luc Godard, while the school's newly created Department of Radio-Television-Film trained aspiring filmmakers. A few freelance production companies stayed busy with commercial work, which helped struggling filmmakers like Tobe Hooper pay the bills and offered access to cameras and other equipment. These various film organizations and institutions nurtured Hooper, Eagle Pennell, and others, who then inspired another generation of filmmakers that included Linklater, Robert Rodriguez, and Mike Judge. This book chronicles the transformation of Austin's homegrown film community, now often called the Third Coast, a term first applied to the state's film industry in the late 1970s; it is the story of how this community began and grew.

The thirty-year history of this regional filmmaking hub involves many converging forces and people, most of whom were (and still are) big personalities. It begins in the early 1970s with the production of Hooper's horror classic *The Texas Chainsaw Massacre. Chainsaw*'s success was integral to the formation and reputation of the local film scene, and its production history reveals the inextricable links among the local and regional film, music, and political communities. For instance, *Chainsaw* had deep ties to state government: Bill Parsley, *Chainsaw*'s primary backer, was a former Texas legislator, and Warren Skaaren, the film's producer's representative, was the head of the Texas Film Commission. Skaaren, who would become a successful Hollywood screenwriter and script doctor responsible for hits like *Top Gun* (1986) and *Batman* (1989), worked behind the scenes to secure *Chainsaw*'s controversial distribution deal with Bryanston Pictures, a company founded by "made men" affiliated with the Colombo crime family.

From *Chainsaw* this story follows the development of the Austin film scene through 2001, a time when the local film community seemed ready to make good on its reputation as the Third Coast. The unexpected success of the first Texas Film Hall of Fame in early March of that year was followed three weeks later by the release of Rodriguez's $35 million action movie *Spy Kids*, most of which was shot, edited, and digitally enhanced in and around Austin. By May, *Spy Kids* had grossed more than $100 million domestically. Tom Copeland, then executive director of the Texas Film Commission, thought the movie had helped Austin's film scene turn a corner. "Outsiders now see Austin as a full-service industry," he said at the time.[3]

In July of that same year, during the tenth anniversary reunion screening of Linklater's first feature, *Slacker* (1991), the signs that Austin's film community had changed significantly were even more visible. Linklater first documented the college town in 1989, but that Austin, as well as most of its hangouts, no longer existed by 2001. And film events like the *Slacker* anniversary screening were no longer the clubby all-night parties they once were, presided over by characters like the late George Morris, a former *Texas Monthly* movie critic, film professor, and Linklater's mentor. Instead, Austin's benefit screenings and movie premieres had become carefully orchestrated events pitched toward a broader audience. They were marketed to appeal to the city's newest residents, many of whom were venture capitalists, entrepreneurs, and young professionals working for high-tech companies like AMD and Motorola and computer giants like Dell. These Austinites were part of the New Texas: geek smart and culturally savvy, they had money to burn.

This is the story of a community that has been shaped as much by Skaaren's creation of the Texas Film Commission in 1971 as by Matthew McConaughey's relocation to Austin in the late 1990s and the blockbuster success that launched the *Spy Kids* franchise. In the decades between these events, Austin's film scene changed radically.

### The Pioneers

Austin's love affair with the movies began long before *The Texas Chainsaw Massacre*. One of Texas's first Kinetoscope parlors opened in Austin in 1894, a mere seven months after the first parlor opened on Broadway in New York.[4] By the 1910s the cinema had begun to replace theater and stage shows as these "live" events became more expensive to produce. Around the same time, film production in Austin became a reality when brothers W. Hope and Paul Tilley relocated their filmmaking equipment from their grandfather's San Antonio garage to Austin in 1911. Prior to their move the brothers had tried to break into the burgeoning freelance market as producers of 35mm newsreel footage. After shooting images of a sixty-foot beached whale and the crowds it attracted when it washed ashore in Port Arthur, Texas, the Tilleys sent their footage to New York's Pathe Freres, the largest newsreel studio at the time. It was promptly rejected.[5]

The Tilleys paired up with movie promoter Charles C. Pyle in 1912. By early 1913 Pyle, who was married to a New York–based actress, had convinced twenty-five Austin businessmen to invest $1,000 each in a local movie production company. Pyle recruited his wife and fourteen other New York actors, named the company Satex (a jumbling of the letters that spell "Texas"), and negotiated a national distribution deal with Warner Bros. Satex set up shop in the Joseph Goodman Building downtown, a few blocks west of the

Capitol and just a few doors down from what in the early 1970s would become the first office of the Texas Film Commission.[6]

Like the local filmmakers who came after them, the Tilley brothers took advantage of Austin's lush natural resources, exploiting the capital city's varied geography of verdant hills to the west and wide prairies to the east, its mild temperatures, and the natural spring that fed into the lower Colorado River. And while many early filmmakers of the time refused to acknowledge public demand for longer movies, Pyle and the Tilleys branched out into longer productions with silent three-reelers like *Their Lives by a Thread* and *Shadow of the Virgin Gold*, which was shot in the nearby Hill Country. The Tilley brothers' homegrown filmmaking enterprise quickly went bust, however. The Satex Film Company closed its Austin office in late 1913 after Warner Bros. went bankrupt and the Satex investors became more and more aggravated with Pyle's shifty accounting.

Two years later, in 1915, Austin's Paragon Feature Film Company made *A Political Touchdown*, a love story that featured local actors and showcased numerous Austin landmarks such as the Governor's Mansion, the University of Texas, and the Capitol. After its sold-out Austin run at the newly opened Majestic Theatre on Congress Avenue, *A Political Touchdown* played in nearly one hundred cities around the country. The stately Majestic was designed by noted Chicago theater architect John Eberson and built for $150,000. Its stage first featured vaudeville acts that gave way to the more popular silent movies and, by the 1930s, sound films. In 1930 the theater underwent a massive renovation after being purchased by the Interstate Theatre Circuit. Upgrades were made inside and out, and the theater was outfitted with air-conditioning and a top-of-the-line sound system that transformed it into a first-run movie palace renamed the Paramount.[7]

Film production would remain sporadic at best in Austin in the coming decades. For a time, the state's larger cities held the most promise of creating and sustaining a regional film center. San Antonio, which boasted the Alamo and Fort Sam Houston as well as several army bases, attracted Hollywood studio films like *Wings* (1927) and *Soldiers in White* (1942). In the late 1940s, Hill Country rancher and businessman James T. "Happy" Shahan began promoting his 22,000-acre Bracketville ranch to these studios, but Shahan's biggest coup was convincing John Wayne to shoot his directorial debut, *The Alamo* (1960), at the ranch. By the late 1960s, most of Texas's film and television industry was centered in Dallas and Houston. Southern Methodist University film professor G. William Jones and Dallasite L. M. Kit Carson co-founded the Screen Generation Film Festival in 1970 and invited director Robert Altman to show a controversial new film called *M\*A\*S\*H*. Carson eventually moved to Los Angeles, and Jones renamed the event the USA Film Festival.[8]

By the early 1980s the state's crew base had swelled to more than 1,000 union members, and Dallas alone boasted more than 300 companies that catered to the film industry. But the real bread and butter of the state's entertainment industry in the 1980s was television work, most of which took place in Dallas. The long-running prime-time series *Dallas* occasionally shot on location beginning in 1978, but it was the many made-for-television movies (MTMs) and movies of the week (MOWs) that brought the most work into the city beginning around 1983.[9]

Like Dallas, Houston also had its share of film and television work in the 1970s and 1980s, and the city also nurtured an independent film scene with the help of several organizations designed to encourage regional filmmaking. The Southwest Alternate Media Project, or SWAMP, was co-founded in the mid-1970s by Rice University film professor James Blue. SWAMP, which became a nonprofit organization in 1977, would provide finishing funds to many Austin-based filmmakers over the next two decades.[10]

As with other states across the nation, Texas experienced a proliferation of film production and studies programs on college campuses by the 1970s. The University of Texas established its own Radio-Television-Film (RTF) program in the fall of 1965 within a new School of Communication. The school's director, Dr. DeWitt Reddick, envisioned an RTF department along with programs in journalism and speech that combined hands-on experience and scholarly research. It was a progressive idea for its time, and it had the potential to differentiate UT's RTF program from its competitors on both coasts. Reddick recruited Stanley Donner (who had been director of Stanford University's radio and television program) to chair the RTF department. Initially the department operated out of the campus Radio-TV building, which also housed local PBS television station KLRN and backed up to the university's main administration building, known as the Tower. When Charles Whitman began shooting from the Tower's observation deck just before noon on August 1, 1966, the KLRN staff took one of their studio cameras, rolled it out onto the roof of the Radio-TV building, and trained its lens on the Tower. The images their camera recorded that day provided the news feed for stations across the country.[11]

Donner eventually stepped down as RTF department chair and was replaced by Rod Whitaker, who arrived to teach in 1966. "Whitaker used to say, 'If you want to contemplate your navel, go to UCLA. If you want to learn to make films, come to Texas,'" remembers production manager Bill Scott, who was one of the department's earliest graduate students. "Whitaker's mandate was to foster production," explains former RTF instructor Ron Policy of Whitaker's somewhat controversial decision to partner with various state agencies in order to supplement the department's insufficient equipment budget. Graduate student Richard Kooris, for instance, made his master's thesis film for the Texas Aeronautics Commission. "They paid us, and since we had free labor and free facilities, about 80 percent of what they paid us was profit. So we took all that money and we used it to buy more equipment."[12]

Whitaker stepped down as chair in 1974 and was replaced by Bob Davis, a professor at Southern Illinois University at Carbondale. Newly graduated with a doctoral degree in film history from the University of Iowa, Thomas Schatz was one of Davis's six new faculty hires in the mid-1970s. Young and ambitious, Schatz represented the department chair's attempts to expand and energize the department. "What Davis was about was socializing and program building," Schatz recalls. Davis threw parties at his west Austin home, where he carried around a pitcher of margaritas, and UT faculty members and graduate students mingled with some of Austin's literary lights like nationally known writers Bud Shrake and Gary Cartwright. Guests strummed guitars and passed joints. One of Davis's most important hires in the late 1970s was former blacklisted screenwriter Edward Dmytryk. Down on his luck in Hollywood, Dmytryk reluctantly agreed to teach film production and screenwriting courses in Texas. Recalls *Austin Chronicle* film critic Marjorie Baumgarten, who was a graduate student at the time, "Dmytryk was one of the first big experiments for the department, to bring in a real professional."[13]

When the university's aspiring filmmakers weren't learning their craft, they were soaking up movies in Austin's four-wall and drive-in theaters. The Varsity and the Texas were located on the edge of the UT campus. The Varsity screened a mix of studio films and specialty releases, while the Texas's schedule of soft-core pornography was interspersed with new foreign films like Ingmar Bergman's *Cries and Whispers* (1972). A handful of university film programs tried to fill the artistic gap with varying degrees of success. In the process, these programs nurtured a generation of passionate filmgoers who became industry leaders, like Sony Pictures Classics co-founder Michael Barker. These university-sponsored screenings also attracted non-students, cultivating a filmgoing culture that still exists today.[14]

The University Film Program Committee (UFPC), formed in 1953, screened foreign classics at Batts Auditorium. Restricted to students, faculty, and staff, the free screenings offered audiences movies from around the globe and were fairly popular until the early 1970s, when the program went under because of financial troubles and an indifferent administration. In 1965 UT students Greg Barrios and David Berman started the volunteer-run Cinema 40 Film Society to bring alternative movies to Austin. Cinema 40 often invited directors to present their films, and in the spring of 1967 French filmmaker Jean-Luc Godard gave a bilingual lecture before he screened one of his own previously unreleased films. Two years later, Andy Warhol showed some of his movies to a sold-out crowd. *Esquire* film critic Dwight MacDonald marveled at the organization's cutting-edge film programming after a visit in the late 1960s: "While I was in Texas . . . I was able to see for the first time some films by Warhol and [Kenneth] Anger, both programs being put on by Cinema 40, a student film club operated with great enterprise."[15]

In 1970 undergraduate students Michael Shelton and Shannon Sedwick (who would later create the long-running local comedy sketch troupe Esther's Follies) organized a film series called the Museum of Light, which programmed experimental and underground films. "This media is not to be confused with the Godards, the Antonionis, the Resnaises, or the Bergmans, who are actually the Establishment with subtitles," opined Austin's underground weekly, the *Austin Rag*, by way of promoting the series.[16] The Museum of Light, which Shelton and Sedwick also created to assist local independent filmmakers by screening their work and paying them directly, lasted only through 1973.

A year after the Museum of Light began, RTF faculty members Richard Kooris and Ron Policy founded a nonprofit film program called CinemaTexas. Run by graduate students for course credit, CinemaTexas initially was designed to screen the films that were being discussed in RTF history and theory classes. "We're talking about a time when the idea of a cinema studies program was still kind of new. We're talking about a time when, without home video, you got excited to get your hands on a 16mm print and be able to play it over and over, and really be able to analyze it," says George Lellis, who served as the program's first editor.[17]

Charles Ramírez Berg had quit a high school teaching job in San Antonio to enroll in the RTF graduate program in the spring of 1972, and he immediately gravitated to CinemaTexas. The series began by showing movies two nights per week and eventually expanded to four weeknights. Lellis, Ramírez Berg, and other graduate students wrote "Program Notes" to fulfill part of their course requirements in film criticism, and these informative and often thoughtful analyses eventually earned the program an international reputation. Reportedly, *The New Yorker* film critic Pauline Kael received the notes on a subscription basis.[18]

Of all the film groups that originated on the UT campus, CinemaTexas and Cinema 40 had the most influence on the film tastes of students, local film aficionados, and Austin filmmakers. Says Cathy Crane, who arrived at the university in 1975 and later worked with Richard Linklater, "You'd be walking around campus and there'd be three or four cool places to see movies. You'd go in and half the people would be film students and the other half would be people who were just interested in movies. Then you'd come out and all these people would congregate and start talking."[19] The RTF program proved to be a training ground for future filmmakers, cinematographers, and other crew as well as critics, writers, and teachers.

But the RTF program wasn't a perfect fit for everyone. Larry Carroll, who edited *The Texas Chainsaw Massacre*, was a master's student in the department in the 1960s. "We decided that making movies was much more fun than being graduate students, and there weren't a whole lot of opportunities to work on theatrical films. Documentaries were a blast, but there was no money in them, even if you could get a grant, so we created Shootout Films," recalls Carroll. He and fellow graduate students Daniel Pearl and Ted Nicolaou went into business with Kooris and sound recordist Courtney Goodin. The group collaborated on freelance film projects in the early 1970s, but they didn't organize formally as a commercial production business until 1974, after Kooris left his teaching position at UT. Kooris and his wife bought out the partners a year later and opened Texas Pacific Film, a production company that continued to expand. By the mid-1980s the company was booking two to three jobs per month and training generations of crew in Austin. Richard Linklater's longtime cinematographer, Lee Daniel, began working there in 1984. Like so many others before him, Daniel trained on the job with Kooris, who had high expectations for his crew and could be demanding and abrasive. Still, says Daniel, "he was mentor and teacher to all these people that came through his company. He gave people every chance in the world to excel. He was very egalitarian."[20]

Feature film work was rare in Austin in the early 1970s, but a number of state agencies supplied enough work to establish a healthy battle between Shootout and its primary competition, Richard Kidd's Motion Picture Productions of Texas, which became Filmhouse around 1970. In the early 1960s Kidd worked as a news cameraman at KTBC, one of the television stations owned by Lyndon Johnson. There Kidd met fellow cameraman Gary Pickle, and the two left the station around 1966 to start their own freelance film production house. They hustled commercial work from banks and other local businesses, occasionally hiring freelancers like Kooris.[21]

A year or so after opening his business, Kidd met filmmakers Tobe Hooper and Ron Perryman. Born in 1943, Hooper grew up immersed in the movies. Around the impressionable age of seven, Hooper began reading the EC comics series. "I loved them," Hooper recalled. "They were not in any way based on logic. To enjoy them you had to accept that there is a Bogey Man out there." These horror tales and the movies he consumed growing up contributed to his later development as a filmmaker, a talent that he began cultivating in high school while making 8mm horror movies. By the mid-1960s Hooper had made a number of his own films, including an eleven-minute period comedy called *The Heisters*, which he shot in 35mm with Perryman acting as director of photography. Perryman and Hooper collaborated on Hooper's 1969 psychedelic art film *Eggshells*. Hooper, who eventually would become best known for a film about cannibals in rural Texas, also worked with Perryman on *Peter, Paul & Mary: Song Is Love* (1970), a PBS documentary produced by Fred Miller about the popular folk trio. "In the 60s Ron was kind of a guru to Tobe," remembered Kidd. "Tobe was a great cinematographer, had a really good eye, but he loved collaboration, which Ron really provided him with— they'd talk over shots for hours, figure out some crazy way to rig the camera, hang the lights, whatever." After Kidd saw *Down Friday Street,* a short film Hooper and Perryman co-directed in the late 1960s about the demolition of an Austin building, he knew he wanted to work with the talented filmmakers. He convinced Hooper and Perryman to join forces with him and Pickle.[22]

While Shootout and Filmhouse provided production services in the mid-1970s, Ivan Bigley's Texas Motion Picture Service (TMPS) functioned mainly as a post-production facility. TMPS, which operated into the late 1990s, provided completion services for nearly three generations of filmmakers. TMPS gave locals like Richard Linklater a place to edit and mix their films and provided out-of-town productions like *The Best Little Whorehouse in Texas* (1982) a facility to screen dailies, which Bigley often projected himself. "Practically everybody who ever did a film, anywhere, any time, went to Ivan," says Tom Copeland, who worked as a makeup artist on commercial shoots in the 1970s before transitioning to location scouting for the Texas Film Commission. In 1967 after Bigley finished his service in the Vietnam War, he relocated to Austin as a cameraman for Earl Miller Productions, which produced programming for KLRN. Miller sensed the industry was moving toward video technology and decided to expand into television production, but Bigley staunchly supported film. In 1975 he was able to create TMPS with backing from an investor eager to branch into the film business. Located northeast of the university, the original facilities included editing equipment, an eight-track mixing board, and a thirty-seat screening room. Joel and Ethan Coen screened footage at TMPS in 1982 while making *Blood Simple* in and around Austin and developed great affection for Bigley, who allowed cash-poor students and independent filmmakers to use his facilities, often at no cost. "Ivan did a good job at servicing UT and the film industry," says Sandra Adair, Richard Linklater's longtime editor. "I don't think films could have been finished in Austin had TMPS not been there."[23]

TMPS, Shootout, and Filmhouse, in addition to the University of Texas's RTF program and its campus film series, made up the initial infrastructure of the Austin film community in the 1960s and 1970s. These businesses and organizations trained many of the cast and crew that Tobe Hooper hired for *The Texas Chainsaw Massacre*, which began principal photography in the summer of 1973. This particular moment in Austin's history reveals the converging forces that helped to nurture the city's vibrant cultural scene.

Young people had been coming to Austin to attend the University of Texas since 1883, but the 1960s marked a gradual shift in Austin's population profile. Although the university more than doubled its enrollment between 1960 and 1970, two-thirds of the city's newest residents in 1970 were not students but young adults, perhaps drawn by the city's newly hip music scene. Austin's City Council noted the typically transient nature of this particular new population group and wondered whether the young people would stay long enough to make significant contributions to the Austin community. "On the other hand," reasoned the council in a 1973 study, "the newcomers bring a vitality to the city, an open mind and a fresh approach. Austin was their 'city of choice.'"[24]

It was at a Willie Nelson concert in 1972 that many people began to see clearly the creative potential in Austin. Nelson's concert at Armadillo World Headquarters memorably brought together country and western and rock 'n' roll fans. "All of a sudden the hippies and the cowboys all looked alike," said writer Bud Shrake.[25] Like many creative types, Shrake moved easily between Austin's music and film scenes. By the early 1970s, he had published a few novels and was writing for *Sports Illustrated*. He was splitting his time between a house in Austin and an apartment in Manhattan. It was in New York in 1969, after seeing *Butch Cassidy and the Sundance Kid*, that he was inspired to write his first screenplay. Originally titled *Dime Box* after the small Texas town where the story took place, the script eventually became *Kid Blue* (1973), a comic western starring Dennis Hopper.

Once Shrake finished *Kid Blue,* he sent it to his New York agent, who eventually got it to Hollywood producer Marvin Schwartz. Schwartz showed the script to Twentieth Century Fox studio head Darryl Zanuck, who greenlighted the project. Although *Kid Blue* was in the can by the end of 1971, the movie's release was held up for more than a year. It eventually opened in 1973, and *Kid Blue* was selected as one of only three American films to play in the New York Film Festival that year. Shrake was convinced that the movie would take off, but it didn't. "When *Easy Rider* came out, Hopper insulted everybody out in Hollywood. And so they were all just waiting for his next movie, which was mine," Shrake said. "*Kid Blue* was a lesson for me that I learned two or three times about how petty or nasty the studios could be."[26]

### Warren Skaaren and the Texas Film Commission

Austin was worlds away from Hollywood, which is one of the reasons writers like Shrake based himself there. But something about the unassuming city with its mix of counterculture wannabes and conservative politicos—a place where hippies skinny-dipping in a local watering hole counted as a tourist attraction—managed to attract a fairly steady stream of film industry insiders. Some of the politicians recognized the inherent business value of this and, in the late 1960s, began actively to cultivate film production by creating the Texas Film Commission. And while this government agency was created to promote film production across the entire state, its location in Austin meant that local filmmakers could more easily establish a relationship with its staff.

Warren Skaaren was a senior at Rice University in 1969 when he first met Jerry Hall, press secretary for Governor Preston Smith. Skaaren, who was student body president, had been invited to spend the weekend visiting the governor's office. The weekend began with a dinner on Friday night, where the governor's staff visited with the students. Remembered Hall, "The next morning, this intent-looking guy came over and introduced himself and said, 'I'm Warren Skaaren.' We talked a little bit. The next thing I know, he turns up in Austin working on the governor's staff."[27]

Skaaren was a quick study of human behavior and seemed to have an uncanny ability to zero in on a person's vulnerabilities, which he related to with empathy. This quality would prove instrumental later in life when as a screenwriter he would interact with Hollywood's powerful but often fragile egos on projects like *Top Gun.* "Warren worked with Tony Scott and Tom Cruise to fix that film," recalls Mike Simpson, executive vice president at

William Morris Agency and Skaaren's former agent. "Tom Cruise was bailing on the picture, and Warren saved the movie."[28]

After Skaaren graduated from Rice in 1969, he moved to Austin so he could begin working within the Texas Department of Health and Human Services. Over the next two years Skaaren would become a valued member of the governor's staff. Ron Bozman, who in 1992 would win a producing Academy Award for *The Silence of the Lambs,* was Skaaren's good friend and college roommate. "Warren was in the inner circle of those guys around Preston Smith," Bozman recalls.[29]

Bill Parsley, a good friend of Hall's and the primary investor in *The Texas Chainsaw Massacre,* moved within this circle as well. A former state legislator who became Vice President of Public Affairs at Texas Tech University in 1965, Parsley first met Hall in Lubbock while they were both students at Tech. Parsley had come from less than humble beginnings in a small town north of Abilene, toiling in the fields pulling vegetables and enduring hard physical labor. But by the time Parsley arrived in Lubbock in the 1950s, he had reinvented himself. He had confidence to spare, and he saw himself as something of a ladies' man. "He hit campus, and word got around immediately that he had worked for Paramount Pictures," Hall remembered, although no one was ever really sure if he had.[30]

One day in 1969, not long after Hall began working as Governor Smith's press secretary, Parsley called from Lubbock. He had seen an item in the newspaper that piqued his interest. "What do you know about film commissions?" asked Parsley.

"Nothing," Hall replied.

"Well," Parsley said, "I'm going to see what I can find out about them."[31]

New Mexico had formed a film commission in 1968 and managed to convince director Sam Peckinpah to shoot scenes for *The Ballad of Cable Hogue* in Santa Fe. After doing a little research of his own, Hall realized that he knew Charlie Cullum, who headed up the New Mexico Film Commission. He consulted with Cullum a few times by phone before he and Parsley presented a proposal to Governor Smith. Skaaren heard about the project and approached Hall about running the operation. Skaaren had some experience with the film business, if only by association with Bozman, his Rice roommate. "I was working in films since 1968, so Warren had been around the film business by just hanging out with me," Bozman remembers.[32]

Governor Smith, a former theater owner, gave Parsley and Hall the go-ahead to draft a resolution. In the end, they wrangled $400,000 from the state's budget surplus to create the Texas Film Commission, which was housed in the governor's office. Hall and Parsley also put together an advisory board with notable individuals chosen primarily to increase the commission's glamour quotient. Actress and Dallas resident Dorothy Malone joined the board, as did former Lyndon Baines Johnson special assistant Jack Valenti, who had since become the head of Hollywood's self-censorship organization, the Motion Picture Association of America (MPAA). Skaaren was just twenty-four years old when Governor Smith officially appointed him as executive director on December 9, 1970.[33]

The commission's first office, opened in May 1971, was on the top floor of a downtown apartment building called The Penthouse, just a few blocks west of the Capitol. Although the building itself was impressive, the office was little more than a couple of desks and chairs and a few filing cabinets. Almost immediately Skaaren purchased a 35mm still camera. He took it with him on road trips throughout the state, photographing possible film locations and slowly building an impressive file.

One of Skaaren's first coups as director of the film commission was convincing producers of *The Getaway* to shoot in Texas. Directed by Sam Peckinpah, the $4 million studio picture filmed in El Paso, Huntsville, and elsewhere beginning in January 1972. Skaaren's business savvy impressed *Getaway* producer David Foster, who had produced Robert Altman's *McCabe and Mrs. Miller* a year earlier. "The thing about Warren is that he understood movies and he understood the problems. A lot of guys just do the job and try to con you into working in their state. Warren actually knew the business of making movies. He sure as hell knew what he was talking about. Or, even if he didn't, he knew what we needed, and that was the important thing for us," recalls Foster. Skaaren arranged for the crew to destroy a bank in San Marcos and other old buildings in El Paso, and he paved the way for the use of the state prison in Huntsville. "He would find places like that where we could do whatever we wanted to do, which Peckinpah loved," Foster says. "Skaaren was like a bulldog, but in a nice way. He had great style and great taste and was a real gentleman. And yet he knew, we needed that prison, goddammit, and he was going to get us that prison."[34]

Skaaren worked tirelessly to please the out-of-towners and ensure smooth sailing on the production, and he did the same for the nearly forty features that came through the state while he was head of the film commission. Sidney Lumet shot *Lovin' Molly* in and around Austin; Steven Spielberg filmed *The Sugarland Express* in Sugarland, Del Rio, San Antonio, and Floresville; Brian de Palma lensed *Phantom of the Paradise* in Dallas; and George Roy Hill filmed *The Great Waldo Pepper* throughout Central Texas. Skaaren's quiet charisma put him on a par with the Hollywood people. He could deal with the outsized personalities and egos coming in from Los Angeles without overshadowing them. "He was like a *Wizard of Oz* character that was very mysterious and able to do these magical things like suddenly showing up at the airport with Steve McQueen," says Bill Broyles, who at the time was preparing to launch *Texas Monthly* magazine. "Warren was moving in a world that none of us could even imagine. He just made things happen."[35] Skaaren was very good at what he did, amassing contacts for himself and the state and bringing in plenty of business. But as the years passed, he felt a growing dissatisfaction about his involvement behind the scenes. Despite the access it gave him to the Hollywood filmmaking community, Skaaren was ambivalent about heading up the state's film commission. He really wanted to write movies but felt not quite ready. His stifled creative side revealed itself in sketches, metal sculptures, and charming letters he penned to friends and associates.

In May of 1973, while still at the film commission, Skaaren used this charm as well as his contacts on behalf of Tobe Hooper, who was planning to direct his second feature from a script he had co-written with Kim Henkel called *Leatherface*. Skaaren sent a letter about Hooper to a Hollywood distributor, and he spent the better part of its three and a half pages extolling the marketing potential of the unproduced script. Skaaren wrote convincingly of Hooper's talent, calling him "straight" and "very bright" with a superior sense of design and layout, as demonstrated in the advertising campaign for his first feature *Eggshells*. That film's fatal flaw, Skaaren wrote, was its artiness and inability to attract audiences. But that would not be the case with the horror movie *Leatherface* (retitled *The Texas Chainsaw Massacre*). Skaaren explained that in exchange for the distributor's help with the project, he was in for a cut of the producer's profits, but he was quick to note that his own work was strictly behind the scenes. "My name will not be on the picture, that would not be a good public first pix for the Ex. Director of the Gov's Film Commission to be involved with," Skaaren explained, and he closed the letter by asking his friend not to reveal his involvement to anyone.[36]

Skaaren met with Austin lawyer Robert Kuhn, a friend of Parsley's who would handle legal work for *Chainsaw* and put up $9,000 of the initial budget. They discussed how to skirt any potential conflicts of interest between Skaaren's involvement in the project and his position at the film commission. "Even though it might have violated somebody's rules, it didn't violate mine. Everybody wanted him to do what he did," says Kuhn of Skaaren's lobbying for *Chainsaw* during his tenure as film commissioner. "He was doing

*Chainsaw* while he was there, but he wasn't doing it by depriving or setting back the film commission," Kuhn insists. Still, Skaaren was uneasy about the potential conflict and would express more than a little ambivalence about the project to industry friends like Foster, who agreed to line up meetings with potential distributors once the film was finished. Kuhn thought Skaaren deserved whatever monetary benefits he might get for all the work he was doing trying to find a distributor for the film, and he helped an anxious Skaaren navigate the legal issues involved. "Relax, Skaaren," Kuhn told him. "You won't go to hell yet."[37]

The Tilley brothers (ca. 1913), two of Austin's earliest filmmakers.
(PICA 20477, Austin History Center, Austin Public Library.)

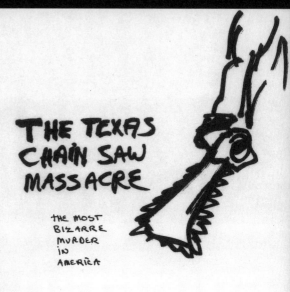

THE TEXAS
CHAIN SAW
MASSACRE

THE MOST
BIZARRE
MURDER
IN
AMERICA

The grapevine on Joe and Lou Peraino

Both have been convicted in New York
Both have a city of new york "B" number (bad guy number)
Both have an FBI number
Joe Sr. Had two sons- Anthony and Joe
Anthony is Joe and Lou's father, Joe is their uncle.
Lou was born June 16, 1940
They are connected closely with the Columbo family.
They are personal freinds of Joe Jr. (Columbo)
They are freinds of the Gangino brothers.
They are alleged to have Drug connections with Robert Leno
Their trade has been stolen goods and Pornography.

*above:* "A director with a real vision": Tobe Hooper, producer-writer-director of *The Texas Chainsaw Massacre.* Courtesy of Austin Film Society.

*facing top:* Promoting *The Texas Chainsaw Massacre*: an early marketing concept sketched by Warren Skaaren. Courtesy of the Warren Skaaren Collection, Harry Ransom Humanities Research Center, University of Texas at Austin.

*facing below:* The fruits of Warren Skaaren's research into the Perainos, who owned Bryanston Pictures and distributed *The Texas Chainsaw Massacre.* Courtesy of the Warren Skaaren Collection, Harry Ransom Humanities Research Center, University of Texas at Austin.

*above:* Sonny Carl Davis (foreground) and Lou Perryman shooting a scene for
*The Whole Shootin' Match.* Photo by Vera Carmignani. Courtesy of Lou Perryman.

*facing above:* Crew and cast members of *The Whole Shootin' Match*: (l to r, back)
soundman Wayne Bell, an unidentified extra, art director Jim Rexrode, cinematographer Doug Holloway, Sonny Carl Davis; (l to r, front) director Eagle Pennell,
Lou Perryman. Courtesy of Doug Holloway.

*facing below:* Eagle Pennell (left) and Sonny Carl Davis on the set of
*Last Night at the Alamo.* Photo by and courtesy of Eric Edwards.

*facing above:* Eagle Pennell (left) and Kim Henkel in Mexico.
Courtesy of Chuck Pinnell.

*facing below:* "He was the teacher of us all": Ed Lowry, a program notes
editor for the fabled University of Texas CinemaTexas film series and the
*Austin Chronicle*'s first film editor. Photo by and courtesy of Martin Chait.

*above:* Nick Barbaro (left) and Louis Black in the early 1980s. Currently
publisher and editor, respectively, of the *Austin Chronicle,* Barbaro and
Black also co-founded the highly successful South by Southwest media
festival. Photo by and courtesy of Andrew Long.

*top:* On the set of *Red Headed Stranger*: (l to r) art director Cary White, production coordinator David Anderson, writer-director-producer Bill Wittliff, star and producer Willie Nelson. Courtesy of Cary White.

*below left:* Willie Nelson and Morgan Fairchild on the Willieville set of *Red Headed Stranger*. Photo by Cate Hardman. Courtesy of Bill Wittliff Papers, Southwestern Writers Collection, Texas State University–San Marcos.

*below right:* After eight long years and countless deals, Bill Wittliff and Willie Nelson finally film *Red Headed Stranger*. Photo by Cate Hardman. Courtesy of Bill Wittliff Papers, Southwestern Writers Collection, Texas State University–San Marcos.

This film has no intention of attracting nor pleasing the spectator; indeed, on the contrary, it attacks him, to the degree that he belongs to a society with which surrealism is at war. (*Un Chien Andalou*)

# MIDNIGHT EXPERIMENTAL FILM SERIES

this weekend—

# SEXUALITY AND BLASPHEMY IN THE AVANT GARDE

Luis Bunuel and Salvador Dali : "Un Chien Andalou"
Kenneth Anger : "Scorpio Rising"
Barbara Hammer : "Multiple Orgasm"
George Griffin : "The Club"
Curt McDowell : "Nudes(A Sketchbook)"

2 $

fri and sat @ midnight    sun matinee @ 1:00pm
DOBIE SCREENS   21st and Drag
MIDNIGHT EXPERIMENTAL FILM SERIES: first weekends of the month at DOBIE SCREENS

A flier promoting the Austin Film Society's first screening
in October 1985. Courtesy of Austin Film Society.

*facing:* Richard Linklater during postproduction on *Slacker.* Courtesy of Detour Filmproduction.

*left:* Cinematographer Lee Daniel, a co-founder of the Austin Film Society and director of photography on six of Richard Linklater's feature films. Courtesy of Austin Film Society.

*below:* Teresa Taylor peddles Madonna's Pap smear in *Slacker.* Courtesy of Detour Filmproduction.

*top:* Carlos Gallardo on the Ciudad Acuña set of *El Mariachi.* Director Robert Rodriguez is behind the film camera (foreground). Courtesy of Carlos Gallardo.

*below:* Carlos Gallardo (left) and Robert Rodriguez toasting the production of *Desperado,* the sequel to *El Mariachi.* Courtesy of Carlos Gallardo.

*facing:* "A shot of adrenaline": Matthew McConaughey reprises Wooderson, his scene-stealing character in *Dazed and Confused,* for photographer Dan Winters in 2003. Photo by and courtesy of Dan Winters.

Frank Kozik's black light poster for *Dazed and Confused,* which Gramercy Pictures did not use to promote the film. ©Kozik. Photo by Stephanie Friedman. Courtesy of Detour Filmproduction.

Tim Dingle's watercolor poster for *The Newton Boys*. Instead, Twentieth Century Fox chose a non-period-specific image to market the movie. Photo by Stephanie Friedman. Courtesy of Detour Filmproduction.

*above:* Richard Linklater (left) and John Pierson at an event for the Texas Filmmakers' Production Fund, created by the Austin Film Society in 1996 to award grants to regional filmmakers. Photo by Chris Caselli for the Austin Film Society.

*below:* King of the hill: Mike Judge filming in Austin. Courtesy of Mike Judge.

Harry Knowles, whose Ain't It Cool News web site first attracted industry attention (and ire) in the late 1990s. Photo by and courtesy of Dan Winters.

*facing above:* A reflective Tim McCanlies (seated on tree limb) on the set of *Dancer, Texas*. Photo by and courtesy of Suzanne McCanlies.

*facing below:* State Highway 166 during the media firestorm surrounding the Republic of Texas militia standoff, which occurred just weeks before the start of production on *Dancer, Texas*. Photo by and courtesy of Suzanne McCanlies.

*above:* State Highway 166, the desolate two-lane blacktop featured in the opening scene of *Dancer, Texas Pop. 81*. Photo by and courtesy of Suzanne McCanlies.

*facing above:* "A real immediate kinship": Robert Rodriguez and Elizabeth Avellán in 1998. Photo by and courtesy of Wyatt McSpadden.

*facing below:* Austin's Congress Avenue hosts a street carnival for the 2001 benefit premiere of *Spy Kids*, which raised money for the Austin Film Society and Austin's Ronald McDonald House. The Paramount Theatre is on the right. Courtesy of Austin Film Society.

*above:* A homegrown blockbuster: Robert Rodriguez and Elizabeth Avellán thank the City of Austin in an advertisement in the *Austin Chronicle* to celebrate *Spy Kids*'s $100 million success. Courtesy of Troublemaker Studios.

*above:* Richard Linklater (left) and Rebecca Campbell pose with director Martin Scorsese and actor Kevin Spacey after receiving the Directors Guild of America's first Honors Award in 1999. The award honored the Austin Film Society for its dedication to regional film culture and production. Courtesy of Austin Film Society.

*below:* If you honor them, they will come: Rip Torn inducts Sissy Spacek at the first Texas Film Hall of Fame, a star-studded fundraising gala launched by the Austin Film Society in 2001. Courtesy of Austin Film Society.

# 1

Tobe Hooper was a director with
a real vision. Even if it meant
killing all of us to get it.
DOROTHY PEARL

# A Living Nightmare

## Tobe Hooper and *The Texas Chainsaw Massacre*

- - - - - - - - - - - - - - - - - - - - - - - - - - - - - - - - - - - - - - - - - -

The white Victorian house at the top of Quick Hill Road reverberated with the sound of a woman's muffled cries. Inside the dimly lit dining room, a pretty blonde struggled against the ropes binding her to a chair. She was seated at the head of a long dining table, its wood splintered and distressed. Streaks of dried blood and dirt caked her light blue tank top and white jeans, and her long hair hung in lank bunches around her face. She could hear faltering footsteps coming down a staircase somewhere to her left. Two figures entered the room carrying a chair that held a decrepit man, his facial features barely visible beneath folds of aged, leathery skin.

The smaller of the two men got behind the woman's chair, reached down and with a pocketknife cut the rope and freed her right arm. The other man, his face hidden by a crude mask made from human skin, reached for a small carving knife that lay on the table. The masked figure reached over and clamped his beefy hand around her wrist. She began to feel faint. He sliced the tip of her index finger, and a bright bubble of blood oozed from the wound. He slowly guided her finger into the dried-out mouth of the old man, who began to suckle it like an infant as the others watched with morbid fascination. Her eyes grew wide at the spectacle, and she screamed with revulsion. Her eyes rolled back in her head as her body slumped forward toward the table.

A wiry, bearded man dressed in a dark workshirt stepped from the shadows at the side of the room and spoke quietly to Marilyn Burns, the actress who was playing the young woman. "Do the fainting again, Marilyn," said director Tobe Hooper as cinematographer Daniel Pearl and his assistant, Linn Lockwood, rearranged themselves on the floor.[1] Burns slumped back in the chair.

They spent nearly an hour shooting ten takes of the harrowing scene, which lasted less than two minutes in the final cut of *The Texas Chainsaw Massacre*. Hooper's meticulousness and relentless drive in capturing the scene, which marked the beginning of the film's "last supper" and penultimate horror sequence, defined the beleaguered two-month production. Within months of *Chainsaw*'s 1974 release, however, the cast and crew's hard work seemed to pay off. The homegrown Austin film exploded at the box office and earned critical praise—and raised some critical ire—that continues to this day. Although *Chainsaw* has its fair share of gore, it also makes effective use of a semi-documentary style realism that intensifies its most horrific scenes. By 1975 the film was playing midnight shows after developing a second life as a cult movie. *Chainsaw* inspired five prequels, sequels, and remakes and numerous documentaries and video games, although none of them has come close to duplicating the splash of the original 1974 film. Thirty years after its initial release, *Chainsaw* still came in at number six in *Entertainment Weekly*'s profile of the top 50 cult films of all time.[2]

*Chainsaw* was the first Austin feature to break out both commercially and critically, and its success shined brightly on the fledgling local film scene. The movie launched the Hollywood careers of cinematographer Daniel Pearl, makeup artist Dottie Pearl, and producer Ron Bozman, among others, and it earned Hooper and co-screenwriter Kim Henkel a multi-film development deal at Universal Pictures. *Chainsaw* gave Warren Skaaren the confidence to cut ties with the Texas Film Commission and become a player in the national film industry. But as many people connected with *Chainsaw* have observed, the real horror unfolded off-screen after Skaaren and others brokered the film's distribution deal with Bryanston Pictures, a company that would be brought up on obscenity charges for distributing the landmark adult film *Deep Throat* (1972). While *Chainsaw*'s behind-the-scenes drama tells a familiar—if uniquely colorful—tale of independent filmmakers making their way in Hollywood, it was an uncommon experience for the film's local cast and crew, one that served to introduce the Austin movie community to the seedy underbelly of the Hollywood film industry.

## A Monster Is Born

The production, whose initial working title was *Headcheese*, began shooting in July of 1973. Within months, *Headcheese* would be renamed *The Texas Chainsaw Massacre*, a stroke of marketing genius ostensibly thought up during a late-night poker game. Its relatively young and inexperienced cast and crew were a cross-section of Austin's nascent film scene. Most were graduates of UT's RTF program, and some had done freelance film and television work for local production companies like Shootout or Filmhouse.

The *Chainsaw* script sprang from the fertile minds of Hooper and Henkel. In a town overflowing with transient residents and newcomers from other places, Hooper was that rare thing: a native Austinite. Born in 1943, Hooper grew up immersed in the movies in part because his father owned a movie theater in San Angelo. Later, Hooper attended classes in UT's RTF program, and he studied drama with director Sidney Lumet's father, who taught in Dallas. By his early twenties Hooper had assembled a body of film work that included commercial projects, documentaries, and short narrative films. His comedic short *The Heisters* (1965) caught the attention of the Academy of Motion Picture Arts and Sciences, who invited the filmmaker to enter the film in their short subject category. (Unfinished at the time of the request, *The Heisters* didn't qualify for that year's competition.)[3] But it was Hooper's first feature, *Eggshells* (1969), described in its press kit as "an American freak illumination" about a group of young people, "undergrounders living in a house which is possessed by a cryptoembryonic, hyperelectric presence," that introduced him to Kim Henkel.[4]

Henkel had been an English major at UT, hoping to become a writer. Born in Virginia, Henkel spent his childhood moving around South Texas and living in small towns thanks to his father's various newspaper jobs. By the time Henkel went off to college in Austin in 1964, he had lived in no fewer than five Texas towns.

Henkel flirted briefly with a military career after graduating from UT in 1969 and then met Hooper through mutual friends that same year, just before Hooper began shooting *Eggshells*. The normally camera-shy Henkel agreed to co-star in Hooper's psychedelic feature, but rather than use his real name, Henkel worked under the pseudonym Boris Schnurr. Wayne Bell, who had met Hooper while working at Filmhouse, served as a "guy Friday" on *Eggshells*, doing a little bit of everything on the production. The film, according to Bell and others, was very much a product of the late 1960s. "It was a very psychedelic, playful film that was dated as soon as it came out," says Bell.[5] Still, *Eggshells* went on to win the gold award at the Atlanta International Film Festival. It also gave Hooper and Henkel a chance to establish a creative rapport.

Not long after Hooper finished *Eggshells*, he and Henkel began to discuss specific ideas for a project they could collaborate on. It was no accident that the result of Hooper and Henkel's collaboration was a horror picture. They realized the majority of independently made movies making it into theaters around that time were of the horror genre, like George Romero's *Night of the Living Dead* (1968). The pair had studied the genre like film theorists before sitting down to write a first draft of a screenplay in early 1973. They watched a bunch of movies, everything from classics like James Whale's *Frankenstein* (1931) to *Night of the Living Dead*, which they saw on the UT campus at one of Cinema 40's sold-out shows. They knew that with no budget and no cast to speak of, they had to rely on the script for marketability.

During the day Henkel drew cartoons for an educational company, and after work he'd walk over to Hooper's house to hammer out the script. After they talked through their ideas in one room, Henkel went into Hooper's kitchen and typed out scene detail and dialogue. Henkel completed the 160-page first draft (retitled *Leatherface*) in about six weeks. "We didn't understand three-act screenplays or anything like that other than we kind of had a visceral understanding from having seen a lot of movies," says Henkel.[6]

They polished the script into a 100-page second draft. It began with a lengthy description of an opening shot of a dead dog (later changed to an armadillo), but the writing also conveyed a taut sense of tension and horror. The story involved five characters out for a drive in the sweltering heat of a summer afternoon in rural Texas. When the group comes upon a graveyard that has been vandalized, they decide to check out the nearby ancestral home of two of the characters, Sally and her handicapped cousin Franklin (changed to her brother in the final version). The script described Sally as a striking blonde, braless under a thin t-shirt. Franklin was written as a somewhat pathetic "Chaplinesque" figure in a beat-up wheelchair. The screenplay also included atmospheric details like sun spots, astrological jargon, and numerous references to the oppressive heat to set an ominous mood and suggest that the events about to transpire went beyond the control of the characters themselves. Henkel took time to describe Leatherface's variable emotional state, noting when he was vulnerable and childlike, frustrated, or murderously angry. Human bones and skulls decorate the dining room of the grandfather's house, where Sally is forced to "dine" with her captors as they prepare to dismember her. The final scene ends with Sally's narrow escape from the chainsaw-wielding Leatherface. As Leatherface performs a gruesome pirouette in the background, the camera zooms in on a dead hitchhiker's unblinking eye.[7]

Hooper and Henkel polished the script a few more times before they met with potential investor Bill Parsley, who by then was Vice President for Public Affairs at his alma mater, Texas Tech University. Warren Skaaren, friends with Parsley since the start of the film commission, had arranged the meeting for the filmmakers sometime in the late spring or early summer of 1973. Over the years Henkel would come to have great affection for Parsley, but his initial impression was that if he became involved, he'd try to control the production. "When we were dealing with Bill Parsley, I definitely felt like it was his intention to keep us under his thumb. I don't respond too well to thumbs."[8]

In 1973 Parsley was 46 years old and spent most of his time lobbying on behalf of Texas Tech. Although Parsley didn't make much money as a lobbyist, he was a shrewd businessman with many deals on the side and, some said, access to his wife's family's money. In the late 1960s, Parsley partnered with a former law school friend, and they started looking at scripts to finance an independent film. They chose one whose main character, a black playboy type, was modeled on Hugh Hefner. The film was targeted toward the African American market, but it bombed at the box office. The pair also got behind a horror movie shot in Dallas, but it tanked as well.

After the initial meeting between the filmmakers and Parsley, things moved quickly. As Parsley said in 1982, "We talked, we got along and finally I told them that for 50%, I'd put together a financing corporation and pro- duce the movie."[9] Hooper and Henkel had drawn up three possible budgets for the project, the highest of which was $60,000. Parsley agreed to this one and invested $40,000 in his name. Henkel approached his sister Katherine, a UT student who put up $1,000. Austin attorney Robert Kuhn, a friend of Parsley's, invested some money as well.

Kuhn credits Parsley with having the idea to form two companies as part of the financing deal, one to represent the investors and handle the busi- ness side of things, and one to represent the filmmakers and the production itself. Parsley became president of the investing company, which he chris- tened MAB. Marilyn Ann Burns at one time claimed that Parsley had named the company for her, telling a reporter, "I am MAB." Parsley himself denied this in 1982, saying, "I can't remember what MAB stood for. It was probably something I couldn't even say in mixed company. But I'm sure it wasn't Mari- lyn Ann Burns." Parsley and Burns were rumored to be having an affair at the time. Decades later, Burns denies their involvement. "Whether or not she was banging him, it was presumed that she was and everyone assumed she was," recalled Bob Burns (no relation), who served as the movie's art director. Whatever their relationship, Parsley thought enough of Burns to make her a partner in MAB along with Katherine Henkel and Robert Kuhn, giving her one-sixth ownership in the company (the equivalent of Katherine Henkel's). The final investor and partner in MAB was Richard Saenz, a friend of camera-man Daniel Pearl's. Hooper had asked Pearl to shoot the film after seeing the work he'd done for Shootout, telling him production would start as soon as they raised a final $10,000. The film would be Pearl's first feature. He knew Saenz, a film buff from a wealthy family (and, allegedly, a very successful pot dealer), so he showed him the script. "He read it, and three hours later he wanted in for more than $10,000, but that's all that was left," says Pearl.[10]

Hooper and Henkel comprised the production company, Vortex, which owned the other half of the film. Henkel was president, with Hooper acting as vice-president. Like MAB, Vortex would earn 50 percent of any profits brought in by the finished film. Initially, Henkel and Hooper were the primary shareholders in Vortex, but as they hired crew and cast the film, they asked many of the participants to defer their salaries to lower initial production costs. In exchange, they offered points, or a percentage of the film's future profits. Because Vortex owned only half the film, however, these points would be worth only a percentage of that 50 percent, a fact that many people in-volved in the film didn't realize when they began production. "It was not atypical, that kind of financing structure, but it just wasn't made clear from the beginning," explains Ron Bozman, who served as *Chainsaw*'s production manager.[11] Before the production was over, about $40,000 in cast and crew salaries had been deferred.

### Because You Filled the Door

One of the first people Hooper approached to work on the film was Bob Burns. He edited the satirical *Texas Ranger* and eventually became manag-ing supervisor of Texas Student Publications. He graduated with a degree in acting and remained in Austin after college to open his own graphic design shop, the RH Factor, which designed posters for the Cinema 40 and Cin-emaTexas film programs. Hooper and Burns had been friends since 1965, but Burns thought twice about doing *Chainsaw*, having worked with Hooper when he designed the press kit for *Eggshells*. "Tobe was always kind of dif-ficult to work with because when he got to doing something, he would throw

himself into production and everything would be crushed under to the production," said Burns.[12]

Hooper hired Larry Carroll to edit *Chainsaw* after Daniel Pearl recommended him for the job. Hooper also brought on Wayne Bell, who had helped
out on *Eggshells*, to operate the boom microphone. Ted Nicolaou, another
Shootout partner and Pearl's best friend, signed on to record sound. He
sweetened his deal with Hooper by lending his green Ford Econoline van to
the production in exchange for about $100 added to his $300 weekly rate.
Nicolaou's then-wife Sally also worked on the movie. She was taking film
classes at UT and liked to throw dinner parties. Hooper and Henkel heard
about her impressive cooking and persuaded her to cater the film.

Dottie Pearl, married to Daniel at the time and an anthropology student at
UT, had helped her husband "age" his actors on one of his student films, and
she read the *Leatherface* screenplay and knew what it would require. At the
end of her husband's initial meeting with Hooper, Pearl told the filmmaker
that she'd like to do makeup for the film and arranged to have him come
back to discuss the position. Meanwhile, Pearl raided her kitchen to create
homemade special effects to impress Hooper. She used the skin of a raisin
to simulate a scab, the outer layer of a golden currant as a mole. "I went into
my kitchen and became very organic with the whole thing. It was like the
Julia Child approach," says Pearl. When Hooper arrived for their meeting,
the willowy blonde had transformed her appearance and answered the door
sporting her own special effects makeup. "He just started laughing and said,
'You're hired,'" recalls Pearl.[13]

Art director Bob Burns started on the production design in April 1973.
He had about $3,000 to spend on props and set decoration. "I was chas-
ing around, finding the parts, and making all the stuff," he recalled.[14] He
spent about half of his budget to construct the grotesque masks that Gunnar
Hansen would wear as Leatherface. Local plastic surgeon Dr. W. E. Barnes,
who assisted with the special effects makeup, made facial impressions out
of dental algenate that Burns then manipulated into the various masks. He
experimented with different materials to perfect the skin-like texture of the
masks and finally settled on a combination of liquid latex and yellow fiber-
glass insulation. After the materials were applied to the impression and had
dried, Burns left the mask to bake in the sun to achieve a leathery, parchment-
like texture. He used thin wire to sew up a "wound" and give the entire mask
a primitive look, as if constructed by the deranged Leatherface himself.

Burns discovered a company in Killeen called Medical Plastics Labora-
tory that manufactured medical-quality plastic skeletons. There was enough

money to buy only one complete skeleton, but Burns negotiated for some random "seconds" of the company's other bone parts as well. An Austin-based company made prosthetics of ears, arms, and other body parts, and they also gave Burns seconds from their inventory. Dottie Pearl was working part-time for a local veterinarian and had access to an animal boneyard on the doctor's ranch outside of town, which produced dog, cat, monkey, and cow bones. One day Burns and his girlfriend, Mary Church, who signed on as script supervisor, found a freshly splattered armadillo as they were driving around on one of their "hunting trips." Burns brought it back to Austin, found a book about taxidermy, and taught himself how to stuff the mangled armadillo, which made an appearance in the movie's opening highway shot and in the infamous dinner sequence, where it sat hunched in the middle of the dining room table.

Burns also was instrumental in securing the production's main location in a relatively remote spot northeast of Austin. Burns met Ron "Smokey" Isgur when the RH Factor sponsored Isgur's softball team. Isgur lived in the white Victorian farmhouse perched on Quick Hill Road, and after checking out the spread, Burns told Hooper and Henkel about it. In exchange for letting the filmmakers use the house for a week or so, they'd pay one month's rent. When the initial shooting schedule ran long, Isgur, who had been living in the house during production, approached Burns about further compensation.[15] Tempers flared when the filmmakers balked at the idea, which added stress to an already tense situation.

Hooper and Henkel held auditions all over town throughout June and July. Marilyn Burns was one of the first actors cast in the film. "I knew Warren Skaaren, so it was natural that I'd go audition for Tobe and Kim," she recalls.[16] This was the University of Texas graduate's first starring role. The year before, she had played Blythe Danner's stand-in in *Lovin' Molly*, a romantic comedy shot in Austin by director Sidney Lumet and adapted from Larry McMurtry's novel *Leaving Cheyenne*. Originally cast in the role of Danner's sister, Burns was replaced by Susan Sarandon but kept on as a stand-in for both actresses.

Marilyn met with Hooper and Henkel a few times, discussing the movie and her character, Sally. Privately Marilyn thought the script wasn't that good, but she was excited about the prospect of a lead role. Later, because she had worked on other features, some of the other cast members assumed she was a screen veteran.

Jim Siedow was a professional actor in Houston who had worked with Henkel, Bozman, and Hooper on a low-budget feature called *The Windsplitter* a few years earlier. He had numerous theater credits and a few features under his belt by the time he was cast as "the Cook," one of Leatherface's brothers.

Allen Danziger had met Hooper through mutual friends who had co-starred in *Eggshells*. When Hooper and Henkel were writing the script for *Chainsaw*, they came to Danziger with a copy and suggested he play the part of Jerry, Sally's boyfriend. Danziger read the script and signed on. They offered him $400 for three weeks of work, payable in two installments, and one percentage point in the film's profits, double what they offered some of the other actors. Like most of the others working on the movie, he believed he owned one percent of the entire production.[17]

Ed Neal was studying acting at UT when he literally stumbled into auditions being held in the drama building one afternoon. He improvised the part of the hitchhiker after scanning the script's minimal description, basing the sketch on his nephew, a paranoid schizophrenic.

Georgetown native Paul Partain was working for a military manufacturer during the day and doing some theater acting on the side when he heard about the independent horror movie. Partain initially read for the role of the hitchhiker, but Hooper was unimpressed. "Well, since you're here," said Hooper, "read this other part."[18] He handed Partain pages for the wheelchair-bound Franklin.

Twenty-two-year-old Bill Vail began his college career at UT as an acting major and then switched to directing. He had heard good things about Hooper and *Eggshells* but hadn't met the director or seen his first feature. Nonetheless he arranged to meet with Henkel to talk about *Leatherface* and the part of Kirk, one of the friends traveling in the van with Sally and Franklin and one of Leatherface's first victims.

Gunnar Hansen was a graduate student in UT's German department when he became interested in acting. That summer an acquaintance had a small part in a horror movie being shot locally, and he said it was too bad that they had already cast the killer because Hansen, a sturdy 6'4", would have been perfect for the role. Hansen ran into the acquaintance a week later. "He told me the guy that they had wanted to cast as the Leatherface character was holed up drunk in a motel." When Hansen got in touch with the filmmakers, he could tell they were intense. Hooper did most of the talking, outlining the plot and describing the other characters. They talked about Leatherface, telling Hansen that he was incredibly violent, but also afraid of his family. He couldn't speak although he could grunt and say a few things, but he was basically unintelligible. Months later, Hooper and Henkel told Hansen about being inspired by the story of Ed Gein, the Wisconsin serial killer who in the late 1950s crafted lamps, furniture, and other household objects from the skin of his female victims. In their script, Hooper and Henkel told Hansen, they distributed characteristics of Gein among the different family members. Once Hooper had Hansen's contract, he told him that he had decided to give him the Leatherface role as soon as he saw him. When Hansen asked why, Hooper replied, "Because you filled the door."[19]

## An Inauspicious Beginning

In the early morning hours of July 15, a sleepy core group of *Leatherface's* cast and crew gathered at the compound on Quick Hill Road. The first shots took place in and around an abandoned stone structure near the Victorian house. The stone house was an appropriately creepy location. Layers of dirt and dust covered the floors, and strips of peeling wallpaper curled off the walls. Whispery spider webs hung in the corners of doorframes, and armies of Texas-sized daddy long legs camped out in every nook and cranny.[20]

Hooper and Henkel made an unlikely team. "Tobe was kind of a crazed hippie type, and Kim was more of a reserved intellectual, Texas-style," Ted Nicolaou remembers. They both tended to be quiet, but Hooper's silence could turn dark and brooding while Henkel appeared introspective. The two often would confer at length about shooting decisions and script changes while everyone else waited. "There didn't seem to be a great plan for anything," recalls Dr. W. E. Barnes, the plastic surgeon who assisted with a few of the masks and special effects makeup. "They didn't even seem to have a regular schedule per day set up. They'd shoot a few shots, and everybody would kind of sit around and talk, then they'd try something else." As graduates of UT's film program, Nicolaou, Pearl, and Carroll had been schooled in the art of pre-planning, so "it was kind of stunning to see guys wasting so many hours in circular discussion," says Nicolaou.[21]

The shoot was beset by problems typical of an independent film: too little time and money. In a few situations, the cast and crew's relative inexperience would also hamper the production. At other times, their ignorance led to inspired screen moments.

The filmmakers spent the first week of production shooting a handful of interior and exterior scenes from the first half of the script, but the dailies revealed a number of out-of-focus and poorly lit scenes. Pearl realized too late that one of the production's two cameras had a faulty lens. Upon hearing of the technical problems and the need to reshoot three or four days' worth of scenes, Parsley and Bozman stepped in. "They said, 'We need to get you guys under control here. You're running around like a bunch of headless chickens,'" Pearl recalls.[22]

According to production designer Bob Burns, an anxious Parsley, concerned about his investment, pushed for the July 15 start date without a grasp of the realities of low-budget filmmaking. Bozman doesn't recall that Parsley pressured the filmmakers to begin shooting, but he does admit to being underprepped and ill prepared for the experience. Neal and the other actors often would sit waiting in the blistering heat while Henkel and Hooper planned the next shot. Says Neal, "This is pretty much how low-budget moviemaking works. It doesn't mean Tobe and Kim are bad moviemakers. It means they were doing it the only way they could. They were probably sleeping eight minutes a day."[23]

So in late July, the *Chainsaw* production shut down after eight days of filming, which yielded little usable footage. During the hiatus, the filmmakers tried to regroup and organize themselves. Hooper and Henkel scouted and nailed down a few more locations for later scenes in the script while other members of the crew continued to prep the Leatherface house on Quick Hill. The cast cooled their heels and waited for the call to go back to work.

During that time the producers also insisted that Hooper make and follow a shot list. The result was a three-and-a-half-page typewritten chart. The production was to regroup on Saturday, August 4, and continue shooting through Tuesday, August 28, with one day off every seventh day. Pearl followed the schedule once the production swung back into gear, setting up the shots as described. But for shot after shot, Hooper walked on set and changed the setup. An aggravated Pearl eventually confronted him. "Why am I setting up the wrong shot?" he demanded. Hooper took Pearl aside. "Daniel, didn't anybody tell you? I didn't even write that. Kim wrote that. I don't even know what's on that damn thing." Henkel does not recall coming up with the list. "If I came up with a shot list, it would have been something that I'd worked on in collaboration with Tobe, and it would have been something that we put together to satisfy somebody that was demanding it, rather than anything that had any reality to it."[24]

It was the fourth day since shooting had resumed on *Leatherface*, and the production miraculously was still on schedule. The crew began setting up for the script's first kill, when Leatherface bludgeons Vail's character, Kirk, with a hammer. Bob Burns's handiwork had turned the Victorian-style house into a vision from hell. Cowhide skins hung from the walls in the first-floor hallway, flapping slightly in the occasional breeze wafting in through the screen door. Burns had painted the small passageway at the end of the hall a deep red.

A large cow skull peered out from the wall along with smaller deer skulls and other assorted animal bones. A lightweight piece of sheet metal, nailed to two 2x4s of framing, hung in the doorway and obscured the red "trophy" wall from view in the initial shot as Kirk entered the house from the front porch. Pillows lay scattered on the floor out of view to soften Vail's fall when Hansen threw his body off-camera at the end of the scene.

This death scene, the first in the film, offered Vail a chance to flex his acting chops. Hooper pulled him aside before the shot and instructed him to run down the hall, trip in the grate, fall forward and let Hansen hit him in the back of the head with the prop hammer. A blood bag in Vail's mouth would add some gore. At the end of the shot, Hansen would heave him off-screen and slam the metal door.

Vail remembered a quotation he'd read in *James Cagney: The Authorized Biography*: "No good actor dies quickly." This was his moment, he told himself. Vail also understood that his scene had some story impact because it was the first killing that audiences would see. Knowing where the rest of the movie was headed, Vail thought the scene should have more drama.[25]

The shot also marked Leatherface's first on-screen appearance. Adrenaline and anxiety pumped through Hansen's body as he waited for his cue. After he heard Hooper yell "Action," Hansen threw open the prop door and bashed Vail's head with the fake hammer. Hansen hit Vail with so much force that he broke blood vessels in the other actor's eye.

After Vail fell to the floor and flailed around for a bit, Hansen leaned over the actor, but instead of dragging him off-screen and tossing him onto the pillows, he picked him completely off the ground and launched him into the wall. Vail didn't have far to go in the small space, and he hit the wall hard.

Even Hooper looked impressed. "It was much more than Tobe was expecting," says Hansen. "When that door slams, you have a sense that that character is immensely strong and huge. He just picks up Kirk like he's a feather and tosses him."[26] Thanks to Bob Burns's design skills, the pieces of plywood and sheet metal looked as if they weighed 200 pounds. At the end of the shot, when Hansen slammed the door, it stopped dead in its tracks with a sickening thud, adding an impressive bit of finality to the shocking kill.

The following day, after the final takes of Vail's scene were in the can, the house was prepped for Pam's scenes with Leatherface and a horrific shot involving a meat hook. Actress Teri McMinn kept coughing between takes, her throat ravaged by the screaming she had to do at the end of the scene, not to mention the overwhelming stench emanating from the props.

According to Bob Burns, Hooper originally wanted to construct a special effect that would allow them to show the hook piercing Pam's chest as blood squirts from the wound. Burns claimed to have talked him out of it. "Subconsciously or not, people will wonder how you did the special effect, and it'll be much more effective without," he argued. This was one of many points of tension between the old friends, whose relationship became badly strained during the course of filming. Hooper liked to work off the cuff and would call Burns at his shop with last-minute prop requests. "I would have to drop everything and try to drag all this shit out there," recalled Burns.[27]

They first shot the sequence from behind the actors, with the hook hanging in the foreground as Leatherface lifted Pam as if to impale her on the hook. Hooper later told Hansen that he made it look as if McMinn weighed next to nothing because he lifted her with such ease. "Part of it was because I had been working out, doing a lot of weight lifting. But the other reason was, I was so full of adrenaline for every shot that nothing seemed to weigh anything."[28]

Hooper enlisted Burns's help to design something that would allow McMinn to dangle from the hook, but Burns objected to the stunt and its potential danger to McMinn. In the end, Dottie Pearl came up with the materials for the harness McMinn wore to make it look as if she was hanging from the hook. She took flesh-colored nylon stockings and cut them into thin strips, wrapped them between McMinn's legs, crisscrossed them behind her back, and tied the ends to a metal ring hidden under the actress's long hair. Pearl placed three sanitary napkins in the crotch of McMinn's shorts to minimize the discomfort of the nylon cutting into her skin. McMinn was then suspended from the meat hook by the metal ring behind her neck.[29]

Vail lay spread eagle on the butcher block as Hansen hovered over him with the saw. Hansen couldn't see out of his mask, and the chainsaw was inches from Vail's head. Although Hansen was using a toothless saw, Vail still felt uneasy as he listened to the whirring of the chain. Hansen maneuvered the saw into the wooden block just below Vail's right shoulder; from the camera's perspective it would look as if the saw was slicing through Kirk's chest. Hot oil splattered off the chain and onto Vail, and wooden splinters bounced off the side of his face. Hooper told Vail not to breathe, and he made Dottie Pearl stand at the foot of the table to watch the actor's chest and make sure it didn't move. McMinn, suspended from the hook, screamed in the background as the camera rolled.

## The Last Supper

*Chainsaw's* cast and crew had been working twelve- to sixteen-hour days for three weeks, with only one day off from week to week. On Saturday, August 18, they were about six or seven days behind as they prepped the dining room of the house for the movie's climactic scene, where Sally is tortured and forced to endure dinner with Leatherface and his family. The scene features the elderly grandfather character played by John Dugan, Henkel's eighteen-year-old brother-in-law. As the day began, Hooper, Pearl, and the others busied themselves shooting other, shorter scenes while waiting for Dugan's makeup to be finished, a grueling process overseen by Dr. Barnes.

As Pearl changed lenses on one of the Éclairs, he overheard a message come through on the walkie-talkie. Dugan had had it with the effects make-up, and he refused to go through another day of the application. Hooper would have to shoot him out that day.[30] They also had to cope with the fact that Jim Siedow was scheduled to do a play and had to leave Austin the following day.[31]

In the script the dinner scene takes place at the end of the first day, so blackout drapes were used to cover the windows, blocking out the summer sun and intensifying the heat in the close room. Additionally, the Éclair cameras required a 16mm film stock that needed twice as much light as 35mm film. They shot the lengthy dinner sequence mostly in order, reframing for different shots rather than stopping the camera. If someone flubbed a line, Hooper would call for another take. The hours crawled by, and the heat from the lights cooked everything and everyone in the room. Neal sat at the wooden table, stifling yawns and trying to stay focused. With the room temperature rising above 100 degrees, the formaldehyde preserving the animal props had evaporated. The heat affected the dead animals' chemical composition, and the props rotted quickly, like a time-lapse photograph. "They'd have to move the props in certain ways and cheat the angle because it looked different than when they had shot it earlier," Neal recalls.[32] Once night fell, someone removed the blackout drapes from the windows, which offered some relief.

Lou Perryman pulled focus on the camera throughout the sequence, which often put him downwind from Hansen. Like the other actors, Hansen had been told not to wash his costume. The noxious combination of sweat and grime, made worse for the towering actor because of the mask and the fact that he was wearing a heavy suit, hit Perryman full force as he crouched in front of the camera. Every time Hansen lunged down the table toward

Marilyn, Perryman quickly pulled focus and then stuck his head out the nearest window.[33]

The decaying head cheese, rotting chicken corpses, and acrid body odor created an unholy stench in the small room. Dottie Pearl hovered just off camera so that she could help Hansen navigate the space and touch up Dugan's and Burns's makeup during breaks. "At one point," says Pearl, "I looked around and thought, 'We are truly living this thing. We aren't making it any more. We're living it.'"[34] The dinner sequence was taking forever, in part because of the long stretches of dialogue. Hooper also wanted to get a lot of coverage—multiple master shots from each end of the table, close-ups simulating character point-of-view shots, etc.—which required extra setups. Lights had to be moved, makeup had to be reapplied, and the prop food, quickly decomposing in the overheated space, had to be replaced.

Shooting continued through the night. In the end, the cast and crew worked on the dinner sequence for more than 26 hours straight. "A director's always looking for his idea of what's perfect in a take. Sometimes it's hard to discern what is. I think Tobe also was insecure and just wanted to get enough material," says Nicolaou. Hooper later admitted that perhaps he had been too much of a taskmaster. "Knowing what I wanted and being a cameraman and editor myself, it was easier at times for me to grab the camera. That may have caused friction." In retrospect, Bozman adds, they could have filmed Dugan's scenes first and returned another day to shoot the other actors. "It was a living nightmare," Bozman admits. But perhaps the twenty-six-hour marathon paid off in other ways, he muses nearly three decades later. "It might have had its own crazy dynamic and made it better."[35]

Drug-taking ran rampant on the set throughout production, but on that particular day a batch of enhanced brownies may have added to the mayhem. Throughout the production Sally Nicolaou fortified the cast and crew with homemade chicken casseroles, lasagna, or chicken pot pie and southern-style biscuits. Prior to that Saturday, Nicolaou reportedly had helped herself to a marijuana crop growing in the backyard of the Quick Hill house and added it to her brownie recipe. After lunch, the remaining dessert was left on the snack table. Hansen helped himself as did others. When he wasn't lounging on the porch and chanting "Time has no meaning" between takes, Hansen sat for what seemed like hours at the dining room table waiting for his next shot as Hooper and Pearl discussed the lighting setup.[36]

By early September cast and crew were in their sixth week of production, with the marathon dinner sequence finally behind them. The twenty-six-hour shoot had been rough on everyone involved, but perhaps no one had suffered

CHAINSAWS, SLACKERS, AND SPY KIDS

more than Marilyn. Physically drained and emotionally on edge, she stood glassy-eyed between takes as the crew set up for the film's final sequence. As written in the script, the scene takes place at dawn, after Sally has spent a horrific night in the Leatherface family house. In reality, Hooper and the others began prepping for the scene late in the afternoon on the second day of September, and they rushed to get all the shots before they ran out of light. As they were preparing to shoot the final scene of Leatherface, Hooper suggested to Hansen that he stamp his feet and gesture with the chainsaw to show his frustration over Sally's escape in the back of the pickup. Hansen ad libbed the shot, stomping around and swinging the saw. Then Hooper and Pearl decided to move the camera 360 degrees around Hansen for a dizzying panoramic effect. They cleared the Quick Hill set of all extraneous cast and crew. Pearl guided the camera around Hansen, with Hooper close behind.

Hansen's movements amounted to a kind of awkward pirouette as he sliced through the air with the saw, the setting sun glowing behind him in the western sky. The shot provides an unsettling conclusion to Sally's story. She escapes, but Leatherface's macabre dance, ominously captured in the movie's final freeze-frame, offers an uneasy catharsis at best. Many *Chainsaw* fans consider it the best moment in the movie.

At the end of the filming of this scene, which essentially marked the end of principal photography, Hansen hurled the chainsaw into a nearby field and walked out of frame.[37]

### Postproduction and P.I.T.S.

In mid-October 1973, Henkel wrote a letter to Skaaren. Henkel's tone was formal but upbeat, informing Skaaren that postproduction had begun and was expected to last approximately four weeks. According to Henkel, he and Hooper were in talks with "several distributors" and "optimistic" about *Leatherface*'s future. "Without your cooperation, many aspects of our production would have been more difficult, if not impossible," wrote Henkel.[38] Skaaren had in fact been quite helpful to the production in a number of ways, not the least of which was putting the filmmakers in touch with Parsley, their primary investor. But as the coming months would reveal, Skaaren's greatest—and most controversial—contributions were yet to occur.

As the film's editor, Carroll had been organizing the dailies throughout the production. Slow and methodical, he made basic choices in order to assemble a rough cut for Hooper. Typically an editor cuts together a version based on a master script with notes about the director's preferences for each scene. It is unclear whether such a script existed for *Leatherface* or whether something happened to the notes, but in the end Carroll worked off of Nicolaou's sound logs, which contained detailed notes about which scenes worked best. The logs also included Nicolaou's frustrated asides about Hooper.[39]

Postproduction began in earnest in October but hit a technical snag that would complicate the film's financial situation and create bad blood among the cast and crew for years to come. Carroll and Hooper edited after hours in the downtown offices of Shootout Films, the freelance production company co-owned by Richard Kooris, Courtney Goodin, Carroll, Nicolaou, and Pearl.

Not surprisingly, Parsley pressured Hooper to finish the film quickly. In addition, he also pushed for the movie to be edited in such a way as to get a more lenient rating from the Code and Ratings Administration. When Carroll heard this, he was incredulous. "This is a film about cannibals—they kill and eat people. It's an automatic 'R,'" he said to Hooper. It was not until years later, while watching a retrospective screening of the movie in Los Angeles, that Carroll realized the payoff of the movie's low budget and Parsley's insistence on the less controversial rating. "The classic moment is when Franklin is attacked in the wheelchair, and you see him waving the flashlight as the chainsaw's going back and forth. People will swear that his arm is cut off. All of the stuff that Tobe had been forced to do because of the backers and the lack of what we could actually do on screen had been done through innuendo."[40]

The postproduction phase quickly surpassed the scheduled four weeks. Parsley continued to push for a completion date, phoning Carroll to check on Hooper's progress when the director himself began to dodge the executive producer's calls. Wayne Bell worked on the film's sound design with Hooper, and the pair spent hours jamming with various instruments and improvising into Bell's tape recorder. Bell also recorded sounds to simulate the on-screen actions, like the crack of a tooth being stepped on.[41]

A few months into the editing process, the phone rang late one night while Hooper and Carroll were working. Remembers Carroll, "Ron Bozman called in the midst of a poker game in Houston and had a good bit to drink, it sounded like, and I handed him off to Tobe. I was looking at Tobe and his eyes suddenly start to glow. He looks at me and says, '*The Texas Chainsaw Massacre.*' My understanding was that Ron was telling people the stories and someone in the poker game came up with the title."[42] Most people connected with the film credit Skaaren for the title change, and nearly everyone believed it was a change for the better. Others like Bob Burns and Carroll expressed reservations about libeling the state's already fragile reputation, which still was trying to shake off the bad press from the 1963 assassination of President Kennedy and Charles Whitman's 1966 shooting spree on the UT campus. But even the naysayers eventually acknowledged the title's exploitation potential.

The editing dragged into 1974, and Carroll left to fulfill another production commitment. Hooper brought in Sallye Richardson, with whom he had worked on *The Windsplitter* and at Filmhouse. According to Richardson, Hooper had summoned her because he was unhappy with Carroll's work. "Larry was not from the kind of thinking process that we had all been in, he wasn't able to work with Tobe the way a lot of us were. That's when [Tobe] called me in, and we tore it all up and started anew."[43]

In early 1974, Hooper again moved the Steenbeck, this time into Bill Wittliff's offices to cut the negative. Wittliff operated a publishing outfit called Encino Press and was beginning to write screenplays. Cutting *Chainsaw's* negative proved tricky because of the film's many quick cuts. Postproduction stalled when it came time to conform the 16mm negative. Recalls Henkel, "Basically, our cutting process had gotten things out of synch. We had cut negative in such a way that things were not going to match up, and it was an expensive error." When Hooper and Henkel realized they needed more money to correct the mistake and finish the film, they went back to Parsley and offered to sell him a 19 percent share in Vortex. Parsley turned them down flat. "He was hard," remembers Kuhn. "Parsley had plenty of money, but he didn't give up any of his shares. He was a Democrat, but he was as Republican a son of a bitch as I'd ever seen."[44]

When Skaaren heard about the filmmakers' predicament, he approached Wittliff, who assembled a group of friends for a pitch to be possible second-round investors. One night in late February, a handful of men gathered downtown in the boardroom of City National Bank. The group included City National's vice president, Richard Logan, who handled the finances of many of those present, and attorney Joe K. Longley, Wittliff's former fraternity brother at the University of Texas. Longley invited friends Tommy Townsend, a state legislator, and Michael Barron, another attorney. Richard Haney, another businessman, regularly played poker with Wittliff. The investment sounded like fun to the men. "It was a lark," says Wittliff, who ponied up $2,000. Longley, who knew Parsley, remembers the investment being pitched as a tax write-off after the filmmakers screened about twelve minutes of the movie's more compelling scenes. "It was just a disposable income investment. We didn't need the money. It was okay if we lost it. It was just fun to say we were involved in a movie." Hooper and Henkel got their money. In the end, eleven individuals contributed investments of $1,000, $2,000, or $3,000 for a total of $24,000 in exchange for 19 percent of Vortex's share of the film's net profits, whittling away even more of the cast and crew's potential profit shares. The investors cheekily dubbed their investment group P.I.T.S., or Pie in the Sky.[45]

## A Deal with the Devil

A few days after the P.I.T.S. group signed their contract, Skaaren announced in the March 1974 issue of *FilmTexas*, the film commission's monthly newsletter, that he would be stepping down from his post as executive director. Publicly Skaaren said that he would spend his time writing and producing feature films and television programs. Privately he often had expressed his ambivalence about the film commission and his growing need to "write to live."[46]

Although it's clear that Skaaren viewed the film commission as a stepping stone to other opportunities in the motion picture business, he may have been encouraged to leave the post by his increasing involvement in *Chainsaw*. In mid-February Henkel had written to Skaaren to discuss the possibility of Skaaren's becoming a producer's representative for the film. After some negotiation, a deal was finalized on April 1 to appoint Skaaren as the film's "sole agent." He received a $5,000 deferred cash fee for his services, payable at the same time as the production's other deferments. In addition to his cash fee, Skaaren would receive 33 ⅓ percent of the film's net profits realized by Vortex (but not MAB), which entitled Skaaren to about 15 percent of the film's total profits.[47]

Meanwhile, with the negative cutting finished, the film's sound needed to be mixed and synched for the 35mm blowup print. Hooper asked Sallye Richardson to accompany the movie to Los Angeles to oversee the process. Robert "Buzz" Knudsen, who a year earlier had won an Academy Award for mixing the sound on *The Exorcist*, also worked on *Chainsaw*. The technicians who worked on the audio mix responded well to the picture. "They seemed to share our belief that we have a very commercial picture," wrote Henkel in a letter to Vortex investors. In a later letter, Henkel wrote that the reaction from major distributors at advance screenings only confirmed their confidence in the horror film. But while initial responses from industry insiders may have been encouraging, the appearance of actual offers was another matter.[48]

One year earlier, Skaaren had secured a tentative distribution deal—solely on the basis of Hooper and Henkel's script—with International Producers Corporation (IPC), a small company located in Los Angeles. By August 1974, however, Skaaren's contact at IPC had moved to Roger Corman's New World Pictures, and the deal with IPC had fallen through. Skaaren continued to mine his Los Angeles contacts in shopping the film, one of whom was old friend and *The Getaway* producer David Foster. Skaaren set up a screening for Foster in Los Angeles. Foster thought the movie looked rough, but he appreciated its clever innuendo and saw potential in its ability to connect with an audience. They worked out a deal in which Foster got one and a half points of the film's back end in exchange for helping to arrange screenings with potential buyers such as Twentieth Century Fox, Warner Bros., Universal Pictures, Columbia Pictures, and other companies. "Frankly, a lot of them passed," Foster recalls.[49]

One relatively new distributor did show interest. Bryanston Pictures was founded by Brooklyn-based brothers Louis (a.k.a. "Butchie") and Joseph C. Peraino in 1971 as a means to distribute "legitimate" (i.e., nonpornographic) motion pictures.[50] Their father, Anthony Peraino, and *his* brother, Joseph S., allegedly were "made men" with connections to the Joseph Colombo mafia family. Before he became president of Bryanston, Louis already had experience in the film industry as a producer (along with his father) and distributor of *Deep Throat*, which became the most successful pornographic film in U.S. history soon after its release in November 1972. The Perainos channeled *Deep Throat*'s profits into Bryanston and rapidly acquired *Return of the Dragon*, Bruce Lee's last film before his death in 1973, and Andy Warhol's *Frankenstein*, among others.

Fred Beiersdorf owned Dal-Art, a Dallas-based distribution company that subdistributed Bryanston's legitimate films. Beiersdorf's father founded Dal-Art after working for Warner Bros., and he cultivated the art-house film business in Texas. The younger Beiersdorf first met the Perainos in the early 1970s when they "invited" him to represent Bryanston's films in the Southwest. The gravelly voiced Texan was a hit with the Perainos. "You can keep Dal-Art," they told him, "but on the door of your office we want 'Bryanston Films.'" The Perainos' purported mob ties, which Beiersdorf knew about when he agreed to work with the company, didn't bother him. "I loved Lou Peraino and Uncle Joe. I was just a raggedy-ass old film peddler from Texas. I mean, these guys were bad news, man, but they couldn't have been nicer to me." Beiersdorf slipped up only once, when he asked Uncle Joe how much the company had made off of *Deep Throat*. Later that day, after an extravagant lobster lunch, Peraino put his arm menacingly around the Texan. "Fred, Lou has eight kids, through different wives. His kids and his grandkids have nothing to worry about the rest of their lives. Does that tell you how much money *Deep Throat*'s brought in?"[51]

On July 19, Lou Peraino sent Skaaren a letter outlining the terms of *Chainsaw*'s deal. Bryanston offered the filmmakers $225,000 up front and 35 percent of *Chainsaw*'s gross rentals, defined in the letter as the proceeds remaining after the costs of "prints, promotion, and advertising" were subtracted from the exhibition profits. The up-front money would cover *Chainsaw*'s investors and deferred salaries for the cast and crew, which amounted to approximately $140,000. According to the contract, Bryanston would handle the film's domestic and international release, opening *Chainsaw* in New York and no fewer than nine of the top twenty-five cities before the end of the year. Releases in Europe and Japan would occur before July 1975, and in "all other countries" before the end of 1975.[52]

On August 28, Bozman and Skaaren arrived at Bryanston's New York offices, a gray stone building at 630 Ninth Avenue. Prior to the meeting Skaaren had drawn up a list entitled "The grapevine on Joe and Lou Peraino." The typewritten document enumerated eleven points about the family and their business dealings. The list mixed banal facts with other bits of information about conviction histories, Colombo family connections, and the fact that both men had a New York City "B" number, or "bad guy" number.[53]

The Peraino brothers were imposing figures who each stood about six feet tall and tipped the scales around two hundred pounds. Lou had black curly hair and could be soft-spoken and charming in a rough-edged way. Joseph's babyish face belied his seniority as the older brother. Both of the men spoke with heavy Brooklyn accents.

Bozman, Skaaren, and their New York–based attorneys accepted the terms of the contract, including a check for $136,000 as partial payment of Bryanston's initial $225,000 offer. Although Bozman admits to having misgivings about Bryanston, he also felt hard pressed to turn down the contract. "You've got all of these people on the line—investors—and here was almost a quarter of a million dollars, against $140,000 owed. There were no other offers. So we took it."[54]

Hooper wrote to the cast, crew, and investors a week after the New York meeting to announce the movie's sale and its impending release. He called Bryanston a "young aggressive organization" and mentioned its box office success with *Frankenstein* and *Enter the Dragon*. According to the letter, Vortex and MAB had agreed to retain the services of Thomas Glass, an accountant in the Austin firm of Glass & Caylor, to distribute the profits as they came in from Bryanston. (Glass's fees would be paid off the top of any incoming profits.)[55]

Hooper's letter also thanked everyone involved for persevering to get the film made despite the production's many challenges. Henkel also wrote a letter to the investors with specifics about the Bryanston contract. The company had agreed to send $89,000 (the remaining balance of the $225,000 up-front money) within a month's time. Not surprisingly, no mention was made in either letter of Bryanston's alleged mafia connections.[56]

The P.I.T.S. investors also received a jubilant letter from banker Richard Logan. "*Chainsaw* has been sold!" he wrote on September 4.[57] His letter also included a check fully reimbursing each of the eleven investors, with information about future payments based on profit participation.

For many of *Chainsaw*'s cast and crew, normal life had resumed after production ended, so by the time Skaaren secured the distribution deal in August 1974, nearly a year had passed since their involvement with the film. The Bryanston deal definitely was good news. Daniel Pearl and Ted Nicolaou had left for Los Angeles by this time, and both men's careers were beginning to take off. Pearl's wife Dottie had begun to receive offers to do makeup on Hollywood features. But rumors about Bryanston's questionable business dealings began to spread among the cast and crew. In Austin Bob Burns, who was designing posters for Steve Bearden and the Cinema 40 film series at the time, showed Bearden his letter from Hooper announcing the sale to Bryanston. "They're mafia," confirmed Bearden, who had been dealing with distributors for years.[58]

### It Was Obviously Very Controversial

On September 4, the same day that Hooper and Logan wrote letters to *Chainsaw*'s cast, crew, and investors, Bryanston ran a full-page advertisement in *Variety* promoting the movie's upcoming release. The powerful illustration featured Leatherface wielding a chainsaw while a terrorized Pam (Teri Mc-Minn) hung suspended from the meat hook. "Who will survive and what will be left of them?" read the ad copy. A box at the bottom of the ad touted the movie's release in 230 Texas theaters on October 11.

Beiersdorf oversaw *Chainsaw*'s release in Texas, Oklahoma, New Orleans, and Memphis, and met with Hooper to discuss plans for the movie's rollout. "He didn't trust anybody," remembers Beiersdorf. He promised Hooper that he'd do the picture justice, and in early October he organized a press conference in Dallas to announce the movie's opening. Bones and other props from the film decorated a room in the ritzy Fairmont Hotel, and regional television stations and newspapers covered the event. Marilyn Burns and Gunnar Hansen joined Hooper and Henkel to answer questions, and Hooper dazzled the crowd with a fast-paced clip from the movie. *Dallas Morning News* film critic Philip Wuntch interviewed Henkel, who played up the movie's tenuous connection to real events and serial murder Ed Gein. "We filmed it in Austin although the actual incident happened in Wisconsin over twenty years ago. A fellow lived on the edge of a graveyard and robbed the graves."[59]

In its first four days of play in Texas, the movie made an impressive $602,133. In addition to the southern territories, *Chainsaw* opened in 105 New York theaters and forty-five movie houses in Los Angeles as well as select theaters in other states. Not surprisingly, the movie received strong local reviews. Patrick Taggart, the movie critic for the *Austin American-Statesman*, praised the film's horror sensibilities despite its low-budget production values. "Grainy and appearing to have been filmed through the bottom of a Coke bottle, it is hardly the technical achievement of *The Exorcist*. But in the perverse sensibilities of horror movies, it's a lot more fun." Taggart's gushing lead sentence, which called *Chainsaw* "the most significant horror movie since *The Exorcist*" and "the most important horror movie since 1968's *Night of the Living Dead*," graced print advertising across the country. *Variety* criticized the movie's "thin, washed-out color" but complimented its overall "look." Most importantly, the reviewer conferred on the film *Variety*'s highest accolade: its box office looked promising.[60]

Not everyone was impressed, however. When audiences at a San Francisco theater were treated to a sneak preview of *Chainsaw* instead of the Walt Disney movie they had paid to see, they reportedly demanded their money back. And on opening day, the P.I.T.S. group headed to the Riverside Twin in south Austin to check out their investment and were fairly shocked by what they saw. They left the theater early and waited outside to gauge audience reaction. Recalls Longley, "People were just disgusted. They were just totally outraged. It was obviously very controversial."[61]

The *Los Angeles Times* blasted the movie, calling it "a despicable film." Although the reviewer credited Marilyn Burns's promising "Cloris Leachman-like quality," she chastised the filmmakers: "Craziness handled without sensitivity is a degrading, senseless misuse of film and time." *Chainsaw* played at midnight in Chicago and a few other cities upon its release, capitalizing on a relatively new exhibition trend of booking exploitation movies as late-night interactive events for a young demographic. Films like *Pink Flamingos* (1972) and *Reefer Madness* (1972) developed cult followings from midnight screenings, and *Chainsaw*'s reputation likewise began to grow. By the fall of 1975, a *New York Times* reporter included the film in an article about the popularity and appeal of midnight movies, calling it "the *Jaws* of the midnight runs" for its sustained terror and over-the-top violence.[62]

### Trail of Tears

While *Chainsaw* was doing very well at the box office, the reality for most of the Texans involved with the low-budget film would prove very different. During the two years between *Chainsaw*'s initial release in the fall of 1974 and December 1976, when *Variety* declared it one of the fifty highest-grossing films of the year, Skaaren, Henkel, and others would wage a protracted and ultimately unsuccessful battle with Bryanston to collect their share of the film's profits. Meanwhile, Bryanston was involved in a lengthy legal trial over *Deep Throat*, and *Chainsaw*'s release schedule became haphazard at best. By 1977, Parsley began referring to the film's dreary financial situation as the "Trail of Tears."[63]

According to the terms of the original contract with Bryanston, *Chainsaw* participants and investors should have begun to receive their initial profit-sharing checks in early 1975. By January, *Chainsaw* reportedly had earned about $5 million. But by late February, Skaaren had made at least three telephone calls to Lou Peraino in New York to discuss the outstanding money owed to Vortex and MAB. When Bryanston finally sent a first-quarter report, Skaaren was frustrated to discover that the information was far too general to determine the movie's actual box office in its first few months of release. Even worse, Bryanston's accounting reflected a deficit: Vortex actually *owed* Bryanston $152,735 according to the report. Skaaren quickly realized that he would have to deal with Peraino in person, and he wrote to Bryanston's president to inform him he would be traveling to New York in late April or early May to discuss plans for the spring and summer release of the film. In the meantime, Skaaren requested and received another profit update, in which Bryanston acknowledged outstanding box office receipts of approximately $340,000. Although Skaaren was disappointed that the report did not include a check reflecting these profits, he expressed optimism in a letter to Henkel about the film's strong performance overseas and the news that *Chainsaw* had been chosen to play as a Director's Fortnight selection at the Cannes Film Festival in May.[64]

Bob Burns, for one, was fed up. Why were they allowing Bryanston to push them around? He particularly couldn't understand why Parsley, whom he considered a fairly astute businessman, wasn't doing more to recoup his share of the profits. "They either allowed themselves to be incredibly stupid or money went under the table," says Burns.[65] And if this were the case, Burns believed Skaaren and Parsley were benefiting.

Skaaren spent a week in New York. During the meeting, Peraino stood by the company's early report that showed the picture actually lost money after expenses. Skaaren couldn't accept this, given how well the movie did when it opened in Texas and other markets as evidenced by the more than $300,000 receipts accumulated by the end of 1974. With the help of attorney Arthur Klein and an audit by the New York firm Main La Frentz (which later became Peat Marwick), Skaaren combed through the documents, discovered "inaccuracies" in the expense list, and determined that the movie had indeed shown a profit. Skaaren negotiated with Peraino, who offered $25,000 in cash and three notes worth $25,000 payable over a four-month period. They finally agreed to two $28,000 checks and three notes of $24,000 each, to be paid out with interest on the first of every month through September 1975. On May 27, a week after Skaaren's return, the cast and crew received their portion, which amounted to only $5,321.33.[66]

Sometime in mid-1975 Henkel began holding "money meetings" with disgruntled members of the cast and crew. From his point of view, many didn't understand the split between Vortex and MAB because they were too inexperienced to realize what their share of the profits actually represented. Ed Neal was among those who attended the meetings. "They were very difficult to go to because what you learned was that Ron Bozman and a couple of other people—not Bill Parsley so much but a couple of other people—were making $7,000 a month monitoring the film."[67] Skaaren's monitoring fee entitled him to three percent of the profits off the top, while Bozman's agreement with Vortex gave him one percent of their shares, or half a percent of the entire profits.

Bob Burns took issue with the fact that P.I.T.S., the group of eleven second-round investors, was getting paid before the cast and crew. Burns alleged that illegal practices ensued, and he sued Hooper and Henkel for drawing up a fraudulent contract. "Everyone on the cast and crew was just incensed, but I couldn't get anybody to go in and sue them because everybody figured Tobe's going to take us all along with him."[68]

Bozman acknowledges that some people, like Burns, felt they were mistreated but insists that all involved received what was due them. "Everyone got their percentage of what came in. No one took anything except what was contractually due them. Everyone got paid about $100 or so," he says of the cast and crew's deferred salaries, and he claims that he made only about $2,000 for a year's worth of work. "I had to stop and go do commercials to make a living."[69]

During the summer of 1975, while *Chainsaw* continued to reap profits at the box office, Skaaren began to make plans for the sequel. He recognized the financial potential in establishing a franchise based on the original movie, and he very much wanted the Skaaren Corporation to helm any follow-up to *Chainsaw*. By August he had negotiated a one-year option with Vortex and Parsley to develop the project. Over the next few months, Parsley bankrolled Skaaren's efforts to develop the sequel to the tune of $3,500.[70]

In early September the *Chainsaw* cast and crew received more bad news from Henkel. Although Vortex and MAB had earned a profit of $5,734, Henkel wrote in a memo, they would not be receiving any disbursements because the funds were needed in escrow to cover the costs of a possible audit. Vortex had requested its final $24,000 payment from Bryanston, who responded that it would be delayed. As with earlier profit summaries, the principals intended to challenge Bryanston's latest report because of its low figures. On September 24, Vortex received its final payment with interest. After Skaaren's monitoring fee and Parsley's half interest were deducted, in addition to the legal and accounting fees, taxes, and other expenses, $8,100 remained to be divided among 81 percentage points, which represented the cast, crew, and other investors.[71]

In October the *New York Times* published a front-page article about Bryanston's ties to the mafia and the hard-core pornography industry. Citing the Peraino family's involvement in the production and distribution of *Deep Throat*, which was the subject of a pending obscenity case in Memphis, the article detailed how the profits from the film had been used to establish Bryanston. It also mentioned *Chainsaw* as one of the company's "legitimate" titles currently in distribution.[72] By November, the balance in *Chainsaw*'s escrow account dipped to a new low. It was clear that something had to be done about Bryanston.

Although their New York lawyers advised against a suit, Parsley, for one, was ready to move forward. He convinced Henkel, Hooper, and the others to hire fellow investor and Austin attorney Robert Kuhn to represent them. In exchange, Kuhn would receive a deferred fee of $5,000 and one-quarter of all monies and property recovered from the distributor. Recalls Parsley's son, Clint, "Kuhn was supposed to be the Wild West lawyer sent to bring justice to the district of New York." The next step required a face-to-face meeting with Peraino, which was scheduled for the following month.[73]

The streets of New York's warehouse district were fairly empty when Skaaren, Parsley, and Kuhn arrived at Bryanston's Ninth Avenue offices on the morning of December 8. The scene inside Lou Peraino's office hadn't changed much from the first time Skaaren and Bozman had met the brothers in August 1974. A few of Peraino's lieutenants positioned themselves around the room. But unlike Skaaren's first encounter with the Bryanston president, this meeting lacked most of the usual social niceties. Kuhn reminded the Perainos that they'd come to audit *Chainsaw*'s books, but Peraino said the bookkeeper was ill and unavailable. Kuhn responded, "If you don't let us examine those books, you don't leave me any choice but to sue you." Peraino looked across his desk at the Texas lawyer. His voice was low and even. "You haven't got enough balls to sue me."[74]

"Well, he was partially right about that," Kuhn recalls years later. "I didn't sue him in New York. I came back to Texas and filed the suit." Six months after the meeting, on May 12, 1976, Vortex, Kuhn, and Katherine Henkel (as former shareholders in MAB, which had been dissolved by Parsley around August 1975) sued Bryanston Pictures for breach of contract.[75]

Skaaren spent the first two months of 1976 placing phone calls to Bryanston and struggling to pull together the funds to settle *Chainsaw*'s overdue bill with their New York legal representation. In early March, Sidney Finger began to audit Bryanston's books in preparation for the Texans' suit against the distributor. Finger would spend six months trying in vain to complete the audit. Years later he described the experience as being "as much of a horror story as the movie."[76]

In late April 1976, a Memphis jury convicted Louis Peraino and his uncle Joseph of "conspiring to distribute obscenity [the pornographic movie *Deep Throat*, which Louis Peraino allegedly co-produced with his father Anthony for $22,000] across state lines."[77] Lou received one year in prison with an additional year of probation, and he was ordered to pay a $10,000 fine. One month later Bryanston closed its doors, but not before it was cited for breach of contract in the lawsuit filed by Texas attorney Kuhn on behalf of Vortex and the former shareholders of MAB. (Although many assumed Bryanston declared bankruptcy, according to a 1982 *Los Angeles Times* article, the company had not filed the necessary papers in either New York or California.)

The legal battles and financial problems swirling around *Chainsaw* had little if any impact on the movie's reputation in Hollywood. *The Exorcist* director William Friedkin championed *Chainsaw*'s director and writer to Ned Tanen, executive vice president of Universal Pictures. By the summer of 1976, Tanen had offered Hooper and Henkel a five-picture deal, and the pair left Austin for Los Angeles.[78]

Bittersweet news arrived two months later. When *Variety* released its list of "50 Top-Grossing Films" in the final week of 1976, *Chainsaw* occupied the twenty-third spot with reported domestic gross receipts of more than $1.8 million.[79]

In February 1977, the Texans chose to settle out of court with Bryanston in an effort to regain some damages. The distributor agreed to pay $400,000 and return all *Chainsaw*-related property to Vortex, in effect returning control of the film to the filmmakers. Bryanston never fulfilled the financial end of the agreement, however, nor did Vortex retain control of *Chainsaw*. The filmmakers discovered that in May of the previous year—a week prior to the filing of their suit, in fact—Bryanston had subdistributed *Chainsaw*'s domestic rights to independent distributor Joseph Brenner Associates for a period of three years. In exchange, the company paid off an outstanding debt of $10,000 that Bryanston owed to a vendor. This agreement was in clear violation of Bryanston's 1974 contract with Vortex and MAB, and it involved an additional suit for the Texans that was finally settled in August 1977.[80]

Decades later, investor David Foster is still fuming. "I hate to be made a fool of. They made a lot of money. No one wanted to release the picture, and I got the damn picture released. That's the thank-you: they screw you." Accountant Glass estimates that he has divvied up approximately two million dollars among *Chainsaw*'s participants and investors over the course of about three decades. "I used to get two- and three-hundred thousand dollar checks once in while," says Glass. "The checks I get now [circa 2003] are $25,000 or $30,000, something like that."[81]

The financial debacle continued into the 1980s with additional suits and countersuits and involved a series of distributors. Shortly after finalizing Bryanston's agreement with Vortex and MAB in 1974, Peraino signed an agreement with JAD, a distribution entity, to handle all of *Chainsaw*'s foreign rights. This agreement eventually led to numerous suits among JAD, a film processing lab, and the Texas filmmakers. By 1978 Brenner's contract to distribute the film in the United States had expired, and Parsley and Kuhn began to negotiate with New Line Cinema, an independent distributor. But the former MAB shareholders didn't get very far in their negotiations. "We were in the process of talking to New Line about them distributing it when we got involved in this lawsuit with Henkel and Hooper," explains Kuhn. The filmmakers were angry that Parsley and Kuhn had moved forward without consulting them, and Henkel felt that as president of Vortex, it was up to him to protect the filmmakers' interests.[82]

The suit languished in the Texas courts for more than two years, during which time *Chainsaw* ceased to be in distribution. Austin-based United States District Judge Jack Roberts eventually settled the case by ruling in favor of the filmmakers. The suit was settled in April 1981 with Roberts awarding Kuhn one-quarter of the film's profits through 1978 (the year Brenner ceased distributing *Chainsaw*).[83]

At the conclusion of the suit, Judge Roberts divided $127,000 in profits among the investors and filmmakers, money which had been placed on deposit with the court for the duration of the lawsuit.[84] Roberts also appointed a young attorney, Charles Grigson, as a trustee. Grigson replaced Joe Longley, one of the original P.I.T.S. investors, who had been appointed by the court during the trial as special master to get the film back from Joseph Brenner and into new distributorship. Longley handled negotiations with potential companies such as New Line, until a court order decreed that Longley be replaced with a trustee who would represent the film's owners, collecting profits due and, if necessary, negotiating future distribution agreements. Investor Kuhn objected to Grigson's appointment and spent two years filing appeals, but Judge Roberts's decision eventually was affirmed.

By 1979, while the Texas suit was still in progress, Skaaren had received letters from at least two companies interested in distributing *Chainsaw* on videocassette in the relatively new home video market. In October 1980, *Chainsaw*'s primary investors signed a distribution agreement with the principals of New Line Cinema to re-release the film in theaters. By the time the Texas suit was settled six months later, according to Henkel, *Chainsaw* had opened in twenty theaters in California and grossed $150,000 in its first two weeks alone.[85]

Between *Chainsaw*'s first release through Bryanston in 1974 and just prior to its re-release in 1981, the film's profits from worldwide distribution—minus bills due, attorneys' fees, and investor payments—reportedly came to about $45,000. If the situation surrounding *Chainsaw*'s initial domestic distribution was fraught with difficulties, its overseas distribution was even more challenging. In England alone, for instance, the film had multiple distributors. Of the $45,000 in profit shares received by Hooper, Henkel, and the other Vortex participants (mostly cast and crew) through 1981, less than half (approximately $20,000) represented the film's overseas release in at least eighty-five countries. At one point during this period, Skaaren made a list of sixty-seven overseas cities and countries where *Chainsaw* was due to play. For just nine of these markets he noted profits totaling in excess of $250,000.[86]

According to New Line Cinema president Bob Shaye, the company's U.S. re-release of *Chainsaw* in 1981 yielded profits in excess of $6 million, which translated into approximately $1 million earned by Vortex and the other

CHAINSAWS, SLACKERS, AND SPY KIDS

Texas shareholders. A later audit of New Line's distribution revealed errors totaling $39,233.40 and unreported revenue of more than $44,000. "They're all thieves," says Kuhn of the distribution side of the film business. Years later, after a similarly protracted experience with a *Chainsaw* sequel and a different distributor, Kuhn would be told by the distributors themselves that he should have bargained for more profits.[87]

### Afterlife

In the year following New Line's 1981 re-release of the movie, Skaaren pressed forward with plans to make a sequel of the film, and by late 1983 it seemed as if *Chainsaw*'s sequel was about to become a reality. On November 2, a full-page advertisement appeared in the *Hollywood Reporter* announcing *The Texas Chainsaw Massacre Part II*.[88] Hooper was listed as the director and co-producer, with Henkel receiving the writing credit and Skaaren assuming co-producing duties. Kuhn objected to Skaaren's involvement with the sequel and in an October 1983 letter had expressed his own interest in purchasing the rights to a follow-up. Delays would hamper the production and release of the sequel, however, which was shot in Austin and distributed through Cannon Films in 1986. *The Texas Chainsaw Massacre 2* was the third in a three-picture deal Hooper had struck with Cannon, having made *Lifeforce* (1985) and remade the 1953 science-fiction film *Invaders From Mars* (1986) with the company's financial backing. Hooper directed the film from a script by L. M. Kit Carson, a screenwriter (he co-wrote *Paris, Texas*) and a friend. Although Henkel and Hooper had worked on a number of drafts for a sequel, Hooper eventually partnered with Carson. (Henkel received a credit on the film based on his co-creation of the original characters.) *Chainsaw 2* featured Dennis Hopper as a Texas sheriff, and Jim Siedow reprised his role as The Cook. Siedow was the only cast member from the original film to appear in the sequel (Lou Perryman, who worked on the original crew, had a small role in *Chainsaw 2*). This was the source of much back and forth in print between the filmmakers and the original cast, and it stirred up old resentments. The sequel opened in August 1986 and earned back more than half of its $4 million production budget on opening weekend. It received mixed reviews but generally disappointed audiences and disappeared fairly quickly from theaters.

In spite of Skaaren's ambivalence about the film, *The Texas Chainsaw Massacre* has withstood the test of time. It is widely regarded as a cult classic and one of the first slasher films, and it consistently appears on "Best Of" lists year after year. Retrospective screenings with various cast members in attendance continue to draw crowds. And despite the fact that the majority of *Chainsaw*'s principals never got rich off the film, *Chainsaw* keeps generating sequels, remakes, and prequels, many of them made in Austin.

In the early 1990s Henkel would reluctantly team as director with attorney Robert Kuhn to make their version of a *Chainsaw* sequel. *Texas Chainsaw Massacre: The Next Generation*, which was eventually released in 1997 after a three-year legal battle, co-starred Matthew McConaughey and Renée Zellweger in a story that introduces a new generation of teenagers to the Leatherface family. *Next Generation* did poorly upon release, but it provided employment to locals like cinematographer Lee Daniel (*Slacker, Dazed and Confused*) and editor Sandra Adair, who a year later would begin her long association with Richard Linklater. McConaughey, who gives an inspired performance as the maniacal older brother to Leatherface, was also grateful for the work. The then-unknown first auditioned for Henkel in a small supporting role shortly after he wrapped Linklater's *Dazed and Confused*. Emboldened by the fact that Henkel had yet to cast the main part of Vilmer, McConaughey read for and won the part. Low on money and en route to California with a U-Haul full of belongings, recalls McConaughey, "All of a sudden, I had what seemed to be a month's work."[89]

In 2003 producer Michael Bay released his version of the original *Chainsaw*, a much gorier remake starring Jessica Biel that was shot in and around Austin in 2002. Henkel and Hooper were co-producers, and cinematographer Daniel Pearl signed on to shoot the film for director Marcus Nispel. This version of *The Texas Chainsaw Massacre* even had its world premiere sponsored by the Alamo Drafthouse Theater, an innovative Austin franchise run by movie fans Tim and Karrie League. Their decision to stage the screening at a former Austin institution for the mentally impaired is typical of the Leagues' cheeky programming.[90] Buoyed by the remake's healthy box office, Bay produced the prequel *The Texas Chainsaw Massacre: The Beginning* (2006) in nearby Granger a few years later. Once again Henkel and Hooper were involved as co-producers, and Kuhn executive produced.

As a co-producer Henkel no doubt profited to some extent from these most recent retakes of his original script, but he seems almost stubbornly proud of the first film's financial legacy, despite having missed out on a considerable portion of its profits. As Henkel observes, "Ask anyone how many independent films have actually made any money, and *Chainsaw* will be one of the few."[91]

2

# Eagle Pennell and the Rise of Regional Filmmaking

A few months after Tobe Hooper and Kim Henkel settled their lawsuit with Bryanston Pictures in 1977, twenty-three-year-old University of Texas film school dropout Eagle Pennell was shooting his first independent feature and using *The Texas Chainsaw Massacre*'s storied box office success to sell his own project. *Chainsaw*'s financial picture in reality may have been bleak for those who made the film, but its reputation already was taking on a life of its own. Pennell and his writing partner Lin Sutherland spent the summer of 1977 calling on friends and family to raise funds for a blue-collar comedy called *The Whole Shootin' Match*. They began filming in the fall, and by December the cast and crew had assembled at Steiner Ranch, about eleven miles northwest of Austin, to shoot the movie's final scenes.

They were running behind as the afternoon light faded and the camera ran out of film. "It was foggy, and if we came back we couldn't match the light," remembered *Chainsaw*'s Lou Perryman, who co-starred in the film. "You all stay here," Pennell told the cast and crew, and he drove back to Austin to buy more film. Pennell arrived at Photo Processors, a lab on Congress Avenue, but couldn't find the owner. Night had fallen by the time Pennell finagled the film stock he needed, and Pennell decided to stay in town. The cast and crew fell asleep waiting for him to return, which he did around five the next morning with a number of 100-foot rolls of film and no explanation for his extended absence. Miraculously the fog had held, and the light remained much the same.[1]

More surprising was the fact that Pennell's cast and crew didn't abandon him and the production, which had quickly spiraled out of control months earlier thanks to Pennell's drinking, drug-taking, and all-around bad behavior. By the time they shot the movie's final scenes, screenwriter Lin Sutherland had broken up with the abusive filmmaker, who began having an affair with lead actress Doris Hargrave. Pennell had alienated nearly everyone on *Shootin' Match,* and yet they waited for him that night and into the next morning.

"That was part of Eagle's charisma," explains Sutherland. "He got everyone believing deeply in this project and committed to it."[2]

Pennell's charisma served him well, but ultimately it was his talent that earned him international recognition and acclaim for *Shootin' Match.* Championed by industry players like Roger Ebert and Gene Siskel, *Hollywood Reporter*'s Arthur Knight, and Universal Pictures executive Verna Fields, Pennell and *Shootin' Match* even inspired Robert Redford's creation of the Sundance Institute after the film screened at the inaugural Sundance Film Festival (then the U.S. Film Festival). And despite Pennell's best efforts to hog the spotlight, the film launched the Hollywood careers of a number of Austin actors, including Sonny Carl Davis (*Fast Times at Ridgemont High, Thelma & Louise*) and Doris Hargrave (*The Hollywood Knights, The Astronaut Farmer*). Decades before Richard Linklater's *Slacker,* Pennell created one of the first regional feature films with national appeal. Released in 1978, *Shootin' Match* depicted a bunch of Texans who were infinitely more realistic and interesting than the Ewing clan, the fictional Texas family introduced the same year in the popular primetime series *Dallas.*

Like *Slacker, Shootin' Match* was a film with enough energy and charm to transcend its low-budget roots. It catapulted Pennell onto a national stage, but he was ill prepared to take advantage of the opportunities success brought. He would manage to direct a handful of films, including *Last Night at the Alamo* (1984) and *Doc's Full Service* (1994), each of which hinted at his early promise. Indeed, *Last Night at the Alamo* mimicked *Shootin' Match*'s breakout success in many ways, but Pennell's self-destructive lifestyle ultimately would destroy his career. Even before his untimely death in 2002 at the age of 49, Pennell had become both a cult figure and a cautionary tale to another generation of filmmakers that included Linklater and Quentin Tarantino. Tarantino saw *Last Night* while clerking at a California video store and drew inspiration from Pennell's low-budget trick of confining most of the action to a single interior set. "I wanted to be a filmmaker, and I'm like, 'I could do that! I could write a movie that all takes place in a bar.' And that's what I ended up doing with *Reservoir Dogs*. Seventy-five percent of it takes place in a warehouse."[3]

## The Pinnells of West Texas

The rangy Pennell hailed from West Texas, living with his three siblings and parents for a time in Lubbock and then moving to College Station, where his father, Charles, taught engineering at Texas A&M University. He was born Glenn Irwin Pinnell on July 28, 1952, but in his early twenties he changed the spelling of his last name and christened himself "Eagle," the story goes, after screenwriter Kit Carson's brother "Goat" observed that Pennell's prominent nose resembled an eagle's beak.

As a child, Eagle spent summers with his grandparents, and he was deeply proud of his Texas roots. Although his father became an academic later in life, Charles Pinnell lived the life of a cowboy growing up in West Texas. English documentarian Brian Huberman met Pennell in the late 1970s and struck up a friendship that hinged in part on their shared love of all things western, especially movies by John Ford and Raoul Walsh. "He was totally connected to that spirit of the Southwest. J. Frank Dobie had to struggle to justify the culture of the Southwest, and I think Eagle liked to think of himself as being with Dobie and Roy Bedicheck and others," says Huberman, who worked with Pennell on his two later films. Ford's film *She Wore a Yellow Ribbon* so inspired Pennell, he would later claim, that he decided to alter the spelling of his last name to resemble that of Lt. Ross Penell, a character played by Harry Carey Jr. The minor change also may have grown out of Eagle's desire to make a name for himself—literally, perhaps—in Austin. "He was proud of his family but at the same time there was a distance," says his younger brother Chuck Pinnell.[4]

## Making a Name for Himself

He enrolled at the University of Texas, choosing to major in film because it seemed easy and sounded sexy. Recalled Pennell, "A friend of mine in the same dorm showed up one night and said that we'd been taxing our brains with all these pre-law and philosophy courses for nothing. That there was a thing called RTF, where you could get a grade for just watching movies. Plus girls love filmmakers. So I signed up the next semester." Pennell's interest in moviemaking dated back to his teen years, when he would borrow his father's Super 8 camera to film his two younger sisters and his brother as they acted out short skits. Still, he dropped out of UT in 1973 during his junior year. Pennell took offense years later when articles reported that he learned filmmaking while a student. "I've heard it said in the press that I graduated from the University of Texas (Radio-Television-Film) department. I take that as an insult. I never graduated from a film school at all," he boasted to a film festival crowd in 1978. Around the time he left UT, Pennell met Lou Perryman, who was living with his brother Ron in the Eastwoods Park neighborhood just north of campus. Pennell frequently dropped by Lou's place, and the two would talk about movies for hours. After UT, Pennell started working for Richard Kidd's production company Filmhouse, where he met other freelancers like Tobe Hooper.[5]

Armed with production skills and access to equipment, Pennell began shooting his first film, a short documentary produced for the Rodeo Cowboy Association called *Rodeo School*. The documentary screened at Austin's first film and video festival in April 1975. Organized by Pennell and local filmmaker Maureen Gosling (who would later co-found Flower Films with independent filmmaker Les Blank), the Change the Reel Festival featured four days of movies, most of them made by Austin filmmakers. A panel of local critics selected an ambitious 60 films including *David Holzman's Diary* (featuring L. M. Kit Carson), *Giant*, and *The Texas Chainsaw Massacre* as well as Hooper's comedic short *The Heisters* and the Peter, Paul, and Mary documentary. The pilot episode of the locally produced musical program *Austin City Limits*, which featured Willie Nelson, opened the festival. Five hundred people packed the Ritz Theater on Sixth Street during the four-day event.[6]

A year or so later Pennell began work on his first narrative short. Originally titled *Saturday Night*, the story was loosely based on a *Texas Monthly* article about rednecks written by Larry L. King. Pennell's script also borrowed from a real-life incident that reportedly occurred at the Armadillo World Headquarters. An angry patron arrived at the club one Saturday night armed with a gun and looking to settle a score with one of the Armadillo's bouncers. After a night of drinking, the customer mistakenly shot and killed one of the artists who designed posters for the club. Pennell cast Perryman and Sonny Carl Davis in the lead roles as two redneck buddies who drown their sorrows after being laid off from their roofing jobs and get into trouble at a local honky-tonk. Davis was an Austin bartender and member of the band Uranium Savages, and he was also an aspiring actor who had heard Pennell was a filmmaker. "He had a cockiness about him that I find offensive in most people," recalls Davis of their first meeting, but he told Pennell to keep him in mind for any future projects.[7]

Davis and Perryman shared an affable on-screen chemistry, despite an inauspicious beginning. One of the first scenes they shot was the climax, where Davis's character dies at the Soap Creek Saloon. "They put this bullet hole on my bald head, and I'm lying out on the cold floor of the bar, dying in Lou's arms." Pennell wanted Perryman to cry in the scene, but the actor, who had never taken a class, didn't know how to cry on cue. "I couldn't weep so I made up this dialogue. Sonny started laughing and reached up and touched his wound," said Perryman. Davis was unprepared for Perryman's improvised speech and thought it was some kind of a joke. "It was pretty syrupy. You could pour his speech over a waffle," remembers Davis. Pennell shot the thirty-minute featurette in black and white for about $1,500, saving money by scamming freebies and borrowing equipment and locations. One day during production the cast and crew were driving around Austin looking for a realistic place to shoot some of the roofing scenes. When they spotted a truck pulling a roofer's rig, they followed it into the parking lot of an apartment building and convinced the driver to let them film a scene next to the tar truck.[8]

They finished the movie within a few weeks, shooting much of it on the weekends. When it came time to record a score, Pennell got in touch with his younger brother Chuck, who by this time was majoring in classical guitar at the University of North Texas in Denton. Eagle described the film to Chuck, who agreed to drive down to Austin with a friend and record the music. "We were told the basic kinds of moods that we needed to create and came up with two or three things that worked reasonably well," recalls Pinnell.[9] The aspiring musicians worked with Wayne Bell, the boom operator who also supplied sound effects on *The Texas Chainsaw Massacre*. Bell oversaw the sound recording, design, and mixing of Pennell's short. The threesome spent one night in an Austin garage composing and recording the songs as Pennell hovered in the background, editing feverishly on a borrowed Steenbeck. Changing its title to *A Hell of a Note*, Pennell screened the short in local theaters to favorable reviews.

Pennell's short film also received a mention in the Texas Film Commission's semi-monthly newsletter. "Big Producers fretting over their multi-million dollar budgets will be shaken to learn that someone in Texas has made a half-hour semi-feature for $1500," the article began. Pennell saved the write-up and mailed a copy to his parents in College Station. "Dear Folks," he scribbled, "there is an article about my film on page 5." For all his bluster and bravado, it seemed Pennell still valued his family's approval. He even signed the note using his given name, Glenn.[10]

## Comin' Back to Go

It was with *A Hell of a Note* in 1977 that Pennell wooed writer Lin Sutherland to work with him on his first full-length feature. One night at the Soap Creek Saloon, Pennell approached Sutherland, introduced himself, and started to tell her about his movies.

Sutherland had no screenwriting experience, but that was okay with Pennell. He couldn't afford to pay a real screenwriter, but he knew he wanted someone with a writing background. Sutherland had graduated from UT with a B.A. in English and Anthropology and then moved to England to earn a master's degree. Upon her return to Austin she found work writing press releases for the county's mental health services department and for St. Edward's University, a local liberal arts college. Born and raised in Austin, Sutherland's family spanned seven generations of Texans. Her aunt Liz Carpenter had been Lady Bird Johnson's press secretary during LBJ's presidency.

Pennell was prone to womanizing, and he fancied himself as a ladies' man despite a self-consciousness about his crooked front teeth, which he hid for a time with a droopy mustache. He pursued Sutherland, which complicated her ten-year relationship with local artist David Elliott. "There was a lot of personal sacrifice in doing this film," she recalls of her eventual split with Elliott.[11] She was seduced by Pennell's talent and the thrill of collaborating on such a creative project. When Pennell showed her *A Hell of a Note*, she fell in love with Skeet and Jimmie Lee, played by Perryman and Davis.

She and Pennell began writing almost immediately. They sat at a table tossing ideas back and forth for each act or "chapter" of the story, discussing what would happen next. Sutherland typed out their ideas, and they'd talk some more. Like the characters in *A Hell of a Note*, Sutherland and Pennell had their own creative chemistry. The experience stimulated Sutherland despite the negative impact it was having on her personal life. They looked to the "real Texans" from their own families to inspire Lloyd and Frank, the two rednecks in a script that originally was called *Comin' Back to Go*. Although Pennell himself came from a decidedly middle-class background, he felt an affinity for blue-collar characters and their struggles.[12]

By the summer of 1977 Kim Henkel and Tobe Hooper were in Los Angeles under contract with Universal. Henkel had met Pennell in 1975 when he was still living in Austin and Pennell was making the rodeo documentary. "Eagle would just drop in periodically. He would just come in, sit down and say nothing. He'd sit there for forty-five minutes or an hour, then excuse himself and leave," Henkel recalls. "I tend to be rather taciturn if left to my own devices, so it didn't bother me in the least." After Pennell and Sutherland finished their script, Pennell sent it off to Henkel in Los Angeles. He read it and made some notes, and the two had a few conversations about it. "There was a basic story there," Henkel recalls. "But the best part of what happened there with the characters is really a product of Lou Perryman, the setting, and Doris Hargrave. There wasn't enough of an overall structure for them to really develop those characters beyond the moment."[13]

Once the script was finished, Pennell offered Sutherland a co-producer credit in exchange for help in securing the movie's financing. Fresh off the thrill of their stimulating collaboration, Sutherland agreed despite having no experience and little desire to hit up her family and friends for money. She wrote a treatment of the screenplay, and the pair made appointments. In July 1977 a lawyer friend helped them set up their own company, Maverick Films, Inc., which they operated out of Pennell's house on Elmwood Place. They "talked" the script to potential investors like Johnny Jenkins, a rare books dealer and local eccentric who had put up $2,000 as a second-round investor in *Chainsaw*.[14] Pennell and Sutherland naively pointed to the low-budget horror movie as an example of the earning potential of an independent production. Their enthusiasm was contagious, and money began to trickle in. Over the course of three to four months, the pair raised about $43,000 from twenty-one investors. (Later Pennell would brag they made the film for one-third its actual budget.)

Pennell found Doris Hargrave, Eric Henshaw, and other local actors, some with previous credits, to fill out the rest of the cast. A thirty-four-year-old mother of two, Hargrave had been acting since the age of ten and forfeited a drama scholarship to UT when she became pregnant and married her high school sweetheart. After living for a time in Europe, Hargrave and her husband returned to Austin, and she was taking acting classes at UT when she heard about *Whole Shootin' Match*. Henshaw had majored in theater at UT and traveled around the country with a touring company before returning to Austin in 1977, where he read about the auditions in the local paper. Wayne Bell returned to supervise sound and music, and Pennell once again turned to his younger brother for the movie's score. Sometime in the late summer or early fall of 1977 Pennell wrote to Chuck, "I'd like for you to begin thinking about the music for the picture, although it can be hard without first seeing it." He wanted original music, country and western songs "but with a twist as I do not want to hear the same ol' CW thing, I'd like to hear CW with other influences in it (Spanish, rock, Neil Young or whatever you think will work). Remember that anything can work as long as it *feels* right and is different," Pennell continued. Although they had worked together on *A Hell of a Note*, their relationship was still tenuous and Pinnell was a little puzzled that his brother sought him out even though he knew many other musicians in Austin. "I think it was his sense of family, or maybe he believed in me. That was one of his strong points: He could read people for what they could give him. He had a strong sense of where to go to get what he needed."[15]

Rehearsals began in early September, with the cast meeting on weeknights to go over the script. The actors would work through scenes, reading their lines into tape recorders to take with them on location. Actual production began in early October and took place over ten weekends, when the cast and crew were free from their day jobs.[16] Everyone but Pennell had employment. Instead he lived off of a portion of the movie's budget and dipped into Sutherland's personal savings.

At first, the set of *The Whole Shootin' Match* was a fun place to be. The tall, good-looking director rallied his cast and crew not unlike a good general rallies a volunteer army. A devoted student of Texas history, Pennell often invoked legendary figures like Sam Houston and Davy Crockett in conversation. Pennell demanded long hours from his actors and the crew, taking up all of their available free time over the more than two months of filming.

Once on location, the actors took inspiration from their tape-recorded rehearsals. For Perryman, it was the best possible acting experience. "We would listen to an improvised scene until it began to build, then we turned off the recorder and took off on our own." He recalled the actors being "off book" for a good chunk of the movie, making it up as they went along. "The script got dumped," insists Hargrave, who felt her character needed some work.[17] "Paulette was an accessory to their story, which is kind of how Eagle treated women," she says. Other actors with more experience resented Pennell's hands-off style of directing, which he later described as "structured improvisation." Pennell believed that by letting the actors use the script as a jumping-off point, he would elicit a more spontaneous, and thus more naturalistic, performance. He wanted real characters, he said, not puppets. "He was not a director who would come in and give you any creative input that made any difference at all," recalls Hargrave. Henshaw, who played Olan in the movie, also thought Pennell could have spent more time with his actors. "The position of his camera, the clarity of his image—that's what worried him," he said.[18]

Strapped for cash, Pennell took a bare bones approach to filming. For a night scene in which Perryman's and Davis's characters argue with one another, the actors sat in the cab of a stationary pickup truck while someone on the crew stood outside the vehicle, swinging a light back and forth to make it look as if cars were passing by. "We didn't have enough crew to have somebody wiggle the bumper so that it looked anything at all like we were actually driving," Perryman recalled.[19] Pennell gave them a thumbs-up after their first take and moved on to the next scene. Overly impressed with their abilities, the actors took to calling themselves the One Take Kings. Years later, they realized there hadn't been enough film to shoot another take.

Toward the end of the shooting schedule, the cast and crew assembled at Steiner Ranch to film the movie's last scenes. The on-set mood had long since soured. Perryman had grown jealous of his co-star because he felt the story privileged Davis's character, Frank, as well as the relationship between Frank and Paulette. "I think once Eagle saw that I could develop the character, he made room," says Hargrave. "I think Doris also drew [the story] away because she was so strong and just wonderful," adds Davis. "It's two good ol' boys inspired by *Hell of a Note*, and all of a sudden there's some other stuff [with Paulette]. I think Lou could feel it."[20]

By this time Pennell also was having an affair with Hargrave. Pennell and Sutherland's relationship had disintegrated into verbal and physical abuse, fueled by his penchant for vodka and drugs. "Lin was the antithesis of Eagle," says Henshaw. "He was the taker, she was the giver." Sutherland claims that Pennell battered her twice, and there was at least one instance when she had to call Doug Holloway, the movie's cinematographer, to intervene. Recalls Davis, who along with the rest of the cast and crew watched the relationship implode, "Eagle never showed too much respect for other people, especially women." Says Sutherland, "Eagle had just been abusive so much to the cast members, to the crew members, and to me. I had just had it with Eagle's drinking and his cocaine habit." As soon as the last scene was shot, Sutherland told him, she was off the project.[21]

True to her word, Sutherland distanced herself from Pennell and the film after production wrapped in late 1977. But Pennell would find reasons to get in touch with her. "He would use the movie to draw me back in, the spider to the web," she remembers. "He cared so little about other people. He was willing to do anything—use people—and I was extremely young and innocent.

I really believe that Eagle was evil. I really believe that. I say that because evil means not caring at all about anyone, and he didn't. Not even himself. He was willing to take anybody down, and he did. Over and over."[22]

Meanwhile Pennell edited the movie while his brother and Bell worked on the soundtrack. Chuck Pinnell had written a few songs in the fall while still in school, and he came to Austin during his three-week Christmas break to record the score and work with Bell to refine the music.

By the beginning of 1978, Pennell had a final cut and began sending it to film festivals around the country. He also spent time trying to convince Sutherland to accompany him to Los Angeles, where he planned to shop the film to distributors. She reluctantly agreed. "Like a lot of abusers, he would weep and say, 'I'll never do that again,'" Sutherland explains. "You wanted to give him a second chance because he had such talent."[23] She arrived in Los Angeles a few weeks after Pennell. As much as she wanted nothing to do with the filmmaker, she was as determined as he to get the movie into theaters.


## Regional Cinema, National Success

*The Whole Shootin' Match* received its first big break when a jury of industry insiders selected the film to play in Dallas's USA Film Festival in March 1978. Advance press materials for the festival described the film, chosen by judge and *Hollywood Reporter* columnist Arthur Knight, as "one of the first truly 'regional cinema' feature films with enough humor and serendipity to appeal to nationwide audiences." Pennell, Perryman, Davis, Hargrave, and other members of the cast and crew appeared with the film, which was embraced by the festival audience. "There was this heady sense of something about to happen," remembers Hargrave.[24]

Knight devoted much of his post-festival column to *Shootin' Match*, calling it "the revelation of this year's Festival." The columnist, who compared Davis to "a young Robert Duvall," observed that festival audiences forgave the film its technical limitations (poor sound quality, dim lighting in some places, etc.) because they related to Pennell and Sutherland's characters. "Both the characters and their milieu are wholly believable, their story unfolding without conventional dramatic values but with a growing tensity," wrote Knight. "The people involved in this film were not merely dedicated; they also had the talent to bring off a regional film that has the potential of reaching a national audience." The problem, Knight observed, would be finding a distributor willing to take a chance on a small film that lacked movie stars and "conventional thrills."[25]

In Los Angeles, Pennell and Sutherland were finding this to be true. They hawked the film to small distributors, distribution houses, and anyone else they could get on the phone, "half of which," according to Sutherland, "were as crooked as a dog's hind legs." By the time the USA Film Festival had chosen *Shootin' Match*, Pennell had inked a deal with New Line Cinema, the same company that would distribute *The Texas Chainsaw Massacre* in the early 1980s. New Line agreed to a limited release for *Shootin' Match*, beginning that summer in New York, in art-house theaters and on college campuses. A European release also was a possibility. Says Sutherland, "We made as good a deal as we could make." Pennell grew unhappy with New Line's promotion of the film (years later he boasted that he threatened to throw a company executive out an office window), but *Shootin' Match* rolled along on word-of-mouth buzz and glowing reviews by Knight and other industry heavyweights.[26]

Meanwhile Sutherland and Pennell's relationship remained strained at best. As they promoted the film, Pennell often neglected to mention Sutherland's or anyone else's contribution during interviews. Davis accompanied Pennell to some of the festivals where *Shootin' Match* screened, and he sat on panels with the director and listened as he took credit for the movie. At other times Pennell seemed to recognize his limitations. After Sutherland arrived in Los Angeles, for instance, he insisted she keep the print of the film. "He would rely on me in ways that were so odd," Sutherland recalls. "He would put the film in my hands saying, 'I don't trust myself with this.' At times he had these flashes of honesty about himself. He knew how much he needed others. But he just was hell bent for ruination."[27]

After *Whole Shootin' Match* opened in New York that summer, it was selected as one of six finalists to screen in September at the six-day U.S. Film Festival in Salt Lake City, Utah. The new festival was the creation of filmmaker Sterling Van Wagenen, whose cousin was married at the time to Robert Redford. One of Van Wagenen's goals in organizing the festival was to spotlight "small regional films being made outside the Hollywood system, mostly in 16mm." *The Whole Shootin' Match* certainly met the criteria for entry. Van Wagenen managed to track down Pennell and convinced him to enter the film in competition. Although Claudia Weil's debut feature *Girlfriends* won first place, *Whole Shootin' Match* garnered a "special second prize" from the jury, who reportedly engaged in a lively two-hour debate over the final decision.[28]

Pennell toasted the film's warm reception at a post-awards dinner and then at a raucous after-party, held at the home of Lory Smith, the festival's programmer and co-founder. "When Eagle Pennell arrived, he took off his sports jacket, whirled it around his head, and tossed it into the bushes," recalled Smith of Pennell's dramatic entrance. When it came time for Pennell to leave, he couldn't find the jacket. Drunk and belligerent, he railed at his host about his missing coat, which he assumed had been stolen. Then Pennell threatened to start a fight.[29]

At the same party Pennell met up with fellow filmmaker Pat Russell, who had recently made her own first feature, a semi-autobiographical narrative called *Reaching Out*. The two spent the night together, and Russell subsequently became pregnant with Pennell's child. Although Pennell would prove to be an unreliable parent, Russell has kept in touch with the Pinnell family over the years.[30]

The 1978 U.S. Film Festival was one of the few instances when Pennell's personal theatrics didn't interfere with his reputation as a filmmaker. Redford attended the festival and was greatly impressed by *Shootin' Match*. A few years later, while in Austin for a fundraiser, Redford told guests that the film was an inspiration for the Sundance Institute. "I'm not just telling you this to be saying it, but that film had a lot to do with our starting the institute. It was an excellent, regional film and our emphasis at the institute is on filmmakers who have things to say about their part of the country," said Redford, who as a child had spent summers visiting his grandfather in Austin. Pennell also charmed Universal Pictures production executive Verna Fields, who was a festival judge. The contacts Pennell made in Salt Lake City led to talks with three of the major film studios, and he began to think about his next feature, which he hoped to shoot in Houston, in color and on 35mm.[31]

One of the studios that showed interest was Universal. Fields championed Pennell to Universal's Thom Mount, executive vice president in charge of production, and after discussions with other studios, Pennell signed a development deal with Mount, announced in January 1979. The deal included Pennell's old friend Kim Henkel, who would co-produce a feature to begin production in 1980. By this time Henkel's development deal with Hooper, also at Universal, had fizzled out. But when Henkel reunited with Pennell in Los Angeles after *Shootin' Match*'s string of festival successes, he noticed a change in his friend's behavior. Prone to his own indulgences and "misconduct" at the time, Henkel observed similar tendencies in Pennell. "The Eagle that I had known, sitting on my couch in silence for hours on end in Austin, had disappeared by that time," observes Henkel. He began to feel uneasy when Pennell talked about their collaboration. "I can't remember what my reservations were, but I was very mistrustful of Eagle. I didn't have a real picture of the deal. My own judgment not being what it should have been contributed as well."[32]

*The Whole Shootin' Match* continued to chug along the festival circuit, making a significant splash in April 1979 when it played in the New Directors/New Films series at the Museum of Modern Art in New York. The *New York Times*'s Vincent Canby loved the movie and gave it a glowing review, calling it "a loving, indulgent, funny, very casual movie about the ups and downs of a couple of innocent, self-defeating American clowns." Like Arthur Knight, Canby warmed to the realistic characters, brought to life by Perryman, Davis, and Hargrave. "The good reviews are what made it," recalls Sutherland. "It was a sleeper, word-of-mouth, popular film. When Canby's review came out, it really helped a lot." New Line re-released the film in theaters that autumn, in part because of its strong festival performance and good notices. Canby gave the movie another boost when he included it in a column six months later about fall films worth noting. "Directed by Eagle Pennell and produced for a reported cost of $30,000, the movie looks every cent of it, which, in this case, is just right," wrote Canby.[33]

Sutherland was shopping film ideas but also frustrated by Pennell's habit of taking all the credit for the movie. After he had inked the deal with Universal, Sutherland vented her frustrations to Fields, whom she had befriended. She reminded Fields of her input on the script and stressed how much she had done to raise money to make the movie. Not only wasn't Pennell giving her the credit, but he had parlayed the film into a deal for himself, which she knew from experience he couldn't fulfill on his own. Fields studied Sutherland for a moment and then patted her hand. "If Eagle doesn't have the talent, time will tell," said Fields.[34]

**The Beginning of the End**

By the start of 1980, Pennell was still living in Los Angeles. He had fallen in with "a bad crowd," according to his brother, and he was living with a cocaine dealer. After more than a year, he had yet to produce an acceptable script for Universal. "He wasn't much for digging in the dirt and nurturing it day to day, the things that you have to do to nurture a project along. He was much more into the flash of the lifestyle—the pretty girls, the booze and the drugs," recalls Pinnell. Eagle decided to return to Texas, uncertain of his next creative move. Henkel, who had found collaborating with Pennell to be difficult, wasn't certain that the filmmaker was ready to do another picture. "Eagle wanted the excitement of making a film more than he wanted anything else. Not even the making of a film so much as the excitement that surrounds that process, the celebrity that surrounds that process."[35]

By this time Sutherland and Pennell had struck a deal with a new distributor, Cinema Perspectives, and throughout 1980 *Whole Shootin' Match* continued to screen in small theaters around the country. The film did acceptable business in places like Atlanta; Santa Fe; Boulder; and Cambridge, Massachusetts. In February of that year the film also played as part of the Berlin International Film Festival, which sparked interest from various German television networks. Without consulting Sutherland or anyone else connected to *Whole Shootin' Match*, Pennell struck a deal with Pahl Film of Germany that allowed the company to broadcast the film on television in seven European countries. In exchange Pennell pocketed the paltry sum of $2,500. Sutherland was livid, especially because the film's distributor was in the process of negotiating a more lucrative agreement with WDR, another German television network. The shareholders of Maverick Films, Inc. confronted Pennell and in July asked for his resignation as vice president of the company.[36]

Lawyers for Maverick were successful in dissolving the contract with Pahl Film, but Pennell's actions put additional strain on his already tenuous relationship with Sutherland. The film eventually sold to WDR for more than four times the amount Pennell had received from Pahl, and shareholders (investors and cast and crew) received their first "substantial" income from the film. In March of 1981 the top-rated PBS program *Sneak Previews* showcased *The Whole Shootin' Match*. Hosted by Roger Ebert and Gene Siskel, the episode featured the film as one of their top five favorite independent American films.[37]

Pennell may have enjoyed the success of *Whole Shootin' Match* and his subsequent fame, but he clearly was incapable of capitalizing on it in the way the industry demanded. UT RTF professor Tom Schatz, who knew Pennell in the years after *Whole Shootin' Match*, thinks that the filmmaker was better suited to working on his own terms, outside Hollywood. He compares Pennell to Tobe Hooper, who by 1980 hadn't directed a project that equaled the commercial success of *Chainsaw*. Says Schatz, "These guys were obviously brilliant, [but] were totally incapable of executing beyond these flashes of genius in industries that were brutally commercial. And they just were not able to take it."[38]

Back in Texas at the start of the 1980s, Pennell struggled to figure out his next move. He eschewed Austin for Houston, which along with Dallas was seeing steady film and television production work. Pennell began to cultivate local film contacts by trumpeting the success of *Whole Shootin' Match*. He reacquainted himself with administrators at SWAMP, which had provided funding for *A Hell of a Note* in the late 1970s. While he was working on the occasional industrial film, he was also dreaming up the story for his second feature film. "I had always wanted to do a piece about a small Texas town in transition, a town like Crosby, which dates back to the Texas Revolution," Pennell told a journalist in 1984.[39] Once again he turned to his friends to assemble the project about a former ranching community that had become absorbed by Houston's sprawl.

One of the first people he approached was Henkel, who by this time had left Los Angeles. "I was very reluctant to do it because I had a better picture of Eagle," says Henkel. But Pennell was persistent, and Henkel eventually agreed. "At that time I knew better than to expect anything from Eagle. I knew if I was going to do anything, it was to ignore Eagle and go off and write the script and then hope we can find a way to make it."[40] Remarkably, Pennell secured a $25,000 grant from the National Endowment for the Arts, and SWAMP contributed about that much in free office space and film equipment. Pennell was ready to embark on his second feature, which would eventually be called *Last Night at the Alamo*. The size of the budget convinced Pennell and Henkel to change the script's focus from a dying Texas town to a dying Texas watering hole whose regulars rally to try to save the condemned bar on the eve of its demolition. Henkel's brother helped them find the Old Bar, an East Houston dive in operation since the 1940s. Its façade, much to Pennell's delight, resembled the Alamo.

Despite the hard feelings still simmering between Pennell and members of the cast of *Whole Shootin' Match*, he managed to convince Davis, Perryman, and Hargrave to appear in *Last Night*. Davis did not want to do the project, but Henkel and Perryman were able to persuade the actor, promising to "cover his back" if things got dicey with Pennell. Says Hargrave, "I just wanted to work with those guys again. And it *was* work."[41]

Production began in May 1982. "Eagle really jumped the gun on the thing and had everything together and started shooting the film before I was even finished with the first draft of the script," recalls Henkel. "Eagle didn't have any idea of what the ending of it was going to be, sometimes not even the next scene." Because the bar where they were filming was still in use, the cast and crew had to be finished by four o'clock in the afternoon each weekday when the Old Bar opened for business.[42]

*Last Night at the Alamo* was finished in three and a half weeks. According to most accounts, Henkel completed the movie because Pennell had stopped showing up to the set. Pennell later disputed this, saying that Henkel directed only the final scene because he was suffering from "the cocktail flu."[43]

*Last Night at the Alamo* played in the fall of 1983 at the New York Film Festival to generally good reviews. The *Village Voice* described it as "a sneakily funny and highly profane exhibit of Texas independent film making," which the reviewer dubbed the "Texas school." The *Hollywood Reporter* also praised the film's regionalism. "Although its profanity and rough language will daunt some people, it has considerable potential for audiences who like their films done with gusto and no holding back." *Variety*'s review was less enthusiastic, decrying the use of foul language and noting that the female characters "are seriously underwritten" although it praised Davis's performance as Cowboy, the lead character. *Last Night* also played at the USA Film Festival in 1984. At a cocktail party during the festival, Davis was accosted by two enthusiastic young men. "Who are *these* losers?" Davis thought to himself as they began to rattle off their various credits in films like *Melvin and Howard* (1980) and *Where the Buffalo Roam* (1980). The fans were brothers Joel and Ethan Coen, and they were at the festival with their first feature, a moody film noir called *Blood Simple* that also had been shot in Austin. Joel had taken film classes at the University of Texas in the early 1980s, and he and Ethan agreed that the gritty streets and empty lofts of the city's Sixth Street entertainment district would make the perfect set for much of the movie.[44]

*Last Night at the Alamo* opened in July 1984 in limited commercial release. *Whole Shootin' Match* fan Vincent Canby raved about Pennell's second feature, calling it a "small, unassuming, all-American classic" and comparing its "idiosyncratic" voice to the writing of Sam Shepard and David Mamet. "It's the kind of low-budget, regional movie that suddenly reminds us that, between New York and Hollywood, there's a vast, unruly, exuberant continent and filmmakers still capable of seeing and hearing what's going on in it."[45]

Canby also noted how reassuring it was that a state prone to hyperbole and legend could also produce a filmmaker like Pennell and a film like *Last Night,* "which is as small as Texas is big." The success of Pennell's second feature was also reassuring to his cautiously optimistic family and friends, whose numbers were dwindling. As Chuck Pinnell says of that time, "Eagle was going to have to evolve as a person and an artist to get to somewhere else with his art. The drugs, the booze, the women, the power, the celebrity—all of that served to keep him incubated in this lifestyle."[46]

Six shortish features and one short culled by Jonathan Demme on a visit to the Lone Star State prove not only that independent features are alive and living on the Third Coast, but that they can outrun those by New York and Los Angeles indies.

*THE VILLAGE VOICE*

# Made in Austin

## The *Austin Chronicle* and *Red Headed Stranger*

oe Dishner was wearing a collared, long-sleeved shirt in the sticky Austin summer of 1981. That fact alone should have conveyed his dedication to the idea of starting an alternative newspaper, but to the gentleman from one of Austin's largest banks with whom he and fellow University of Texas RTF dropout Nick Barbaro were having lunch, Dishner looked just like any other young entrepreneur eager to convince backers to invest in his project.

The young men made quite a pair. Barbaro wore a suit and carried a battered leather briefcase in an attempt to look more professional, while Dishner toted a plastic Samsonite case.

Still, the lunch meeting had gone fairly well, Dishner thought. He and Barbaro had made an impassioned case for why Austin needed a biweekly paper that would focus on politics and entertainment. The banker seemed mildly interested in the idea. But as the three stood up to leave, with Barbaro continuing to elaborate on one final point, the slightly wild-looking thirty-year-old reached across the table and grabbed an uneaten pickle off the banker's plate.

Dishner watched in horror as Barbaro first wagged the pickle to emphasize his point and then bit down on it with a loud crunch.

"Well, we're fucked," sighed Dishner to himself. "This guy will never talk to us again."[1]

The pickle incident notwithstanding, Dishner, Barbaro, and other former UT film students still managed to sell the idea of the *Austin Chronicle*, which published its first biweekly issue in September 1981. Conceived of by Dishner and initially overseen by CinemaTexas's Ed Lowry, Louis Black, and Nick Barbaro, the *Chronicle* would help to solidify the infrastructure of the Austin film community. Lowry, Black, Barbaro, and others literally chronicled the development of the Texas film community, focusing specifically on Austin and celebrating its emerging local scene. Friendships with important independent filmmakers like Jonathan Demme and John Sayles brought increased national exposure to Austin filmmaking and established significant connections such as the New York-based "Made in Texas" screening of Austin work curated by Demme in 1981.

Equally important to Austin in the 1980s was the production of *Red Headed Stranger* (1986), a period western starring Willie Nelson and written and directed by Bill Wittliff. Based on Nelson's wildly successful 1975 concept album of the same name, *Red Headed Stranger* would by no means achieve the critical or commercial success of *The Texas Chainsaw Massacre* or *The Whole Shootin' Match*. Its preproduction odyssey, which lasted nearly a decade, reveals the challenges Austin-based filmmakers like Wittliff faced in the 1980s, particularly in working with Hollywood studios that were more interested in high-concept films than "small" stories with a regional slant. But like the *Chronicle*, *Red Headed Stranger* would nurture and sustain Austin's film community at a time when most of the state's film production—local and otherwise—was happening elsewhere. Wittliff and Nelson employed a mostly local crew base and trained a generation of electricians, grips, and other key personnel like production designer Cary White (*Mean Girls*, NBC's *Friday Night Lights*) and location manager Eric Williams (*Where the Heart Is*, *The Alamo*). More important, a homegrown project like *Red Headed Stranger* allowed technicians to remain in Austin at a time when Dallas and its new studio complex Las Colinas offered the most work. These crew members not only would become nationally known but would "pay it forward" by working in the 1990s with Richard Linklater and Robert Rodriguez at critical points in their careers.

The *Chronicle*'s development in the early 1980s paralleled Wittliff's first Hollywood successes, and the alternative paper covered his career with interest. Unlike a lot of Austinites at the time, Wittliff had had enough experience with the studios and the industry to be realistic about the local scene's filmmaking development. "Hollywood is here," he told the *Chronicle* in 1987, "but that is not, by any stretch of the imagination, the same thing as having a film industry in our state."[2]

CHAINSAWS, SLACKERS, AND SPY KIDS

## When Film Criticism Really Mattered

The *Austin Chronicle*'s founding members all met at the University of Texas in the 1970s. Joe Dishner had grown up in Dallas and moved to Austin in 1972 to attend UT, where he helped to program the university's Cinema 40 Film Society with another student named Steve Bearden. Dishner made Super 8 films in his youth, but his early film education really came from seeing movies at various theaters around Dallas.

Like Dishner, Bearden was from Dallas and discovered art films in high school. He began reading the *Village Voice* and film journals like *Sight and Sound,* hungry for information about directors and distributors. He wasn't interested in reading reviews, which to him seemed written mostly by middle-aged critics hopelessly out of touch with the rock 'n' roll subculture, but he devoured information about the filmmakers themselves and the business of distribution.

Bearden began running Cinema 40 (which eventually became the Student Association Film Program) full-time after Dishner graduated and moved to San Antonio in 1976. Bearden loved movies, but he was learning to strike a balance between his own occasionally offbeat tastes and the films that would bring in money. He gambled unsuccessfully on Fassbinder's *The Merchant of the Four Seasons* and discovered that, in the mid-1970s at least, Godard's films weren't commercially viable with his particular audience. Generally, however, he ran a profitable business. "He really understood the commercial side and really understood the relationship between taste cultures and markets," remembers RTF professor Tom Schatz, who tried to diffuse the growing tension between Bearden's operation and a new group of graduate students who by the mid-1970s were programming and publishing notes for RTF's CinemaTexas film series. "The CinemaTexas group saw themselves as vastly cooler and more important to the film culture. It was a combination of the films that they brought in and the notes. This was back when criticism really mattered," Schatz says. Bearden considered their tastes to be more mainstream, more American than his own. And he didn't put much stock in their program notes. "They wanted to explain movies. I wanted to show movies."[3]

By 1975 the founding members of CinemaTexas were moving on. Charles Ramírez Berg finished his RTF master's degree and left to enroll in a film studies program at USC. CinemaTexas founders George Lellis and Ron Policy both left UT in 1976. Graduate student Ed Lowry took over as editor after Lellis's departure. Lowry's enthusiasm and likability impressed everyone who came into contact with him. He liked pushing the limits of film theory

**66**

and critical practice. By the early 1980s, Lowry would become an important national figure in the field of film studies. Remembers Lellis, "He was constantly reading and constantly going to the movies. It created this very fertile environment for ideas. It was the kind of thing that grad school should be."[4]

Lowry taught undergraduate film history classes while finishing his degree, and he dazzled his students with his extensive film knowledge and the exuberant way he acted out movie plots. He also united the CinemaTexas group when he took over in 1976. By this time CinemaTexas included Lowry's classmates Marjorie Baumgarten, Louis Black, and Nick Barbaro. A New Jersey native and graduate of Grinnell College, Baumgarten arrived in Austin in late 1974. Having no job and a lot of time to kill, she wandered into one of the CinemaTexas screenings at Jester auditorium, where Mae West wooed a young Cary Grant in *She Done Him Wrong* (1933). She read Lowry's program notes for the film, which included an essay about West's star persona. It was the first serious film criticism she'd read.

Like Baumgarten, Louis Black also grew up in New Jersey but his introduction to movies happened much earlier. In the seventh grade he met classmate and fellow film buff (and future film critic) Leonard Maltin. Together they split memberships to various New York-based film societies and would plan their weekends around what films were showing at theaters and museums throughout the city. "Len was totally aggressive, so we were always meeting people," recalls Black of the time, for instance, when Maltin discovered that Buster Keaton was shooting a movie in New York and managed to get himself and Black onto the set to meet the pioneering silent film comedian.[5] Black ran a film society for a couple of years in college and nurtured equally passionate interests in rock 'n' roll and comic books. He made his way to Austin in 1974 drawn by the city's thriving music scene, left in 1975 but returned a year later, when he enrolled as a graduate student in English and eventually migrated to the RTF department.

Barbaro grew up in Dallas but went west to California to earn a degree in English at UCLA. He minored in film history and gravitated toward foreign movies, especially Italian cinema. His mother worked in the Italian film industry after World War II, and his parents had met in the early 1950s while working on Roberto Rossellini's *The Machine That Kills Bad People* (1952). After graduation Barbaro moved back to Texas, and he arrived in Austin in 1975 to pursue his master's degree in film, the same semester that Baumgarten enrolled in the program.

While Lellis and Berg may have preferred classic Hollywood and European art movies, Lowry, Black, and the others loved B movies, exploitation films, experimental stuff. They all agreed about what they didn't like, however. "The real thing we all hated," recalls Lellis of the overarching CinemaTexas aesthetic, "were sort of middle-brow works like the *The Lion in Winter* (1968) or the kind of historical movies that won Oscars. We all preferred down and dirty genre films or blatantly sentimental genre work to things that were in good taste. Or we liked the complete opposite, which would be the kind of rarefied stuff that would push the edges of the medium."[6]

By the mid-1970s CinemaTexas was operating out of a former hotel UT inherited from past university president Frank Erwin directly across from the new RTF building. Rumors circulated that Erwin had hosted wild parties in the place. Indeed, one of CinemaTexas's two offices was covered in zebra-striped wallpaper.[7]

Lowry's editing style was tough but fair, and he presided over the CinemaTexas group like a benevolent buddha. According to Schatz, "He really ran that operation. He had a more rigorous sense of what that whole taste culture was about, whereas for Louis and the others, I think it was more intuitive." Films like *Easy Rider* and *The Graduate* promised to take American cinema in a new direction in the late 1960s, and, although the promise remained essentially unfulfilled (witness the 1980s), 1970s movies like *Jaws, The Godfather*, and *Mean Streets* did signal a shift in American cinema. "You could feel things changing. It was very intense. There was still a sense that criticism mattered to the world of filmmaking," Schatz remembers. The CinemaTexas writers shared this feeling, and their passion for movies inspired some of their best writing. In the early spring of 1976, Lowry wrote a two-and-a-half page essay about *Jaws*, which had opened the previous summer and become the first movie to gross over $100 million. He compared the film's horrors to Vietnam, Watergate, and the Manson murders: "For this reason, *Jaws* seems peculiarly *our* film. Like Roy Scheider, we sit on the beach trying to look comfortable while we secretly scan the waters in search of shark fins."[8]

Although Dishner worked with Bearden and the "rival" Cinema 40 program, he befriended Lowry and the other members of the CinemaTexas crowd. After graduation Dishner moved with his wife to San Antonio so she could attend medical school while he taught high school. Eventually he decided to return to UT for a graduate degree in film production, but it didn't take Dishner long to decide that this degree was essentially worthless. Not long after, he moved to Dallas and found work as a location manager on various runaway productions.

By 1980 Barbaro had also dropped out of the UT program when Dishner approached him about starting an alternative newspaper in Austin. Dishner's rationale for starting the paper had as much to do with channeling his UT friends' creative energy as anything else.

Austin seemed like the logical place to launch the newspaper. "It had cheap labor, overly qualified writers, people who wanted to be in the scene," Dishner recalls.[9] Once there, he and Barbaro brought Black and Lowry on board. Dishner and Barbaro approached Black first, but they asked Lowry to be film editor and Black to handle promotions. The decision and other tensions eventually would create a long-standing rift between the roommates and friends. "I was just so pissed because I wanted to be film editor. I did not want to do marketing. I didn't want to do what I ended up doing," says Black. "Which was fine because if Ed hadn't been there, the *Chronicle* probably wouldn't have survived."[10]

A natural organizer, Dishner cajoled the ragtag group forward. "Part of it was just getting everybody to take themselves seriously." Together Dishner and Barbaro pooled $2,000 of their own money to form a corporation. Barbaro approached his mother for half of the start-up money after showing her their business plan.[11]

The proposed paper's editorial board drew from the people who wrote and edited the CinemaTexas program notes as well as UT's campus newspaper, *The Daily Texan*, a prestigious publication that claimed alumni Bill Moyers and Walter Cronkite as former staffers. Recalls Marge Baumgarten, who eventually became the *Chronicle*'s film editor, "We knew so many people who were really smart about popular culture and were good writers, and they couldn't write for the *Texan* or CinemaTexas forever."[12]

Dishner and Barbaro found office space in a warehouse just north of the downtown business area. The staff shared the space with a collective of artists, many of whom had worked out of Armadillo World Headquarters before its demise in 1980. After taking another loan from Barbaro's mother, they bought a $24,000 second-hand typesetting machine, a necessary piece of equipment that became obsolete within a few years. The temperamental machine had to be kept at a consistent temperature, so a three-room, air-conditioned "house" was built to enclose it and the other equipment necessary to produce the newspaper.[13]

In addition to the handful of individuals Dishner and Barbaro recruited from UT to make up the six-person editorial board, they also solicited contributions from writers who had written for other alternative Austin publications like the defunct *Austin Sun*. Margaret Moser, for instance, had written for the *Sun* and was a fixture on the local music scene. Like Black, Barbaro, and the others, she hung out at Raul's, a punk club near the university.

Countless meetings took place in the late spring and the early summer of 1981 as the group prepared to publish its first issue under the working title *The Austin Reader,* which was eventually changed to *The Austin Chronicle.* A prototype issue went out that summer boasting a cover that featured a bespectacled Barbaro, wearing a shirt and tie and an old-fashioned newsman's porkpie hat and floating in an innertube as he pounded away on a manual typewriter.

**Trumpeting Texas Film**

On September 4, 1981, the first biweekly issue of the *Austin Chronicle* hit the streets. Although a printing mistake led to a garish cover, the rest of the twenty-four-page issue was in pretty good shape. The editor's note on the inside page, a space that would become Black's "Page Two" column by June 1987, encouraged its readers to offer feedback. The masthead listed the six members of the editorial board (Barbaro, Black, Dishner, and Lowry along with the *Daily Texan*'s Sarah Whistler and Jeff Whittington). Barbaro was the editor and Dishner the business manager, and the two shared the title of publisher. Lowry handled the managing editor duties. Twenty-four locals, including former Armadillo World Headquarters artist Jim Franklin and cartoonist Sam Hurt, contributed articles, reviews, and artwork. The Austin slant reflected the *Chronicle*'s belief that the writers should be "of the same firmament" as the magazine's readers.[14]

For the first issue, Lowry and Barbaro interviewed independent filmmaker John Sayles. The two-page feature was an in-depth conversation with Sayles about making the transition from writing novels and screenplays to directing. The insightful interview would become a *Chronicle* staple, offering readers a chance to "visit" with a nationally known filmmaker, writer, or musician. Many of these stories were made possible because of relationships forged by Barbaro, Black, and others on staff who were tireless fans of popular culture.

Two weeks later, the *Chronicle*'s second issue came out. It trumpeted Texas movies in a four-page spread that included an article on the production of the film *Raggedy Man.* "When we decided to highlight Texas filmmaking in this issue, it wasn't entirely because of this week's premiere of *Raggedy Man,* a film shot around here, based on a screenplay by local native Bill Wittliff and starring an East Texas actress named Sissy Spacek who happened to win an Oscar last year," wrote Lowry. "It was also because Texas has become one of the hottest regional film centers during the past few years." A sidebar article chronicled the making of *Raggedy Man*, a story Wittliff based in part on his mother, Nita. The production made use of local crew and actors in minor supporting and extra roles and shot in a soundstage that was part of 501 Studios, Richard Kooris's rapidly expanding production company just east of IH-35. Those interviewed for the article, like production assistant Sam Balkam, championed Austin's thriving movie community. Balkam predicted that Austin would become a "major entertainment center" within five years. Larry Reinninger, who moved to town from Los Angeles a few years earlier, argued that Austin already had become a thriving film center. "It won't take three or five years," he told the *Chronicle*. "It's happening here, and it's going to come fast now."[15]

And it wasn't just Austinites who thought so. In early October "Jonathan Demme Presents—Made in Texas—New Films from Austin" had its New York premiere thanks to *Chronicle* pal Demme. Members of the CinemaTexas crowd were huge Demme fans, and Barbaro had met the filmmaker at the Venice Film Festival where *Melvin and Howard* (1980) was screening in competition. Then Demme visited Austin in early 1981 just after *Melvin and Howard* had won two Academy Awards. He arrived in town, according to the *Chronicle*, "to consult with a local screenwriter and to hear some local New Wave music." The screenwriter was Bud Shrake, who had a script called *The Big Mamoo* that Demme was interested in directing. On that trip Demme also asked if he could see some local films, and a screening was hastily arranged that included Brian Hansen's *Speed of Light* (1980) and David Boone's spacey sci-fi masterpiece, *Invasion of the Aluminum People* (1980). Demme respond-ed enthusiastically to the work—a snippet of Boone's film would appear in Demme's 1986 film *Something Wild*—and asked if he could program the films as a New York screening the following year. "Made in Texas" premiered at the Center for Living Cinema on October 10, 1981, the first night of the center's fall season. Four other films were included with *Speed of Light* and *Invasion*: *Fair Sisters* (Missy Boswell, Ed Lowry, Louis Black), *Mask of Sarnath* (Neil Rut-tenberg), *Leonardo Jr.* (Lorrie Oshatz), and *Death of Jim Morrison* (Tom Hucka-bee and Will Van Overbeek). The program received tremendous advance no-tice in the New York press, with write-ups appearing in the *Village Voice* and *New York* magazine, and as a recommended pick in the *New York Times*. The screening sold out to an enthusiastic and appreciative New York crowd.[16]

But there was at least one person living and working within the local film community who wasn't buying the hype. Bill Wittliff, who by 1981 had established a successful screenwriting career while remaining based in Aus-tin, took a more realistic view of the situation. "Outside productions come here to shoot," Wittliff told the *Chronicle*. "But the deals and decisions are made elsewhere, and after the shooting, all the postproduction work goes elsewhere. Furthermore, there's no structure for distributing from here. So realistically, how could you say there's an industry developing here?"[17]

### The Voice of Experience

By this point Wittliff was about four years into a project with Willie Nelson to turn *Red Headed Stranger* into a feature film. Actual production on the movie was still another four years and about twice as many deals down the road. If anyone understood Austin and its film community's place with respect to the industries on both coasts, it was Wittliff.

After countless unsuccessful attempts to turn Nelson's *Red Headed Stranger* album into a motion picture, the two men had finally found the funds to make the movie the way they wanted. One of their first investors was an entrepreneur they called the Chicken Man, who raised chickens for the Army. (The Chicken Man's company grew up to become Tyson Foods.) A used-car salesman from Fort Worth kicked in some money, as did Bud Shrake and Nelson's friend Darrell Royal, the former UT football coach. Banking on a promise of a million dollars from another group of investors, they started shooting the movie.

Wittliff and Nelson first met at a Mexican restaurant in Austin around 1977. According to Nelson, their mutual friend Bud Shrake introduced them. Recalled the singer, "I liked Bill and [his wife] Sally right off. I had seen a TV movie Bill wrote with Johnny Cash in it, and I knew he and Sally owned and operated Encino Press, a very high-class regional book publishing house, which impressed me."[18]

Wittliff started Encino Press in 1964 at the age of twenty-four after working for two university publishing outfits in Dallas and Austin. "The truth of the matter is I didn't have the courage enough to try to write myself. Starting the Encino Press was a way to be involved with writing but not to personally be at risk," he admits.[19] Wittliff studied journalism at the University of Texas and palled around with a group of fraternity brothers, including *Chainsaw* investor and attorney Joe Longley.

Wittliff's Texas roots ran deep. Born in Taft, in South Texas, he moved to Blanco as a teenager. Wittliff drew from his family's history to write his first screenplay, a period western that he began in the early 1970s while making numerous driving trips to Dallas for a visual history of the city being published through Encino Press.

Wittliff made the 200-mile drive back and forth from Austin to Dallas many times over the course of a month, collecting old glass plate negatives for the photo book. Every time he got back in the car, he'd pick up with his story. "And by the time I finished gathering the negatives, I had also 'seen' the story, in a very unformed and crude fashion. And so because I'd seen it, I decided to write it as a screenplay."[20] Wittliff finished the script on April 25, 1973, the day Sally gave birth to their daughter.

The next day, Shrake stopped by Wittliff's office and noticed the script sitting on his desk. Wittliff told him he was just fooling around. Shrake took the script with him and called his friend the next morning, offering to send the screenplay to his New York agent. She agreed to send it to Barry Weiss and Philip D'Antoni, who had produced *The French Connection* (1971) and were traveling the country promoting its sequel, *The Seven Ups* (1973). They loved Wittliff's western and invited him out to Los Angeles to turn it into a series—they had a deal with one of the television networks—but he declined. With two young children and a small business, Wittliff had no desire to move to L.A. "He knew immediately, I think, that to keep his feet firmly in Austin was the way not only to keep himself sane, but also to make him more attractive and more intriguing to people for whom writers in L.A. were a dime a dozen," recalls screenwriter Bill Broyles, who had co-founded *Texas Monthly* magazine years earlier and followed Wittliff's career with interest.[21]

Weiss and his partner kept calling, and Wittliff kept turning them down. Eventually, the phone stopped ringing. Wittliff had tremendous self-discipline, and he was less concerned with selling something than honing his craft. For the time being, it was enough that local writers such as Shrake liked his work.

It was around this time, in the mid-1970s, that Wittliff decided to invest a small amount of money in Tobe Hooper's *The Texas Chainsaw Massacre.* Wittliff heard about the opportunity through Warren Skaaren, whom he had met sometime before Skaaren started the Texas Film Commission. After Skaaren left his post in 1974 to try his hand at writing, Wittliff offered one of the upstairs rooms in his Baylor Street office as a writing space. The two even began to collaborate on a screenplay together but never finished the project. "Even then, Warren was thinking on a much grander scale in terms of the size of movies," says Wittliff, referring to the blockbusters for which Skaaren would become best known. "I was interested in doing the smaller, more intimate character-driven things."[22]

They eventually had a falling out a year or so later after Skaaren bought an option on Wittliff's script for *Raggedy Man.* Skaaren used his contacts in

Hollywood to try to sell the screenplay but was unable to find a buyer, and Wittliff "exercised a provision in the option contract" and eventually got the movie made without Skaaren's involvement. Skaaren bitterly alluded to the rift in a letter to his New York attorney, Arthur Klein. "I learned a painful lesson, unfortunately it involved the loss of an alleged friend. The writer, (whose work I had so carefully encouraged, whose naïve approach to the business I tempered) took devastating advantage of the only weak spot I had in my option." The two friends never quite repaired their rift, according to Wittliff.[23]

In the early 1980s Wittliff traveled to Los Angeles to work with director Irvin Kershner, who directed *The Empire Strikes Back* (1980) and *Never Say Never Again* (1983). A friend of Kershner's had optioned one of Wittliff's scripts, and Kershner came on board to work with Wittliff on the polish. Kershner walked Wittliff through the script, pointing out what would work and what wouldn't, saying things like, "An actor's never gonna do that," and explaining the ins and outs of the movie business.[24]

It was an instructive introduction to Hollywood and the business side of moviemaking, but a few of Wittliff's later industry experiences would be less so. Hired to write and direct *Country* (1984) starring Jessica Lange, Wittliff ended up leaving the project, which would have marked his directorial debut. Cinematographer Neil Roach, who had worked with Wittliff on earlier projects, was fired from the picture, and Wittliff quit soon after. "I think they fired me to get Bill to quit," says Roach. "Bill never seemed to believe that, but I did."[25]

Wittliff was dissatisfied with the release version of *Barbarosa* (1982), based on his first script and starring Nelson, so he hired an editor to re-cut the movie in his Austin office. He also didn't like *Honeysuckle Rose*, which came out in 1980. Wittliff wrote the script based on many conversations with Nelson, who essentially played himself in the movie. Says Wittliff, "*Honeysuckle Rose* was supposed to be the true life of a road musician, but it's not because they had ideas of what would put butts in chairs in front of screens, and so they didn't want to make the hero be a true example of that life. Which is, road musicians don't go home." Wittliff's introduction to Hollywood happened at about the same time as "baby moguls"—powerful young turks such as agent Michael Ovitz and Disney executives Michael Eisner and Jeffrey Katzenberg—were gaining a substantial foothold in the industry, and he learned by observation. "It's not about movies first. It's about money and power and ego, and movies come out of it. Sometimes the movies are great, most often they're not."[26]

### *Red Headed Stranger*: Take One

By the time Nelson met Wittliff in the late 1970s, the musician had been living in Austin for about six years. He had moved to the capital city from Nashville based in part on the suggestion of friend Darrell Royal, who told Nelson that in Austin he'd find "brothers under the skin" in addition to pretty scenery, lively music halls, and decent barbecue. The singer played his first Austin gig at the Armadillo World Headquarters on August 12, 1972, and by the time Nelson hosted his first Fourth of July picnic in Dripping Springs a year later, his popularity had mushroomed. The very successful release of the *Red Headed Stranger* album in 1975 cemented Nelson's rising profile.[27]

Once Nelson met Wittliff, the two went for a drive and listened to a tape of the album. Afterwards, Wittliff agreed to write a script, and then Universal gave the pair a development deal. Just a few months after Eagle Pennell's deal with Universal was announced in early 1979, Wittliff finished a draft of the *Red Headed Stranger* script. By this time Wittliff also had signed a two-picture development deal with Warner Bros. The arrangement had Wittliff listed as writer and co-producer, a combination that he hoped would give him more control over his studio projects and the opportunity to write smart Texas-based stories that didn't pander to Hollywood's notion of the West.[28]

Meanwhile over at Universal, the studio budgeted the *Red Headed Stranger* project at $14 million and sent the script to Robert Redford. Redford and Nelson had ranches near one another in Utah, and the two would appear together in *The Electric Horseman* (1979), Nelson's first movie role. Although Nelson liked Redford, he imagined himself in the starring role of *Stranger*. Recalled the musician, "Giving the script to Redford froze the project at Universal. The moguls said our movie would only be made if Redford would do it." But Redford was in no hurry to decide on the project. Two years later, he finally turned it down.[29]

Nelson came to the conclusion that Universal probably never intended for him to carry the picture in the first place. Instead, he discovered, they gave him the development deal in 1978 because they wanted him to sign with MCA Records, which was part of the MCA, Inc. corporation that had merged with the movie studio in the early 1960s. "Basically, I think they wanted my music contract a lot more than my classic profile on the screen."[30]

In order for Nelson and Wittliff to buy back *Red Headed Stranger* from Universal, they had to repay their advances. "All of a sudden, Willie and I had it," says Wittliff of the turnaround. "And then there were any number of times when people were going to put money in it. Independently, or with some small production group, or whatever."[31]

In the early 1980s HBO expressed interest in the project and put up $5 million. Director Sam Peckinpah also was attached at one time, a year or so before his death in 1984. The infamously ornery filmmaker flew into Austin to talk to Nelson and Wittliff, who met him at the airport. Before they even shook hands, Peckinpah demanded his $300 per diem. During the course of their visit, as Peckinpah increased the movie's costs with demands to add his daughter to the payroll as dialogue coach and so on, Wittliff kept reminding the director of the $5 million budget. "He finally got mad and left," Wittliff remembers.[32]

Eventually the project died at HBO. Now well into the early 1980s, Wittliff and Nelson tried to raise the $5 million on their own. One day Wittliff called Nelson and told him what they should do is figure out how much money they could realistically find, then make the movie for that amount. In the end they put together a budget of $1.8 million, with Wittliff as director and Nelson as leading man. Together they would share the main producing credit.

But the movie once again ran into financial difficulties. Together with Royal, Bud Shrake invested around $25,000. "That was enough to get them through a day or two," remembers Shrake. "Then out of nowhere, this woman showed up. As I recall, she said she had a vision or something that Willie Nelson needed her."[33]

Nelson did need the woman's help with *Red Headed Stranger*, but their serendipitous meeting was grounded in reality, according to Wittliff. The "angel," who lived on the East Coast and came from a wealthy family, had heard about the project through mutual friends. Impressed by Nelson's gifts as a songwriter and musician, she instructed her financial advisors to invest in the film.

By this time Wittliff and Nelson had spent nearly eight years trying to get *Red Headed Stranger* to the screen. And within the span of about five minutes, they finally had all of the pieces of the puzzle. Wittliff and Nelson's "angel" arrived in Austin and went out to the set to meet with the pair. "Basically, she got a handshake from each one of us and put up a half million dollars the next day or two, and we made the film," says Wittliff.[34]

### We Were All Neophytes

Production designer Cary White hadn't been in Los Angeles long before he realized he needed to get back to Texas. White arrived in California around

1980 to work on a low-budget exploitation movie called *Demonoid*. *Chainsaw* art director Bob Burns was handling the show's special effects and hired White to do props. A graduate of UT's RTF graduate program, White had made a pre-thesis film entitled *Persistence of Vision*, which had won a special jury award in the 1976 student Oscars sponsored by the Academy of Motion Picture Arts and Sciences. White followed *Demonoid* with fairly steady work on after-school specials. Around that time he started to read about Wittliff, who was getting attention for his work on films like *The Black Stallion* (1979), executive produced by Francis Ford Coppola, and *Raggedy Man*. White envied the screenwriter's ability to live in Austin without sacrificing his career, a decision that impressed many in the industry as well as more than a few Texans struggling to find movie work in Los Angeles.

A few years after White landed in Los Angeles, Wittliff and Nelson had succeeded in raising money to make *Red Headed Stranger* and had begun to assemble a cast and crew. Wittliff had heard good things about White's design ability and that he was looking for any excuse to get back to Texas. The next time he was in Los Angeles, he called White. At the time White was working on the annual Academy Awards telecast as an assistant art director.

Although White was nervous—he really wanted the job—the gregarious Wittliff immediately put him at ease. Recalls White, "I was just sky high because I was going to get to come back to Austin, I was going to get to do a feature, which I had not done, with these guys who were making movies in Texas."[35]

White commuted between Texas and Los Angeles for a time, and once the project seemed assured, he moved his wife and young son back to Austin. One day as they were getting ready to go into production, Wittliff walked into Richard Kooris's office, which was being used as the show's production headquarters. Kooris, the former UT RTF instructor who co-founded Shootout Films in the early 1970s, had signed on as the movie's cinematographer.

"I have good news and bad news," Wittliff told White. "The bad news is we're pulling the plug on this right now. We're not gonna do it right this minute. But the good news is we want to keep you working and keep you building the sets."[36]

For the next year or so, White and a few others worked full-time to build the 1880s western town that Wittliff had so vividly created in his script for *Red Headed Stranger*. They constructed the storefronts and structures across the road from Nelson's Pedernales golf course, about thirty miles west of Austin in what came to be called Willieville. The entire process took two years. On an average day, White would head out to Willieville, decide what needed

CHAINSAWS, SLACKERS, AND SPY KIDS

to be built, and get going on the project. Or he'd scour Central Texas antique shops, looking for props and furniture suitable for the movie's period set. Nelson would come out from time to time to check their progress, and he did his best to keep the project afloat. If he played a gig and had some extra money, he'd throw a few bucks toward the construction of the set.

For White and a majority of the movie's crew, the production marked their first big break into feature filmmaking. Nearly all of Austin's crew members—grips and such—clamored to work on the film. A few department heads came from Dallas and Houston, but the bulk of the crew were local. Others, like assistant director Tommy Thompson and production manager Dick Gallegly, were grizzled industry veterans. In his late fifties by the time he worked on *Red Headed Stranger*, Thompson had produced Lucille Ball's television show in the 1960s and worked as an assistant director on numerous other TV series and features, but he was probably best known for his long-time collaboration with director Robert Altman, which began with *Brewster McCloud*, shot in Houston in the early 1970s.

Like Thompson, Gallegly met Wittliff while working on *Barbarosa*. A few years older than Thompson, Gallegly got his start as a production manager on movies like *To Kill a Mockingbird* (1962) and *Little Big Man* (1970) and was "a real been-there, done-that kind of guy," according to Roach.[37] He worked on a number of television series in the 1980s and would team again with Wittliff on the *Lonesome Dove* miniseries based on Larry McMurtry's novel, which Wittliff adapted for television in 1989.

"They were the voice of doom, but they were also the voice of reason," recalls Roach. "Dick would constantly say 'There's just no money for this,' and we would shortcut the traditional Hollywood way of doing things, and Tommy would get really unhappy with some of the ways we tried to do stuff. They ultimately, I think, had a good time." The fact that these two veterans signed on to work with mostly amateur crew personnel on a scrappy independent movie spoke volumes about their confidence and affection for Wittliff. Says Cate Hardman, who had spent a decade as an editor before becoming a script supervisor, "Bill had a vision. People respected him, and they wanted to do things for him."[38]

Connie Todd was Wittliff's assistant and did casting on the project. "One of the interesting things about *Red Headed Stranger* was that very few people had ever done the jobs they were doing before. So we were all neophytes."[39] Although Todd hadn't cast a movie prior to *Stranger*, she had a few years' industry experience by the time production began in 1985. In 1983, she accompanied Wittliff on location for the shooting of *Country*, where she met casting director Liz Keigley. Watching Keigley, Todd developed an affinity for many of the detail-oriented aspects of production such as casting, screen-writing, and editing. For *Stranger*, Todd put out casting calls for the movie's various supporting and minor roles. Sonny Carl Davis, who had moved to Los Angeles after positive reviews for *The Whole Shootin' Match*, heard about *Red Headed Stranger* and wanted a role. He had met Wittliff, who had seen and liked him in Pennell's film, so he peppered the writer-director's office with calls. In the end he auditioned on tape for Wittliff, who gave the balding actor the role of the youngest Claver sibling, a character originally written as a teenager.

Todd ran into problems as she began to cast for extras in the movie. Many of the actors who read were too pretty and their teeth looked too perfect. "This was supposed to be a real down-at-the-heels town," she recalls. "I needed some real character faces, and nobody was showing up."[40] When Todd arrived at Nelson's ranch, she found her extras. Many of the musician's bandmates and members of his entourage had long, scraggly hair and faces that showed the wear and tear of life on the road. Todd was in heaven.

### The Willie Zone

The *Red Headed Stranger* project officially began production on April 29, 1985. Wittliff's excitement trumped any anxieties he had about directing his first movie. Plus, it was Wittliff's story, and he knew what he wanted on film. He was smart and had surrounded himself with good people like Thompson and Gallegly. He also hired Neil Roach, who had been camera operator on Wittliff's first television project *Thaddeus Rose and Eddie* and worked on *Barbarosa* and *Honeysuckle Rose*, to replace cinematographer Richard Kooris after he and Wittliff had a falling out.

Roach was shooting a picture in Dallas during *Red Headed Stranger's* preproduction in early spring, but he flew to Austin every Sunday to go over shot setups with Wittliff. Roach had been based in Dallas since the 1970s, and his solid ties with equipment rental houses like Victor Duncan secured camera upgrades and price breaks on rental fees for Wittliff's first feature.

Veteran actors Morgan Fairchild and Katharine Ross were cast, respec-tively, as Nelson's uppercrust Philadelphia bride and the single mother who brings the preacher back to the land of the living. A native of Dallas, Fairchild had been friends with Nelson for years and agreed early on to do the project. "Willie would keep calling and saying, 'Morgan, what are you doing next April?'" says Fairchild, who read several drafts of different scripts over the years. "Everybody loved Willie. Everybody wanted to pull together, especially those of us that are native Texans, and make it happen for him."[41]

Ross had recently given birth to a daughter, and she and her husband, actor Sam Elliott, and their three-month-old relocated to Austin for three weeks. Ross had liked the script and, as a new mother, was intrigued by the role. "Laurie was an idealized character. She was every woman's fantasy, to be so together. She was the woman of the earth," says Ross. "Willie was the hometown boy, so it was very much a labor of love for Willie and the people that he surrounded himself with."[42]

Shooting would take place in nine different locations, but Wittliff filmed the majority of scenes in Willieville. The cast and crew spent the first week or so shooting scenes on Wittliff's farm east of the airport, where Ross's character lived in a cabin built specifically for the movie. Wittliff had insisted on certain touches to make the cabin and its surroundings look as lived-in as possible. Recalls Roach, "From the outset of building the cabin, they brought a bunch of chickens out there and fed them so that they would hang around and be 'yard chickens.' Bill wanted them to run around and do what chickens do when they're comfortable and they're used to living in a yard." Art Rochester, a sound mixer brought in from L.A., hated the chickens' clucking and what it was doing to the soundtrack. As the weeks went on, fewer and fewer chickens roamed the yard. "At lunch Rochester was catching two chickens and taking them out in the woods and killing them," says Roach. "So by the time we left, there was, like, one chicken there."[43]

The climactic shoot-out between the Claver clan and Nelson's Stranger, scheduled for the end of production in mid-June, took three days to film. Wittliff and Roach had worked out the choreography for the complicated sequence, which unfolded in the main street, alleyways, and buildings of the western town. "We took each piece as it would be used editorially and shot it," says Roach. The cast and crew plowed through seventy to eighty setups per day using only one camera. Actors were moved around like chess pieces, and Thompson, the first assistant director, groused about the lack of coverage. "It became kind of miserable," recalls Hardman. In addition to the many actors required for the scene, farm animals and various perishable props were used to dress the set. Everything and everyone began to cook under the hot June sun.[44]

Nelson's daughter Lana worked on the costumes although Fairchild had chosen many of her period dresses at Western Costume, a Los Angeles wardrobe house that worked with most of the studios in Hollywood. Like the rest of *Red Headed Stranger*, much of the wardrobe was done on the cheap although the final result was fairly impressive. Once again, the limitations enforced by the budget paid off in surprising ways on-screen. Plumber's tape was used to repair the holes made in the actors' costumes during the shoot-out sequence. After each take, assistants would rush to the actors and tape closed the holes made by the blanks. Wittliff was pleasantly surprised when he watched the dailies. "There's one scene where somebody gets shot and when it comes through their back, it looks like this huge piece of flesh," he remembers.[45] In reality the detritus was a chunk of plumber's tape, propelled through the air by the sheer force of the impact coupled with its own weight.

Nelson's bandmates proved to be some of the most inspired casting choices. Longtime drummer Paul English played one of the Claver brothers as did Bee Spears, Nelson's bassist. Before English started playing in Nelson's band in 1966, he had done jail time for picking locks and other assorted misdemeanors. One day on the set, an actor was having trouble with his character's death scene. Wittliff wasn't satisfied with the results, but he wasn't sure what about it didn't work on camera. "Jack Bennett, the special effects guy out of Dallas, was very opinionated about [an actor] dying: how a person should react and how the bullet should hit him and what should happen when the bullet hits him," says Roach. Suddenly English spoke up. "Well, the first guy I shot, he just fell to the ground. He just dropped like a sack of potatoes. And then the second guy I shot, he danced around." English continued to elaborate on the details of each man's death while the cast and crew listened, transfixed. "And the point of the story," English concluded, directing his comments to Bennett, "is you don't know what happens. And you don't know what's gonna happen. So anything that somebody wants to do could be right." English took the actor aside, gave him some tips, and they did another take.[46]

Midway through the film, in the days leading up to the scene in which Nelson's Preacher shoots Fairchild's Raysha when he discovers his wife with an old beau, Nelson expressed doubts about the scene to Fairchild. He worried that the audience would lose sympathy for a character who shoots his wife. "I'm not sure how we get around that," he said to Fairchild, who was enjoying tremendous success as an actor playing assorted vixens on television programs like *Flamingo Road* and *Falcon Crest*. "I play bitches. You're the best guy in the world. Everybody will forgive you for shooting me," said Fairchild. But Nelson was still dubious. "Willie, believe me," deadpanned Fairchild. "No one in America will hate Willie Nelson for killing Morgan Fairchild."[47]

At the end of each day, the cast and crew would gather to watch the dailies in Nelson's recording studio, which overlooked the rolling hills of the country club's nine-hole golf course. "Typically it would be Willie and Bill and maybe any of the band members who happened to be around. There'd be

14 to 16 people there, and then there'd be friends of Willie's—the governor, Darrell Royal," recalls Roach. After a long day on the set, the informal evening gathering offered a convivial way to wind down while preparing for the next day's shots. "It was not like some Hollywood shows where they're sort of stratified above the line and below the line," says Fairchild of the open, relaxed atmosphere.[48]

Nelson was such an avid golfer, Fairchild recalls, that he often snuck in a few rounds between takes. "As soon as Bill would yell 'Cut!' Willie would strip off his Western garb and down to his little jogging shorts, and he and Darrell Royal would run over and play golf. Then you'd have to wait for Willie to come back."[49]

One evening Hardman looked around the studio and noticed Royal sitting along the back wall next to the musician. Royal often stopped by in the evenings to check out the movie's progress—he had invested some money, after all—and say hello. Marvels Hardman, "Where else in America could you see a coach for a football team sitting next to this musical star smoking a joint and [the coach] not even saying anything?"[50]

"You were in the 'Willie Zone,'" says Roach, "and the Willie Zone was a world unto and of itself."[51]

### Made in Texas, Part II

Production wrapped on Friday, June 14, 1985. Wittliff took time off and got back into some of his unfinished screenplays. In October, he joined Bud Shrake and others to take part in "Independent Images," a three-day conference about regional filmmaking held on the lush grounds of Austin's art museum. Co-sponsored by the museum and Houston's Southwest Alternate Media Project (SWAMP), the conference featured seminars about financing, producing, and distributing low-budget and independently made films. The weekend of panels, seminars, and screenings featured filmmakers Jonathan Demme and John Sayles as well as Horton Foote (author and co-producer of *Tender Mercies, Trip to Bountiful*), Frank Daniel (former head of the Czech Film School, newly affiliated with the American Film and Sundance Institutes), Carlin Glynn (actress and member of Actors Studio), Peter Masterson (director, *Trip to Bountiful*), local producer Ross Milloy, Dallas producer Martin Jurow (*Terms of Endearment*), and others.[52]

Demme screened one of his earliest features, *Citizen's Band* (1977). Since programming "Made in Texas" in New York in 1981, Demme had stayed in touch with the *Chronicle* crowd and in particular Louis Black. Sayles also maintained an ongoing connection to the *Chronicle,* and he screened *The Brother From Another Planet* (1984) at the Varsity Theater as part of the conference.

The CinemaTexas film program, along with the *Chronicle,* sponsored a screening of Shrake's film *Kid Blue* to coincide with the "Independent Images" conference. At the event, Shrake ran into Warren Skaaren, whom he hadn't seen in a few years. The former executive director of the Texas Film Commission arrived in a beat-up car and was dressed shabbily. "Poor Warren," thought Shrake. "Since he left the film commission his life has really gone to hell."[53]

Actually, the opposite was true. Skaaren's screenwriting career had really begun to take off by the fall of 1985. After a decade of serving as chairman of FPS, a Dallas below-the-line film production services company, and working on screenplays, Skaaren was on the verge of making it in Hollywood. Skaaren's screenplay *Of East and West* had Hollywood studio heads talking thanks to William Morris agent Mike Simpson. By the time Skaaren ran into Shrake in October, Skaaren had just come off an intense few months rewriting the *Top Gun* screenplay for Don Simpson and Jerry Bruckheimer.

The weekend conference benefited the Austin film community in a variety of ways. It brought important American independent filmmakers like Demme and Sayles back to town, and it inspired Demme to organize another program of Texas films called "Made in Texas, Part II." At the time of the "Independent Images" conference, many of the *Chronicle* staff were still reeling from the loss of good friend and *Chronicle* co-founder Ed Lowry, who had died a few weeks earlier from complications related to AIDS. The week before, they previewed the conference in a two-page spread, with sidebars about Demme and Sayles. Recalls Marjorie Baumgarten, "It was the first thing I remember as far as Austin being of interest to the outside world. It was an important thing, partly because it cemented relationships with Demme and Sayles that last to this day." The reality was that a handful of Austinites already had piqued the interest of film communities in Los Angeles and New York. The names of Wittliff, Shrake, and Skaaren may not have been as recognizable as those of Demme, Sayles, or the other conference participants, but they all had accomplished some measure of success in Hollywood. More important, they had achieved their success while working from their home base of Austin.[54]

Soon after the conference Wittliff returned to work on *Red Headed Stranger.* Wittliff wanted to use editor Artie Smith, who had been hired to edit *Country* but had left the production when Wittliff quit. When Todd reached Smith, however, he was already committed to *Back to the Future* (1985). Wittliff found Stephen Purvis, whose experience at the time was as a sound editor on movies like *Body Double* (1984). The director then hired prop wrangler (and Wittliff's former production assistant) Eric Williams to help Purvis.

Wittliff converted one of the first-floor rooms in his historic Baylor Street office into an editing suite. A KEM flatbed editing table sat in the front of the room and an ancient Moviola was set up toward the back. The editing gradually shifted to more of a team effort with both Purvis and Williams cutting film separately.

According to Williams, Wittliff eventually asked him to take over the bulk of the editing, while Purvis shifted his focus to the sound editing. They worked for months on the footage with Wittliff supervising the process. Wittliff didn't hover over the editors the way some directors do. Instead, he would come in periodically to check their progress and watch the edits. Wittliff would say, "Let's not cut film, let's look for the essence here," which might mean distilling a few lines of dialogue into a simple look to preserve the meaning and power of a shot or scene.[55]

Shortly after New Year's, they finished *Red Headed Stranger*'s music mix with edits, and by late January 1986 they had stitched together a first cut of the film. A month later they had trimmed the first cut and synched the music, which Nelson had worked on with Wittliff a few months earlier in a marathon session in South Padre. By late February Williams and Purvis had finished editing the second cut. They spent the summer tweaking the length and tightening the story, and by early October 1986 they had cut together a trailer in anticipation of the movie's fall release.

Wittliff and Nelson worked out a deal with Wrangler Jeans to produce a ten-minute "Making of" video, which featured interviews with Nelson talking about the genesis of the movie, beginning with his 1975 album. R. G. Armstrong, who played the sheriff, Royal Dano (Pops Claver), and other cast members told behind-the-scenes stories, which were edited with footage of Wittliff directing scenes on the set. The cable television music channel VH-1 taped a special edition of their popular "One on One" interview series out at Willieville. Nelson talked to reporter Bruce Leddy about going to the movies as a child and his dual desire to make music and have an acting career. A music video tied into one of the movie's songs also was in the works.[56]

*Red Headed Stranger* had its first screening at the Denver International Film Festival in mid-October. Critic Michael Healy, writing for *The Denver Post*, praised the *Red Headed Stranger* album but not the movie it inspired. "Unfortunately, when those great country songs are used as the basis for this insipid story, they become ridiculous." The *Variety* review ran two weeks later under the headline "Feeble Willie Nelson vehicle." The write-up cited Nelson's acting and Wittliff's direction as two of the movie's weaker points. "Nelson sings frequently but not enough to alter the dull tone of the action," the critic wrote. "There is an effort to frame the narrative in a ballad but it does not work."[57]

The movie fared better in Texas when it opened in February 1987. *Red Headed Stranger* had a splashy local premiere at the Arbor Cinema Four in North Austin. Nelson and Fairchild made a grand entrance at the event, with the singer-songwriter decked out in a top hat and tails. Cast members Royal Dano and Brian Fowler, Nelson's fifteen-year-old grandson who was cast as Ross's son, also appeared. After two screenings of the film, Nelson hosted a dinner and performed a concert for friends like University of Texas president Peter Flawn. Proceeds from the event, which raised about $175,000, benefited local public television station KLRU.[58]

The *Austin Chronicle* devoted two pages to an interview with Wittliff in which, among other things, he continued to challenge the idea that Texas even had a film industry. Louis Black reviewed the movie, calling it "perhaps the best western of the decade (though given the competition, that isn't saying much)." Although he praised Wittliff's direction, he also wondered in print what the infamous Peckinpah might have done with the material.[59]

*Red Headed Stranger* had a limited national release, playing in cities such as Kansas City, Minneapolis, Philadelphia, and Seattle. By its second week, the film had grossed around $24,000.[60] Critics in general were lukewarm about the movie. But Wittliff and Nelson had accomplished what they set out to do nearly a decade earlier: They had made their movie on their terms. They had also given a lot of Central Texans the opportunity to work on a feature film without leaving their homes. In the process, Wittliff and Nelson helped to train a new generation of film crew, people like Eric Williams and Cary White. In White's case, they allowed him to return home without giving up the work he was trained to do.

Their expertise in turn would allow Austin to capitalize on a shift that was taking place in the Texas film industry. Once the state's major film center, Dallas had by 1986 become unionized, and many producers of runaway film and television productions began to look elsewhere in an effort to find inexpensive crew. Former Texas Film Commission executive director Tom Copeland credits a number of small Hollywood projects for capitalizing on the Austin crew base established by *Red Headed Stranger*. In 1987 former *Happy Days* actor Anson Williams brought a low-budget feature called *The*

*Lone Star Kid* to town and asked the TFC for help in assembling a local crew. "From that point on," says Copeland, "when somebody would call the commission to ask if we had a crew down here, we'd tell them to call Anson Williams."[61] Williams continued to praise Austin to his colleagues in Los Angeles, which led to a steady stream of television movies being shot in the area into the 1990s. These projects became Austin's bread and butter and would sustain the local film community for many years.

*Slacker* resonated for me because Richard Linklater had found the way to express the authenticity of Austin life for a certain type of people that lived there. It wasn't too American, it wasn't too European. *Slacker* was very idiosyncratic, like Austin.

MICHAEL BARKER

# Slacker

## The Least Auteur Film Ever Made

In October 1985—the same month that Bill Wittliff and Warren Skaaren participated in the "Independent Images" conference featuring Jonathan Demme and John Sayles—twenty-five-year-old aspiring filmmaker Richard Linklater was preparing to screen a collection of experimental films at Austin's Dobie 1 & 2 theater. He and Lee Daniel, who shot commercials and made Super 8 films on the side, had convinced Dobie owner Scott Dinger to show the series on the first weekend of every month that fall. Linklater, who had underwritten much of the cost, grew increasingly worried as the initial screening approached. He became convinced the event would tank and he would lose his money even though the *Austin Chronicle* had agreed to run a free advertisement and a friend had designed an eye-catching flier playing off the program's tantalizing title, "Sexuality and Blasphemy in the Avant Garde." The flier featured a provocative image—a man's hand cupping a woman's bare breast—from Luis Buñuel and Salvador Dalí's *Un Chien Andalou* (1929), one of the films in the program.[1] Borrowing a grassroots promotional technique favored by local bands, Linklater and friends papered the University of Texas campus with the flier.

On October 4, the first midnight screening sold out the Dobie theater. In all, two of three screenings sold out, which impressed Dinger. "To be honest, the films that Rick and Lee were showing were ones that I hadn't heard of. I appreciated what they were doing, but I couldn't really get behind the films."

What Dinger could understand, however, was the "event" status their marketing efforts conferred on the series. "They created the excitement around that. They packaged that in a way by getting these films and giving it a certain title and going out and plastering the Drag. I knew that they created something that I couldn't do."[2]

Part of Linklater's inspiration for the series was a successful UT Cinema-Texas program of locally made short films at the Dobie in the spring of 1985. "People showed up, and they made money," recalls Linklater. The Dobie's "Sexuality and Blasphemy in the Avant Garde" program marked the start of the Austin Film Society (AFS), and it allowed Linklater not only to pursue his love of film, but also to network in what was a rapidly changing American independent film scene. Says screenwriter Clark Walker, who would work with Linklater on *Slacker*, "Rick saw very clearly that if you wanted to get involved with film, you had to start somewhere. Getting to know distributors was as good a way as any."[3]

Influential producer's representative John Pierson (*She's Gotta Have It, Roger & Me, Slacker,* among many others) has referred to Linklater as "a charmed underdog."[4] But even before Linklater achieved success with the independently made and idiosyncratic *Slacker* (1991), he revealed a shrewd business sense and tremendous self-discipline that seemed the antithesis, for example, of Eagle Pennell. These traits were visible as Linklater, Daniel, and others nurtured the Austin Film Society, which would become an internationally recognized nonprofit organization that in 1999 received the National Honoree Award from the Directors Guild of America.

*Slacker*'s stream-of-consciousness narrative belies the planning that went into its production. In a college town where student films often were started and then abandoned, Linklater would surprise many with his dedication and organization. Years later, he would refer to the experience as "chaos by design." Linklater's production of *Slacker* would coincide with a second generation of independent filmmakers who followed 1980s "pioneers" like Demme and Sayles. Low-budget, independent black-and-white movies like Jim Jarmusch's *Stranger Than Paradise* (1984) and Spike Lee's *She's Gotta Have It* (1985) had landed national distribution, and Linklater paid attention. "There were distributors, there were theaters, so it was easy to have your eye on the prize," he remembers. And in 1989, the same year that Linklater began making *Slacker*, Steven Soderbergh's debut feature *sex, lies, and videotape* transformed the reputation of the Sundance Film Festival.[5]

From *Slacker*'s grassroots beginnings and festival success to the film's distribution deal with Michael Barker's Orion Classics, the film put Linklater into the same generation of promising 1990s filmmakers as Soderbergh, Quentin Tarantino, and Allison Anders. Linklater's reaction to his success was a lot like writer director Bill Witliff's a decade earlier. Linklater chose to stay in Austin, creating Detour Filmproduction in a two-story house just north of the University of Texas and shooting subsequent features like *Dazed and Confused* (1993) and *The Newton Boys* (1998) in and around his home base. It was a decision that would transform the Austin film community in ways large and small, from increasing the national profile of the city's film scene thanks to Linklater pals and frequent visitors like Tarantino and actor Ethan Hawke, to convincing directors like Soderbergh to shoot in Austin and hire local crews for projects like *The Underneath* (1995). Linklater's determination to stay in town encouraged aspiring directors like Robert Rodriguez and Mike Judge to remain local, but it also contributed to Linklater's rebellious "outsider" reputation among some Hollywood department heads and studio executives.

### Happy Years of Total Focus: The Creation of the Austin Film Society

Richard Linklater arrived in Austin from Houston in the fall of 1983 after working on an offshore oil rig. He had spent much of his downtime in Houston schooling himself in the history of cinema. He read books and, when he wasn't working offshore, spent entire days in movie theaters viewing up to four films in one sitting. Although he knew he was on a path to become a filmmaker, Linklater held himself back from making his own movies. "I was still absorbing the history of cinema very systematically. I had waited to jump in technically because I knew I would have to devote myself fully to it."[6]

Once in Austin, he used some of the money he had socked away to purchase Super 8 film equipment and then embarked on a crash course in self-taught film production. He took advantage of UT's Union and CinemaTexas film series, bulking up on foreign films, Hollywood classics, and new independent and art-house fare. At night, he edited his own footage and read. "Looking back," says Linklater, "they were very happy years of total focus. Every waking second I was doing something to do with film."[7]

His savings supported him for a time while he acclimated to the Texas capital, which he had chosen over New York, Los Angeles, and San Francisco because he knew people in Austin, it was affordable, and it had something of a film scene. While living in Houston, Linklater had seen and been impressed by David Boone's *Invasion of the Aluminum People* (1980) and Brian

Hansen's *Speed of Light* (1980), and he had heard that Boone and Hansen took classes in the UT RTF program. Linklater assumed he'd end up in the film program, but when he did apply, he was rejected because his grades—for work completed during a few semesters at Sam Houston State University in Huntsville—were too low.

Instead he enrolled at Austin Community College in the fall of 1984. While Linklater had been turned off after sitting in on a UT production class in which the instructor and other students critiqued one another's films, he blossomed in the film studies courses taught by Chale Nafus, a longtime ACC instructor who would come out of retirement nearly two decades later to program the Austin Film Society. The class's written assignments forced Linklater to articulate his ideas about film, which he had formed over the years he spent reading and watching movies.

Around the same time, Linklater met Lee Daniel through the Heart of Texas Filmmakers, a loose collective of Super 8 filmmakers who occasionally put on small festivals of their work. Ray Farmer co-founded the group in 1982 with fellow Super 8 enthusiast Austin Jernigan, who later became involved with the comedy troupe Esther's Follies. Filmmaker David Boone was also part of the collective.

Daniel began making Super 8 films as a teenager in Dallas. He arrived in Austin in the early 1980s to attend the university, and his film career began with a craft services (catering) assignment on a historical documentary produced by Richard Kooris's Texas Pacific Film for local PBS affiliate KLRU.

By the time Daniel and Linklater met, Linklater hadn't really shown his work to anyone. The two went back to Linklater's apartment in West Campus, where he had converted his closet into a projection booth. "It was all completely soundproofed, and it had a little window that he had made. I'd never seen anything like it. He had his own cinema, and it was just this efficiency apartment on the second floor of a frat house," Daniel remembers. "Rick hadn't gone to film school, but he was making better stuff than I saw at UT."[8] Soon they began showing their work around town as part of live shows with local bands like the Texas Instruments.

Linklater also met Gary Price, a fellow film lover who moved to town in 1984. Recalls Price of his introduction to Linklater and friend Jack Meredith, "One Saturday I'd gone to five movies in a day, and I was getting up to leave the last one and these two guys came up to me and they said, 'We've been to five movies today, and you're at every single movie theater we're at. Who are you?'" Price was impressed by Linklater's ability to live cheaply. "He lived in what he called 'The Five Percent Club.' There's a five percent margin of people who can live off the fat of the land. He knew all these tricks about how to get money or make money or stay afloat," recalls Price. For instance, Linklater and Daniel came into possession of a copy key that allowed them to make free Xeroxes at their local Kinko's. He also observed in Linklater a desire to move beyond his current circumstances. "Even when he didn't have any money, he was taking me around and looking at houses and wanting to buy real estate," says Price, who had a background in construction.[9]

When director Sam Peckinpah died in January of 1985, Louis Black wrote a passionate obituary that ran as the *Austin Chronicle*'s cover story. One night soon after, Linklater was hanging out at Liberty Lunch, a popular live music club near the river. He wandered over and introduced himself to Black, complimenting him on the Peckinpah piece. Eventually Linklater mentioned his idea for a screening of experimental films at the Dobie. Black told him to stop by the *Chronicle* offices and talk to Chuck Shapiro, a contributor who wrote a video column and had programmed for CinemaTexas. Shapiro in turn suggested distributors who could rent films to Linklater and Daniel. The networking and new faces energized Linklater. "After working privately for so long, it was fun to start putting my film energy in a more social direction."[10]

The summer of 1985 shaped up to be a busy one. Linklater worked with Daniel to secure the films for the Dobie experimental series, scheduled for the fall, and the two also attended the annual Woodshock music festival just outside of Austin, which they documented on 16mm.

Around this time Linklater and Price met George Morris, a former New York-based movie critic. Morris was teaching film classes at ACC and threw fantastic parties that brought together like-minded film lovers in Austin. He could be difficult and temperamental, but he, Linklater, Price, and Meredith bonded quickly. Morris began having them over to his house, where the group would watch and discuss multiple movies. He also made available his extensive library of film history books. Recalls Linklater, "This sounds corny, but he was the first gay man I really knew well. I'd been to college, obviously I knew gay people, but not someone that I actually worked with, got to know really well." Morris became a mentor to the aspiring director, pushing him to watch specific movies and re-evaluate genres in which he had little interest. "No, really watch this. Check this out," Morris would say, and Linklater paid attention. "He just really opened up my eyes to a lot of cinema." It was Morris, in fact, who encouraged Linklater and his friends to start a film society.[11]

By the fall of 1985 Linklater and Daniel had become roommates. Like the CinemaTexas crowd had done decades earlier, they screened 16mm films in their living room. The experimental series at the Dobie was an extension of these living room film screenings. The midnight film series continued throughout the fall and into the winter of 1986. Energized by the films and their positive reception by local audiences, Linklater planned more screenings for the spring while simultaneously beginning to edit footage he had shot the previous summer during a train trip to the Pacific Northwest. With support and encouragement from Morris and Chale Nafus, the film society partnered that spring with Austin Community College to sponsor a screening of films by French directors Carl Dreyer and Robert Bresson. Linklater also met with Judith Sims, director of the Austin Museum of Art. While a student at UT in the 1970s, Sims had been involved with the Union Film Committee and remained an avid filmgoer and champion of new filmmakers. Sims agreed to allow the film society to use the space in the museum's off hours that summer. Linklater and Daniel programmed their most ambitious series yet, a retrospective of ten films by German director Rainer Werner Fassbinder. Local press coverage helped to create a buzz around the event, which kicked off with *Fox and His Friends* (1975). The screening sold out, the series eventually paid for itself, and the event served as a model for later series built around the work of a single director.

By this time Linklater and Daniel had begun calling the organization the Austin Film Society. Although they tossed around more inventive titles, they agreed that they needed something descriptive, even bland, in order to apply for grants. "I always liked the name of the Collective for Living Cinema in New York. But you're not going to get Austin's Parks and Recreation Department to give you money with a name like that," recalls Daniel.[12]

In less than a year, the Austin Film Society had shown forty films and enjoyed healthy and, in some cases, sold-out attendance. Linklater felt grateful for the enthusiastic support they received from the Austin community. In the fall of 1986, Linklater met Jim Jackson, a local administrator with ties to the Texas Commission on the Arts. Jackson encouraged the film society to apply for city funding, so Linklater began the lengthy process of securing nonprofit status. Again and again, people reached out to assist the fledgling organization, including then-state representative Jake Pickle. Recalls Linklater, "I learned so much about how to get things done. You really rely on community and help and favors. It's a real world of reciprocity."[13]

It was during a series on Bresson that Linklater met Clark Walker. Walker came from a long line of archetypical cowboy types in Texarkana; his rancher grandfather took him to *Last Picture Show*-type movie houses to see classic westerns like *Red River* (1948). While attending high school in Bartlesville, Oklahoma, he frequented the local film society run by filmmaker and Austinite Terrence Malick's parents. Although Walker took a few film classes in college, like Linklater he taught himself much about film history by reading. Walker was impressed by Linklater's encyclopedic knowledge of film, which he nurtured through a filing-card system listing all of the movies he'd ever seen.

Walker quickly became part of the expanding group of volunteers who helped to run the film society. "It just seemed like a great scam to us, honestly, to see the movies we wanted to see, and if we could get 12 people to come by virtue of putting up fliers, we could pay for the shipping."[14] Daniel had connections to experimental filmmaker Craig Baldwin, who was based in San Francisco and had started an alternative film program called Other Cinema. The two groups often exchanged programs, promoting each other's regional cinema and splitting the rental fees.

In the spring of 1987 Linklater met art student Denise "D." Montgomery at one of George Morris's film parties. "She was the girl who always had a video camera to her eye," Linklater remembers.[15] Montgomery was an extremely charismatic and intense personality. Linklater and Montgomery hit it off, and he asked her to appear in his unfinished first feature. Montgomery also became a regular fixture at film society events, and her involvement would transform the organization's scope over the next few months.

With Jim Jackson's help, Linklater applied for and received a $4,000 Texas Commission on the Arts grant for AFS. He, Daniel, and their friends used the money to renovate loft space above Captain Quackenbush's Intergalactic Café, a popular student hangout located on the Drag across from UT. They ripped out the carpet, sanded and painted the floors, built a projection booth, and installed a movie screen. At the same time, Linklater began programming for the grand opening of the new space in the spring of 1988. He scheduled five separate film programs to screen between late January and May. Although some were skeptical that the ambitious programming would make back its money, Linklater reasoned that the location of the new space, so close to the UT campus, would attract large-enough crowds. A solid audience turned out for the first night of the season's initial program, a reconfigured "Sex & Blasphemy" lineup similar to the film society's 1985 screening. By the following week, however, the crowd had dwindled. Each week, the numbers got worse.[16]

AFS lost money that season, having quickly burned through the grant to program and run the series. Linklater dipped into his own financial reserves, but these also had dwindled substantially since he first arrived in Austin. When his savings finally ran out, he took a job working the graveyard shift at a local hotel.

By his own admission, Linklater's ambitious programming choices nearly collapsed the film society that spring.[17] His frustration about his own film-making only added to his disappointment. After two years of work, Linklater had finally finished his first feature, an "oblique narrative" entitled *It's Impossible to Learn to Plow by Reading Books*. Shot by and starring Linklater, the meditative film explores the nature of travel and loneliness in extended long shots Linklater photographed while touring the country by bus and train. Although he had finished the film, he had no idea what to do with it. When the hotel laid him off, he decided to leave town for the summer and go to New York, where he lived off his weekly $125 unemployment check. He thought seriously about not returning to Austin.

But the summer had given him time to re-charge and re-think, so he returned to town in August and to programming the film society. The fall line-up, while much reduced from what it had been the previous spring, included an impressive twelve-film series entitled "The Black Image in American Film," curated by friend John Slate. Lee Daniel's brother Bill returned from San Francisco to show some of that film community's latest Super 8 work. Documentaries, experimental film, Cuban video, and performance pieces rounded out the schedule.

Linklater also began thinking about his second feature, which he planned to shoot in Galveston. "I had written a script and was vaguely location scouting, trying to raise money although I didn't really know how to do that."[18] He tried to attract potential backers by screening *Plow*, but no one showed any interest. Over the Christmas holidays, Linklater took stock of his situation. The film society was digging itself out of the financial hole he helped create earlier that year. He had finished his first film but had no way to distribute it. And after four months, he was nowhere closer to getting his second film off the ground. It was then that he realized that, as a filmmaker, he had failed.

## Chaos by Design

After deciding in the final months of 1988 that his second feature wasn't going to take off, Linklater turned his attention to another idea that had been percolating for years. Still living in Galveston during the week, he spent most nights working out the details for a movie set in Austin in which the camera follows multiple characters in relay-like fashion, similar to Max Ophuls's *La Ronde*. "I was just making it to make it, because I had to make a film. I had been shooting *Plow* and editing it for a few years, finished it, and I just wanted to make another film *so* bad."[19]

Months earlier Linklater had returned to New York to attend the Independent Feature Film Market (IFFM), a conference where filmmakers and screenwriters pay to have their completed films, scripts, or works in progress shown to distributors with the hope that a sale might be made. He went with the vague notion that he might make some contacts to get his second feature off the ground. Sitting in on panel discussions by industry professionals, Linklater discovered the ins and outs of distribution and publicity.

When he began to work on a treatment for his next project, which he tentatively entitled *No Longer/Not Yet*, Linklater had few illusions about its ever being purchased by a distributor. "Every year there were a few big independent success stories. You could make a film that could actually show at the Varsity Theater or the Dobie. [But] I had zero confidence it could ever get a national distribution the way *Stranger Than Paradise* or *She's Gotta Have It* did." For starters, he worried that the film's lack of a conventional storyline would be seen as a drawback. As with *La Ronde*, Linklater's earliest treatment amounted to a series of linked episodes involving disparate characters. The first of the forty-five scenes began late at night with two young men partying in a car. Eventually they pick up a hitchhiker on his way to Austin, where the rest of the story's action takes place.[20]

But Linklater's research trip to the IFFM the previous fall had him thinking from the start about ways to sell the film. Walker remembers reading an early treatment of *Slacker* that contained a scene with an explosion at a gas station. "Rick could give this little pitch to non-existent investors about how it had sex, it had an explosion, it had a car chase." According to Walker, Linklater invoked Martin Scorsese's experience of trying to find a distributor for *Who's That Knocking at My Door?* and how the filmmaker went back and shot a sex scene to appease its distributor.[21]

Linklater's treatment described events or ideas that he had experienced, been told, or dreamed up and written down over the years. One scenario involving a son who runs over his own mother grew out of an event that occurred decades earlier near the Austin house Linklater shared with Daniel. Another scene, in which a woman sits at a lunch counter babbling about never traumatizing a woman sexually and purporting to be a "medical doctor," happened to Linklater while in New York. Explained Linklater years later, "Some were inspired by or adapted from bookish ideas or pre-existing texts, like a spoken-word performance by Jim Roche or a few short stories by my friend Jack Meredith. I had a meeting with a friend named Sid Moody about various conspiracy theories I had heard him talk about before." Whereas Ophuls employed recurring motifs of a waltz and a narrator to link *La*

*Ronde*'s various episodes, Linklater would rely on the fluid camera and a kind of "baton-passing" among the characters as they ran into one another or their paths crossed in the same location. The treatment's final sequence featured a car full of people, joyously heading off into the hills overlooking Austin with their Super 8 camera. The sequence took inspiration from one of Daniel's experiences when he and his brother Bill and their girlfriends spent an afternoon atop San Francisco's Twin Peaks.[22]

Linklater gathered around him a crew of people culled mostly from the film society. "It was purposefully designed around the limitations of its budget. I figured I could get some people to work on it, a real small crew, working sporadically over a two-month period," says Linklater. With his extensive commercial experience and his own 16mm Arriflex camera, Daniel came on board as the movie's cinematographer. Richard Kooris, Daniel's former boss, generously agreed to defer payment on all of the necessary lighting and sound equipment. Daniel's connections also allowed him to "borrow" a dolly from public television station KLRU. Linklater and Daniel shared a 16mm editing bed that would get them through most of the film's postproduction.[23]

Montgomery became the film's sound recordist and also helped Deb Pastor with art direction. Meg Brennan, another film society regular, handled script supervisor duties. Clark Walker, now married to Anne Walker-McBay, had returned to Austin from San Francisco that spring. Walker-McBay suggested that it would be an interesting film to cast, and without any kind of formal arrangement, she became the production manager and co-casting director. With some experience as a grip, gaffer, and camera assistant, Walker also signed on to assist Daniel.

Although Linklater didn't realize it at the time, most of these individuals would become key collaborators in Detour Filmproduction, the production company he co-founded with Daniel, and they would continue to work on many of Linklater's future films. And although there was no mistaking that the project was Linklater's, for some of those involved it felt like more of a collective endeavor, an extension of the film society itself. Recalls Walker, "I think our hope was that one of us was going to do a film, then another of us would do a film—we just would all help each other finish our first features in the same semester-based fashion that we learned from college and booking film series."[24]

During preproduction Linklater assembled a list of production guidelines pulled from the notebooks he had kept over the years. Covering the movie's narrative structure, camera movement, and dialogue, the list was like a non-visual storyboard to keep everyone on the same page. He envisioned the film as "one long sequence" and expected viewers to assume "causal relationships" among the different scenes. The script was meant only as an outline. Daniel's camera was to be "quiet but eloquent," the colors "muted, not bright," and the entire film should have a documentary feel. Linklater's list of rules addressed every aspect of the project, down to its eventual reception. "It's okay for the viewer to be aware that they are watching a construct," he wrote. "The form of the film makes the viewer experience the discomfort and alienation/disorientation of the characters."[25]

Given the movie's structure, much of the film's personality and energy would rely on its multiple characters. Linklater had taken acting classes over the years, and he had very specific ideas about what would work for this project. The characters purposefully lacked backstory or history. That May, he and Walker-McBay began the lengthy casting process. He had a few individuals in mind for the film, people he knew or actors he had met in his classes. He approached, among others, local actor Charles Gunning and friend John Slate, who had a penchant for conspiracy theories. Linklater and Walker-McBay briefly flirted with the idea of using an agency to find their characters, but instead they created typewritten cards bearing a brief description of the project and explaining that they were hoping to find interesting-looking people to interview—no acting experience necessary. "Just come prepared to talk about yourself to help us match personalities with characters in the film," they wrote.[26]

Linklater and Walker-McBay conducted most of the casting interviews in the Austin Film Society space above Quackenbush's. If the selected individuals showed up—a true test of their commitment, as far as Walker-McBay was concerned—they were videotaped answering random questions about their lives, political beliefs, and so on. Linklater and Walker-McBay conducted a staggering three to four hundred interviews, the majority of which took place between May and July 1989, when production actually began.[27]

On the first day of shooting in early July, a seven-member crew assembled just after five in the morning at the Greyhound bus depot in North Austin. With Daniel's camera mounted onto the hood of Rudy Basquez's taxi, they shot their first take of the scene, in which Linklater's character arrives at the bus station, hails a cab, and then proceeds to chatter pleasantly as the driver stares silently ahead. The project didn't have a title, but it did have an opening scene captured on film. Production had begun.

Linklater's Shell gasoline credit card provided the movie's craft services, such as they were. With no pre-set spending limit, the card allowed virtually unlimited supplies of convenience store snacks and beer. Homemade peanut-butter sandwiches also were a staple. They filmed the movie mostly in sequence. One of the earliest scenes required a Steadicam that followed actors Jerry Delony and Tommy Palotta through the streets of Austin's West Campus neighborhood. During the talky scene a hilariously dramatic Delony peppers a nonplussed Palotta with his ramblings about the government and life on the moon. Linklater manned the slate and then crept alongside the group as he monitored the actors' progress. He also became aware of a police car slowly circling the block and keeping tabs on their activity, a humorous parallel to the scene's rant about an insidious and suspicious government. The crew worked quickly, keenly aware that they didn't have "permission" to be shooting on the street although in the late 1980s it was relatively easy to film without permits in Austin.

At Liberty Lunch, the crew gathered to shoot what would become one of the film's most talked-about sequences. At the time Austin's downtown area remained fairly deserted during the day, which made for easy filming. The shuttered businesses and empty warehouses were ghostly reminders of the economic recession that still gripped the city and much of the rest of the country in 1989. Linklater had asked Butthole Surfers drummer Teresa Taylor to appear in the film. "We talked about doing a drugged-out freak kind of character, going on about Madonna," Taylor recalls of her initial conversations with the filmmaker. At the time, Taylor cultivated a "rock star attitude" and an ego to match thanks in part to the underground success of the band, who spent much of the 1980s touring punk clubs across the country. She arrived on the set and immediately demanded a hat and sunglasses as part of her wardrobe. Given the parties she had frequented with the movie's crew, she expected a very different vibe. "I got there and thought it would be a party scene. I was like, where's the beer? And they said, 'Teresa, it's noon. You look like hell. Put on your hat and sunglasses and do your scene.'"[28] Taylor's performance was an inspired marketing riff about Madonna's Pap smear delivered in an awkwardly compelling sing-song style. Taylor was on set for just half a day, but her wacky monologue would prove integral to the film's audience appeal.

By late July, Linklater figured they had enough footage to submit the movie as a work in progress to the SWAMP Independent Production Fund. SWAMP was the same Houston organization that years earlier had funded Eagle Pennell's first short film, *A Hell of a Note*. Linklater requested $5,000 to finish the project. He described the film as an experimental narrative about people in their twenties, "people on the fringes of any meaningful participation in society." He called the project *Slacker*, a title that hadn't won universal appeal among the cast and crew but somehow seemed better than *No Longer/Not Yet*. Daniel's suggestion, *The Day Before Tomorrow (The Day After Yesterday)*, was as pretentious as Linklater's original choice.[29]

In the fall of 1989 Katie Cokinos was working for SWAMP and organizing the Independent Images conferences. Cokinos had met Eagle Pennell a year earlier and co-produced *Heart Full of Soul* (1990). Like Linklater, Cokinos had created a film society as an undergraduate at Texas A&M University. When she reviewed Linklater's application for the Independent Production Fund, she was riveted by the production stills that accompanied the work in progress. "It was all these kids my age, mid-twenties and just scruffy-looking, this group of people making a film. They were just doing it by the seat of their pants," recalls Cokinos.[30]

Production on *Slacker* continued into August. When Linklater's sister Tricia learned that her brother needed money to pay for a shipment of processed film, she advanced him the cash. "My family has been so supportive," he wrote in his journal. "They must sense I'm desperate. I hope I can pay them back some way." Gary Price, who had recently returned to town after a three-year absence, also put up some money for the film. Meanwhile, the cast and crew—all working on deferred "salaries"—were reimbursed for their time in the form of breakfast tacos, a cheap and plentiful staple of the Austin diet.[31]

Working with a small crew and only a few actors at a time, the production remained mostly under the town's radar. The manager of Les Amis, the café just around the corner from Linklater and Daniel's apartment, generously agreed to let them film in the café during and after hours. The treatment called for Daniel's camera to glide among the tables, capturing two guys debating the philosophical underpinnings of *The Smurfs* and recording a discussion among three women about the disappointing nature of relationships and their potential for enslavement. Kim Krizan, a master's student at Southwest Texas State University who appeared in the scene, recalls that when she showed up for rehearsals, she and the other women began making small talk. Linklater listened for a while and then assigned them roles (Krizan was "the negative one") and had them write down specific "lines" that then became their dialogue in the film. The combination of the lengthy, dialogue-heavy scenes and the café's cramped physical space took its toll. As Linklater later recalled, "Timing's everything when you're working with drunk and high people."[32]

For Linklater, filming the finale was one of the most enjoyable moments of the production. Over the years Daniel had played around with inventive shooting techniques, such as casting a loaded camera from the roof of his apartment using a toy fishing reel and building a catapult and launching a Super 8 camera across the street. He devised a similar technique for the final scene, in which a convertible full of friends drives around town filming passersby. Once they arrive at Mt. Bonnell, a local landmark overlooking Lake Austin, they scramble up the hill to the scenic spot where they film one another mugging for the camera. The scene ends when one person jubilantly pitches the camera over the edge of a cliff. During filming, Daniel tied fishing line to the camera so that they could recover it and the film inside after the drop of more than seven hundred feet into the water below.

Given the various challenges of the two-month shoot—filming around everyone's disparate schedules, casting during production, the occasional external difficulties—the production itself went relatively well. As Walker recalls, "It wasn't hard at all until we started having to cut parts of the film out."[33]

### It's My Film

During preproduction in June, Linklater had asked editor Scott Rhodes to help with the project. Rhodes had taken a couple of film classes at Austin Cable Television (ACTV) and had begun editing friends' music videos. Rhodes had pitched in throughout production and appeared on-camera as the "Disgruntled Grad Student."

Rhodes had done some assembly during production, but he and Linklater edited the bulk of the rough cut in the fall of 1989. They worked at ACTV, where they had access to free equipment but were at the mercy of temperamental machines and restricted to four-hour editing blocks. Linklater had transferred a 16mm work print to videotape so they could edit on video, which allowed them to preview the cuts. The long takes and connectivity of the individual scenes made cutting difficult. "It wasn't your typical editing job where you just cut [scenes] out and show it to people," says Rhodes. "In order to justify taking a scene out, I'd have to suggest a scene that would work in order to put parts A and B together." The collective nature of the endeavor also complicated things. "I got frustrated because every time I wanted to make an edit, it had to pass the group," says Rhodes.[34] But the real editing challenge would come months later, when the finished cut exceeded two hours.

In October 1989 Linklater returned to the IFFM in New York, but this time he had a film in tow. Although *Slacker* was far from finished, they had about an hour of edited footage to screen as a work in progress.[35]

In 1988, Michael Moore had shown *Roger & Me* as a work in progress at the IFFM, but few paid attention. He returned the following year in triumph with a much-buzzed-about documentary. As producer's representative John Pierson fielded various offers for the film, Moore cheekily advised distributors to catch a few of that year's works in progress. The *Slacker* screening was fairly well attended. "Many seem to like it (at least they laugh a bit) but don't really know what they're watching," Linklater wrote in his journal. "There is a little hostility ('They don't DO anything!' I overheard right after), but I'd be surprised if there wasn't."[36]

Producer Otto Grokenberger, who had executive produced two films with Jim Jarmusch, had told Linklater during a lunch meeting that he liked the film and might be able to provide the funds needed to finish the project. But by the time Linklater returned to Austin and began to shoot pickups in November, he noticed a distinct mood change. The energy that had sustained everyone during the intense two-month summer production had since evaporated.

Grokenberger eventually changed his mind about investing in the project. Linklater was completely out of money—a fact he decided not to share with the crew—even with a nearly $2,000 grant he received from SWAMP.[37] Sucked dry of financial backing and optimism, Linklater couldn't believe his good luck when a letter arrived from German television producer Werner Dütsch. According to the terms of the contract with WDR—the same German television network that invested in *Whole Shootin' Match*—Linklater would not receive any money until the film was finished. Still, he was able to use the contract as collateral to borrow enough money to complete the movie over the next couple of months.

The holidays came and went. Editing continued into early 1990 in an effort to shorten the film to less than two hours. Discussions about specific scenes continued to cause friction within the group. "I made this big chart and I did these scenes in a bar graph, scenes that were always getting laughs," says Rhodes. "I had to explain to people why some parts were really slow." The scene that elicited the most debate featured Walker and another person in a San Antonio theatrical supply house having a conversation about classic movies while Walker tinkered with an old projector. The scene began as a lengthy tracking shot photographed with the camera on an elaborate dolly. "It looked processional. This was like the crane coming down in *Intolerance*," explains Walker, who initially opposed the decision to cut the scene. Rhodes lobbied for it to come out, having thought the movie already had too many film references. "It was three against three," says Rhodes. "Me, Rick, and D. Montgomery against Lee, Clark, and Anne."[38]

SWAMP's Katie Cokinos had begun dating Linklater in November and immediately assimilated into the *Slacker* group. "Anne and I really loved that scene. We thought it was beautiful and the one positive scene in the whole film—where someone's actually doing something—and we had a big argument. And Rick just said something to the effect of, 'It's my film,' and he was absolutely right."[39]

Linklater had sent the film to a number of festivals, including Sundance and Berlin. Both rejected *Slacker*. Festival programmers encouraged him, however, to show the film in the open market section of the Berlin Film Festival. He would have to pay all travel and lodging expenses and an additional $200 fee to screen the movie, but he decided to do it. By this time Cokinos was helping to prepare publicity materials for the film and decided to accompany Linklater to Berlin.

Once in Germany, the pair trudged through the snow as they made the rounds of various hotels to drop off press packets for key industry people attending the festival. *Slacker*'s first public screening in Berlin got off to a rocky start when only two people—one a friend of Linklater's—arrived at the venue. Afterward a miserable Linklater wandered around the city and tried to consider other career alternatives. Linklater told Cokinos that he didn't want to be like James Benning, the highly regarded experimental filmmaker who had a loyal following in high-art circles. "Rick didn't want to just make these alternative films that only a handful of people were able to see. He really didn't want that, which I thought was really interesting because the films he wanted to do at that time were kind of like that." He was cheered by the film's second screening, attended by only a small group of people but lively enough to generate conversation afterward.[40]

Upon returning to the States, Linklater sent a letter to Grokenberger, the producer in New York who had withdrawn his offer to finance the film, telling him about the somewhat favorable response *Slacker* had received in Berlin. Grokenberger fired off a rather nasty reply, suggesting that Linklater didn't understand movie audiences and that *Slacker* wouldn't find a distribution outlet beyond "a quirky TV program." Its chances were doomed, wrote the producer, because of the film's length and absence of compelling dialogue. "And that is what you do not want to accept, your film has no theme." Linklater's depression eventually gave way to a kind of cocky rebellion: "I fantasize that anyone who doesn't like the film will have to answer for their cowardice or incompetence."[41]

In April 1990 Linklater traveled with Cokinos to Dallas for the USA Film Festival. Like Eagle Pennell before him, Linklater was using the festival to unveil his feature to U.S. audiences. *Slacker*'s first review, however, published in the *Dallas Times Herald* on the morning of its screening, was less than enthusiastic. The critic's lead sentence was devastating: "This stream-of-consciousness film threatens to render its audience unconscious."[42]

"I remember waking up that Saturday morning and reading the capsule review," says Linklater. "It was basically our first review, and it was this little, dismissive capsule saying this film basically would have been a good short, but it sucks. I was like, 'Fuck! Do I even go to this screening?'"[43] Despite the lukewarm critical response, the audience warmed to the film.

The following month *Slacker* received an invitation to the Seattle International Film Festival. The festival's director and members of the selection committee responded enthusiastically to the movie. Linklater's hunch that *Slacker* had finally found its audience was confirmed when the *Seattle Times* critic wrote a positive review that generated even more interest in the festival screening. "*Slacker* was preaching to the choir in Seattle," recalls Cokinos. "It was 1990, the grunge scene—everything was just about to open up. And I remember talking to Todd McCarthy, the *Variety* reviewer, at one of the parties, and he was so excited about *Slacker*."[44]

More good news arrived in the form of a note left for the filmmaker by Robert Horton, a young writer who wanted to interview Linklater for *Film Comment,* the prestigious film journal put out by the Film Society of Lincoln Center. Horton's interview with Linklater appeared a couple of months later. The piece, which quoted Linklater as dismissing film school—a statement that would not go over well with the UT RTF department faculty—offered some insight into Linklater's background and the movie itself, which Horton found unexpectedly moving: "Linklater has a deadpan but always sympathetic approach to his people; his frequent method of playing scenes in long takes allows the characters to find their own rhythms, and eschews editorial comment."[45] Although other journalists would later gloss over this information, Horton took pains to point out that the film's "improvised look" was anything but spontaneous, thus immediately debunking the notion that Linklater and his tiny crew were slacker filmmakers.

### How to Make Something Work in Austin

Thousands of miles away in Maine, producer's representative John Pierson had read Horton's article with interest. By 1990 Pierson was known in film circles as the guy who had shepherded a handful of important independent films into theaters. *Parting Glances* (1986), *She's Gotta Have It* (1985),

*Working Girls* (1986), *The Thin Blue Line* (1988), *Roger & Me* (1989)—all of these films benefited from Pierson's distribution savvy. While Linklater was sitting in on distributors' panels at the 1988 IFFM, Pierson was in attendance, mourning that year's lack of quality independents while moderating an acquisitions panel. A year later, Linklater returned to IFFM with *Slacker* as a work in progress, but Pierson was otherwise engaged, trying to keep Michael Moore's ego from sabotaging a $3 million deal with Warner Bros. for *Roger & Me*.[46]

Cokinos read an article about Pierson in an industry magazine and showed it to Linklater. In early July he called Pierson, who coincidentally had read the *Film Comment* article a day earlier. Linklater promised to send a copy of *Slacker* to Pierson, who was teaching a summer workshop in Maine. Meanwhile, Linklater turned his attention to Scott Dinger and the Dobie. Dinger agreed to let them use one of the theater's two screens for a private *Slacker* screening in mid-July, but Linklater, Daniel, and Walker-McBay had to work a bit harder to convince Dinger to let *Slacker* screen for paying audiences. Although Dinger had confidence in Linklater from working with him on AFS screenings, he was reluctant to hand over one of the theater's two screens for this offbeat, virtually untested movie. Instead he agreed to program *Slacker* for up to two shows per day for approximately four weeks beginning in late July.[47]

Using printed fliers and stickers, the *Slacker* crew employed the same DIY marketing techniques to promote the Dobie screenings that had proven fairly effective for the AFS screenings. Although Dinger had his initial doubts, he began to sense the buzz building around town. He knew from experience that strong opening nights for local films proved little. The real test would come in the days and weeks following the first screening. Sure enough, the movie popped on opening night during its cast and crew screening, but *Slacker* continued to do well in subsequent screenings. The usual Dobie crowd, full of faces Dinger recognized, gave way to a completely different audience of people who may have never been to a movie at the smallish theater near the UT campus. "That's really where it had that almost water cooler kind of thing. It became *the* movie in Austin to see. It took on a life of its own," recalls Dinger.[48] By the end of the extended eleven-week run, *Slacker* had sold out the first twenty-two of its shows at the Dobie thanks in part to strong local reviews and phenomenal word of mouth.

It was no surprise that the *Austin Chronicle* raved about the movie, given the newsweekly's affection for and support of Linklater and the film society over the preceding years. "When I saw the movie, everybody I knew was in it," recalls contributor Chris Walters, who had befriended the CinemaTexas crowd when he moved to Austin as an undergraduate in 1979 and would later frequent AFS screenings. Walters watched *Slacker* on videotape before interviewing Linklater for a feature about the production. But Walters's essay did more than simply praise the film; it tapped into the movie's larger cultural issues and contextualized its characters' yearning within generations of individuals struggling with similar issues. "The drift, the eternal unchanging bohemia and the lonely people in the really compulsively social town. That really struck me," says Walters. Writing for the city's daily newspaper the *Austin American-Statesman*, Patrick Taggart also gave *Slacker* a glowing review. "In its own, odd and endearing way, *Slacker* is as fine a first feature as Spike Lee's *She's Gotta Have It* or Steven Soderbergh's *sex, lies and videotape*," wrote Taggart, perhaps already sensing Linklater's ascension into the next generation of American independent filmmakers.[49]

Not everyone loved the film. As one irritated Dobie regular wrote to Dinger, "Why are the lives of these unproductive, pretentious, and boring people documented on film? What have they done to make the world or even the city of Austin a better place?" But as John Pierson would later observe, the letter writer's beef about the apparent "documentation" of these individuals (actors and mostly nonprofessionals reading scripted lines) is less an indictment of the film than a testament to *Slacker*'s realism and Linklater's abilities as a narrative filmmaker.[50]

In the midst of preparations for the Dobie run, Linklater had finally put together a package for Pierson. He wrote that the immensely positive reception the film had received at the cast and crew screening—a no-brainer, he admitted—assuaged his anxieties about the movie's potential and again made him realize "that *Slacker* is a definite crowd-pleaser for a particular niche of the population." Linklater included a recent *Time* magazine cover story about the twentysomething generation, suggested other potential target demographics for the film and mentioned the possibility of a cover story in *Film Threat* magazine. "And in the year of the 50 million dollar budgets," concluded Linklater, "I can already feel people going out of their way to support this $23,000, out-of-left-field, genre and plot denying, first time film (that in reality wants to be liked)."[51]

Pierson was charmed by the letter and impressed with Linklater's grassroots market research. "He, even then, quickly adapted to the idea that there might be some larger cultural trend to hook the wagon to," recalls Pierson. "He certainly had a notion, an acute awareness how to make something work in Austin."[52]

In early August Pierson hosted a screening of *Slacker* on videotape for Michael Barker, who had arrived in Maine to guest lecture at Pierson's summer course. Barker was a UT grad and former programmer of the Texas Union Film Program who by 1990 was running the distribution company Orion Classics with Tom Bernard, who also had Austin connections. "We watched the tape, and everyone there fell asleep but me and John. [The film] really captured Austin," recalls Barker, who admits that his own relationship to the city probably predisposed him to the film.[53]

Barker's only concern was how to convince his partners, Bernard and Marci Bloom, to back the movie. "You know, this 'slacker' thing is a real generation, a big group of people," Barker told Bernard, who responded that he thought his brother might be a slacker. "So we called his brother on the phone and his brother was like, '*Slacker*, yeah, it's cool'. So that kind of put Tom over, like, 'We've really got something here'." Barker claims that he next called his relatives in Austin and asked them to check out the movie and confirm its well-attended Dobie screenings, but Pierson insists that Barker had done this before he traveled to Maine in early August.[54]

Says Cokinos, who recalls Barker's "plant" arriving at the cast and crew screening in July, "I was surprised when Orion Classics wanted to distribute it. I didn't think a company like that would see a real audience for *Slacker*, but I think it hit them at the right time. They were known for the European Merchant-Ivory kind of film, and I think they wanted to do more American-type stories."[55]

Meanwhile, Pierson officially offered to represent *Slacker*. Orion made their offer, which included a $100,000 advance and $50,000 to finish the film. (The finishing costs—a 35mm negative to strike prints, an answer print, etc.—ultimately came in at $60,000.) Initially thrilled, Linklater soon realized the money wouldn't cover all of the necessary costs and the deferred cast and crew salaries. Remembers Clark Walker, "It was sobering to learn that this big advance was actually going to be eaten up by the price of finishing the film and postproduction costs."[56]

With Pierson's help, Linklater had submitted *Slacker* to the top three fall festivals, and he hoped that an acceptance to the Toronto International Film Festival might work as a bargaining chip with Orion. Yet even as the movie continued to play through September to enthusiastic Austin audiences, it received firm rejections from Toronto, Telluride, and the New York Film Festival.

The hint of a cultural context, supported by the *Time* cover story about twentysomethings and further underscored by a September *New York Times* feature about campus café society, had helped to convince the folks at Orion. The challenge was getting Orion to increase their initial offer. "It was the way they always approached buying a film," says Pierson, who had last dealt with the company when he was fielding offers a year earlier for *Roger & Me*. "They were probably still at $100,000 [for *Roger & Me*] when everybody else was close to a million. They just had this fixed model of being very low-ball. And since they got a film like *My Beautiful Laundrette* for that little money, why not think that that was an appropriate amount to pay for something that had cost as little as *Slacker*?"[57]

While Linklater ran the numbers and meditated on Orion's offer, Pierson capitalized on the "window of opportunity," letting it slip to a few other distributors that a low-budget film screening in Austin, Texas, was doing very well. At the Dobie, Dinger began fielding distributors' phone calls and questions: Was the film selling out? How many shows per day?[58] But while other distributors may have been interested in the movie, no one else was making an offer.

### *Slacker* beyond Austin

After eleven successful weeks, *Slacker* ended its Austin run at the Dobie Theatre (formerly the Dobie 1 & 2) on October 11, 1990. Linklater spent most of that fall focused on postproduction, trimming some of the scenes and finalizing the soundtrack. He also used a portion of Orion's $100,000 advance to pay the movie's deferred cast and crew costs, which totaled just over $40,000. "It was an extremely socialistic way to hand out the money. It was generous to a fault. Literally, we had to chase all these people down to give them their $200 check," says Walker. "I more than got my money back," says Price, who to this day continues to receive dividend checks from his initial investment.[59]

But editor Rhodes recalls a meeting where Daniel asked Linklater about an original plan to split the film's profits among the group. Linklater began asking people to tally the hours they had worked on the project. "There was a hush in the group when Rick said that. Lee was the only one that spoke up. They were living together at the time. No one else said anything," says Rhodes.[60]

"Rick is a born accountant," shrugs Daniel. "Everything is about the bottom line." Three years later Amy Lowrey would work at Detour first as an office manager and then as Linklater's assistant, and it was her responsibility to mail out dividend checks—some as small as $30—to the *Slacker* cast and crew. "People had so many expectations of what Rick should do for them. I personally oversaw the money, and there was a specific formula Rick worked out to pay people, and that's what they signed on for. You worked a day, you got a certain percentage."[61]

Meanwhile Pierson turned his attention to the Sundance Film Festival and trying to convince Competition Director Alberto Garcia to accept *Slacker*. It was a tough sell despite the fact that Garcia's age (mid-twenties) targeted him as the movie's key demographic. Somewhat grudgingly, perhaps, Sundance extended an invitation.

In the months leading up to the January 1991 festival, Linklater made additional cuts and reshot two scenes, shearing almost seven minutes from the film. One of the reshoots involved a new scene to bridge the gap created by the controversial removal of the theater supply store sequence. Linklater also spent just over a week overseeing a new soundtrack mix, engineered by Fred Remmert at Austin's Cedar Creek Studio. Thanks to his and Daniel's connections with many Austin bands, Linklater was able to infuse the movie with local music by groups like Poi Dog Pondering and Texas Instruments. From the start he had wanted to include local music, which was very much a part of the Austin vibe (not to mention its cultural history), but he intentionally kept it in the background, secondary to the images and dialogue. "You get the sense you're in a 'scene,' but it's not about the music or about being in a band."[62]

*Slacker*'s ebullient final sequence was matched with an equally bouncy and virtually unknown single called "Skokian." They lifted the song, scratches and all, for the movie's soundtrack during the Dobie release. When Linklater began the process of securing rights to keep the song in the Orion release, he discovered that the group's record label had tanked decades earlier, and they were charged $8,000—one-third of the film's much-publicized but inaccurate budget—to use the song.[63]

Linklater also planned to use Peggy Lee's rendition of "Is That All There Is?" behind *Slacker*'s final credit sequence. It appeared on the original 16mm print at the Dobie, but Linklater hit a brick wall when he approached Lee's estate to secure the rights for the official Orion Classics release. It wasn't even a question of money; the estate turned him down flat. Appearing on the soundtrack immediately after the final sequence, the song's wry, somewhat bemused lyrics and Lee's bluesy tone trumped the final scene's ebullient mood. Says Daniel, "It makes the movie entirely different. It completely changed the meaning of the movie for me. And I think Rick recognized that, too."[64]

Although the film society had taken time off during the summers of 1989 (*Slacker* production) and 1990 (*Slacker* promotion and screening), it continued to chug along with its eclectic programs and visiting filmmaker series. Despite the distraction of making and finshing *Slacker*, Linklater managed to program a fall series in 1989 and a spring 1990 lineup of documentaries and experimental films. Bill Daniel's San Francisco connections helped to bring in that city's Found Footage Fest, which included works by experimental filmmakers Bruce Conner, Greta Snider, and Craig Baldwin.

Cokinos effectively took over Linklater's duties as administrative director after moving to Austin to live with him. She focused on bringing in filmmakers to show and discuss their work, people like Gregg Araki, whom she and Linklater met while attending a film festival the previous summer. By this time, AFS had a core audience of about twenty regulars and was still using fliers to advertise the free cinema screenings. Linklater segued from programmer to artistic director and a less hands-on role in the film society's evolution, turning his attention to his budding film career.

In late January 1991, Michael Barker accompanied the film to the Sundance Film Festival. "We got there and of course the second screening was half full, and the third screening was almost full, and the final screening, you couldn't get in. So the word of mouth on the freshness of the movie just kind of grew," Barker recalls. Sundance represented *Slacker*'s first official screening since being picked up by a distributor. *Slacker* won no prizes at the festival, but Linklater basked in words of praise from jury member Gus Van Sant. A positive review in *Variety* capped the Sundance experience. Although the reviewer also noted that *Slacker*'s "nonnarrative, noncharacterization approach" would limit its audience, it predicted good business in college towns and at festivals.[65]

*Slacker* really hit its stride two months later as an entry in the New Directors/New Films program co-presented by the Film Society of Lincoln Center and the Museum of Modern Art. As with Eagle Pennell and *The Whole Shootin' Match* more than a decade earlier, Linklater enjoyed the enthusiastic audience's warm embrace of the film. The good feelings continued through the postscreening Q&A. Despite his usual anxiety about public speaking, Linklater warmed to the appreciative crowd. Pierson laughed when Linklater explained that he convinced his mother to put up the same amount of money for the film that she invested in his sister's wedding. Unfortunately, the love the audience bestowed on *Slacker* was not reflected in the *New York Times* review the following day. The similarities between Linklater's and Pennell's festival experiences ended with Vincent Canby's ambivalent assessment of *Slacker*. Canby may have appreciated the Texas ramblings of Sonny Carl Davis and Lou Perryman in *The Whole Shootin' Match*, but he had less interest in

Linklater's more unusual and philosophical characters. "It isn't easy being eccentric, and it's even more difficult to remain eccentric in the company of other eccentrics. A terrible transformation occurs: the unusual begins to look numbingly normal," wrote Canby.[66]

### A Real Aura of Cultism

Linklater spent the next few months before the film's July release trying to stay on top of the marketing campaign. In April after viewing Orion's rough cut of the *Slacker* trailer, he faxed a shot breakdown to Pierson, which included his suggestions about how to make the trailer more provocative. Orion wanted humor and action, and cut the trailer to highlight the movie's pithiest moments. Words of praise from three reviewers with varying degrees of clout were interspersed among the shots, ending with Teresa Taylor's Madonna Pap smear bit. Linklater believed that the film's diversity of characters and snippets of dialogue would be enough of a draw to appeal to *Slacker*'s ideal viewers and pique their interest. He also voiced his concern about the "generic dance club" background music, which seemed much more conventional than *Slacker*'s carefully selected and locally based soundtrack.

Linklater watched the "final" version of the trailer on another trip to New York before the *Slacker* summer opening. He was surprised and disappointed to see that nothing had changed since his first viewing, and he made his feelings known in a detailed letter that barely contained his anger. "It is not accurate to think that because people laugh at the few funny parts of the trailer that the trailer itself is a smashing success," he began. Linklater felt the trailer misrepresented the movie, and he disliked its appeal to the lowest common denominator. "A trailer that features canned dance music and milks every snippet of 'action' and presents it in lieu of substance is ultimately condescending to an intelligent audience—slackers or not." Also, he wondered, did the "full and meaningful consultation" clause in his contract give him only the right to complain?[67]

The company's perceived lack of interest in his suggestions frustrated Linklater. As with their acquisitions strategy, Orion Classics favored pretty much the same promotional model for every film and even relied on the same individual to put together each trailer.[68]

Plans continued apace for the July 1991 release. Once again Taylor's riff on Madonna represented a kind of unsubtle comedic touchstone for the film, and Taylor's visage, complete with the sunglasses and hat she insisted on wearing for her scene, graced the movie's one-sheet. "We had a promotional item, the Madonna Pap smear, which was pretty funny," recalls Barker. "I think what we wanted to do was create a real aura of cultism around *Slacker*, which is what happened."[69]

Barker and Bernard's *Slacker* marketing campaign also included radio ads. In the fall of 1990 Orion had released *Dances with Wolves*, which went on to win seven Academy Awards at the 1991 ceremony. Barker and Bernard were very proud of one aspect of that movie's marketing campaign, which featured radio spots read in the Lakota Sioux language and aired on select Native American radio stations. They devised a similarly targeted campaign for *Slacker*. "At that time radio was very important, so we had radio campaigns in a number of the cities. Seattle was particularly successful," recalls Barker. Pierson, for one, didn't put much stock in the spots, which were so infrequent as to be virtually ineffectual in his opinion. Years later Pierson says, "Everything must have helped, but I would have a hard time singling that out as a special component of the *Slacker* release."[70]

Prior to *Slacker*'s July 5 opening in Austin and New York, Linklater attended benefit screenings in each of the cities. The Austin premiere raised money for the film society, and it offered a template for the organization's "benefit premiere," a fundraising model that would come into its own three years later with a sold-out screening of Quentin Tarantino's *Pulp Fiction* on the UT campus. As a thank-you to Scott Dinger and his years of support, Linklater insisted that *Slacker*'s Austin run begin at the Dobie Theatre.

*Rolling Stone* critic Peter Travers praised the filmmaker's satirical gifts although he admitted the movie's long takes and "randomness" could become "monotonous." *Newsweek*'s Jack Kroll warmed to *Slacker*'s characters and its director, favorably comparing Linklater to "offbeat" filmmaker Tim Burton. And *The Nation*'s Stuart Klawans was practically exuberant in his review of *Slacker*, calling it one of the "joys of the summer movie season." Some critics were more begrudging in their praise, such as Stanley Kauffman of the *New Republic*, who suggested the film could be shorter.[71]

Linklater embarked on a fifteen-city press tour during the first two months of the movie's release. Even though Linklater often responded to reporters' questions by using collective pronouns like "we" and "our" to describe the film's collaborative production team, the focus always came back to him. "It was a weird thing," says Cokinos of the subsequent national media attention and its focus on Linklater. At one point, Cokinos recalls, there was talk that Jodie Foster had expressed interest in buying Douglas Coupland's bestselling *Generation X* for Linklater to direct. Published four months earlier, Coupland's novel featured three characters who represented roughly the same generation that Linklater profiled in *Slacker*, and the author and filmmaker found themselves on the same talk show together.[72]

"On the one hand you were really happy that it was getting noticed," Cokinos says. "But on the other hand, it really felt like a group effort. And I think they even talked about that before they went up to the IFF market [in 1989]. That *Slacker* was a group effort, but Rick was going to be the person who was out in front." Back in Austin, some members of the *Slacker* contingent harbored mixed feelings about Linklater's good fortune. "I wanted Rick to be the auteur, but I was really attracted to what was going on with this movie. The film is more European and more social-minded, and the way Rick talked about the group was more of a collective," says Rhodes. But at the same time, he recognized Linklater's ambition. "Rick told me early on that he wanted to be a player. He knew that he had a vision or style that he could sell, and he was right. It worked."[73]

According to more than a few *Slacker* intimates, Jack Meredith, Linklater's high school friend, became angry with Linklater over the origins of specific scenes in the film. Meredith was cast in *Slacker* in one of the later scenes as a "Get-away Accomplice." "There's always a 'Jack-like' character in Rick's films," says Gary Price, who hung around with both of them. "Jack and Rick always tried to write stuff together, but I don't know how far they got on their collaboration. Jack supposedly had written some stuff and just left it or threw it in the trash, and Rick kept some of it." According to Price, Linklater and Meredith had "nasty" arguments about Meredith's credit on *Slacker*. (He received a credit for additional dialogue.)[74]

"A lot of people like to use the 'auteur' word, but *Slacker* was the least auteur film ever made," says Daniel.[75]

By mid-August, *Slacker* was playing on screens in six cities including Los Angeles, San Diego, Dallas, and Houston. The *New York Times* had proclaimed it a sleeper hit, with box office receipts totaling over $200,000—more than nine times its much-publicized $23,000 production budget. "*Slacker* had real 'quality' to it, and so we kind of rode on a lot of the good reviews that transpired," says Barker. Less than one month later, Pierson told a reporter for the *Dallas Morning News* that the film was on its way to grossing more than $1 million. "And nobody should be guffawing if they hear $2 million." Orion's strategy of "going heavy into the college towns" once students returned for the fall semester began to pay off. The turnout resulted in an eventual domestic gross of $1.2 million. "That's one of those pictures," says Barker years later, "that people remember as having done a lot more business than it did. It's because it keeps getting followers over years of time."[76]

## Falling Through the Cracks

Linklater continued to do press for the movie throughout the fall of 1991. In October, two years after his first visit with *Slacker* as a work in progress and three years after his initial visit as a wannabe filmmaker, Linklater returned to the Independent Feature Film Market. Pierson compared the trip to Michael Moore's triumphant return two years earlier with *Roger & Me*.[77]

As 1991 came to a close, discussions turned to Orion's plans for *Slacker*'s home video release, and a tie-in book project with St. Martin's Press created a mini franchise and the potential to attract even more viewers upon the movie's video release. All of this became secondary when on December 11, 1991, Orion Pictures declared bankruptcy.

The news stunned Pierson and other *Slacker* intimates, but in reality the company's financial situation had been going downhill since late 1989, when rumors of a sale to Japanese investors began circulating on a regular basis. Box office receipts remained low throughout 1990. Even the tremendous success of *Dances with Wolves* in November 1990 did little to ease Orion's downward slide. The strong release of Jonathan Demme's *The Silence of the Lambs* in February of 1991 provided some relief, but by then the studio had incurred more than $500 million in debt. Before the end of the year, Barker and Bernard were in talks with other companies, and they eventually landed at Sony Pictures Classics.[78]

With Barker and Bernard gone, Pierson summed up *Slacker*'s future at Orion: "They got out. We were in for a long-term screwing." Both Pierson and Linklater tried unsuccessfully to convince Susan Blodgett, vice president of Orion's Home Video division, to consider the film's good press and tremendous cultural impact as they planned the release of the *Slacker* videocassette. Linklater argued that an untapped audience existed who was unfamiliar with the movie but aware of the word "slacker" and its cultural connotations, but his words fell on deaf ears.[79]

Linklater researched the home video market and estimated that by the early 1990s about thirty thousand video stores existed in the United States. "We're doing calculations. Thirty thousand stores, every store has to get at least one copy. We get 12%, that'll be a couple of hundred thousand," says Linklater. But Orion shipped only about seven thousand units, the same figure they used for foreign-language titles, according to Pierson. "They saw no evidence that *Slacker* should be treated any differently, especially since the entire company was poised to collapse and they were about to concoct a plan to sell hundreds of thousands of *Dances with Wolves* videos for $5.99 at McDonald's." Back in Austin, the only places that carried the title were the independently owned video stores located near the university. One day Linklater wandered into a Blockbuster a few blocks north of UT and asked for the film. The young clerk responded that they didn't carry *Slacker*, but a lot of customers asked for it.[80]

"That's where Orion blew it," sighs Linklater. "That's where the money was not made. We had sort of broken even. They hadn't spent much on P[rints] and A[dvertising], and the film did okay. It was all kind of geared up to make money on video, and they totally blew off the video release. Right at this crucial moment, we just fell through the cracks."[81]

In contrast, the uniquely designed *Slacker* book received an aggressive push from St. Martin's Press. Overseen by D. Montgomery, the book's content consisted of excerpts from Linklater's journal detailing the movie's two-year journey and interviews with various slackers and crew members by *Austin Chronicle* writer Chris Walters. An introduction penned by *Generation X* author Coupland provided the perfect cultural tie-in. "Everybody got behind it and it sold—the number I always heard—20,000 copies in its initial release. Orion shipped 7,000 videotapes. Three times more books than videos? That's not the America I'm familiar with," says Pierson.[82]

He didn't begrudge Barker and Bernard their move to Sony, but he was frustrated by the way in which Orion basically dumped the film after their departure. "They were good at what they did—although they didn't seem to know they were about to go out of business. Michael's very fond of the film and proud of the film. He's got rationalized reasons why the Chapter 11 filing of Orion is nothing that they could control and/or why Orion Home Video is nothing that they could control."[83]

The *Slacker* video and the book both hit stores in the summer of 1992, approximately one year after the movie's national theatrical release. But even as Linklater was gearing up for the *Slacker* press tour in the summer of 1991, he was thinking about his next project. When asked during interviews the inevitable question about a follow-up film, Linklater remained somewhat guarded, especially about his willingness to embrace "the Hollywood dream," although he admitted he had ideas that might work for wide release and some that were better suited to smaller audiences.

As he told the *Los Angeles Times*, "I know it sounds sort of dopey but I really just want to keep making films. There's still some things I'd like to play with back in Austin, and I hope that this helps put me in the position to do that."[84]

By the fall of 1991, months before Orion declared bankruptcy, Linklater's hopes would be fulfilled.

Our movies were a reaction to all that crap that we watched in the Eighties, where everyone played it safe. So when Robert and I first bumped into each other, we talked as if we had grown up in the same house together.

QUENTIN TARANTINO

# The Mariachi Kid

Robert Rodriguez and *El Mariachi*

- - - - - - - - - - - - - - - - - - - - - - - - - - - - - - - - - - - - - - -

**A**t 8:30 in the morning on April 23, 1992, the telephone rang in one of the single-bedroom suites at the Westwood Marquis hotel in Beverly Hills. A groggy twenty-three-year-old Robert Rodriguez picked up the receiver. "Have you seen the trades?" asked Robert Newman, one of Rodriguez's agents at ICM.[1]

Rodriguez panicked. Was something wrong? He was in Los Angeles to negotiate the final details of a development and production deal with Columbia Pictures after a seven-week flurry of meetings with some of Hollywood's top studios and executives. "The Chase," as he would later refer to this period, began the previous December after he dropped off a videotape of *El Mariachi*, his first feature film, for Newman to review. The agent was impressed by the self-taught filmmaker and his Spanish-language action movie about a mariachi player and a case of mistaken identity. Newman quickly signed Rodriguez and then began championing him and the film around town.

Rodriguez left the hotel and found a newsstand. He had made the front page of the *Hollywood Reporter*. "Young Director Rodriguez Wins Col Film Deal," blared the headline. The article mentioned his background in cartooning, his award-winning short film *Bedhead*, and that he was enrolled at the University of Texas at Austin. This last detail must have amused the young filmmaker, who less than twelve months earlier had had to beg to be admitted into the university's competitive Radio-Television-Film Department.[2]

*Daily Variety* also carried the announcement on its front page. The brief article observed that Columbia's signing of Rodriguez, a Latino, was in line with that studio's focus on "emerging talents" and filmmakers of color.³ A year earlier, Columbia had signed African American John Singleton, who was also twenty-three at the time, on the strength of his first film, *Boyz N the Hood*.

Later that day Stephanie Allain, Columbia's vice president of production, took Rodriguez to visit the set of Singleton's second movie, *Poetic Justice*. "I wanted to show him how it was done," says Allain, who watched the two filmmakers hit it off. "But I do remember Robert was somewhat incredulous that things were taking a long time. It seemed to him like nothing was going on. I think he made up his mind right then that he was going to run his set in a different way."⁴

Rodriguez's success story would further shape Austin's reputation as a scrappy independent filmmaking hub in the 1990s. Rodriguez intended *El Mariachi* to be an experiment, the first in a trilogy of straight-to-video action films that would allow him to polish his filmmaking skills in relative obscurity. Instead, his "experiment" landed him representation with one of the top agencies in the industry and a multi-picture deal with Columbia Pictures. Rodriguez was courted by some of the biggest names in Hollywood, including Dawn Steel and Harvey and Bob Weinstein. Figures in the hundreds of thousands were being tossed around for his film, which had cost him an initial $7,000 to produce.

Rodriguez also redefined low-budget filmmaking by spending less (up front, at least) and assembling a crew even smaller than Richard Linklater's seven-person *Slacker* contingent. Over the years Rodriguez learned to pare his operation further by doing nearly everything himself, a practice that would not endear him to unions or Austin crews. Although Rodriguez and Linklater would prove to be very different filmmakers, both men demanded a certain amount of control over their projects. To achieve this, Rodriguez teamed with Miramax so he could afford to build an Austin-based production facility that would allow him to stick close to home. He also relied on the nascent producing talents and quiet diplomacy of his then wife, Elizabeth Avellán.

## Now This Is a Muchacho Who Can Direct

Rodriguez and his friend Carlos Gallardo began planning *El Mariachi* in May 1991, but their collaboration actually started much earlier. The two had met as teenagers when they attended St. Anthony's, a private high school in San Antonio where Rodriguez lived with his parents and nine brothers and sisters. Like Rodriguez, Gallardo had spent his adolescence in Mexico fooling around with film and video equipment and making short movies.

Inspired after watching John Carpenter's *Escape From New York* (1981), Rodriguez and his friends attempted to make stop-motion and live-action movies using his father Cecilio's Super 8 camera. But the temperamental technology frustrated the budding filmmaker. When Cecilio purchased a new-model videocassette recorder and camera for his sales business, his third child quickly took over the equipment and began shooting short video narratives starring his siblings.

As Rodriguez immersed himself in the workings of his father's video equipment, he discovered a passion for technology and a talent for mastering new applications. Rodriguez taught himself how to edit in-camera and layer a soundtrack over the images. He learned that he should make movies using less footage, which would pay off in postproduction. He received additional encouragement from Mario Riojas, his first boss, who ran a photo lab where Rodriguez worked during high school. He told the teenager that many creative talents lacked the technical savvy to make them truly successful. Rodriguez took the advice to heart, realizing that he could use a smaller film crew—and trim a feature film budget—if he knew how to do most of the work himself.

At the beginning of their sophomore year in high school, Gallardo returned to school having made a short action movie called *The Guy From the Land Down Under*. Gallardo's movie inspired his St. Anthony classmates to make their own action film, but most of the students lost interest and only Gallardo, Rodriguez, and another friend stuck with the project. While Gallardo was eager to tackle feature-length movies, Rodriguez convinced his friend to focus instead on two-minute trailers and short films so they could perfect their skills. And thanks to Gallardo's connections, many of these short works played at dance clubs in his hometown and aired on the local television station. "I think we hit it off because he was very technical, and I was the other side," says Gallardo of their collaboration, a partnership that would be mirrored in the working relationship Rodriguez and Avellán created years later.[5]

Rodriguez went on to enroll at the University of Texas in 1986 and by 1990, with the help of a couple of impressive, award-winning short films featuring his younger siblings, he had squeaked into the film production program with less-than-adequate grades. His first class effort, a short film entitled *Bedhead* featuring a character based on his youngest sister, wowed the department and began to accumulate awards at festivals around the country.

The attention and accolades secured his place in the UT film program, but it was a trip to Gallardo's hometown of Ciudad Acuña, Mexico, in 1991 that really inspired the budding filmmaker to take some risks. Mexican director Alfonso Arau was in Acuña shooting a big-budget adaptation of *Like Water for Chocolate,* the bestselling novel written by his wife, Laura Esquivel. Gallardo had been hired to work on the movie because he knew the town and, like Rodriguez, he had a background in filmmaking. Rodriguez spent a week on the set, videotaping the production and becoming friendly with Arau and his wife. The couple watched *Bedhead,* and Esquivel told Rodriguez that after seeing the short her husband exclaimed, "Now this is a muchacho who can direct."[6]

### A Real Immediate Kinship

Rodriguez first met Elizabeth Avellán when he found a part-time job as a file clerk in the office of the university's executive vice president and provost, where Avellán worked as an administrative associate. Born in Caracas, Venezuela, and five years older than Rodriguez, Avellán was one of seven children and came from a privileged family. Despite their age difference, Rodriguez and Avellán became friends and began spending time together outside of work. They understood each other's backgrounds, both having grown up in large Hispanic families. "I already felt like a dad by the time I got to college. I practically raised my younger brothers and sisters. Because she was much more mature than other college girls, it just felt like a real immediate kinship. She felt a lot like my family," says Rodriguez. They also shared a love of movies and a deeply ingrained work ethic. Says Avellán, "I think that's where Robert and I are so solid. Creativity's great, but there are parts of it that are not so creative. It's literally work, and you have to be able to just push through." Rodriguez recognized early on how they complemented one another. "I work hard at stuff I like, but she was able to show up at five in the morning and do this and that. I always admired that. She saw my movies and she saw how she could focus all the attention so that I could get more into that."[7]

Much to the surprise of even those closest to the couple, the twenty-one-year-old Rodriguez and the twenty-six-year-old Avellán eloped in early 1990. Even though they had been dating for about eighteen months, none of their co-workers knew about the romance. The couple's union would mesh both their professional and personal lives, a balancing act Rodriguez and Avellán would seem to excel at for the next sixteen years.

Rodriguez planned to major in film at UT, but first he had to apply to the university's RTF department and would gain admittance only if his grade point average met their requirements. The film program had become increasingly popular and more competitive over the years. By the 1990s more than one hundred undergraduate students were applying for thirty seats at one time, and a process of consent was created to determine which students were allowed in. "You had to find some arbitrary way to let people in, keep people out. And they had all of these formulas," remembers Steve Mims, a filmmaker and graduate of the UT RTF master's program who returned to teach production courses in the late 1980s.[8]

By Rodriguez's junior year, he discovered his GPA was not sufficient to allow him entry into the RTF classes, so he took art courses to boost his grades. He also began drawing a daily cartoon for the *Daily Texan* campus newspaper. "Los Hooligans" drew on Rodriguez's family for creative inspiration and featured a character based on his youngest sister, Maricarmen.[9] Rodriguez also continued to make videos, and one, a trilogy called *Austin Stories*, won the Eighth Annual Third Coast Film and Video Competition in the spring of 1990 after Avellán read about the competition and encouraged Rodriguez to submit his work. Even before she began working as his producer, the organized and efficient Avellán pushed her new husband to get his work seen.

### The Research Hospital, Take One

Newly inspired, Rodriguez met with Mims, who would be offering a film production course that fall. "His grades weren't that great, but his movie was great. When I got the chance to see the films he had made, I was like, there's no way he can't be in the class," says Mims.[10]

Rodriguez spent the summer preparing. He wrote the script for *Bedhead*, about a young girl (once again featuring sister Maricarmen) who takes revenge on her bullying older brother by using telekinetic powers. After rehearsing his "actors" and storyboarding the movie, he shot a version on videotape, which he planned to remake on 16mm film during Mims's class. Even then, Rodriguez was thinking about his future and planning accordingly. He wanted to make a film that would showcase his best work to date, and he wanted that work to lead to something concrete. "I did that short film to sort of get out of film school," he says years later. "I thought, this is my chance to enter real film festivals because I'll have something shot on film rather than video."[11]

Rodriguez had enrolled in his first drug study at Pharmaco, a local research hospital, in 1989. Although he initially chided his then roommate for participating in the potentially harmful tests, he found himself eating his own words when he ran short of money. Rodriguez was chosen for a trial that tested a speed-healing drug. He earned $2,000 and a matching set of scars on the backs of his upper arms. Six months later he participated in another trial to fund his filmmaking efforts. This second test, for which he evaluated an antidepressant and was paid $1,000, allowed him to purchase a camcorder. After years of borrowing video equipment, he finally had his own.[12]

By the end of his first semester in the RTF program in the fall of 1990, Rodriguez had reshot *Bedhead* on film for $800 and sent the finished short to fourteen film festivals around the country. The entertaining movie began to rack up prizes. Rodriguez realized that it was a successful project not only because he had kept costs low by using locations, actors, and props already available to him, but the movie also represented years of experience he had accumulated while making short videos and drawing his daily comic strip. The next step, he reasoned, was to venture into feature films and to do so in the same way that he had learned to shoot and edit short videos.

In March of 1991 Rodriguez received the call from Gallardo about *Like Water for Chocolate*. One day while Rodriguez was hanging out on the set and videotaping interviews, he recorded a conversation between Gallardo and a crew member, who produced movies for the Mexican video market. The producer suggested that the younger men could make a low-budget $30,000 feature film for him. Although they wouldn't receive any money, he said, they would gain experience in making a full-length movie. Rodriguez had no intention of making a movie for someone else for free, but the conversation sparked his interest. He made plans to research the Spanish-language straight-to-video market, and he began to flesh out an idea for a movie about a mariachi character who toted a guitar case full of weapons. Says Rodriguez, "I figured out I could make real low-budget movies for the Mexican video market, turn them around, and sell them for maybe $20,000 more than I made them for."[13]

Rodriguez knew he wanted to shoot his feature on film, but the 35mm Bell and Howell and Bolex cameras he and Gallardo considered were simply too expensive. Although Rodriguez had held down two part-time jobs while going to school, most of his earnings went to tuition, rent, and living expenses. He barely had any money left over to fund a movie. Even if they borrowed a camera and kept costs under $10,000, they still had to raise the money.

Gallardo contributed around $3,500 to the budget, and for years both he and Rodriguez claimed in interviews that his share of the money had come from the sale of a family ranch. In reality, Gallardo supplied his half by cashing in a $5,000 bond that had been put up by his family after he was involved in a drunk driving accident in Del Rio, Texas, in October 1990. After Gallardo was acquitted of the charges in court, the bond money was returned to him.[14]

Raising the remainder of the movie's budget was up to Rodriguez, who also needed a block of time to write the script, something he couldn't do while working two jobs. Once again he turned to the Austin-based Pharmaco research facility for help.

### The Research Hospital, Take Two

The hospital was offering $3,000 for a month-long drug study during the first part of the summer in 1991. To Rodriguez, the study meant free room and board, time to write the *Mariachi* script and watch countless movies as research, and earn a chunk of the movie's budget for his trouble. He could arrange to take a month's absence from his jobs and make money in the process.

Rodriguez treated his five-week stay at Pharmaco as a working vacation. He arrived with a single bag that contained lined index cards, blank legal pads, drawing tools, paper, and a paperback copy of Stephen King's novel *Dead Zone*. His days consisted of meals, medical procedures, blood draws, urine and fecal analyses, and meetings with a study coordinator. He began to flesh out his script about the anonymous Mariachi character, who would be played by Gallardo.[15]

On June 20 Rodriguez celebrated his twenty-third birthday at Pharmaco, which put him in a reflective mood. He noted that Orson Welles was the same age when he made *Citizen Kane*, and he had only a few years left to match Steven Spielberg's success with *Jaws* at the age of twenty-six. Like Richard Linklater, who had felt the pressure to make his first feature while still in his twenties, Rodriguez saw time slipping away.[16]

When Rodriguez left the facility in early July, he had a finished screenplay for his first feature film with most of the scenes completed and blocked for shooting. During the course of the five weeks, he also had managed to cast one of the key roles in addition to earning nearly half the budget for his movie.

Rodriguez had made the eight-minute *Bedhead* for about $800. Using that formula as a model, he estimated that if they minimized expenses on

*Mariachi*—using virtually no crew, making use of available props and locations, shooting as few takes as possible to keep production costs low—they could make a feature-length movie for about $8,000.

Gallardo had scouted potential locations while Rodriguez did his time in Pharmaco. A letter from Acuña's mayor also helped to secure the necessary permits. Most of the "sets" were all within a two- or three-block radius in the small border town. Gallardo's "producing" duties also included meeting with various government officials to borrow weapons. When they turned him down he contacted the city's authorities and played up the "cultural" aspects of the project, including the fact that an American was coming to their Mexican town to shoot a movie. "The guns were the most important thing, and finally we did have the guns. Sometimes we didn't have [the government officials] with the guns, so we started calling the cops, who would come to take care of the guns," says Gallardo.[17] When they needed additional bodies in the movie, Gallardo and Rodriguez convinced the policemen to pose as extras.

Back in Austin, Rodriguez called Keith Kristelis, a friend from the department who owned a 16mm Arriflex camera. Although Rodriguez had hoped to buy or rent a film camera, he knew they couldn't afford to spend nearly half their budget on one piece of equipment. Kristelis planned to take his camera on a road trip that summer, but Rodriguez convinced him that he and Gallardo would put it to better use.

**Down Mexico Way**

*El Mariachi*'s principal photography began on the morning of July 31. Rodriguez, who had arrived in Mexico a few days earlier, came to the first location with a do-rag tying back his shaggy curls. (It was an accessory that would later come to define his directorial style as much as his rapid-fire editing and DIY mantra.) All of the actors supplied their own wardrobe, and crafts services consisted of a gallon of watered-down Gatorade. Most of the props had been found or borrowed, and Rodriguez achieved his tracking shots using a wheelchair "dolly" on loan from the local hospital. Because he and Gallardo had spent so many summers making movies in Acuña, the locals were used to seeing the two young men running through the streets with a camera. Raoul Falomir, an effects specialist whom they had met on *Like Water for Chocolate*, offered assistance by providing contact information and instructions on how to use the small electric devices, or squibs, that would simulate on-screen explosions. Says Gallardo, "Falomir gave me a phone number so we could get the squibs. So I called the number and somebody at Paramount Pictures answered. I tell him about Falomir, he says, 'No problem. Send me $300,' and they sent us explosives by Federal Express."[18]

Rodrigucz was a machine, plowing through each day's setups and spending his nights planning the next day's shoot. But on Friday, August 16, Avellán called with bad news. Rodriguez's friend needed the camera back earlier than expected, so the filmmaker had only four days left to finish his movie.

Rodriguez grabbed as many shots as he could in the final two days before he had to deliver the camera back to Austin. He and Gallardo were forced to cut some scenes, including a spectacular car explosion that showcased a disembowled Chevy from a friend's junkyard. He worked until 3:30 in the morning on August 20. He had shot twenty-five rolls of film in twenty-one days and logged about four hours of footage. Now all he had to do was cut it together. He had spent approximately $2,400 to purchase the twenty-five rolls of 16mm film, which cost an additional $1,300 to be developed. He asked the lab to transfer the 16mm footage to three-quarter-inch videotapes, which he hoped to use as his master copy if all went well during postproduction.[19]

### This One's Killing Me

Rodriguez planned the editing as meticulously as he had the production of his first feature. Like Linklater before him, he would use ACTV, Austin's cable access television facility, in its off hours to edit free of charge. After making VHS copies of the four hours of footage, he would edit a rough cut using his own videocassette recorder and a Pro-Edit video camera. He would then use the rough cut as a guide when he began to edit the final version.

Rodriguez understood himself well enough to know that he needed an incentive to get through the lengthy editing process. Adept at editing short films after two decades of experience, Rodriguez decided to cut a two-minute trailer before he plunged into the actual editing of his first feature-length movie. The trailer would serve multiple purposes: It would force him to study his footage and determine the best shots, it would provide an action-packed blueprint for the film itself, and it would serve as a teaser for anyone interested in watching the actual movie.[20]

Rodriguez spent the first three weeks of September 1991 working at home on his rough cut of *Mariachi*. On September 23 his friend Keith Kristelis, whose camera he had borrowed to shoot the movie, invited Rodriguez to air the trailer on Kristelis's public access television show. Viewers loved the trailer and called in with questions, so Rodriguez went on the air to talk about the project.

The positive feedback energized Rodriguez, who was gearing up for the next phase of the editing process. During production in Mexico he had recorded all of his sound separately, and now he had to transfer the best tracks to the three-quarter-inch backup videotapes he had made at the station. The process took more than twelve hours, and the actual synching of the dialogue would drag on even longer. He spent days hunched over the editing equipment at the public access station. Plagued by back problems, Rodriguez developed a nagging pain that only grew worse. By the first week of October, as he was struggling to finish synching the dialogue, his back finally gave out completely. And, as he was nursing himself with back medication, he learned that the station would be closing for renovations in mid-November, giving him less than eight weeks to finish the movie. He also realized that some of Gallardo's dialogue was unsalvageable and he would have to return to Acuña to re-record his friend's lines.

He had been working nonstop for nearly four months straight. Although he and Gallardo planned to make two more straight-to-video features, the stakes had been raised with all of their hard work. Instead of simply breaking even, Rodriguez decided that they had better make a profit if they were planning to exhaust themselves on Part II of the Mariachi trilogy. "This one is killing me," he wrote in mid-October. "My back hurts, my eyes hurt, my head hurts, my wallet is empty. I keep trying to remind myself that I'm single-handedly replacing a crew of about 100 people, trying to feel good about that, but it's not working. The movie is starting to feel like work now. It was never that before."[21]

By the end of the month, Rodriguez was able to finish his rough cut, which meant he could move forward on the editing of his master tape. During the first week of November, Dominic Kancilla happened to glance into the editing room as he passed through the hallway. Kancilla worked for the Texas Film Commission, which had recently undergone a housecleaning of sorts with the arrival of Ann Richards in the Governor's Office. The two men had never met, but Rodriguez's dynamic close-ups of the Mariachi had caught Kancilla's eye. Rodriguez showed him the trailer as well as some of his short films, and Kancilla told him about the commission's upcoming twentieth anniversary party. He asked the filmmaker if he could screen some of his work for the Hollywood agents and executives who would be flying to Texas for the event, telling him that it might help him make contacts with people like ICM's Robert Newman, one of the top power brokers in Los Angeles.[22]

## Ann Richards and the Texas Film Commission

In September as Rodriguez was beginning work on his *Mariachi* rough cut, Ann Richards was settling into her role as governor. One of the first directives she issued was to move the Texas Film Commission into the Governor's Office from the Department of Commerce, where it had been since 1988.

"When I came into office Texas's budget was $6 billion in the hole. The number-one thing had to be economic development. I like the movie industry because it offers an opportunity to showcase your state. It is a high-employment industry. It provides a lot of local employment, and then they clean up their mess and leave town. It's not [the same as] recruiting a manufacturing facility that's going to pollute and leave you with a mess. And I had always felt that Texas had the potential to be the second L.A.," said Richards.[23] She also believed that the film commission, which had been run since 1990 by Tom Copeland, needed to establish stronger ties to Hollywood.

Copeland started at the commission in 1982 and within three years had worked his way into the position of assistant director. His years of experience finding locations for regional and out-of-state productions gave him a familiarity with the state, its landscape, and its crews that was invaluable. But when Richards took office in 1991, she decided to appoint an energetic thirty-two-year-old named Marlene Saritzky.

Saritzky was the complete opposite of Copeland. She hailed from Los Angeles, which immediately rankled many native Texans working for the film commission. Saritzky was the first executive director of the Hollywood Women's Political Committee, and she first met Ann Richards when she attended an event in honor of U.S. Representative Barbara Jordan in Los Angeles. But it wasn't until after the 1988 election cycle that Saritzky had the chance to spend time with Richards while she was in Los Angeles to raise money for her gubernatorial campaign. Although she tried to schedule meetings for Richards with local donors, they were reluctant to sit down with the Texan. "No one thought she was going to win," says Saritzky. "Then she gave that speech in Atlanta at the 1988 Democratic National Convention and everyone in the Hollywood political community wanted to meet her."[24]

Saritzky's appointment gave Tom Copeland two options: he could take a lateral move and remain at the film commission, or he could leave. He chose to stay and hoped for the best. "On paper, it should have worked. Marlene was very good at what she did. She was extremely smart, extremely intelligent. But she knew nothing about managing people. About forty years of experience walked out when she came in," he says.[25]

"Tom says people left, and he says they left because they were miserable. Some of them did," admits Saritzky. But she wasn't necessarily sad to see all of the defectors leave. "Some of them, I'm glad they left."[26]

Saritzky agreed with Richards's vision for the state's film industry and knew it was her job to make it happen. "She told me that one little part of her economic development agenda was to increase the visibility of Texas as a film location, to much more aggressively market the state, to much more aggressively try to get media attention for the industry, to pass whatever legislation we could think of to make it economically feasible and attractive for film companies to shoot on location."[27] Saritzky's value was such that she could cultivate her Hollywood contacts to learn about projects in the earliest stages of their development rather than waiting for a producer to approach the film commission once a project had been greenlighted.

Saritzky weathered an unpleasant transition period that included a letter-writing campaign to Richards railing against the governor's appointment of the California native. The state's film and television industry prospered at least on paper during Richards's and Sartizky's tenures. Production within Texas increased from $118 million in 1991 to $189 million in 1994. Legislation was passed for a sales tax exemption that would make shooting in Texas more attractive financially to out-of-state productions. And between 1992 and 1994, Austin led the state with the highest production revenues. These figures also coincided with the rising national profiles of filmmakers like Richard Linklater and Rodriguez. Recalls Julia Null Smith, whom Saritzky hired in 1992, "The film commission wasn't effective in driving business to Dallas or San Antonio or Houston. Everybody wanted to be shooting in Austin because it's like the cool kids were hanging in Austin."[28]

One of the first events planned during Saritzky's tenure was "The Texas Celebrity Homecoming," a party featuring Hollywood bigwigs with ties to Texas. As Dominic Kancilla had explained to Rodriguez in October 1991, the event would celebrate the film commission's twentieth anniversary and also give the state an opportunity to charm movie industry insiders like William Morris agent Mike Simpson and Robert Newman. But days before the scheduled party, it was called off for unspecified reasons.[29]

Kancilla told Rodriguez to hold onto the list of invitees and contact a few of them when he arrived in Los Angeles with his demo tape of *Mariachi*. He particularly encouraged Rodriguez to get in touch with ICM's Newman.

## California Here We Come

Rodriguez finished *Mariachi* two days before Thanksgiving. Now that he was done, Avellán wanted to see her husband's movie. Rodriguez was nervous. She more than anyone knew how much effort he had put into the film, but what if she hated it?[30] But Avellán's final review was overwhelmingly positive; her only suggestion was that he fix certain inaudible lines of dialogue. Still, Rodriguez couldn't help but wonder if the movie really was any good.

At the end of the holiday weekend Gallardo arrived at the Rodriguez family home, and the two friends decided to leave for Los Angeles that evening. They drove through the night and arrived on the evening of December 2, 1991. They had two goals for their visit: they hoped to find a Spanish distributor for *Mariachi*, and Rodriguez wanted to meet agent Robert Newman. They brought a demo tape of *Mariachi*, the movie's two-minute trailer, and a copy of *Bedhead*. They hoped to be back in Texas by Christmas at the latest, and with a deal in hand.

The first distributor on their list, which they had compiled from renting and watching Spanish-language videos, was a company called Film-Mex. When they arrived at the company's office, the owner feigned a meeting and pawned them off on a secretary. Gallardo and Rodriguez had better luck at Mex-American, where they met with one of the distributor's reps and screened the trailer. The woman seemed to like what she saw but remained noncommittal. She scheduled a meeting for them with her boss, the company's owner, for the following week.

The next morning, December 4, the pair left Los Angeles for San Diego, where they had an appointment at Cine-Mex, another of the top video distributors. The company's president listened to their pitch and agreed to watch some of the video, which was transmitted onto all of the television screens in the Cine-Mex showroom. As images from *Mariachi* played on the screens, the handful of customers slowly began to wander over to watch Rodriguez's movie. The president took notice and made the pair an offer to buy the movie, but he wouldn't include an advance. They turned it down but were buoyed by the audience response.

After returning to Los Angeles and striking out with another distributor, they decided to focus instead on Mex-American and their meeting a few days later with the company co-president. On December 9, Rodriguez and Gallardo sat down with the gentleman, who seemed eager to watch their trailer. He guessed that the movie cost as much as $80,000, and the pair tried to remain poker-faced as they discussed the budget. Eventually he offered them $25,000, but Rodriguez and Gallardo didn't commit immediately. They decided instead to continue shopping the movie and to use Mex-American's offer to leverage a better deal with another distributor.[31]

Over the next couple of days they tried to arrange meetings with other companies, many of which weren't panning out. Rodriguez also decided to call Robert Newman. Newman's assistant told him to drop off his tape. Two days later, Newman's office called to request another video to replace the first, which had been ruined by the agent's VCR.

It was a fortuitous accident that landed Rodriguez an impromptu meeting with Newman when he arrived at the agency to deliver a replacement tape. Rodriguez explained the work that was on his tape and asked Newman to watch it and offer feedback about his master plan to make three movies on his own before he tried to work in Hollywood. The agent seemed impressed when Rodriguez told him how much they had spent to make *Mariachi* and that they already had a $25,000 offer on the table.

"I was, at the time, doing a lot of direct-to-video sales and distribution deals like that," says Newman, who was unfamiliar with the Spanish-language market for action movies and therefore intrigued that Rodriguez had discovered the niche and tailored his first feature to a specific audience. "He had a point of view of the kinds of things he was trying to create and he actually had identified where people might actually see them. So to have someone with a point of view of what they're doing at that point was interesting."[32]

Rodriguez's five-minute visit to ICM had taken place on a Friday. By Monday, Newman was on the phone. He loved both *Bedhead* and the trailer, and he was eager to watch *Mariachi* in full and asked Rodriguez if he could send a subtitled version. Rodriguez said that he would as soon as he returned to Texas.

He and Gallardo decided to take Mex-American's offer for $25,000. When they arrived at the company to sign the contracts, however, they discovered that the money was to be paid in two separate checks by their U.S. and Mexican offices. The Los Angeles office could offer the filmmakers only $10,000 immediately. Gallardo and Rodriguez decided to wait the extra few days for the remaining $15,000. They were still waiting by Monday, December 23. The representative at Mex-American encouraged them to sign the U.S. contract and return to Texas with the $10,000 check, and she promised to notify them as soon as the Mexico contract arrived.[33]

The two young men had spent more than three weeks in California, alternately pounding the pavement and spinning their wheels. Now the Christmas holiday was only days away, and they were absolutely broke. As tempting as it was to take the $10,000 and turn a $3,000 profit on the movie, they agreed to wait and leave empty-handed for the time being. Although Rodriguez was encouraged by Newman's response at ICM, he was angry that they didn't have a deal and worried about the situation in general.[34]

### ICM and the Chase

The weeks immediately following the break were relatively quiet, but in mid January ICM began to court Rodriguez aggressively. The office called to remind Rodriguez to send the subtitled version of *Mariachi*, and then Newman himself phoned to tell the young filmmaker how eager the agency was to represent him. But while ICM was wooing Rodriguez, he was hearing nothing from Mex-American about the outstanding Mexico contracts.

Three weeks later in early February, after watching the subtitled version of *Mariachi*, ICM made Rodriguez an official offer.[35]

During Gallardo and Rodriguez's initial meeting with Mex-American, the company's co-president had suggested they send a copy of *Mariachi* to Miramax, the distribution company created in 1979 by brothers Harvey and Bob Weinstein and named for their parents, Miriam and Max. The Weinsteins had made a name for themselves and an unknown filmmaker named Steven Soderbergh in 1989 when they purchased *sex, lies, and videotape* for an unprecedented $1 million advance after it won the Audience Award at the U.S. Film Festival (later changed to the Sundance Film Festival). Rodriguez asked ICM for advice about sending his tape to Miramax. Newman, himself a former Miramax executive, didn't think the Weinsteins would be interested in a Spanish-language action film without stars, but he gave Rodriguez the go-ahead to approach the company anyway.

Suddenly, it seemed, everyone was interested in *Mariachi*. In Austin, Dobie Theatre owner Scott Dinger asked Rodriguez if he could shop a copy of the film at the Berlin Film Festival. Although Dinger wouldn't receive any firm offers for the movie, he did run into producer's rep John Pierson, who asked to screen a copy. In late February, Rodriguez's work received a mention in the *Austin Chronicle* in connection with an article about his film teacher, Steve Mims. Mims's short film *Aunt Hallie* was being aired as part of *The Territory*, the long-running PBS showcase co-produced by UT's Thomas Schatz, the Austin Museum of Art's Judith Sims, and SWAMP's Ed Hugetz.[36]

Also included on *The Territory* was *Bedhead*, which *Chronicle* editor Louis Black wrote about in a sidebar to the Mims piece. After Rodriguez read Black's

*Chronicle* piece, he called the editor to thank him, and Black told him that Warren Skaaren, who had been a judge with Black when they chose *Austin Stories*, had been very impressed by Rodriguez's work. Recalled Rodriguez, "He said how they talked for a good while about how good [the film] was before awarding it first place, and how Warren Skaaren wondered aloud how the filmmaking would be affected if I ever moved to Hollywood and started making bigger movies with bigger equipment." It would be Black's final conversation with Skaaren before the screenwriter's death from cancer in December 1990.[37]

Also in February, Newman told Rodriguez that he had decided to bring *Mariachi* to the Cannes Film Festival three months later. Interest in *Mariachi* grew as *Bedhead*, which had been on the festival circuit for nearly a year, continued to earn top awards. Things were nearly perfect except for the fact that Mex-American was still dragging its feet over the $15,000 Mexico contract.

If the buzz around *Mariachi* and Rodriguez grew louder in February, by March it had become a cacophony. Newman and David Wirtschafter, another ICM agent who signed on to represent Rodriguez, had effectively whipped the studios into a frenzy. Calls from TriStar Pictures, Columbia Pictures, Walt Disney Productions, and Steel Pictures (created by producer Dawn Steel, former head of Columbia) kept ICM's phones ringing steadily. It was decided that Rodriguez would visit first with TriStar, and ICM would spread the word that he was available for other meetings while in town. He was scheduled to leave Austin on March 15.

In the meantime, Rodriguez checked in with Miramax's Mark Tusk, who was head of Acquisitions. Tusk expressed skepticism about a foreign-language action film's box office potential and mentioned *La Femme Nikita*, a sexy French thriller released that same month, as one of the few films of its type that had successfully crossed over. Recalls Avellán, laughing, "He told Robert, 'It ain't no *Nikita*.' We came to find out much later, they passed on *Nikita*."[38] Unbeknownst to Rodriguez at the time, Miramax was floundering under the weight of too many acquisitions. In the first few months of 1992 when Rodriguez initially contacted Miramax, its chief executives were preoccupied with whether or not to pick up a low-budget movie by another first-time director. The film, a gritty all-male ensemble called *Reservoir Dogs*, had played in January at the Sundance Film Festival. Rodriguez could have no way of knowing it at the time, but his career path would eventually lead him back to Miramax and *Reservoir Dogs*'s director, Quentin Tarantino.

Rodriguez spent two days in Los Angeles. He met with his agents, the principals of Trilogy Entertainment production company (*Robin Hood: Prince of Thieves, Backdraft*) and TriStar Pictures, and charmed the executives by showing them *Bedhead*.

Rodriguez's meetings set off a hyperkinetic buzz among the other studios and production companies. "It was very competitive," recalls Newman. "There were a lot of people who were very angry. I remember Jeffrey Katzenberg calling up [ICM chairman] Jeff Berg from the opening of Euro Disney, which was a big darn deal at the time, saying, 'What do we do to be in business with this Rodriguez guy?'"[39] Despite the interest building on the West coast, however, Rodriguez spent the rest of March working at the university and waiting for the Mex-American contracts to arrive in the mail. Encouraged by his meetings earlier in the month, he still wasn't taking anything for granted.

He returned to Los Angeles for a five-day visit in early April. This time he was to meet with representatives from Steel Pictures, Disney, Paramount Pictures, and Columbia. He felt most comfortable in a meeting with Columbia executives, a young group that included Stephanie Allain, the studio's vice president of production. Newman had sent Allain a tape of *El Mariachi*, which she popped into her VCR one day while working from home. Rodriguez's fast-paced visuals caught her eye. "I don't even think I was reading the subtitles. I felt, 'Wow. This guy's a filmmaker,'" recalls Allain, who immediately called Newman to hear Rodriguez's backstory. At the Columbia meeting, Allain and the other executives seemed interested in the *Los Hooligans* comic strip, and they warmed to Rodriguez's other ideas.[40]

Later that evening Newman took his new client to the Hollywood premiere of *The Player*. Robert Altman's slyly funny movie followed a Hollywood studio executive being blackmailed by a jilted writer. Its send-up of the movie industry couldn't have been better timed given Rodriguez's own situation. Watching *The Player* in the Directors Guild theater with his own ICM agent and being surrounded by many of the well-known actors who appeared in the film was like an out-of-body experience. Los Angeles truly felt like a surreal environment. Rodriguez made a mental note to add a rider of sorts to whatever deal he signed: it would have to allow him to live in Texas. Technically, his request would be honored, but it would be another four years before he and Avellán would really be able to call Texas home.

After Rodriguez returned to Austin in early April 1992, interest among the studios ratcheted up a notch. He fielded calls from many of the executives he had met, each one eager to make another pitch for their company. Columbia made what was perhaps the smartest move when they decided to fly Allain and Trilogy Entertainment's Richard Lewis to Austin to hang out with Rodriguez on his home turf. Says Allain, "At the time I think Robert was being courted by TriStar and other places, so I just decided I had to get on a plane and go down there. I needed to connect." On April 7, before they had even left L.A., Columbia made an official offer. Their deal would pay Rodriguez approximately $350,000 up front to write and direct a remake of *El Mariachi*. It also included a guarantee of about $475,000 for a second picture. Rodriguez was in a state of shock.[41]

A day later, Rodriguez and Avellán met Allain and Lewis's plane when it landed in Austin. Their visit allowed them to court Rodriguez away from the craziness of L.A., where he clearly didn't feel at home. It also gave them a chance to pitch themselves to Rodriguez's parents and siblings, who had driven up from San Antonio. "I think she had done that with John Singleton," says Rodriguez of the visit. "Stephanie had seen her success with Singleton and thought, 'Well here's a Latin filmmaker. Maybe he'll do something cool for us.'"[42]

Says Allain, "I told him we wanted him to be a filmmaker at the studio and that we'd try to do for him what we did for John. And he said yes."[43]

Back in L.A., Newman and Wirtschafter had made a counter-offer to the studio, which it accepted. By April 10, exactly three months since Rodriguez had signed with ICM, he decided to go with Columbia. Although Miramax had made an offer of more money, Newman advised his client to sign with the more established Columbia, a studio with the ability both to produce and distribute his next feature. The final deal gave the young filmmaker a remarkable amount of money and degree of control.[44]

The weeks following the Columbia deal were a blur of activity. Rodriguez paid a thank-you visit to the university's Dean of Students, who had been instrumental in allowing him to enroll despite his less than acceptable grade point average. The story of how he made *Bedhead* and *El Mariachi* and his newfound success flabbergasted the dean, as it would some professors in the RTF department who had cautioned Rodriguez against making the feature without a crew. ("Everyone in the RTF department came from the world of film. They didn't know the impact of video yet," explains Rodriguez.) Rodriguez also flew to L.A. for the official announcement on April 23. He returned to Austin a few days later a hometown hero and took a call from Richard Linklater, who invited him to visit the Detour offices. The two filmmakers had never met, but they chatted easily about their moviemaking interests. Rodriguez had just begun to edit *Mariachi* when Linklater released *Slacker* the previous fall. Recalls Avellán of that time, "Robert began to have doubts. 'Am I doing the right thing? I should have gone and just done a movie about Austin.'"[45]

In mid-May, Miramax expressed interest in obtaining the distribution rights to *El Mariachi*. A few weeks earlier, Harvey Weinstein had been in Los Angeles on business and finally had seen *El Mariachi*. Recalls Weinstein's brother and business partner, Bob, "After Columbia bought *El Mariachi*, Harvey subsequently saw the movie and just went, 'Oh my god. How could somebody pass on *this* movie?' So we both saw it, fell in love with Robert, realized he was a great filmmaker, of course tried to get the film. Film was sold. Couldn't do anything about it, but we realized this is a guy that we wanted to do business with."[46]

Rodriguez had mixed feelings about the entire situation. If *Mariachi* was released and did poorly in the theaters, wouldn't it ruin his chances to make another movie no matter what his Columbia deal stipulated? Rodriguez compiled what in his mind was an outrageous wish list of conditions upon which he would agree to release the original version. He figured his ace in the hole was the fact that *Mariachi* had been cut on videotape, and therefore no film print existed. He knew how expensive it would be to make a print from his original video master. But even this did not deter the Columbia executives.

"That was the brainstorm of Peter Guber," says Allain of the Columbia Pictures studio chief's decision to release Rodriguez's "practice" feature. "Once the tape made its way to the top and Robert had a little buzz on him around town, Peter Guber saw the movie and said, 'This is brilliant. We're going to release it just like it is.' Peter just saw a raw opportunity to exploit the fact that he'd made it for $7,000, sold his blood as a lab rat, and just saw the showmanship of doing it that way." Guber's decision shocked Allain, who considered *El Mariachi* a "template" and shared Rodriguez's doubts about releasing the movie. "I remember being slightly disappointed. Although it was clearly the work of a talented filmmaker, it was low, low, low, low budget."[47]

Rodriguez's schizophrenic existence was beginning to wear on him. Despite meetings about six-figure payouts and back-end points, he and Avellán were cash poor. He had not received any of his advance from the Columbia deal because his lawyer worried that it might negatively affect the ongoing *Mariachi* distribution negotiations. Finally, he was forced to pawn his beloved video camera. "It's a strange split," Rodriguez observed at the time. "Here in Texas my wife and I can barely buy lettuce but as soon as I get to L.A. I'm eating like a king 'cause it's all free."[48]

Rodriguez finally received his first check in late May 1992. It amounted to $13,000 after commissions and deductions.[49]

### Riding the Festival Circuit

A couple of weeks later, Rodriguez flew to L.A. to spend about a month supervising the conforming and blowup of his original film to 35mm. By the end of the first week, he and veteran editor George Hively had made it through only one minute of film. The process was excruciating, especially for someone like Rodriguez who was used to doing his own cutting. He asked for a separate editing bench so that he could cut alongside Hively to speed up the editing, which raised some questions about union violations. The more time Rodriguez spent on the Columbia lot, the more he began to observe what he considered to be the studio's Byzantine bureaucracy and wasteful habits, something Linklater was only beginning to encounter as he began production in Austin that summer on *Dazed and Confused* with Universal.

Although *Mariachi* originally cost only $7,000 to make, like most big-budget action films it contained a large number of edits to enhance the pacing and intensity of the action sequences. The movie's two thousand cuts complicated *Mariachi*'s re-editing process, but by the first week of July the film finally was edited and the soundtrack nearly synched. But just when Rodriguez thought he could return to Austin, he discovered more technical problems in conforming the sound from the original version, which would require him to stay in L.A. for another three weeks. During that time he also received some good news. *El Mariachi* had been selected as one of the opening night films for the Telluride Film Festival, and the Toronto International Film Festival of Festivals also wanted to screen the movie. A well-received screening of the *Mariachi* work print for Columbia executives also boosted his spirits.

By early September while work was still being done on the 35mm blowup, Rodriguez was on his way to Colorado for the first public screening of his movie. Rodriguez and Avellán's Telluride trip was a blur of exclusive parties, dinners, screenings, and interviews. What Rodriguez dreaded almost more than his movie bombing with an audience was the prospect of speaking in public about the film, which was scheduled to screen three times. Rodriguez freaked out when the couple arrived at the theater for the first screening. More than six hundred festivalgoers were lined up outside the venue. Inside, the crowd included Hollywood heavyweights like producer-director Kathryn Bigelow. Scanning the full house, Rodriguez noticed the audience's slightly older demographic and worried that it was the wrong crowd for *El Mariachi*. Before the start of the film, Rodriguez was brought up to the front to give a brief introduction. Back in the audience, Avellán grew anxious as her husband approached the microphone. She knew he was nervous. Although Rodriguez had made extensive notes about what he wanted to say, she had never seen him speak in public and feared that he might make a fool of himself.

Quite the opposite was true. "Robert gets up there and he was like a stand-up comic. It was shocking. He told the whole story. He made everybody laugh. He primed them for the film," recalls Avellán. Aware of his flaws as a public speaker, Rodriguez had slipped into a couple of screenings before his own to watch how other filmmakers introduced their movies. He wanted to avoid the stammering, shuffling persona of the first-time filmmaker, so he scripted the entire story of how he made the movie.[50]

Like Newman, Allain recognized in Rodriguez an attractive and appealing personality that would translate well on stage. "He took to it like a fish to water. He's gorgeous, and very 'of the people.' That's why people liked him. He didn't pretend to be anything. He played it like, 'I don't know what I'm doing, but I'm just doing it.' And people loved that," recalls Allain.[51]

The audience embraced Rodriguez and the movie, which eased his fears somewhat at the next screening. In the crowd he spotted Roger Ebert, whom he had met the previous evening at the opening night party. After the screening, Rodriguez was approached by Michael Barker and Tom Bernard, the pair who had picked up *Slacker* for Orion and were now at Sony Classics. "They said, 'You should stop telling people the movie's $7,000. No one's believing it,'" recalls Rodriguez, who realized later that they thought he was trying to pass off all costs—striking a film print, etc.—within the $7,000 production budget. But he also wondered if their comment was the beginning of a subtle backlash against him and the film. "They're nice guys, but there's a lot of jealousy [in the industry]. I felt that right away."[52]

Ebert's review ran the following week. Although Ebert had hinted to the filmmaker that he liked the movie, Rodriguez still was relieved to read the review, which included excerpts from his introductory speech and described the movie as "better directed and more entertaining than a great many of the movies I see." Todd McCarthy's *Variety* review ran a day later. It also praised the movie and its director, but where Ebert lightly criticized the movie's cheeky overuse of fast-motion sequences, McCarthy wondered about the story's "calculated" quality: "Pic feels like a technical exercise well executed, but one with little emotional conviction or p.o.v. behind it."[53]

Rodriguez and Avellán were back in Austin for only a few days before they jetted off with Gallardo to Toronto, where Rodriguez was scheduled to appear on a panel of young filmmakers with *Reservoir Dogs* director Quentin

Tarantino. After seeing the movie at Telluride, Rodriguez was looking forward to meeting the director. When they finally met in the lobby of a Toronto hotel, the two quickly bonded over their love of martial arts movies and a mutual appreciation for the other's hyperactive filmmaking sensibility. Recalls Tarantino, "It's happened a few times in my life but not that often. There were people all around us and we just kind of blocked them all out and just proceeded to talk and bullshit and geek out."[54]

In Toronto Rodriguez also finally met Miramax co-chairman Harvey Weinstein at a festival party, and he enjoyed listening to Weinstein grouse about not being able to buy *Mariachi*. "He told me how much he loved *Mariachi* and that it was a 'great fuckin' movie' and that he wished he had seen it first, instead of the 'bunch of idiots' working for him."[55]

At the end of September Rodriguez flew out to L.A. for a test screening of his movie, which went over well with the predominantly Hispanic audience recruited by the studio. Eventually Columbia executives decided that *Mariachi* would have a limited February release in six U.S. cities including New York and L.A., and then be given a larger rollout depending upon its initial performance. From the original list of cities, San Antonio was dropped in favor of Austin. Rodriguez, a native of San Antonio, was actually pleased that Columbia had decided to open in Austin because he understood the marketing implications of such a decision. "I told [Columbia] it was a mistake to ignore Austin, that the movie could do great here. Even though I was born in San Antonio, Austin claims me as one of their own."[56]

Rodriguez spent most of the fall of 1992 in L.A., where he supervised the sound transfer and other final postproduction details and tried to begin work on his next screenplay. He had decided to write two different scripts: a remake of *El Mariachi* and a sequel, which would explore a "new Mariachi adventure." By writing two versions, he reasoned, he would cover his bases in case Columbia changed its mind about the original release. He set up housekeeping in the Myrna Loy Building on the Columbia Pictures lot. Ever the cost-conscious multi-tasker, Rodriguez scrimped on his per diem by sleeping on his office couch and showering at the studio's gym.

In an office next door to Rodriguez, Tarantino was working on his own follow-up to *Reservoir Dogs*, an ambitious narrative with more than ten principal characters who weave in and out of separate vignettes. The two filmmakers would spend their days writing in their separate offices, then meet for dinner at a Cuban restaurant down the street or grab a quick hamburger at a nearby In 'N Out. "We'd talk about movies, and I'd read him a scene or two. He'd tell me about his shit. Robert would just act out one of his sequences.

He would usually have cartoon drawings," says Tarantino, who fantasized that their creative exchanges were like something out of the French New Wave. Having both spent time on the festival circuit with their first films, Rodriguez and Tarantino were beginning their careers at about the same time and going through similarly unique and intense experiences that cemented the friendship quickly.[57]

Despite this seemingly cushy setup, however, the months Rodriguez spent in L.A. were dogged by postproduction technical difficulties and distractions that kept him from writing. Problems with Foley sound effects, a ratings dust-up, and miscellaneous meetings plagued the filmmaker as he tried to meet a January 1993 writing deadline. One piece of good news did come during the fall, however, when Allain informed the filmmaker that *Mariachi* had been invited to screen at the Sundance Film Festival.

By December he was in danger of not making his deadline with Columbia. When the color correction of his film's negative dragged on for weeks, Rodriguez knew it was time to leave. On December 21 he returned to Austin and began work in earnest on a sequel to *Mariachi*. The follow-up would again star Gallardo, a decision that was not popular with the studio. "Robert wanted to use Carlos, who was his friend, but I knew that a sequel really needed to cross over. We needed to introduce an element that Hollywood was already familiar with," says Allain, who suggested Antonio Banderas. The Spanish-born actor was a familiar face from director Pedro Almodovar's movies and had crossed over to English-language films with *The Mambo Kings* earlier that year. But Rodriguez, a third-generation Mexican-American, says Allain, was "dead set against it. Robert said, 'He's Spanish, he's not Mexican!'"[58]

After about two weeks of marathon all-night writing sessions, Rodriguez had completed a first draft of the follow-up to submit to Allain. With a background in story development, Allain was somewhat alarmed when she received an eighty-page script bloated with big action sequences.

"Robert, you have to write it out!" she exclaimed after seeing the skimpy dialogue and character development.[59]

"But I know what it's going to be. I've already cut it in my head! Why do I have to say what it is?" Rodriguez considered the extra steps a waste of his time. Unlike Tarantino, for instance, who loved writing dialogue, Rodriguez would rather sketch out a scene with a drawing. Rodriguez once asked Tarantino about his technique, to which Tarantino responded, "Well, I just get the characters talking to each other. And then I just write it down. I've got to kick it off, but then they start talking to each other and they do the work." Rodriguez just stared at his friend, a blank expression on his face.[60]

On Thursday, January 21, Rodriguez and Avellán arrived in Park City, Utah, excited but with low expectations about the film's prospects of winning any awards. *El Mariachi*'s first screening took place the following day at the 360-seat Prospector Square Theatre, where they learned that all six of the movie's festival screenings already had sold out. Rodriguez took the stage before the film and spent ten minutes describing the movie's journey, including its "birth" in an Austin research hospital and the fast and furious two-week shoot in Acuña. During the lengthy question-and-answer session following the screening, Rodriguez tried to debunk any lofty notions about his cinematic style by explaining that *Mariachi*'s widely praised fast pacing and quick edits were the result of having to shoot mostly single takes and to cut around inexperienced actors and a lack of props.

The budget-conscious *El Mariachi* wasn't the only movie that generated buzz at Sundance that year. Other first-time filmmakers in attendance included Robb Weiss, who made *Amongst Friends* with backing from his father's gambling contacts, and Jennifer Lynch, the daughter of director David Lynch and the writer-director of *Boxing Helena*, a controversial film about an obsessive surgeon who amputates the limbs of his gorgeous girlfriend. Both filmmakers joined Rodriguez, Bryan Singer (*Public Access*), Tony Chan (*Combination Platter*), and Leslie Harris (*Just Another Girl on the IRT*) on a panel entitled "Twenty Somethings: The New Generation." Producer's rep John Pierson, at Sundance to push Weiss's film, moderated the panel.[61]

*Mariachi*'s final Sundance screening was on a Saturday, the same day as the festival's awards ceremony. Never much of a public event, the more formal 1993 ceremony featured speakers and a program and attracted media and crowds. When actor Seymour Cassel announced that *El Mariachi* had won the coveted Audience Award, Rodriguez and Gallardo floated to the stage to accept the honor.

Other festivalgoers were shocked by the announcement. Pierson and the *Amongst Friends* camp were "fully expecting" to win the Audience Award thanks in part to their grassroots marketing campaign during the festival. Indeed, Weiss's film was rumored to have missed the award by a hair. Observed Pierson, "The agents from ICM and the executives from Columbia Pictures had been working hard for Robert Rodriguez." Recapping the event for the *New York Times*, Bernard Weinraub wrote that an influx of Hollywood players had begun to change the festival and, in 1993, the awards seemed to recognize more "mainstream" films. But in an article that ran a few weeks after *El Mariachi*'s general release, film critic Peter Travers defended *Mariachi*'s win. "*El Mariachi* won't change your life, but in its own modest way the film earns its place at Sundance by celebrating the joy of making movies at a time when the pressures of the marketplace have damn near squeezed out all the fun."[62]

### You Don't Have to be an Executive to Like *El Mariachi*

Rodriguez had little time to savor the accolades. Two days after returning to Austin, he was back on a plane to New York and his first stop in a month-long publicity blitz. On the first leg of the tour, Rodriguez did interviews with CNN and Howard Stern. When a reporter from the *Daily News* expressed doubts about *Mariachi*'s low-budget backstory, Rodriguez demonstrated his cost-cutting camera moves by showing the interviewer unedited and edited footage from the movie. This "show-and-tell videotape" became a staple in the filmmaker's press kit, a handy visual that he used to convince the skeptics.[63]

Rodriguez then flew to L.A., where photographer Annie Liebovitz shot him along with Linklater, Todd Haynes, and other young filmmakers for an upcoming photo spread in *Vogue* magazine.

*El Mariachi* had its West Coast premiere on February 18. In keeping with most of Rodriguez's surreal L.A. experiences, his screening took place at the Directors Guild of America Theatre on Sunset Boulevard, the same venue where he had attended the premiere of *The Player* in 1992. This time a raging hailstorm delayed Rodriguez's arrival at the screening. Klieg lights illuminated a soggy red carpet, and a mariachi band played inside the theater lobby.

A week later he was back in Austin, where a camera crew from *Entertainment Tonight* shadowed his every move for an upcoming "Day in the Life" segment. From there he returned to New York, where even the bombing of the World Trade Center on February 26 couldn't derail the *Mariachi* PR express train. Rodriguez taped appearances on late-night television talk shows with veteran interviewer Charlie Rose and host David Letterman.

Columbia Pictures spent approximately $107,000 to produce a theater-ready version of Rodriguez's $7,000 *El Mariachi*. It opened on February 26, 1993, in ninety theaters. Although it didn't crack the weekend's top ten list, *Mariachi* did take in an impressive opening weekend gross of $312,000, for an average of $3,466 per screen.[64]

Mention of Rodriguez's rags-to-riches success story appeared in nearly every review of *El Mariachi*. Many critics went out of their way to note the film's limitations—"crude" technique, "makeshift" budget and props, "home movie" aesthetic—but celebrated its pacing and entertainment value as well as Rodriguez's youth and future promise. The *Atlanta Journal and Constitution* expressed a common theme: "One doesn't want to oversell *El Mariachi*—it's a diamond in the rough, with the emphasis on rough. But its pulpy charms and makeshift ingenuity are undeniable—as is the sheer pleasure of watching a fresh young talent flex his muscles with such unbridled high spirits." The *New York Times* took a similar tack: "'El Mariachi' is a skillful, familiar-feeling hybrid of film noir and western conventions, with a hint of futuristic nihilism in its final scenes," wrote Janet Maslin. "It is also visually primitive, with a home-movie look that would be distracting if Mr. Rodriguez's storytelling skills were not so keen." Citing the film's comedic timing and Rodriguez's "hip awareness" of cinematic storytelling conventions, the *Boston Globe* described the movie's universal appeal most succinctly: "You don't have to be an executive to like *El Mariachi*."[65]

Even in an article about Hollywood's then fascination with low-budget filmmaking, *Mariachi* was singled out for its ability to deliver on-screen. "This isn't a good film because it's cheap," wrote Caryn James in the *New York Times*. "It's cheap *and* good because Mr. Rodriguez has wit and style, and is accomplished enough to know exactly what he wants on screen. The budget may be a selling point, but behind the hype is talent."[66]

One reviewer in particular even offered some context for Rodriguez's DIY filmmaking aesthetic. "Is Austin a hotbed of low-budget cinematic creativity?" mused Gary Arnold in the first sentence of his *Mariachi* review. Two years earlier Arnold had written favorably about *Slacker* and even had a hand in connecting Richard Linklater with Universal Studios. Arnold also liked *Mariachi* and praised the "comic logic" underlying its "violent agitation."[67]

By April Columbia had added more cities to *Mariachi*'s release schedule, and by the time the movie had wrapped up its North American run, it had grossed more than $2 million. In the summer of 1993 Rodriguez traveled overseas to promote *El Mariachi*'s international release in more than ten countries. Toward the end of the year the film was released on videotape, in both subtitled and dubbed versions, and earned more than $1.5 million in sales.[68]

At the Sundance Film Festival earlier that year, Rodriguez had told *Rolling Stone*'s Peter Travers that his future plans did not include a move to Los Angeles. "I'm staying in Austin with my family, where my inspiration is," explained Rodriguez. By the time *El Mariachi* was released in 1993, Rodriguez had met plenty of people in L.A., but he still had no desire to live there. Plus, he told *Rolling Stone*, "I want my family to see me finish school. I'm only half a semester away—otherwise I might blow it off." But as much as Rodriguez wanted to set a good example for his younger siblings, he was eager to get on with his career. And with the exception of instructor Steve Mims and RTF professor (and former CinemaTexas graduate student) Charles Ramírez Berg, who also offered ongoing encouragement, Rodriguez didn't have much good to say about his experience in UT's film school. By the fall of 1990, when he took his first film class, he considered himself more experienced than his classmates and doubted that he would learn anything he couldn't teach himself. "It was more about using the free equipment. Then once I made *Mariachi* and made the Columbia deal, there was no reason to stay in school any more. I was already working," says Rodriguez of his decision not to finish his degree at the time. (Rodriguez eventually earned a bachelor's degree from the university in August 2008.)[69]

### The Next *Mariachi* Adventure

Meanwhile executives at Columbia had yet to greenlight Rodriguez's next project, which left the filmmaker uncomfortably spinning his wheels. Columbia chairman Mark Canton, says Allain, had begun to "balk" about the project. "Robert was getting very frustrated because he'd never asked permission before. He just didn't understand that this is how it goes in the studio. Sometimes they say yes, sometimes they say no," says Allain. But according to Gallardo, the project had been delayed because of the scandal that broke in the early summer of 1993 concerning twenty-seven-year-old Heidi Fleiss and her illegal call-girl service. At the time Gallardo, Avellán, and line producer Bill Borden had begun preproduction on the *Mariachi* sequel. In Mexico Gallardo introduced Borden to key union people, and they began to negotiate deals on behalf of the production. "We were already spending money, we were in preproduction. Then in late August, we stopped hearing from the studio. So Bill Borden called me and said, 'I haven't heard anything from the studio but there's a big scandal going on,'" recalls Gallardo.[70]

By August of that year at least two of Columbia's top executives had been linked to Fleiss in the press. "In my memory, nothing of that affected *Desperado* at all," says Borden, who recalls that casting decisions ultimately pushed the project's start date. "I'd gone and scouted Ciudad Acuña, and then the whole movie was put on hold for a while." For the time being, at least, the *Mariachi* follow-up would have to wait.[71]

In the meantime, Rodriguez decided to accept a smaller project. In January 1994 he spent less than two weeks shooting *Roadracers*, a period piece set in the 1950s for the cable television channel Showtime. Rodriguez shot the ninety-five-minute feature on 35mm for $1 million as a "warm up" to his *Mariachi* sequel, scheduled after a series of delays to go before the cameras later that year. The *Roadracers* project offered him the opportunity to work with a film crew, to make something within the system. "People in Austin take each movie as if it's amazing to get a job here in town. [In Hollywood] it was, 'Yeah, we're slumming it on cable, and this movie's gonna suck anyway.' The attitude was completely different." As far as Rodriguez was concerned, many people on the crew acted as if they were just punching the clock. The "Hollywood way," he decided, wasn't for him.[72]

By the summer of 1994, after a delay of more than a year, Columbia had finally given Rodriguez the go-ahead to make the follow-up to *El Mariachi*, originally entitled *The Return of El Mariachi* but now called *Desperado*. The decision came soon after a trip Allain had made to the Cannes Film Festival in May, where she ran into Rodriguez fans Harvey and Bob Weinstein. They had heard about Canton's reluctance, and they told Allain they'd be more than happy to make the movie. "All it takes is a little bit of pressure, and the next thing I know, we had a greenlight," says Allain.[73]

Allain's earlier suggestion about casting Antonio Banderas had become a reality. Rodriguez initially had been reluctant to have a non-Mexican in the role, but the studio refused to bankroll a lesser-known actor. The studio tested other actors, according to Borden, but both he and Allain were pushing for Banderas. Months earlier Allain had arranged a screening of *El Mariachi* for Banderas. Afterward she called Rodriguez. "He loved your movie, and he wants to meet you," she told him. "And I think that was pretty much it," says Allain.[74]

Gallardo had hoped to resume the lead role, but after an executive reshuffling at Sony/Columbia, he was told, that was no longer an option. "I didn't make any fuss because we were trying to get the movie made, but I've always felt that Stephanie Allain had something to do with that," he says.[75] No longer the star, Gallardo did remain on board as co-producer.

Salma Hayek, whom Rodriguez had first cast in *Roadracers*, played Banderas's love interest. Steve Buscemi appeared in the movie's opening sequence, a humorous part Rodriguez had written expressly for the actor after meeting him in Toronto. Even Tarantino had a cameo. *Desperado* was budgeted at just over $7 million and had the filmmaker returning to Acuña to use the same locations as in his first feature.

Avellán, who was credited as an associate producer on *Mariachi*, became a co-producer on her husband's second feature film after leaving her full-time position at the university. "Very early on Robert said, 'My wife is going to be producing it.' And that was very unusual. No one comes in and says, 'Oh by the way, my wife, who's never made a movie, is going to be my producer,'" recalls Allain. The two women were around the same age, however, and Allain appreciated that Avellán was trying to learn the ropes. "I was pretty young in the business myself, and it seemed like we'd broken every rule with *Boyz N the Hood*, so it didn't seem that foreign to me. Plus, it was obvious that he liked having her around and that she did serve in capacities that were producer-oriented and could be beneficial."[76]

After the sale of *Mariachi* Avellán and Rodriguez had talked about her own career path. Avellán was attracted to producing, and her managerial skills and experience handling large budgets at the university suggested she might be good at it.[77] Her husband encouraged the decision, he says, in part because their respective jobs were keeping them apart. Plus, Rodriguez told Avellán, if he could figure out how to make a movie, she certainly could master producing. He liked the idea of his wife being able to look out for him, and he had seen her manage budgets in her position at the university and in their own relationship.[78]

On the set of *Roadracers* Avellán met longtime Hollywood producer Debra Hill, who had first worked with John Carpenter and later partnered with producer Linda Obst. Hill became a mentor to Avellán and even helped the younger woman gain admittance into graduate-level production courses at UCLA's extension program so she could "learn the language" of the business. As time went on Avellán was thankful that she had kept her maiden name because she noticed that people didn't immediately make the connection between director and producer.[79]

Rodriguez loved being back in Acuña, but the *Desperado* shoot was challenging. Members of the cast and crew were being housed on both sides of the border, and equipment was being shipped in from Mexico City as well as the United States. And in Acuña, it was as if the prodigal son was returning after his $7,000 triumph, and everyone who had helped him and Gallardo on *Mariachi* wanted a piece of the action. Says Gallardo, who handled pre-production details in Acuña, "I had to talk to a lot of people because now we had money and everyone wanted money."[80]

The studio also was putting pressure on the filmmaker. "The first week they were ready to come down and fire everybody. After that, they started seeing the dailies, and I cut a couple of trailers together," said Rodriguez. Having Avellán on the production helped, as did working with Gallardo, who also had a small part in the sequel. But despite Rodriguez's success as a one-man band on *El Mariachi*, Columbia insisted he work with a more traditional

**143**

setup on *Desperado*. He hired some of his crew in Mexico, but as is typical of most studio films shot on location, the department heads came in from L.A. Not surprisingly, some members of the crew, who were used to working on sets where the lines of demarcation among positions were more clearly drawn, had difficulty understanding Rodriguez's all-encompassing directorial style.[81]

Although the production was more or less on schedule, word filtered back to the executives at Columbia that Rodriguez was throwing tantrums and kicking cameras and that key personnel, including director of photography Guillermo Navarro, were about to jump ship.

Avellán claims Borden, *Desperado*'s line producer, invented scenarios and created problems on the set, "badmouthing" Rodriguez to the studio. "He wanted to be in the business of Robert Rodriguez, and at the same time make the studio think that was the only way to manage that wild, renegade horse of a boy."[82]

"We had difficulties in the beginning with Bill," agrees Gallardo, "but it became worse." Indeed, the miscommunication and conflict began to take its toll on the friendship between Gallardo and Rodriguez and Avellán. "Bill was just putting us against each other. I was very mad, but I didn't find out until years later."[83]

One day Avellán took a conference call from her agent and Allain, who had been so enthusiastic about signing Rodriguez two years earlier. They asked Avellán for an update, and she told them the shoot was going well and everyone was having fun.

Allain explained to Avellán that they were hearing reports of Rodriguez's bad behavior and about disgruntled crew members and that Borden "has had to calm people down."

"I've known Robert for six years," Avellán told Allain. "We've been married for five. He's never screamed at me. He's not a screamer. So that's incorrect. And number two, how could it be that the DP is about to quit when the DP's just signed on to do *Four Rooms*? So, I don't know who's feeding you this bullshit, but it's not the truth."[84]

Instead of confronting Borden, Avellán alerted Rodriguez to the situation and suggested they generally steer clear of Borden but monitor his actions. In her mind, at least, Borden was working for hire; they were in control. Gallardo disputes the description of Rodriguez as a tantrum-throwing filmmaker on *Desperado*, although he acknowledges his friend's moodiness, which he has witnessed since they were teenagers. "He just becomes somebody else. It's like a change in personality."[85]

Says Borden, "There was one incident in the bar or something when Robert lost his patience and did something and somehow the studio found out about it and thought he was throwing tantrums, but it was really minor." He adds, "Robert was always a pro. Maybe it was an issue that got blown out of proportion."[86]

The tense situation between Rodriguez and Avellán and Borden was made more difficult because of Borden's close friendship with Gary Martin, who was head of physical production at Sony Pictures, Columbia's parent company, and was one of the executives overseeing *Desperado*. "I think we tried to model that film as much as we could on the way Robert actually wants to work," says Martin, who describes the *Desperado* shoot as a "tough show." Recalls Avellán, "Basically, [it looked like] Robert was insulting Gary's friend. It took a long time to heal the wounds between Gary Martin and us."[87]

At another point in the project's development, Avellán and Martin sat down for a meeting at Sony. Columbia executives Allain and Lisa Henson (daughter of Jim Henson) joined Avellán and Martin. According to Avellán, Martin had called the meeting because he wanted Avellán to understand why the studio didn't want Rodriguez to edit his own film. Martin, who was sitting to Avellán's left, turned to her and smiled. "Honey, just like when you go to a beauty parlor, and somebody does your nails because they specialize in that and somebody does your color because they specialize in that, it's the same in the movie business."[88]

Avellán was dumbfounded. She stared at Martin, and then turned to the two other women at the table. She could tell they were equally insulted. "We do things differently," Avellán wanted to tell Martin at the time. "Robert's the *Mariachi* kid. Who, by the way, will do nails and hair all at the same time, okay?"[89]

Instead, she bit her tongue. "I didn't know what to say, and I wanted peace. And I thought, 'Someday this man will know that I was right and he was wrong. Someday,'" she says. "It was one of the hardest things I had to go through."[90]

Says Martin, who confirms that a meeting took place, "That sounds like me but I can't recall the specifics."[91]

By November of 1994 Avellán and Rodriguez had returned to Los Angeles for postproduction on *Desperado*. After production on *Desperado* wrapped, Rodriguez had jumped to the project *Four Rooms*, which featured four interlocking storylines set in a hotel on New Year's Eve and written and directed by Rodriguez, Allison Anders (*Mi Vida Loca*), Alexander Rockwell (*In the Soup*), and Quentin Tarantino. (Richard Linklater had originally agreed to direct a segment but pulled out at the last minute, a "smart decision," observes producer's rep John Pierson of the poorly reviewed film that tanked at the box office.) All four filmmakers had released their first features at about the same time and had gotten to know one another on the festival circuit. Three of the four filmmakers began work on *Four Rooms* while Tarantino was in Sweden promoting *Pulp Fiction,* and by the time Tarantino returned to L.A., tensions had erupted on the project. "It started off four friends making the movie and now me and Robert are the only guys who stay in touch," says Tarantino. He blames the difficulties on Anders's and Rockwell's jealousy of his success with *Pulp Fiction,* while both Anders and Rockwell have cited Tarantino's inflated ego and Miramax's favoritism of the other two filmmakers as contributing to the problems. From Tarantino's perspective, however, the difficulties only cemented his and Rodriguez's friendship. "Everyone but Robert was giving me static. We were the only ones having a great time," says Tarantino.[92]

When Rodriguez finished shooting his part of *Four Rooms,* he turned his attention back to *Desperado* and encountered more resistance from the studio. Says Rodriguez, "They had never had a director edit his own movie." Gary Martin explains, "The concern going into a film with Robert at the beginning of his career was, we only have one guy because he's doing all the jobs. When you have one man, and you're putting all your eggs into that one man's basket, and there is no other point of view, it makes you concerned, particularly when you're talking about the first major film."[93]

A compromise was reached: Rodriguez could edit the film, but he had to post in L.A. Despite initial resistance from Martin and others, Rodriguez had converted one of his rental house's bedrooms into an editing suite so he could work nonstop on the film's rough cut. At one point an anxious Martin went by the house to check out the footage. "You see exactly what he does and how fast he does it and all your fears, if you have any, go away. He had a point of view and he kept it with him and he was very focused on it. And it worked."[94]

### The House That Miramax Built

By February of 1995 Rodriguez was finishing the edit and preparing to oversee the mixes on both *Desperado* and *Four Rooms,* which were done in adjacent mixing rooms at Twentieth Century Fox. Simultaneously he began preproduction on the horror movie *From Dusk Till Dawn,* written by Tarantino, and organized the journal entries he kept during the making and selling of *El Mariachi* into a book to be published along with the release of *Desperado.*

Rodriguez's pace may have seemed baffling to others, but he had his own reasons for juggling multiple projects. "I knew people would be watching for that sophomore slump," Rodriguez said at the time, "so I figured that instead of making one film and putting all the eggs in one basket, I would simply confuse the marketplace by putting out four films quickly."[95] It also gave Rodriguez the opportunity to hone his filmmaking skills, something he had originally planned to do by making three movies back-to-back for the Spanish-language video market.

But Rodriguez hadn't been back in L.A. for more than a few months before he decided he had had enough. One day in February he looked over at his wife, three months pregnant with their first son, Rocket. "Go back to Austin and find some land," he told her. "I'm not staying here."[96]

Avellán lost no time in placing a call to Robert Steinbomer, an Austin architect who introduced her to an associate who helped her find a sixty-acre tract about thirty miles west of downtown. Avellán and Rodriguez purchased the land on May 1, 1995, just before they left for the south of France and the Cannes Film Festival, where *Desperado* was scheduled to have its premiere. Rodriguez was putting down roots, and not just in his personal life. The release of *Desperado* marked the end of his two-year contract with Columbia, and he was able to ink a new deal around *From Dusk Till Dawn* that would guarantee him the creative control he desired while also providing the financial backing that would allow him to make his kind of movies without studio interference. The arrangement teamed Rodriguez with the Weinsteins of Miramax. The deal gave the filmmaker final cut, among other things. Rodriguez's agents shopped it to other studios before Miramax said yes. Recalls Avellán, "Fox really was interested because they had been wanting to work with Robert. But when they saw the deal, they all went, 'Too rich for us.' There were too many precedent-setting things [in the contract]. And Harvey and Bob said, 'We'll take it.' And they walked away with it, like that."[97]

Observes Sony's Gary Martin, "Getting Robert used to the studio system, if you want to call it that, was a chore. And I think Miramax probably gave him a lot more latitude than most major companies would do."[98]

On the brink of bankruptcy by 1992, Miramax had struck a deal with the Walt Disney Company in 1993 that finally allowed the distributors to branch out into production. Around the same time, Rodriguez was working on the *Desperado* script on the Sony lot in an office next door to Tarantino, who was writing *Pulp Fiction* for TriStar. "They passed on *Pulp Fiction*—they thought it was too long and weird. So Quentin took it to Miramax, which had just been bought by Disney, and so they had money to make it. And I saw how well that went for him over there," says Rodriguez, who was impressed by the

Weinsteins' independent-minded style and seemingly renegade approach to running their company.[99] *From Dusk Till Dawn* would become one of the first movies the Weinsteins produced through Miramax and Bob Weinstein's exploitation division, Dimension.

"When *Desperado* was going to be shown at Cannes, that got them motivated to get me over to the new Weinstein company, so they offered a great deal to try to surpass the Columbia deal," says Rodriguez of the exclusive agreement that would allow him to write, direct, and produce for Miramax in an arrangement very similar to the one Tarantino and producer Lawrence Bender had negotiated with the company. It gave Rodriguez approval over final cut and merchandising decisions and a stake in the sequel rights. ("We share the sequel rights," explains Bob Weinstein. "He can't go and do it [without our approval] nor can we go and do it.") Rodriguez and Avellán's Los Hooligans production company, named for his *Daily Texan* cartoon strip, would be brought under the Miramax banner as well.[100]

Rodriguez's deal had been finalized shortly before he and Avellán left for France, and it was announced in the trades a day before *Desperado* played at the festival on May 25. A triumphant Rodriguez received a standing ovation after the movie's screening. Back in the audience, Harvey Weinstein rose to his feet beaming, recalls Avellán, "like he had been the producer of that movie. Like a proud papa!"[101]

By the mid-1990s it had become very clear that the Weinsteins loved to make money, and stories about their slippery accounting strategies were legendary. They had also earned a reputation as threatening bullies. As one former Miramax executive would later say, "This business is about ego and greed. Harvey is ego, Bob is greed."[102]

Avellán views their relationship differently but acknowledges its restrictions. "They love each other, Harvey and Bob, and we understand that the language of family is so important. When they say to me, 'You are our family,' now, they mean it. But it's like a mafia family in a way." She laughs, "But you know what? When I saw *The Godfather* I *wanted* to be a mafia princess! There're some pluses to being a mafia princess."[103]

For the time being, at least, the deal suited Rodriguez just fine. And years later when he wanted to spend a sizable amount of money to make *Spy Kids*, a family-friendly film that would exploit a relatively new filmmaking technology, the Weinsteins signed off on the risky project with little hesitation.

But what was most important about the Miramax deal for the young couple, about to start a family, was that it finally allowed them to return to Austin for good. Bob Weinstein, who visited the couple in L.A., was surprised to see Rodriguez editing on an Avid set up in their rental house. "Don't they have, like, a studio over there?" he kidded Rodriguez, referring to Columbia's facilities. Says Weinstein, "You could just see that he was out of place, and I could just feel that he didn't like being in L.A."[104]

By 1996, three years after Rodriguez had first insisted to *Rolling Stone*'s Peter Travers that he was staying in Texas, he finally made good on his word. Beginning in May 1995, with his wife's blessing, Rodriguez had spent eighteen months commuting between Los Angeles and Austin to supervise the construction of a 6,000-square-foot Mediterranean-style house. After finding the land herself, Avellán had entrusted every aspect of the home—design, construction, etc.—to her husband. She chose not to see the house until it was finished. "Do whatever you want, babe. I'll pay the bills," she had told him. In a sense the arrangement mirrored their working relationship: he "directed" the project while she "produced" it. And although Avellán loved the finished product, with its dark, painted interiors and castle-like exteriors built from native Texas stone, she immediately realized that all of the light switches and other fixtures had been positioned to accommodate her husband's much taller frame.[105]

Years later she would observe, "That's part of how our relationship tends to work. It's his way or the highway."[106]

In November of 1996, Rodriguez carried his wife across the threshold of their new Austin house. They were finally home.

Rick never said he was going to make a movie about growing up in Huntsville, Texas, about the quarterback who didn't really want to be one. He never vocalized it, but it materialized in *Dazed and Confused*. It could have been called *The Reluctant Quarterback*.

LEE DANIEL

# The Reluctant Quarterback
## Richard Linklater and *Dazed and Confused*

- - - - - - - - - - - - - - - - - - - - - - - - - - - - - - - - - - - - - -

**B**y July 1992, while a frustrated Robert Rodriguez was overseeing the 35mm blowup of *El Mariachi* on the Columbia lot, Richard Linklater was just weeks into production on his next movie, a teen comedy set in 1976 on the last day of school called *Dazed and Confused*. Its $6.9 million budget was modest by Hollywood standards, but in many ways a lot was riding on the film. Despite an amicable beginning, the relationship between Linklater and his Austin-based crew and the executives at Universal Pictures quickly turned sour, and the studio forced the filmmaker to trim his budget and his shooting schedule. And to the L.A. members of the *Dazed* crew, Linklater's laidback directorial "style" was a joke. "The truth is he's an amateur and it shows," scoffed one crew member. "We're shooting half the scenes we could be shooting, exactly half."[1]

Night shooting had begun, and one evening the crew assembled at the Top Notch hamburger stand in North Austin. Twenty-two-year-old UT RTF undergraduate Matthew McConaughey arrived on the set for a hair and wardrobe test. "I wasn't scheduled to work that night but I had come down to do a makeup and hair thing just to walk out in front of Rick and see what he thought," recalls McConaughey of his role as David Wooderson, a character slightly older than the others in the movie. The aspiring actor stepped out of the wardrobe trailer dressed in peach-colored polyester slacks, a tight white t-shirt with a silkscreen of Ted Nugent's *Cat Scratch Fever* album cover, leather motorcycle boots, and a pot pipe dangling from a leather cord around his neck. Shaggy, dirty-blonde waves and a thin mustache completed the seventies look. When Linklater first caught sight of the actor in wardrobe, he decided to expand that night's scheduled scene from a quick drive through the hamburger stand's parking lot. He pulled McConaughey aside. "Hey, there's a beer bust going on later in the movie, and we need a character to get that information to some of the other characters. Maybe Wooderson is the guy to do it," Linklater explained.[2]

They conferred about the changes to the scene, and thirty minutes later McConaughey slid behind the wheel of a vintage Chevelle. He played the scene with Marisa Ribisi, who was cast as one of the three brainy sophomores hanging out at the Top Notch and looking for a party. McConaughey improvised his dialogue, inviting Ribisi's character to the keg party that evening and even offering her a ride, despite the obvious fact that both characters were driving their own cars. The line worked: It was goofy without detracting from Wooderson's aura.

The shooting of the scene was a turning point for the rest of the cast and crew as well. Linklater maximized the tight shooting schedule by grabbing extra moments when he could, filming improvised scenes not written into the script. Many of the actors hung around the set whether or not they were written into that day's shots, so nearly the entire cast was on hand for McConaughey's first scene. After weeks of tension, the congenial actor's inspired bit seemed to unite and energize everyone. "It was like a shot of adrenaline," recalls production designer John Frick. Admits assistant director John Cameron, "It was one of those times on any film where the crew just stops, everything clicks. Each take was good, and there was a lot of applause and good feeling afterward." Even Linklater, who had been spending his lunch breaks justifying his shot list to the studio naysayers, sensed a change. "I can feel the crew completely catch a groove that will be with us the rest of the way." Unfortunately, the good feelings wouldn't last.[3]

Linklater partnered on *Dazed and Confused* with former studio executives Jim Jacks and Sean Daniel, who by 1992 had created their own independent production company and had a distribution deal with Universal Pictures. The filmmaker had first sensed trouble during preproduction discussions when Universal suggested he use the same editor who cut the lampoonish *Police Academy* movies. Instead he hired local editor Sandra Adair, which meant that for most of the picture's production and postproduction he could remain in Austin and away from Universal's meddling studio executives.[4] With

*Dazed,* the filmmaker insisted on an Austin-based crew that included Adair, producer Anne Walker-McBay, and cinematographer and former roommate Lee Daniel. Having established the production company Detour Filmproduction while making *Slacker,* Linklater now created his own studio unit while shooting *Dazed.* But he also faced many struggles while he tried to learn how to negotiate the studio system. The question was whether or not Linklater and his friends could make a bankable genre movie for a major Hollywood studio without completely sacrificing the film's independent spirit. The process of releasing *Dazed* was disappointing for Linklater as he struggled to work with a studio that didn't "get" his film. Despite a tepid box office return, the movie eventually found its audience and launched the careers of many of its unknown actors, including McConaughey, Ben Affleck, and Renée Zellweger. Veteran casting director Don Phillips, who had met McConaughey in an Austin hotel bar during preproduction, would fill the *Dazed* ensemble with fresh young talent in the same way he had cast *Fast Times at Ridgemont High* a decade earlier.

Meanwhile, as Linklater and his inexperienced crew became more organized and professional during the making of *Dazed,* longtime members of the Austin film community seemed anything but as they battled to establish competing film festivals. *Dazed and Confused*'s 1993 release coincided with the *Austin Chronicle*'s launching of the South by Southwest Film Conference and Festival and the creation of the Austin Film Festival by relative newcomers Barbara Morgan and Marsha Milam. Both festivals would become nationally respected and have since come to define Austin's ability to attract top industry talent and host world premieres of the latest independent and studio films. But the behind-the-scenes pettiness leading up to these inaugural festivals in the mid-1990s serves as a reminder of how small and inherently local Austin's film community really still was.

### A Better Next Movie

In the beginning of July 1991, as Richard Linklater began a two-month press tour to promote *Slacker,* he was also itching to begin his next project. By early fall he was in talks with Ted Hope and James Schamus of Good Machine, a small, relatively new independent production and distribution company that would earn a reputation for nurturing the work of unknown writer-directors. Linklater was interested in reviving the failed project that had preceded *Slacker,* a "modernization" of Norwegian writer Knut Hamsun's novel *Hunger,* about a young writer trying to maintain his dignity in the face of poverty and homelessness. While commuting between Galveston and Austin in 1988, Linklater had written a couple of drafts of a script that updated the story, first published in 1890, for contemporary audiences. As with *Slacker*, Linklater had tapped Lee Daniel to be the cinematographer. "We were poised, ready to shoot it for about $250,000 on Super 8, blow it up to 35mm," Daniel recalls. The artiness of the project appealed to Daniel, whose own photographic style had been inspired by the vivid abstract imagery of American avant-garde filmmakers like Stan Brakhage and Kenneth Anger.[5]

Then one day Linklater asked Daniel to take a look at another script. The title page read *Dazed and Confused*. Daniel recognized the title immediately (a reference to a Led Zeppelin song) and knew without reading the first page that the script was based on conversations they'd had about their similar Texas high school experiences.

Linklater had been working on the script, set in 1976 at a Texas high school on the last day before summer vacation, but had kept it mostly to himself. During the *Slacker* press juggernaut, Linklater met and was impressed by Gary Arnold, a film critic writing for the *Washington Times* who seemed to understand *Slacker* better than most reviewers. In response to Arnold's question about his next film, Linklater revealed details about the project closest to him. "I tell him I want to capture the moment-to-moment reality and energy of being a teenager. Like *Slacker*, it will have a lot of characters and not a lot of plot but if I set it in the Seventies, everyone will at least think it's 'about' something," he later recounted.[6]

A few weeks after this conversation, Linklater took a call from Jim Jacks, who had been president of development at Universal. Jacks had seen *Slacker* at Sundance: "The first time I saw *Slacker* I walked out of it, only because at some point it became kind of repetitive and I had to move on to the next movie. But I said, 'This guy knows what's funny.'" Jacks also had heard about Linklater through friend and critic Gary Arnold, and he invited the filmmaker to Los Angeles to discuss the idea for his next movie. Jacks then touched base with Michael Barker and Tom Bernard at Orion. "They said, 'Rick's great. A little full of himself right now, but he's great.'"[7]

Anxious to begin production by summer 1992, Linklater agreed to a meeting with Jacks and his producing partner, Sean Daniel. Linklater weighed the pros and cons of getting involved with Universal during his mid-September lunch with Jacks and Daniel. Despite his innate distrust of Hollywood politics, Linklater liked the fact that Daniel and Jacks had produced *Animal House* (1978) under Universal's radar. By the end of his visit, he had agreed to deliver a finished script within the next couple of months.

Linklater took *Slacker* to the London Film Festival in late October. He also brought along a first draft of a script that ran more than 160 pages. It was upon his return to Austin that he first showed the script to Lee Daniel and a few other AFS intimates.

"We'd talked about our high school days when we were roommates. But the idea of going to a studio and making a representation of his own experience growing up in a small town in Texas, with high school hazing and football—a teen high school coming-of-age movie? It's been done a million times," says Daniel. Although he didn't say the words aloud to Linklater, he thought, "You fucking sellout." He had difficulty, initially, understanding Linklater's decision. "To me we were so much more of a team. That's the way I saw it. He had bigger ideas. He never let on that he was ever going to do anything remotely Hollywood at all. All we ever talked was Europeans— François Truffaut, Andrei Tarkovsky, Vittorio De Sica. But maybe in Rick's own mind, he thought, 'Hey, I'm an American. I can't make a foreign movie. I'll make a story about my own experience.'"[8]

Explains Linklater, "I had this idea [for *Dazed*] before *Slacker* even, and then it just seemed like a better 'next' movie, more of a logical next movie I could get made. That I could get money for to do it right."[9]

During their conversations about high school, Daniel had shared with Linklater his own experiences of going to rock concerts and working on his GTO "project" car. Together they came up with an idea for a conceptual film, shot in a single take, that followed two high school guys cruising around at night, "probably smoking some pot." Filmed with a camera mounted on the hood of the car, the circular story's running time would match the duration of ZZ Top's *Fandango* album, and the first image of the movie would be of a hand popping an 8-track cartridge into a player. The concept was quintessential Daniel, an inspired narrative experiment in the tradition of the camera catapults he built on the roof of his Austin apartment. As with that experiment, which inspired *Slacker*'s final scene, Daniel's "concept film" eventually worked its way into *Dazed*.

Linklater turned to his AFS cohorts for help with the *Dazed* screenplay. Says Clark Walker, "We were all reading Rick's early drafts of the script and helping him. The film has too many characters as it is, and it had twice as many at the beginning. He needed somebody to bounce ideas off of and to encourage him in the right directions, where the stronger material was."[10]

Eventually Daniel came around to the film. "How was I going to argue if he was going to hire me to shoot it?" he admits more than two decades later. "I wanted to do the other one much more, although I wouldn't have made nearly any money."[11]

Says Walker-McBay, "I didn't have that same connection to *Hunger*. I thought it was kind of a difficult film to make. We had a script and Rick had been talking about it for a while, but he obviously let that go at some point since he didn't pursue it."[12]

### Preproduction, *Slacker*-style

In December 1991, Universal responded favorably to Linklater's script for *Dazed* although they had yet to commit to the film. By February of the following year, the filmmaker decided to proceed with preproduction duties even though the studio still hadn't officially greenlighted the project. He and Daniel took advantage of the time and began to map out the shoot. Although they were no longer roommates, their collaboration harked back to the early days of their friendship and the endless discussions in which they debated formative film influences.

Linklater once again turned to Walker-McBay for help with casting. She canvassed Austin *Slacker*-style, handing out business cards to teenagers, while Linklater hired "scouts" to frequent area high schools. Walker-McBay discovered local high school freshman Wiley Wiggins on the Drag at Quackenbush's café, where some of *Slacker*'s scenes had been filmed. The fifteen-year-old had had some acting experience, most notably playing a character on a PBS series in the 1980s. Walker-McBay thought his name alone was terrific, but she also recognized that his long hair and slight gawkiness were perfect for the part of Mitch, a freshman-to-be who is stalked in the movie by paddle-wielding seniors. Wiggins immediately warmed to Linklater. "He seemed to really care what we had to say, and I never felt like he was judging me somewhere in the back of his mind."[13]

While waiting for word from the studio, the Austin crew also began preliminary location scouting. Shooting during the summer meant they could film in a deserted junior high in Northwest Austin, which stood in for the movie's main high school setting. The quiet suburban neighborhoods surrounding the Austin school, many of which had been built in the 1950s and 1960s, offered wide streets and ranch-style residences with the appropriate architectural details for the movie's mid-1970s time period.

During this time Linklater also made as many crew decisions as possible. He hired local production designer John Frick, whose credits included *Nadine* and the *Lonesome Dove* miniseries. Debbie Pastor, a Linklater intimate who had appeared in *Slacker*, came on board as the art director. In addition to Daniel and Walker-McBay, other returning AFS/*Slacker* cohorts included Clark Walker as second assistant camera, D. Montgomery as assistant art director, and Keith Fletcher as extras costumer. Recalls Fletcher, who shared the job with his wife Melanie, "We thought we were interviewing for the position, and we walked in and were talking to some people and they just made us fill out some forms and gave us a big stack of twenty-dollar bills and keys to a station wagon and told us to start shopping." One *Slacker* intimate who was not included in Linklater's next movie was editor Scott Rhodes. Rhodes had distanced himself from the *Slacker* crowd after the film sold to Orion, but he stayed in touch with Linklater. Before *Dazed* went into production, Linklater contacted Rhodes and told him he probably couldn't get him a position editing the movie. "Of course I knew that was bullshit," recalls Rhodes, who believed Linklater really didn't want to work with him because of their falling out on *Slacker*. "My attitude was really bad. It's no wonder that he wouldn't want to edit with me." Still, Rhodes wanted Linklater to acknowledge their rift. "He didn't want to address it at all. And that's part of his talent—let people think what they need to think. Rick's a survivor. He doesn't get emotionally wrapped up in things."[14]

At the suggestion of the studio, Linklater hired Alma Kuttruff as *Dazed*'s production manager. The Austin-based Kuttruff brought a decade of experience to the project. A Louisiana native, she had built a career as a production manager after working on Bill Wittliff's *Red Headed Stranger* and Joel and Ethan Coen's *Blood Simple* in the 1980s. Her initial work for the Coens led to positions on their later films, and it was Jim Jacks, whom she met on *Raising Arizona*, who recommended her to Universal for *Dazed*. "I know he called me to do the budget," says Kuttruff of Jacks's decision, which reflected the studio's determination to keep Linklater and the film in line. Eventually she had lunch with Linklater and Walker-McBay in Austin. Kuttruff's ability to shave production budgets had earned her a generally favorable reputation by the early 1990s. "In my mind," she says, "being a good production manager is finding a way to be able to steal from here to spend it there." Indeed, with *Dazed*'s rapidly shrinking budget and ever-expanding soundtrack, Linklater would rely on her to squirrel away money during production for later use in acquiring music rights.[15]

Another industry veteran favored by the studio was casting-director-turned-producer Don Phillips. Jacks and Daniel knew Phillips from his work on *Animal House*, and the fifty-two-year-old had also cast *Serpico* (1973) and *Dog Day Afternoon* (1975). Phillips's former assistant Nancy Nayor was by then head of casting for Universal, and she called him about the *Dazed* script because it reminded her of Phillips's last casting project, the successful teen comedy *Fast Times at Ridgemont High* (1982). The ensemble had launched the careers of many of its young actors, including that of Sean Penn. Any reluctance Linklater may have felt about Phillips disappeared after their first meeting at the Universal commissary. Phillips's enthusiasm was legendary. He had once protested Universal's decision to shelve Jonathan Demme's *Melvin and Howard* (1980), which Phillips produced, by stripping down to his underwear during a heated meeting with studio executives. (Universal agreed to give the movie a limited release, and it went on to win two Oscars and numerous other awards.) "I was very enthusiastic with those kids," recalls Phillips, who felt an immediate connection with Linklater and Walker-McBay and saw *Dazed* as a challenge to duplicate the casting success he had had with *Fast Times* a decade earlier. Phillips was someone Linklater respected and came to rely on for his expertise and understanding of the industry.[16]

Other crew decisions were more difficult. Universal insisted that Linklater use an assistant director and other department heads out of Los Angeles. Explains Jacks, "Rick wanted to use a lot of his people from Austin. The problem was, at that point, they had done *Slacker*, but kind of like, well, slackers. It was kind of catch-as-catch can and nobody was very professional."[17]

"Rick had a choice," Lee Daniel recalls. "He had to hire one out of basically a lineup of assistant directors and producers who were basically yes-men to the studio. Rick had never worked with an assistant director before. So we got one of their guys that had done a movie with them before." Assistant director John Cameron had worked on a few Sam Raimi films and knew Jacks through a Raimi–Coen brothers connection. Cameron met with Linklater and Walker-McBay and, despite tensions that would surface during production, recalls the initial interview as friendly. "Rick had the story down cold. And he had an approach down that he was very articulate about, in terms of working with raw young actors who didn't have a lot of film experience." Says Daniel of Cameron, "He was extremely condescending. He didn't think we had a clue, and vice versa." No more than a few weeks into production, Cameron and Daniel were barely speaking to one another, a not atypical situation given their respective crew positions. "Lee Daniel was kind of lucky to get the job," counters Jacks. "I like Lee, and I know Rick still works with him, but if I had it to do over again, I think I would have insisted on a more experienced DP. But in the end, maybe [the movie] would have lost its energy."[18]

### We've All Got Our Work Cut out for Us

In May of 1992, after months of grassroots preproduction in Austin, Universal faced a deadline. With the help of entertainment attorney John Sloss,

Linklater had negotiated an option on the project with the studio, which meant that they had to decide whether or not to fund the picture or return it to Linklater, who would then shop the project to other interested parties. (Paramount Pictures already had expressed interest in the story.) Universal asked for a few more days to decide, and Linklater agreed but he also sensed a distinct "chill" from the executives, who had finally viewed *Slacker*. He could tell they feared *Dazed* would turn into an "art film," despite what it looked like on paper. "If I wanted to do an art film (whatever the fuck that means anyway), I wouldn't be getting in bed with them," vented Linklater at the time. According to Jacks, the studio really didn't want to make the film. "We had forced Universal into making it. [Sean Daniel and I] actually had the right to put one $5 million movie to them, but they really didn't want us to do *Dazed*, so they finally gave us a greenlight without us saying, 'You have to.'"[19]

Universal's concerns and cautiousness irritated Linklater and frustrated others in the *Slacker* circle, and some did not give credit to Sean Daniel and Jim Jacks for ultimately supporting *Dazed*. Says Kuttruff, who had known Jacks since the early 1980s, "Jim had a real eye for spotting winners for the theater." Indeed, Jacks had broken into the movie business by picking films for Circle Releasing while also working as an entertainment analyst at Paine Webber. One of his most successful decisions was picking *Risky Business* (1983). "It actually had tested very badly and Warner Bros. was saying bad things about it," says Jacks. Instead, *Risky Business* launched Tom Cruise's career and became the tenth highest grossing movie of 1983.[20]

Making *Slacker* had had its difficult moments for sure, but when Linklater approached his AFS friends with the initial treatment, the feeling had been that they were all going to make the film no matter what. With little to lose, it was easy to view the entire process as a thrilling experiment. After the studio greenlit *Dazed*, however, everyone began to realize that the stakes were much higher on this next project.

Recalls Walker, "The movie existed on the edge of a watchable narrative that you could judge against other movies. Suddenly you think, 'Wow. This is a teen comedy. Universal's going to want a scene where the girl flashes her top. They're going to demand that the football game come in the final act. We've got to figure out how to trick them into thinking that this is entertaining.'"[21]

When Universal asked Don Phillips to help with casting on *Dazed*, he stipulated that he'd take the job only if he could hire unknowns. He and Linklater held rounds of open calls and auditions in New York, Chicago, Austin, and Los Angeles. Jason London, who had earned good reviews for his sensitive performance in *The Man in the Moon* (1991), auditioned for the part of Linklater doppelgänger Randall "Pink" Floyd. After narrowing their choices somewhat, Phillips hosted a final casting pizza party, a technique that he had originated on *Fast Times*. One Saturday, he and Linklater commandeered a nearly deserted building at Universal Studios, where they assembled a large group of actors and mixed and matched them for different parts. A pizza delivery person arrived around noon. "We had, like, 36 or 38 people for 18 parts. The kids had a ball. There was a lot of kissing," recalls Phillips. The pizza party worked well for him and Linklater, a one-stop casting call that gave them the opportunity to see a number of actors reading together for a variety of roles.[22]

Adam Goldberg, who would be cast as the sarcastic honors student Mike Newhouse, had only a few roles to his credit at the time. He ran into Link-later in the bathroom before things got underway, and the director told him that he already had been cast. "The good news is that you got the part," said Linklater. "The bad news is you've got to read with a lot of people today." Goldberg never knew if Linklater had been serious or had simply been try-ing to put the young actor at ease for the audition. "Rick told me before we started that I had the part, but I still had to read with people. So I kind of had this little secret, but clearly I had to test for it because apparently Nicky Katt had the part too."[23]

By the start of rehearsals in June 1992, Linklater and Phillips had met with a number of up-and-coming young actors and relative unknowns who would eventually achieve recognition for other roles. Ben Affleck had ap-peared in some television series and a few features by the early 1990s, but when his agent sent him the *Dazed* script, he had to be convinced. Explained Affleck, "It was the bad guy part. I didn't want to play the bad guy, but I fig-ured I'd do it anyway."[24] Ashley Judd, Vince Vaughn, and Claire Danes had all auditioned at some point but did not make the final cut. Another unknown, Texas native Renée Zellweger, so impressed Phillips and Linklater that they created a small, uncredited part for her in the movie's comical hazing se-quence. Linklater also had chosen a few actors prior to the marathon casting session, like newcomer Parker Posey. By 1992 Posey's most notable work was as a recurring character on the television soap opera *As The World Turns*. In *Dazed*, Linklater cast her as the bitchy senior Darla, who takes sadistic pleasure in hazing the soon-to-be freshmen girls.

Before principal photography began in Austin in July, Linklater got word that not only was his budget being sliced, but he was also losing more than two weeks from the production, trimming the already tight schedule to just thirty-two days. "At the time the budget was $7 million, and that was the lowest we could figure out how to make it," says Walker-McBay, who also assumed co-producing duties. (The budget eventually hovered just under that amount but was often reported as either $5 million or $6 million.) "It was non-union, nobody got paid that much. The actors all worked for SAG [Screen Actors Guild] scale. But it seemed like a lot of money to us. I just felt we were really lucky. We made *Slacker*, and now we get to go and make this other, really cool movie." But Linklater resented what he saw as the studio's scapegoating *Dazed*, a relatively small film in terms of Universal's other projects, for the excesses of bigger-budget movies already in production as well as the studio's 1992 box office disappointments like *Dr. Giggles* and *Far and Away*.[25]

Cuts to the production schedule also forced him to trim rehearsals. "That was indicative of the whole shoot," says Linklater. "Whatever I asked for, I got a percentage of. Why give a director what he thinks he needs to make the best movie possible? Certainly he's indulging himself needlessly." The film-maker valued rehearsals and had taken acting classes years earlier in part to learn how to direct and understand the process of developing a character. The improvisational style achieved in *Slacker* grew out of Linklater using the script as a jumping-off point and working with the actors to loosen them up and encourage feedback, a method he would continue to use throughout his career. In mid-June Linklater sent a letter to his cast preparing them for the shoot. "We've all got our work cut out for us on this one. There's nothing easy about what we're trying to do here—getting cast was the easy part," wrote Linklater. "Know your character so we can forget about it and build something new, something special, in its likeness. As I've said before, if the final movie is 100% word-for-word what's in this script, it will be a massive underachievement."[26]

Linklater often rehearsed with the *Dazed* actors at the Sheraton Crest Hotel downtown, where the entire cast was housed for the duration of the shoot. The young actors basically ran wild in the hotel, bonding with one another and partying into the night. "I remember more about that than the actual production," says Goldberg of the highly charged atmosphere. "I remember thinking this was the college experience I never had. It felt like that fraternal atmosphere but probably better because you're making a movie and don't have to study." Says Phillips, who became a kind of surrogate uncle to many of the actors, "I'd already turned 50, but I felt like I was 22. It was amazing. And the kids were really responsible. They would party, and then they would stop at a certain hour, go to bed, and be ready and be prepared to go to work." Linklater pal Kim Krizan, who appeared in *Slacker*, was cast in *Dazed* as Ginny Stroud, the cynical high school teacher who cautions her students against the commercialism of the country's Bicentennial celebrations. As Krizan waited to film her scenes, she perched on a desk at the front of the classroom set and observed the actors who were playing the students drawing graffiti on the desks and generally acting out. "It was interesting how we were all falling into our roles," says Krizan. "I remember thinking, 'Oh, how to keep order in here?' And then I was like, 'Wait, this is a movie!'"[27]

The script's hothouse atmosphere of high school politics soon materialized in real life among the actors. Says London, "The groups that were in the movie became those groups outside of the movie. Everybody got along, but it was this natural thing to happen. And it was very true that I was very much like Pink that I hung out with every single group at different times. Certain other people never hung out with other people at all."[28]

One of the actors, however, failed to win over the group. Shawn Andrews, an unknown who was cast as one of Pink's running buddies, had taken to tearing his hotel bed sheets into squares, autographing them and selling them to the hotel's maid staff claiming that he was going to be "as big as Brando someday." He also began a steamy relationship with the underaged Milla Jovovich that resulted in an elopement after production wrapped and, less than two months later, an annulment demanded by the sixteen-year-old's mother. During production Andrews's part began to shrink as Linklater fed more lines to McConaughey's Wooderson. "Rick started cutting the lines away from the other guy, giving them to Matthew. And Matthew ended up having the third largest part," says Phillips.[29]

During rehearsals Linklater would sit across from the actors in a bare conference room while they ran through various scenes, and he encouraged contributions from the young cast. "There are so many scenes that started as one thing but turned into something else," recalls London, who received backstory about his character from Linklater. "He basically said, if you look at Wiley Wiggins's character and then you look at my character, Wiley is Rick as a freshman, and I was him as a senior. And the way that happened for Pink is that he probably had older guys like Wooderson, when he was a freshman, be cool to him." The improvisational spirit extended into production. The actors scripted a few of their own scenes, and if Linklater liked what he read, says London, "we could take the B unit crew out and film it." Recalled Affleck years later, "And he was true to his word. I would write stuff, and it appeared in the movie. I felt empowered to have a voice in that, and it gave me the notion that you could make movies that way."[30]

"To me that's where I kind of decide what the movie's going to be, how to shoot it," Linklater says of rehearsals. The process allows him to spend time with the actors and lets them develop chemistry with their characters and one another. Clark Walker also sees the rehearsals as an indication of how much affection Linklater has for the characters in his movies. Their overall likability is another Linklater hallmark. "His films don't have bad guys. *Dazed* has cartoon bad guys, but he loves them just as much. After Ben Affleck's character gets humiliated, he's back at the party afterward. He went home and changed his clothes. Forgiveness abounds," Walker observes. "I called it the benevolent high school."[31]

Prior to any of the actors arriving in Austin for rehearsals, Linklater had made mix tapes with musical selections tailored to each character's personality as a way of prepping the actors for their roles. "I wanted them to own their characters, so I gave them music to listen to. 'Cynthia, you're listening to Joni Mitchell and Carole King, but Simone, you're listening to KC and the Sunshine Band,'" explained Linklater. "That's a great way to direct somebody, but allow their imagination to create their own vision and to embody the character," says McConaughey. Linklater's efforts also impressed Phillips. "Immediately they trusted him. They saw that he wasn't just their director. He was their mentor, and he was their big brother. He was all those things, and yet he was still a kid. He dressed like a kid and had this high-pitched voice. But he's a real leader."[32]

Once the actors were in Austin, Linklater asked them not to listen to any music that wasn't specific to the period. Even members of the crew steeped themselves in the 1970s, playing the cassettes while they built and dressed the various locations and sets. Linklater's attention to detail was so exact that no matter how much he liked a song, if it had been released *after* the month and year in which the movie takes place, he did not include it on the tapes.

This meticulous preparation meant little to Universal executives. Indeed, they viewed Linklater's requests for more rehearsal time as indulgent. Walker-McBay also noticed some red flags during preproduction. "Because of our inexperience, even though we hired the crew, we ended up with a first assistant director, John Cameron, and then Alma Kuttruff and then an accountant who sort of pulled together and didn't allow us any real authority. It was very disturbing and very frustrating because we were being ignored on a lot of stuff." As the first day of production drew closer, tensions increased between Linklater and the studio, particularly when word leaked to the filmmaker in Austin that the studio had labeled him "difficult." Despite his initial favorable impression of Jacks and Sean Daniel less than a year earlier, he now saw them as the enemy. "The lines are clearly drawn: all they care about is money and all I care about is wresting my movie from the jaws of their compromised, mediocrity machine."[33]

### Fighting the (Studio) System

Each day Linklater spent his meal breaks fighting to preserve the ambitious shot list, which amounted to a day and a half's worth of work condensed into one because of the reductions to the original shooting schedule. Recalls Walker-McBay, "From the beginning Rick always had in his mind that he wanted a helicopter shot for the last shot of the movie. The production managers would just never schedule it. Or, if [a shot] was in a montage and didn't have dialogue attached to it, they didn't see it as that important. Rick and I were like, 'Excuse me, that's the movie! At the beer bust scene, Wiley Wiggins walking through the party is as important as anything with dialogue.' But they want to check off 'Dialogue done' at the end of the day."[34]

In response, small "guerilla" groups of actors and one or two crew people would occasionally break away from the production and shoot scenes on the fly. "There's a camera off shooting actors in a parking lot somewhere," recalls Cameron, "and I'm like, 'Who's with the actors? Who from production knows about it?' And the response was, 'Nobody.'" In reality Cameron and Jacks were only a few years older than Linklater, Walker-McBay, and the other Austinites, but the great divide between the groups seemed almost generational. "I probably personified something of 'The Man' to Rick," says Cameron. "There's a little bit of 'fight the system' in Rick and Anne, and the system is such that it's a heavily unionized business. We were working with a lot of minors, and there were a lot of rules. I think Rick felt constrained sometimes by the system of making a studio picture."[35]

As was his style, Linklater vented his frustrations to Jacks in a handwritten memo. "Whether this is an okay movie or a great movie, your job is to enable me room to make a great movie. Two weeks in, I'm making a compromised piece of shit." On the same piece of paper Linklater included a list of what he perceived to be Jacks's flaws as a producer, which included his drinking and socializing with the cast and being too judgmental during dailies screenings. Members of the Austin crew began calling the producer Jim "Phone" Jacks behind his back because of the ever-present cell phone that seemed glued to his ear. Recalls the producer, "To be fair, it was my first movie after five years of being a studio executive. Sean Daniel and I had just started [the production company] Alphaville. So I was probably a little more on top of Rick than I would have been a few years later. It was very important that this movie do well and come in on budget."[36]

As a director Linklater liked to leave room for inspiration while filming, comfortable with the idea of going in a slightly different direction with a scene or line of dialogue if it improved the original idea. But on the *Dazed* set, there was little time for this kind of experimentation. He sensed disapproval from Cameron, the first A.D., if he did multiple takes of a scene. It didn't help matters that Lee Daniel barely communicated with Cameron and the other production heads from Los Angeles, which Cameron attributes in part to the fact that Daniel, like Linklater and the other *Slacker* crew members, had never worked with the kind of stratified crew common on studio productions. "I think Lee was new to that, so his ability to communicate what he needed was sometimes impeded by the feeling of this large structure," says Cameron. "Hollywood is make-believe land," insists Daniel of what he considered the studio's unrealistic expectations. "We have to do it and it has to come in on this budget. And we succeeded in that. But what we sacrificed is all the shots of the guys driving around endlessly to convey the message that there's nothing to do [in high school]."[37]

Linklater felt it was his job to protect the actors from the behind-the-scenes battles with the studio. "The only time I ever sensed tension was because I heard raised voices coming from the trailer one night," recalls McConaughey. One day, after Wiggins shot a scene, he watched as Linklater hurled a paper cup to the ground. "That was the extent of his showing his frustration at the other stuff that was going on," recalls the actor. "He created a bubble around us where we could just play and create these characters and come up with all sorts of interactions between them."[38]

Kuttruff admired Linklater's ability to work with the large ensemble cast and to encourage their participation. "When you think about that casting and the performances, it's like every young star came out of that movie." Although Zellweger didn't have a part per se, she was one of the young actors who most impressed the crew. "This spunky, young girl would continually present herself in front of us to do whatever we asked," recalls Cameron, who marveled at Zellweger's innate talent and sweetness. "A lot of the kids got bored and tired, but Renée stuck in our minds because she was always there and always willing to do anything we asked—fall down drunk, act silly, or walk into a tree—so we ended up putting her in a lot of different scenes. The beer bust, especially, because all of the other kids were asleep or they'd gone home or they were passed out behind the trees. It's one of the surprises of that film."[39]

Production proceeded apace into August with Linklater continuing to feel pressure about the shooting schedule, particularly from Jacks, who was on the Austin set for most of the shoot. Linklater bristled when Jacks suggested changes to two of the filmmaker's favorite scenes. One of the sequences involved the postgame ritual of baseball players lining up to say "good game" to one another and knock each other's mitts. To a former athlete like Linklater, the scene conveyed not only a sports ritual but also the deep camaraderie among athletes, a connection that transcends competition. To a budget-conscious producer like Jacks, the scene added little to the overall story and was expendable. When Jacks left the set to spend a week back in Los Angeles, Linklater reportedly put up a small photogaph of the agitated producer looking at his watch. "I think it was supposed to be sarcastic," says Jacks of the photo, which was taped to the side of Daniel's camera. "But actually I kind of liked that."[40]

Just when Linklater didn't think things could get any worse, he was told that Universal executives had objections to what they considered the overuse of foul language in the film. Indeed, most of the studio heads' original script notes had concerned the characters' swearing, and Jacks took issue with the language as well. "Rick just made the characters so profane. They said, 'You're trying to make this PG.' And I said, 'No, I'm not. I'm just trying not to make it *Mean Streets*. Kids in high school don't talk like they're New York street punks in the Sixties.'" At the time Linklater had remained noncommittal about making changes to the dialogue. Recalls Walker, who read the notes, "That was wonderful to see Rick learn how to give 'the Hollywood no,' which is to never actually say yes." When the expletives became an issue again in August, Linklater felt beaten down by what he considered to be Universal's ridiculous arguments that junior high school students didn't curse as much in 1976. The studio argued that they'd have difficulty booking the film into theaters in the South if the number of "fucks" wasn't reduced. Recalls Goldberg, "While we were shooting, we were protected from everything but [tensions over] the word 'fuck.' Jim Jacks would just brush right past Rick and tell us directly. I don't know how many 'fucks' it takes to get an X-rating, but I didn't understand what the issue was, exactly." Says Jacks, who graduated from high school in the mid-1970s, "It didn't seem real to me, but then again, I didn't hang out with kids who were potheads. Although I thought that was supposed to make you more mellow."[41]

That month they also shot the late-night beer bust sequence, which was the movie's penultimate scene and one of the most challenging to film. In the story it brought together the key characters as the various cliques and groups converged in a darkened field on the edge of town. Conflicts erupted and were resolved, and characters paired off romantically. The scene required most of the principal actors and many extras, all of whom waited around for night to fall before shooting could begin. One of the scene's highlights was the fistfight between Goldberg's Mike and Katt's much tougher character, Clint, which eventually was broken up by Wooderson and Pink. Sitting in his tiny dressing room before the first take, Goldberg psyched himself up by blasting Neil Young's "Cowgirl in the Sand" through his headphones. Many of the male actors were obsessed with Nicholas Ray's *Rebel without a Cause*, and the sequence seemed like a throwback to Ray's elegantly choreographed fistfights. "That was, to me, what [*Dazed*] was all about. And it was getting to do this thing I never did in real life," says Goldberg, who surprised himself and the filmmaker by bursting into tears at the end of the take, a spontaneous response that worked perfectly for his overly intellectual character.[42]

Said Linklater of the challenges inherent in the scene, "I wanted a montage sequence at the beer bust to give the essence of the party. But it's hard to script the essence of a party, and if you don't have it in the script, you don't have it on the shooting schedule." With only about a half hour to capture the sequence on film, Linklater and his crew re-created a party atmosphere with loud music and encouraged the actors to mill around. The filmmaker mixed among them, whispering directives as Daniel and various assistants recorded the action with multiple cameras. And in the background, with the cameras rolling, Jacks could be heard yelling into his cell phone. "You couldn't see him because it was pitch black and there were trees, but you could hear him yapping at somebody out in L.A.," recalls Fletcher.[43]

Principal photography concluded in the final weeks of August 1992, finishing only one day behind schedule. For many of the actors, the end of production marked the conclusion of one of the best experiences of their professional—and personal—lives. Because Linklater was shooting mostly in sequence, one of the last scenes to be filmed was also one of *Dazed*'s final scenes. After the party, Pink and his pals meet on the football field to decide whether or not he should sign the anti-drug pledge for his coaches. While the quarterback anguishes over the situation, Wooderson puts the experience in perspective when he offers some advice to Pink and his running buddies.

McConaughey, moved by the death of his father, who had passed away suddenly during the production, was in a philosophical state of mind when he and Linklater discussed the scene just prior to shooting. Recalled McConaughey, "And he reminded me that one time I had gone to him and said, 'Well, basically, man, it's just about livin', isn't it? Just keep livin'.' So we went out there and we shot it, and it became the thing that Wooderson told 'Pink.'"[44]

## They Didn't Get *Dazed* at All

The next two months on the movie would be for Linklater a stark contrast to the unpleasantness of the previous summer. He had resisted Universal's suggestions to hire an editor out of Los Angeles and instead brought in Sandra Adair, a seasoned cutter who had just recently moved back to Austin from California. "It was kind of a political thing on my part," says Linklater of hiring Adair, which would keep the movie in Austin for the bulk of its postproduction. "I was nervous about making a studio film."[45]

In 1991 Adair and her husband, Dwight, a UT RTF graduate and freelance filmmaker, returned to Austin to raise their two young children in the city where Adair had spent part of her childhood. Looking for work, Adair heard that the filmmaker who had made *Slacker* was directing his first studio movie. She wrote a letter to Linklater and mentioned that she knew how to cut on the relatively new nonlinear editing systems beginning to be used in Hollywood. Weeks later she met with Linklater and Walker-McBay. Linklater had recently purchased an EMC, the first digital video nonlinear editing system designed to work with personal computers, and he was anxious to use it on *Dazed*. When Adair flew out to L.A. to interview with Jacks and Daniel, they made her promise to edit on film rather than video. "You can use the EMC to cut montages or whatever it is you guys want to use it for, but you've got to promise us if that thing doesn't work, you'll tie it to the back of your car and drag it around the streets of Austin," they told her.[46]

Adair's team included long-time editor and Austinite Sheri Galloway, who was married to Ivan Bigley of Texas Motion Picture Service. By the 1990s Bigley had worked with three generations of Austin filmmakers, and he ran dailies for *Dazed* at TMPS in North Austin. Documentary filmmaker Don Howard also assisted in post. Linklater relished the "cooperative and creative" mood in the editing room, a stark contrast to his experience on the set itself.[47]

As Adair and the others sculpted the first cut from the footage, they began to zero in on Mitch, Wiley Wiggins's character. "Sometime in that first cut, I saw the glimmer of it being Mitch's story," Adair recalls. "If it was in the script, it didn't reveal itself the way it did when Wiley Wiggins took on the character."[48] Indeed, the story as scripted by Linklater pivoted on Pink. But

Wiggins's quietly memorable performance, which gave Mitch an unexpected sweetness and captured the awkward transition between junior high geekiness and high school conformity, stood out on-screen.

By the end of October Adair and her assistants had completed a rough cut. After struggling with the multiple characters' plotlines, Adair and Linklater decided to intercut the various stories so that the plotlines appeared to be happening simultaneously, which picked up the pace of the overall film. Linklater was happy with the edit, but he knew it ran too long and dreaded the process of cutting more scenes to bring it to an acceptable length. "I saw an early rough cut that was 30–45 minutes longer than the original film. We probably edited *Dazed* more than any other film," says Walker-McBay.[49]

While Adair was working on the edit, Linklater turned his attention to the task of securing *Dazed*'s many song clearances. Harry Garfield, a music supervisor based in Los Angeles, oversaw the process. Linklater planned to use thirty songs in the film, which pushed the project about $200,000 over its official budget. Although he had compromised on other aspects of the movie, Linklater stood firm on his music choices and was willing to do whatever it took to secure the carefully chosen songs.

By the end of November 1992, the film was ready for its first preview. Linklater traveled to Dallas for the screening, which was held in a theater in a suburban shopping center. The theater wasn't full, but Linklater noticed that the audience reacted positively to the movie. Their response cards told a different story. In the movie's defense, Linklater pointed out to Universal that the screening conflicted with a Dallas Cowboys football game, which may have explained the lackluster attendance. The studio was nonplussed, and they decided that Linklater and his editing team should relocate to Los Angeles to complete postproduction on the film. It was a decision, according to Jacks, that said less about Universal's view of the film at that point than the studio's general desire to keep tabs on its projects. Recalls Jacks, "If nothing else, they feel like it intimidates the filmmaker to make [the film] a little more like they want it. The problem was, in Rick's case, he reacted the other way—to make it less like they wanted." Linklater resented the studio's justification that the move was for the good of the film and disagreed with their philosophy that comedies could be made in post. "I never got this thing that a director doesn't know where his joke is. If a director is not editing in his head as he goes, then he doesn't have a film anyway."[50]

The preview and Universal's dictum that they finish the film in Los Angeles ended the year on a sour note, but Linklater tried to remain upbeat. In January 1993 he and Adair flew to California and took up residence in

168

a building of depressing apartment suites. "It's rare to ever have a conversation with anyone there," Linklater recalled. "People just have these dull distant stares as they pass each other in the halls like ghosts in the night." Says Adair, "It's like the exact opposite of Austin."[51]

Their workspace was not much better. The studio assigned the editing team to a deserted, decrepit building at the very back of the Universal lot. In the studio's heyday it had housed the wardrobe department, and Adair's assistants would take breaks and riffle through old costumes stored on the upper floors. The weeks dragged on as the film went through multiple preview screenings. "We'd preview the film and then we would wait, like, a week. They we'd get notes, and then we'd make the changes in a day. So we'd have to remix the film and wait for another preview. In between each set of changes there'd be these big gaps of waiting. And I think that that made it seem like it was a really long post," says Adair.[52]

Linklater's outlook continued to dim when he learned that the Universal executives were giving serious thought to releasing *Dazed* through Gramercy Pictures, the studio's relatively new distribution company. Gramercy was created in 1992 to distribute Universal's smaller-budget films and its "specialty" releases. Russell Schwartz, who had been an executive vice president at Miramax, was chosen to run Gramercy. "There were a lot of grumblings inside Universal about what to do with the movie, and I respected that. I know a lot of the production execs just wanted to get rid of it. They didn't get [*Dazed and Confused*] at all," says Schwartz.[53]

Explains Jacks, "Gramercy was a relatively new entity at the time, and Universal was selling it like it was going to be Miramax. And you think, 'Miramax handling *Dazed and Confused* would be a great idea.' The way Universal explained it was Gramercy was going to give the movie this really good handling."[54] But the news infuriated Linklater, who imagined his follow-up to *Slacker* having a much wider audience. Although *Dazed* certainly had its Texas focus, the movie's themes of high school conformity and peer pressure and its coming-of-age rituals transcended any kind of regionalism. Linklater also believed that a wide release would somewhat justify all of the struggles he had endured while making the movie.

Linklater learned another lesson in studio politics when he discovered that during production the studio had been unimpressed with the dailies. "They were concerned that Rick wasn't getting enough coverage," says Adair. "The way Rick shoots, his whole style is to do long takes that have a beginning, middle, and end. That was his style on *Slacker*, and some of the coverage for *Dazed* was similar. The executives sitting at the studio are thinking,

'We've got to be able to cut this as a faster/funnier/stupider comedy, we need close-ups, we need inserts, we need medium shots. We need tons of coverage so we can get in there and cut it up." Admits Jacks, "I don't think Universal ever quite got the movie. Even when they saw the finished movie, I don't think they quite got it." After an early morning screening for a handful of Universal executives, the response was cautiously encouraging but essentially noncommittal.[55]

A marketing meeting in early February only heightened Linklater's disgust. When someone floated a question about the film's release date, he couldn't believe what he was hearing. It made complete sense to Linklater to open the movie around the end of the school year to match the time period of the movie. Schwartz's observation that a May release gave Gramercy less than adequate time to prepare nearly sent Linklater through the roof. "Is this going to be the same wall of indifference and outright incompetence I encountered at the end of my *Slacker* journey (via the Orion Home Video idiots)?" he wondered. The marketing meeting concluded with a decision to release *Dazed* in September 1993. Linklater braced himself for another six months of battle.[56]

## Lose the Songs or Cover the Costs

He spent the next few months focusing on the movie's soundtrack. Universal decided to let its own music division, MCA Records, handle the album and its release. Linklater met with Kathy Nelson, who headed up the label's soundtrack division, only to be told that a double CD would be out of the question, and the soundtrack could feature only 11 songs (less than half of what he had envisioned) because of royalty issues. Linklater argued the soundtrack's case. "People are going to watch this film, and then they're going to *not* have all of this music unless they go back and tediously buy all this stuff. The soundtrack will actually be a good place to get a lot of that music." He projected that a *Dazed* album could do very well. "It's like a one-stop shopping for all that music that people of a certain age just don't have," he reasoned. Universal disagreed, pointing to the recent *Reservoir Dogs* soundtrack, which they claimed hadn't sold well despite the movie's tremendous success.[57]

When he wasn't dealing with details surrounding the movie, Linklater tried to keep busy in Los Angeles. "I was miserable," recalls Linklater of his time in L.A. "That was a low point, but I think part of me wanted to have a bad time so I wouldn't be tempted to work out there. 'Fuck this place.' I had a real chip on my shoulder, I think, as far as getting along." Remembers his friend Kim Krizan, who kept in touch with Linklater by phone during post-production, "They stuck him in an apartment complex where, it seemed, they stick directors they're mad at. He sounded pretty beaten down and kind of depressed."[58]

At some point during his three-month stay in Los Angeles, Linklater heard from Garfield that Nelson wanted to have the heavy metal band Jackyl re-record a Seventies song for the album. They could then release the track as a single and cross-promote the movie with a music video and, more important for record sales, gain radio airplay. The idea reeked of marketing to Linklater. It also violated the musical guidelines he had so carefully devised before production even started: songs had to reflect the time period of the movie and could not be used if they had been released after May 1976. "Kathy Nelson was the one actively trying to fuck with me and the film, certainly through the soundtrack," says Linklater. Recalls Walker-McBay, "It felt like a big betrayal. From the beginning, any time we had a meeting with anybody, it was 'We want original music from the period. We don't want to cover anything.' So for Jim [Jacks] and Sean [Daniel] to go and make this whole deal based on sticking in this bad cover for our closing credit song, it was really insulting."[59]

Although Linklater may have tried to protect his cast from the behind-the-scenes battles with Jacks and the studio, he chose a different tack once postproduction began. "We became much more aware of the tensions afterwards when Rick would write us these letters," recalls Goldberg. "He would be very honest with us about his struggles with the studio, largely regarding the music."[60]

Other news put Linklater in a much better frame of mind. He found out that Led Zeppelin guitarist Jimmy Page had agreed to let them use "Rock and Roll" on the *Dazed* soundtrack. He considered this a huge victory given the band's notoriously stingy policy about permissions for their songs. Despite having been told "no" many times over, the savvy filmmaker had created a five-minute videotaped "letter" requesting to use the song and arguing his case. He sent the tape along with a copy of the scene to show exactly how the music would work within the movie. In response, Page communicated to Garfield that he did indeed understand why the song needed to be used and that it was "important to the artist's vision."[61]

In May, Linklater attended yet another preview set up by the studio in part because audience feedback to previous screenings hadn't been good. "They were sort of right in the middle," says Schwartz of the responses up to that point. "They were not bad enough to say, 'This movie's horrible. Let's forget it.' And they were not good enough to say, 'We should really push it.'

It sort of falls into a void of half-assed support. And that's a bad place for a movie to be." This time, however, the audience clicked with the movie, a connection helped in part by a more polished sound mix. Linklater savored the congratulatory remarks offered by the many studio executives who attended the successful Marina del Rey screening. After months of feeling like the lone voice in the wilderness, he viewed their support as an affirmation of his original vision for the movie. Assistant director Cameron, who saw a final cut at some point in L.A., loved the film. "I have never liked it more than the first time I saw it," recalls the A.D. "I thought, 'Oh, he really *does* know what he's doing.'" Despite three difficult months living out of a suitcase at the depressing Oakwood Apartments, Linklater left California feeling upbeat about the film.[62]

He had another reason to celebrate. Later that month Linklater's first child was born in San Miguel de Allende, Mexico. He and Tina Harrison, whom he had first started dating in 1991, welcomed their daughter Lorelei on May 29. Linklater had met Harrison on Labor Day weekend in 1991, just a few days before leaving for L.A. to pitch *Dazed* to Jacks and Sean Daniel. Harrison, at the time a graduate student in the art department at UT–Austin, ran into Linklater at a concert featuring local hardcore punk band Moist Fist ("She likes to tell that story," he laughs).[63]

Upon returning to Austin in early June, Linklater recalls, he felt cheerful and optimistic. But he had barely unpacked when he heard that Jackyl had proceeded to record "We're an American Band" by Grand Funk Railroad, which the music executives suggested could appear over *Dazed*'s closing credits. He fired off daily faxes to Nelson to make his case that a video featuring images of the cover band coupled with clips from the movie would misrepresent the film's story. In response, the executives argued that the re-recording would bring in a younger audience for the movie, encourage Universal to put more muscle behind the film's release, and boost record sales of the soundtrack. Says Jacks, "It was about a song that was over the back half of the closing credits! I said, 'You know, people will have decided whether they like this movie by then.' And Rick's argument was they were going to do a music video and that'll be the song people hear, and it's a cover song. He was probably right about that, but then you would have had publicity. It's an arguable point."[64] Eventually the executives in charge of the album turned a deaf ear to Linklater's protests. His phone calls went unreturned.

He flew back to Los Angeles to meet with Nelson in early June. It was in this meeting that Linklater was told that Jackyl's recording of the song had been written into the terms of the soundtrack deal. Although Linklater believed on some level that Nelson and all of the other corporate executives thought they were making decisions that benefited *Dazed*, he felt betrayed and swallowed whole by the corporate machine that, in his mind, had replaced the Hollywood studio system.

One bright spot was *Dazed*'s screening at the Seattle Film Festival, where three years earlier *Slacker* had finally found an audience beyond Austin. Linklater's follow-up was warmly received at the festival although its first industry review in *Daily Variety* ran hot and cold. "Richard Linklater's followup to his no-budget 'Slacker' is sure to attract support from urban Gen-Xers," it began, but the critic also noted that the film's "unrelieved nihilism" (the hazing, "rampant" pot smoking, and "f-word frenzy") might keep it from its target audience in mall movie theaters, an observation that no doubt irked the Universal executives who had lobbied against the script's drug use and foul language during production a year earlier. The reviewer also criticized the film's large ensemble but praised the actors' performances, prophetically observing, "In the sense of career-launching potential, 'Dazed' could be a 'Diner' for the '90s." Given his actual behind-the-scenes struggle over *Dazed*'s music, Linklater could take some solace in the review's praise of the movie's "pivotal" soundtrack.[65]

Back in Austin, Linklater made one last-ditch effort to remedy the soundtrack stalemate with MCA. His most recent Los Angeles meetings had left him feeling helpless and cut off from the project. He decided to appeal to Jackyl directly and wrote a letter to its members explaining his position. After all, it had worked with Jimmy Page.

The letter was a success of sorts. The band decided not to participate in the project, which also meant that the terms of the original album deal had been violated. "We were both really pleased and surprised when they pulled out based on that letter," recalls Walker-McBay. But with the cover song and music video no longer part of the package, the entire deal fell through. Says Jacks of Linklater, "He basically cost us our music deal, which was a substantial way we were going to pay for all the music. Sean and I had to give up $500,000, part of our back end, to pay for the music." Although Linklater doesn't recall that Jacks and Daniel had to relinquish a portion of their back-end profits, he admits that that could have been the case. But, he adds, "Everyone can say they gave up back end, but I don't really know if there was a back end to give up." MCA's executives placed the blame squarely on Linklater's shoulders, but all the filmmaker felt was relief. He had succeeded in protecting the integrity of his movie. Now all he had to do was find another label to produce and release the soundtrack.[66]

But more bad news was on its way. Two months before the movie's scheduled September release, Linklater learned that he would have to cut "Rock and Roll" from the film. Despite Jimmy Page's support for the project, neither Led Zeppelin frontman Robert Plant nor his handlers were moved by the director's impassioned video plea. With only two days left before the final sound mix, Linklater admitted defeat. Although his second-choice song, Foghat's "Slow Ride," proved to be a more than suitable replacement, providing an effective musical bridge between the movie's final shots and the closing credits, he struggled to accept the fact that the situation hadn't turned in his favor. "I've never worked so hard for something like this and not gotten it," he reflected at the time.[67]

Before the end of July, a relatively new music label showed interest in the soundtrack. Medicine Label was formed in 1992 as an imprint of Giant Records, a label that had begun to expand its soundtrack division and was partially owned by Warner Bros. Records. Larry Jacobson was an ambitious young attorney for Giant who had first heard about the soundtrack a year earlier from his sister Nina, a senior vice president of production at Universal and the executive in charge on *Dazed*. Jacobson, who had grown up in California and graduated from Palisades High School in the mid-1970s, related to the story. Through his sister, he kept tabs on the project until one day in the summer of 1993, she mentioned that the soundtrack might be in distress. "She went back to the office and she spoke to their head of music supervision and he called me immediately," says Jacobson. "The story goes that at MCA, the suits there had seen the movie and didn't get it. But they were committed to paying a lot of money for the rights to the soundtrack. In other words, they still had to pay for it. And they didn't feel it was worth that much."[68]

Jacobson arranged to screen the movie, and he responded to the soundtrack even more. "The music really reflected those times. 'Stranglehold' by Ted Nugent was a classic album track, six to seven minutes long. It was perfect. That was the brilliance of what Rick did. He didn't just understand the hits of the time. He understood the songs that really did comprise the album of our lives at the time." The attorney had no experience bringing in a record, so he brought the company's head of marketing to see the movie. "And he went back and reported to [Giant owner] Irving [Azoff] that it was a great movie, and I got the greenlight to go ahead and try to get it."[69]

Although Medicine specialized in alternative acts, it made an offer for the *Dazed* soundtrack. The original advance proffered by MCA, according to Jacks, was around $750,000. Jacks says Giant then offered $100,000, but

Jacobson claims the advance was "significantly less." ("I always heard Azoff got the soundtrack for $35,000," says Gramercy's Schwartz.) According to Linklater, the advance shrunk even more after MCA's Nelson made a phone call to share her thoughts about the project. But if Nelson had called Giant, says Jacobson, she would have called Azoff. "The advance to my recollection was a reflection that the movie, in terms of its soundtrack rights, in terms of their pure value on the free market, had gone down because there were no buyers."[70]

A reduced advance meant more money was needed to pay for the rights to each song. Universal stepped in and demanded that Linklater cut some of the songs, including Bob Dylan's "Hurricane," which cost around $80,000. Linklater flew to Los Angeles to discuss the situation with his lawyer, John Sloss.

Together they spent two days trying to negotiate with Universal, but the studio offered only two alternatives: lose the songs or cover the costs. The money that had been saved during production, which Linklater believed he could use in post to pay for the music costs, no longer existed. It had been spent on overages incurred while editing in L.A., on preview screenings, and on other expenses Linklater considered wasteful and unnecessary. Although the studio had at one time promised to make good on the money they had originally cut from the film's budget a year earlier, they explained to Linklater that the collapse of the album deal with MCA negated this promise. With the release date less than two months away, the clock was ticking. The studio upped the ante, threatening to replace six songs with "Seventies-sounding guitar licks." After learning that this music already had been recorded, Linklater realized that they would indeed remove the specific songs. He felt just like Mitch and his junior high friends being hazed in *Dazed*. "I'm living through an abuse of power that is in every way analogous to that depicted in the film," he observed.[71]

Eventually the studio presented another option: they would supply the money if Linklater would relinquish his soundtrack royalties.

### Neither Fish Nor Fowl

This solution clearly didn't favor Linklater, but he could live with it if it meant the movie was protected. With the final mix nearly finished, Linklater began to breathe easier. The end of the summer also involved more meetings about the marketing of the movie. The filmmaker didn't completely understand Gramercy's campaign, which pivoted on the idea of pitching *Dazed* as a "pro-reefer movie" and featured a stoned-looking smiley face on the poster. "I hated that smiley face," says Walker-McBay. "We had a really cool black light poster that [well-known poster artist] Frank Kozik made for us that they wouldn't pay any attention to." Not surprisingly, Linklater thought Gramercy was underselling the movie. "I sensed there was a much bigger market than they were ever attempting to go after. To me [the marketing campaign] was just going for the lowest elements of the stupid teen comedy/party movie." Explains Schwartz of the marketing budget, which was reported to be $3 million, "Universal gave the movie to Gramercy, but it was always with a moderate amount of support in terms of how much money is available for P[rints] & A[dvertising]. We realized if it's going to work, you've got to sell it to the kids. The whole stoner mentality was very much alive and still drifting from the Eighties, and we wanted to go out pretty aggressively."[72]

He continues, "At the same time, the movie was not a teenage romp per se. It was obviously a much smarter, much better-made movie. So the question, in Universal's mind, was whether it was an art movie or a commercial movie. We pushed for commercial. They did not want to spend the commercial support."[73]

*Dazed and Confused* played in the Toronto Film Festival's "Midnight Madness" program in mid-September 1993. Linklater flew to Toronto to do press for the film, and he wasn't shy about airing his dirty laundry with Universal. In talking about the film's rather harsh depiction of high school hazing, the filmmaker compared the ritual to his own experience while making the movie. "I got beat up on this film because I'm the new kid," he explained. "You're nobody until you prove yourself. You have this trial by initiation."[74]

Gramercy ran print and television advertisements one week prior to *Dazed and Confused*'s opening on September 24 but was forced to retool its copy when the Motion Picture Association of America (MPAA) objected to the ads' suggestive references to drug use ("Finally! A Movie for Everyone Who DID Inhale!") and a witty pull quotation from an *Us Weekly* magazine advance review that read, "Deliciously accurate in its portrayal of the generation that fell between LSD and R.E.M." The new print copy featured a less obvious drug reference ("See it with a bud . . .") and glowing quotes from seven advance reviews (but not from *Us Weekly*), including the mass-market stamp of approval, "Two thumbs up" from Gene Siskel and Roger Ebert.[75] The ad also touted the *Dazed* companion book, a "nostalgic scrapbook" published by St. Martin's Press, which hoped to capitalize on the movie in the same profitable way they had with the *Slacker* book a year earlier. Linklater cohort D. Montgomery oversaw the production of the *Dazed* book, but its jumbled collection of essays "written" by the movie's characters and 1976-specific nostalgic references lacked any real point other than to push the movie. Unlike the comprehensive *Slacker* companion piece, the *Dazed* book didn't offer coveted behind-the-scenes information.

On the Thursday before the film's release, the *Austin Chronicle* published a feature article comprised of lengthy excerpts from Linklater's diary, which he kept during the making of the movie. The six-page piece spared virtually no one connected to Universal and was at times scathingly funny and blisteringly candid in recounting Linklater's trials and tribulations during the production, editing, and marketing phases of the project. His disclaimer at the very end ("I know this one piece of venting brain-snot in no real way credits the many people who made *Dazed* what it is") did little to temper the rather obvious "fuck you" tone of the piece. Linklater claims to have thought few people outside of Austin would read the excerpt and was surprised to get a phone call from his father, who lived in Oregon and had read an article that described the excerpt as "career-ending." After getting a hold of the *Chronicle* piece out in Los Angeles, an angry Jacks confronted Linklater long distance. "I said, 'I know that we had our differences making this, but basically I thought we were on the same side.'" To Jacks the article was more posturing from Linklater. "He was just puffing out his chest, saying, 'They didn't scare me.'" But in reality the producer's feelings were hurt, and when he expressed this to Linklater, he says, the filmmaker wasn't sympathetic. "When you really work hard for something, and then somebody acts like, 'We made it despite you,' you're like, 'Bullshit. This movie's a lot better because of me.' And I was justified because his next three movies weren't nearly as good."[76]

Producer's representative John Pierson understood from working with Linklater on *Slacker* that the filmmaker often expressed himself by leaving a "written trail." Says Pierson of the published *Dazed* journal, "That was pretty out there for a relative newcomer, but it was honest in the best possible way and probably educational as well."[77]

The following day, on September 24, *Dazed* opened in limited release, playing in fourteen cities (including college towns like Madison, Wisconsin) and showing on 183 screens. On its first weekend, the $6.9 million movie grossed a solid if unimpressive $865,000 and landed at number thirteen in the weekend's Top 20 highest-grossing films at the box office. The studio, says Schwartz, was hoping for a per screen average between $5,000 and $7,000. The reviews generally were positive. Not surprisingly, more than a few critics mentioned *American Graffiti*, a comparison that actually irked Linklater, who believed that *Dazed* was much more cynical and less commercial than

George Lucas's 1973 hit. *New Yorker* critic Anthony Lane appreciated the difference: "If *American Graffiti* turned high jinks into epiphanies, *Dazed and Confused* moves in the opposite direction: fuelled by joints, the characters yearn for significant events that never quite arrive." And Dave Kehr, writing in the *New York Daily News,* said *Dazed* was "smarter and tougher" than the Lucas film, "but just as much fun."[78]

Comparisons to *Rebel without a Cause* also cropped up. But unlike Nicholas Ray and other directors who "looked back on their adolescence," said the *Village Voice,* Linklater was able to depict teenagers without moralizing. *Rolling Stone*'s Peter Travers also praised *Dazed and Confused*'s accurate depiction of high school horrors: "Linklater, 31, is a sly and formidable talent, bringing an anthropologist's eye to this spectacularly funny celebration of the rites of stupidity." The young filmmaker's "deceptively laid-back style," wrote the *Boston Globe,* "proves that Linklater is a man with more than one film in him."[79]

The movie was also getting rave reviews from its cast. A formative experience for many of the young actors, *Dazed* represented all that they hoped their acting career would bring, including creative collaboration with a promising director and an intense off-screen bonding experience that cemented friendships. Back in L.A., Goldberg, Katt, McConaughey, Rory Cochrane, and Cole Hauser continued to hang out and went to see the movie often during its theatrical release. Toward the end of its run, the group showed up for a midnight screening at the Beverly Center. Remembers Goldberg, "We were the only people in there and we were smoking and drinking beer. It was just like we couldn't get enough of it. And I think that goes for everybody [in the cast]. We were talking about it for the entire year that it took to come out."[80]

Despite the majority of good reviews, Universal considered the movie a flop after it returned just $7.9 million at the box office, only about $1 million more than its production costs. "If it had done $40 million domestic, it would have made it profitable," says Jacks. "But it was never in the cards. The distribution pattern was god awful. The movie actually did business. It got incredible reviews. We had such good reviews, but they weren't prepared to broaden [the release]. They were caught with their pants down because they didn't expect it to be a hit," says Jacks.[81]

"We didn't have enough money to really sell it," counters Schwartz. "And at the same time, the problem with a release pattern like that is it's neither fish nor fowl. You're not wide enough to be wide, and you're too wide to be exclusive."[82]

### It's Not About the Money, Man

Linklater had had high hopes for the film but by this time understood that the studio had basically dumped it by restricting its initial release. In print, at least, he waxed philosophical about *Dazed*'s box office performance. "It doesn't change how you feel about it. Or shouldn't," he told a reporter for the *Houston Chronicle* a few weeks before the movie opened. "That's a real Hollywood thing. A film's not very good, but if it makes a lot of money it becomes better. Or vice versa. That's how the industry thinks. Rule No. 1 in Hollywood is never mention films that didn't make it."[83]

Ben Affleck, for one, took note of the filmmaker's relatively indifferent response to the movie's disappointing box office performance. Linklater seemed to measure a movie's success in other terms. Years later Affleck observed, "He had a '70s deal going on, a kind of anti-authoritarian, throw-back mentality, like, It's not about the money, man, people liked the movie."[84]

People did like *Dazed*, which stayed in theaters through March 1994 but played on fewer than three hundred screens even during its widest release. Recalls Walker-McBay, "It's funny because so often I run into people who think that *Dazed* was a theatrical success, and it wasn't at all. But that's the perception. It just took years on video [to become a success]." Linklater bumped into Parker Posey in New York a couple of months after *Dazed and Confused*'s theatrical release, and she told him a story that hinted at the movie's burgeoning popularity. She had attended a Halloween party and was shocked to see another guest dressed as Darla, her character from the movie. Years later, high school teenagers and college students would continue to discover the movie on video—despite another minimal release—and host *Dazed* parties complete with drinking games predicated on the characters' idiosyncrasies.[85]

The film rounded out *Rolling Stone*'s 1993 Top Ten list by Peter Travers, who placed the "acutely observant comedy" next to picks like *Schindler's List* and *The Piano*. Reflects Jacks, "*Dazed and Confused* should have been a giant success, and we would have made a lot of money. We didn't and the studio didn't. What happened was the record company made a lot of money."[86]

Despite its ominous drama during production, the *Dazed and Confused* soundtrack did indeed prove very successful. "From the time the movie came out in September to March when it was put out on video, we sold 125,000 records, give or take," says Jacobson. "All of the other millions that were sold? Started the day the video came out. We're talking massive sales once that video came out."[87] The album went double platinum and was so profitable that in 1994 it spawned a sequel of sorts, *Even More Dazed and Confused*. The second soundtrack featured twelve tracks, more of the same from Edgar Winter, Foghat, Black Oak Arkansas, and Peter Frampton. It eventually went gold.

The albums' success didn't surprise Linklater, but it did offer bittersweet affirmation. "Universal gave away the *Dazed* album. Boom—double-platinum album. They gave it away for no money because they didn't think it would do well. They released the film minimally, they undershipped the video. You get these confirmations when the album *does* go double platinum. You think, 'Okay, I think I was right. I'm not living in my own self-deluded world.'" Jacks estimates that fifty thousand units ("not very many") were shipped upon *Dazed*'s video release in January 1995. "They sold it in dribs and drabs. And even after the movie became a bigger deal, they dropped the ball on video."[88]

But by the end of 1993, Linklater already had moved on to his next project. While promoting *Dazed* in October the filmmaker had revealed that one idea under consideration involved two people who meet while traveling on a Eurail train. Soured on Hollywood, he planned to return to his DIY roots with a low-budget, two-character romance co-scripted by friend Kim Krizan. Walker-McBay and Lee Daniel signed on as producer and director of photography, respectively. Linklater would spend nine months casting the leads, and in the summer of 1994, he and a small production crew traveled to Austria to begin shooting *Before Sunrise*.

### Life Imitating Art: The South by Southwest and Austin Film Festivals

By the fall of 1993 the heightened drama and bad behavior that played out among the high school characters in Linklater's *Dazed and Confused* was about to take place off-screen in Austin's film community. In mid-September Barbara Morgan and Marsha Milam approached Texas Film Commission Executive Director Marlene Saritzky about an idea they had for starting a film festival in Austin. Morgan and Milam knew practically nothing about the film industry, but they were both ambitious and successful local businesswomen.

Morgan graduated from UT in the early 1980s with a degree in math and started a finance company whose clients included radio and television stations. Eventually she got involved in booking musical acts and had great success in 1993 with a thirty-five-city tour that exported Austin to the rest of the country and featured local musicians David Halle, Jimmy LaFave, Jo Carol Pierce, and Michael Fracasso.[89]

Milam also first came to Austin as an undergraduate, studying education at the university and graduating in 1979. Eventually she became director of promotions and public relations for Chuy's Restaurants, a successful regional Tex-Mex franchise, and she had a reputation for being able to put together an impressive affair. She and Morgan met through mutual friends, and after Morgan had developed a business plan she approached Milam about co-founding the festival.

The initial idea for their festival came from a radio station owner and friend of Morgan's who remarked that it seemed strange that a movie-friendly city like Austin lacked a film festival. But in reality Austin did have a film festival by 1993.

Five years earlier Dobie Theatre owner Scott Dinger had started the Austin Gay and Lesbian International Film Festival (AGLIFF). When Dinger first purchased the two-screen theater on the edge of the UT campus in 1984, the university film series—so integral to the film education of students and residents alike since the 1970s—were just beginning to feel the effects of the blossoming home video market. Dinger programmed the Dobie with movies like *Brazil* and *Blue Velvet* that wouldn't necessarily go over at the more mainstream theaters in town. "I began cultivating that little niche," says Dinger, who had first supported the Austin Film Society by allowing Richard Linklater and Lee Daniel to screen films at midnight.[90] Dinger, who started packaging individual films by theme, once again took a chance in 1988 when he decided to book an unknown British drama called *The Everlasting Secret Family*. He wanted to program the gay-themed movie but wasn't convinced he should tie up one of the theater's two screens for an entire week. Drawing on his past successes with packaging separate titles, he decided to program three other similarly themed films and bill the series as a gay and lesbian film festival.

"This thing just built," Dinger recalls of the crowds that seemed to come out of nowhere. Even when an ice storm hit the city on the festival's final day and a water pipe broke inside the theater, a larger-than-normal audience still turned out for the final screenings.[91]

AGLIFF was preceded by several other Austin festivals like Eagle Pennell and Maureen Gosling's Change the Reel in 1975 and the Austin Fantasy Film Festival. This latter festival ran for a couple of years; in 1976 it featured seventeen films including *Invasion of the Body Snatchers* and *Vampire Lovers*, six episodes of *Star Trek,* and numerous special guests, like a sculptor who worked with famed special effects veteran Ray Harryhausen. The Texas Film Festival was held two years later on the UT campus. Sponsored by the university, the Austin Film & Video Society, and the Texas Education Agency, the first Texas Film Festival featured video and filmmaking seminars and screenings with filmmakers in attendance. In the early 1980s the Heart of Texas Film Festival also began to screen local work on an annual basis. In 1986 the festival featured Linklater and Daniel's *Woodshock*, a documentary about a local music festival. That same year Liatris Media held its first Third Wave International Women's Film and Video Festival, which would occur annually through 1990. The festival adopted a global approach and showcased films by women, gay and lesbian filmmakers, and Third World artists. Unlike AGLIFF, however, which continued to flourish, the other festivals typically ran for no more than a handful of years before economics or management shifts led to their demise.[92]

By the fall of 1993 when Morgan and Milam first approached Saritzky, AGLIFF was Austin's only long-running film festival. But instead of organizing their festival around films or filmmakers, Morgan and Milam decided on a different approach. Fred Miller, who had produced *Peter, Paul & Mary: Song Is Love* (1970) with Tobe Hooper and had done some research on film festivals throughout the country, suggested they focus their event on screenwriters as a way to distinguish the festival from others then popping up around the country.[93] They named it the Republic of Texas Film Festival and scheduled the event for the following April.

In September 1993 Morgan and Milam invited Saritzky to dinner. They proposed their idea and shared their business plan. "What Barbara and Marsha were trying to do was create something that was different, that wasn't just a film festival, where people could really hear from the pros about the craft of screenwriting. They wanted to be associated with the best screenwriters, the people who were sort of revered," recalls Saritzky.[94]

Shortly after that evening, Saritzky was having dinner at *Austin Chronicle* editor Louis Black's house. As Black remembers it, "I mentioned that we were going to start a film festival. Marlene sort of turned six different shades. It turned out that Marsha and Barbara had approached her, and she had forgotten that we planned to do one. They had a business plan, stuff like that, and so it was one of these deals where I just went back and just started freaking out and feeling like, 'Hey wait. *We're* doing this.'"[95]

By 1993 the South by Southwest Music Festival (SXSW), which Black and *Chronicle* publisher Nick Barbaro had helped to create in 1987, had become a success. Inspired in part by New York's New Music Seminar, the festival of musical showcases and conference panels fairly quickly made a name for itself. For years Black had been telling everyone, including Saritzky, that SXSW was going to incorporate a film component. He had talked about the idea so frequently—but without acting on it—that he had become convinced that people were no longer taking it or him seriously.

The behind-the-scenes showdown between the proposed festivals went public in an October 22 *Austin American-Statesman* article entitled "Coming Soon: 'Clash of the Film Fests.'" Written by *Statesman* film critic (and Morgan's good friend) Michael MacCambridge, the article stated that both groups had revealed plans that week to start film festivals in 1994. MacCambridge interviewed all of the participants, including Saritzky, who were on their best behavior in print. Black claimed, a bit disingenuously, that while the SXSW founders had always wanted to incorporate a film festival, they decided just that summer to hold the first festival the following year.[96]

Saritzky had arranged a meeting between Black and Morgan in an attempt to broker some peace. The newspaper article described the meeting as an attempt to get the separate festival directors to consider collaborating. But in actuality at their meeting days earlier, Black seemed to have made it clear, at least to Morgan, that there would be no room in Austin for both festivals. "In his words, 'We're the festival people in this town. Who are you?,'" Morgan recalls.[97]

Black admits to making stupid, juvenile comments at the time. "I just didn't want them to do it. *I* wanted to have the film festival. I think it was because it was my territory. This was just primal. I was just a jerk. Any version you hear that makes me sound like a jerk is accurate," he says more than a decade later.[98]

Not only did the *Statesman* article aim a klieg light's worth of attention on the unprofessional rift between the groups, but it also forced Morgan and Milam to move forward with their festival, something they really weren't prepared to do. The one concession Morgan and Milam had made to Black and SXSW was to reschedule their event for the fall instead of the spring as they originally had planned. They may have been undeterred by Black's threats, but they weren't oblivious to SXSW's established reputation. Says Morgan, "It would have been pointless to compete."[99]

They took their cues from the local music scene, recognizing that while Austin may have the talent, the music industry itself resided in Nashville and Los Angeles. One of their goals was to bring the film industry to Austin by inviting producers and established screenwriters to the festival. They also wanted to offer exposure to unproduced writers and were determined to have at least one writer's script sold by the end of the first festival.

These were lofty goals for any festival just starting out, but especially for one created by two individuals without ties to or experience within the industry itself. As MacCambridge observed, Morgan and Milam were facing an uphill battle made more difficult because their festival didn't have the connections or "name recognition" of SXSW.

"I think those women could do anything," says Bill Broyles, who was one of the first screenwriters to agree to participate. Broyles co-founded *Texas Monthly* and by 1993 had become a respected writer after creating the television series *China Beach*.[100]

In the end both festivals did take place the following year but during different months. Black stopped speaking to Saritzky although she did participate in one of South by Southwest's film panels. Relations were also strained between Saritzky and Morgan and Milam although she would use her Los Angeles contacts to help them secure a few industry insiders for the inaugural festival.

"It was wild for a while. People took sides," admits Milam years later. "I do think people were asked early on to pick sides," agrees Morgan. "I feel like Austin is a very, very difficult place if people perceive you as an outsider, and it's not just in film and music. It's weird to see that here because it's such a smart town."[101]

The South by Southwest Film and Media Conference (initially dubbed SFMC) was scheduled to coincide with the music festival in the second week of March 1994, leaving Black and his SXSW staff less than five months to prepare. He approached Austin Film Society's Katie Cokinos about running the festival, but she had qualms about piggybacking a film component onto the fast-growing music festival. "You've got the music festival and now you're going to show films? It's too much," she thought to herself.[102]

Instead Cokinos passed along the name of Nancy Schafer, whom she had met when the two worked as locations manager and production coordinator, respectively, on Kim Henkel's ill-fated *Return of the Texas Chainsaw Massacre*. Before arriving in Austin a few years earlier, Schafer had worked at the Telluride Film Festival. The day after Black and Barbaro interviewed Schafer, they offered her the job of running the SFMC.

The inaugural South by Southwest Film and Media Conference kicked off on Friday, March 11. The conference itself lasted three days over the second weekend (to coincide with the music portion of the festival), with the film screenings running throughout the week. The conference included case studies, workshops, and multimedia panel discussions. Films showed at the Dobie Theatre and the Hogg and Union theaters a few blocks away on the University of Texas campus. Eagle Pennell's latest, *Doc's Full Service*, which reteamed him with Henkel, had its world premiere with Pennell in attendance. The movie was Pennell's fifth feature but was in many ways much like his earlier films with its washed-up characters and Texas backdrop.

A retrospective program, entitled "A Celebration of Texas Independents," featured Bill Wittliff's *Red Headed Stranger* and *Barbarosa* (the version recut by Wittliff); *Kid Blue* and *Songwriter* with introductions by screenwriter Bud Shrake; and Linklater's first two features, *It's Impossible to Learn to Plow by Reading Books* and *Slacker*. Early films by noted Austin independent filmmaker and documentarian Hector Galán and Dallas-based filmmaker Ken Harrison were also on the program.

Four hundred registrants attended the event, most of them brought in as panelists, according to MacCambridge, who covered the first festival for the *Austin American-Statesman*. He dismissed the film lineup as a "retrospective-laden mélange of tangentially related films," but Black defended the regional focus as a strategic move that mimicked the way he and Barbaro cultivated the music conference and festival. "A lot of what we did in the early days was use the music angle to get films," explains Schafer, a fact that was certainly reflected in choices like *Red Headed Stranger* and *Songwriter*. "Austin was not renowned for being able to launch a movie, so we needed to do what we could to get the films we wanted. We did a lot of music-related stuff that put us on the map and opened some doors for us."[103]

Seven months later on October 13, the Republic of Texas Film Festival began its three-day conference. By this time, Morgan and Milam had changed its name to the Austin Heart of Film Festival. The conference included a screenplay contest and a schedule of panels, case studies, and craft sessions that featured about sixty screenwriters, producers, and studio executives. Morgan knew locally based screenwriter Al Reinert, a *Texas Monthly* contributor who had directed the documentary *For All Mankind* and had recently finished the *Apollo 13* screenplay with *Texas Monthly* co-founder Broyles. Robert Draper, a writer for the magazine and Morgan's boyfriend at the time, introduced her to Bill Wittliff, who like Reinert signed on to participate. Singer-songwriter Jimmy LaFave put Morgan in touch with producer David Valdes, who worked with Clint Eastwood and had produced *A Perfect World* in Austin a few years earlier. And Saritzky offered an introduction to Barry Josephson, who was then senior vice president of production at Columbia Pictures. The lineup also featured three Academy Award–winning screenwriters: Robert Towne (*Chinatown*), Kurt Luedtke (*Out of Africa*), and Frank Pierson (*Dog Day Afternoon*). "All of these people came in because everybody wanted to get to a writer. We had three Academy Award–winning writers that first year because usually nobody talks to them. Nobody ever called on those people and asked them to do anything. They were grateful," says Morgan of the relative ease with which they secured panelists and speakers. "At one point," recalls Milam, "we had more speakers than registrants."[104]

In addition to the panels and speakers, the Austin Heart of Film Festival threw a welcome party at the Governor's Mansion, which overlooked the grounds of the Capitol. A laidback picnic with plenty of barbecue and alcohol, the event effectively showcased Austin's appeal as a non-industry town. The party also allowed writers and conference registrants to mingle indiscriminately. Screenplay judge Valdes had read one of the nearly 1,200 submissions, a dark comedy called *Excess Baggage* by Mikhaila "Max" Adams of Sandy, Utah. Valdes liked the script and passed it to Josephson, who was also impressed. Then Valdes made a point to introduce Adams to the Columbia Pictures executive at the Governor's Mansion, which eventually led to a sale for Adams. (The bar at the Driskill Hotel would serve a similar networking purpose when the festival moved its base of operations there in 1995.)

Screenings were held at three theaters spread throughout Central Austin. Premieres included Warren Beatty's remake of *Love Affair* and Alan Parker's *Mrs. Parker and the Vicious Circle* as well as *Hoop Dreams*, a documentary by Steve James that had won the Audience Award at the Sundance Film Festival earlier that year.

The conference portion of the festival took place at the Austin Opera House, located just south of the river. The building had seen better days, a fact that became painfully apparent throughout the rainy weekend. Screenwriter Tim McCanlies, who by 1994 had moved back to Texas from Los Angeles, recalled speaking as a panelist when the room's ceiling began to leak.[105]

The festival received a wealth of coverage from Austin's daily newspaper—six articles in seven days—much of it written by Morgan's friend MacCambridge. Coverage of the festival by the *Austin Chronicle* was a much different story. Publisher Barbaro made a mention of the festival in the paper's September 30 "Page Two" column, writing that there would be more information in the coming weeks "as soon as their screening schedule is firmed up." The *Chronicle*'s minimal attention to the festival was made worse by the fact that one of the ads purchased by AHFF was placed next to a promotion for the following year's SXSW Film Conference. MacCambridge called it a "graceless stunt," but Black claims it was a mistake. At the time he tried to rectify the issue by writing a letter to Morgan. "I explained what had happened, how we hadn't been trying to screw them. Of course a lot of the information in their ad was wrong, but that was their fault. They weren't on top of their shit. So I was about to send the letter, and Nick [Barbaro] said, 'No, don't send it. I should write something [as the publisher].' And then he never did. So it looked like we were trying to fuck with them."[106]

At the very least, the fact there even were competing festivals signaled that, by the early 1990s, the Austin film community was finally beginning to come into its own. Wittliff, who had participated in both SFMC and the Austin Heart of Film Festival that first year, continued to play a significant role in the development of Austin film. Although Wittliff himself had always thought it ridiculous to refer to Austin or even Texas as the "Third Coast," he was one of the talented few whose film and television credits could actually justify the nickname. By 1992 he had written and produced a two-hour television movie for CBS called *Ned Blessing: The True Story of My Life*. It was based on a series of unpublished short stories Wittliff had written in the 1980s. The western starred Daniel Baldwin and gave work to many of Wittliff's original local crew from *Red Headed Stranger,* people like production designer Cary White, line producer Bill Scott, and prop master Eric Williams. (Wittliff assembled a similar crew of locals for the incredibly successful 1989 miniseries *Lonesome Dove,* based on Larry McMurtry's novel and filmed partially in Austin.) *Ned Blessing* was reconfigured as a series after CBS ordered six episodes for the following year. Baldwin was replaced by former rodeo-star-turned-actor Brad Johnson, and all six episodes were filmed in and around Austin and again employed many locals. *Ned Blessing: The True Story of My Life & Times* debuted in August 1993 as part of an experimental CBS programming strategy that tested new series during the typically dormant late summer television season. The first episode finished in the top ten and received some good notices, but CBS chose not to extend its order for new shows.[107]

"A lot of great things have happened for Austin's film community over the past few years," wrote then Governor Ann Richards in a congratulatory note to Wittliff, "and you've been a big part of making so many of them happen. Don't think for a minute that I don't know it."[108]

7

# Winning the Battle, Losing the War

## *The Newton Boys*

n the summer of 1994, while Robert Rodriguez was in Mexico embark-
ing on *Desperado,* his first big-budget studio film, Richard Linklater was
recovering from his own studio experience on *Dazed and Confused* by
traveling to Vienna, Austria, to shoot a two-character romantic drama entitled
*Before Sunrise*. The $2.5 million production was the first film in a two-picture
deal with Castle Rock, an independent production company co-founded by
Rob Reiner. Linklater signed with the company in March 1994 after meeting
with other studios in Los Angeles. The deal allowed Linklater to retain creative control of his projects and to continue to base himself in Austin. By this
time he had also moved his production company, Detour Filmproduction,
from rented offices near downtown to a 7,000-square-foot, two-story building
just east of the interstate that he purchased for about $200,000.[1]

While *Before Sunrise* and Linklater's next film, *SubUrbia* (1997), seemed
like typical Detour projects in terms of their smallish budgets, limited sets,
and personal stories, *The Newton Boys* (1998), which he would also begin
planning in 1994, seemed to represent a complete departure. The epic western was based on the true story of the Newton brothers, a band of Texas
bank robbers. Co-starring Matthew McConaughey and distributed by Twentieth Century Fox, *The Newton Boys* had movie stars and action scenes and,
at $27 million, it was the closest thing to a blockbuster that Linklater had
ever worked on (and that Austin had ever produced). Argues Ethan Hawke,

who would co-star in *Before Sunrise* and play the part of Jess Newton in *The Newton Boys*, "Everyone thought it was so different for Rick to be making a western. If you know Rick, it seemed completely appropriate and just a personal movie. He's such an anti-authority guy."[2]

Nationally, the movie failed to capture an audience, and Linklater's experience making *The Newton Boys* would have a profound effect on his career. Meanwhile in the mid to late 1990s, the local film community prospered, which was somewhat ironic given Linklater's influential role in this development even as his own career was stalling out after *The Newton Boys*.

The Austin Film Society, which Linklater had co-founded in 1985, was flourishing even as federal monies for the arts were becoming increasingly scarce. This development was mainly due to the phenomenon of AFS's celebrity-studded benefit screenings, which took as its model the 1994 Austin premiere of Quentin Tarantino's *Pulp Fiction*, with Tarantino in attendance. Film and television production in Austin also was on the upswing in the late 1990s. In 1996, the city celebrated its most lucrative year ever, with twenty-five projects lensed inside its boundaries. The university's RTF production program also beefed up its faculty and facilities, attracting even more interest for Austin as it trained young filmmakers who demonstrated the potential to become the next Richard Linklater. And in 1997 Harry Knowles launched the Ain't It Cool News online movie site, which reviews upcoming releases and provides juicy scoops about the film industry. Knowles's brash enthusiasm and unfiltered opinions made this a unique enterprise that strengthened—and occasionally jeopardized—Austin's hard-won Hollywood connections.

### Someone Should Make a Movie out of This

*Before Sunrise* co-starred Ethan Hawke and French actress Julie Delpy. Linklater had first met Hawke before the release of *Dazed and Confused*, when he was in New York to see *Dazed*'s Anthony Rapp in a play put on by Hawke's theater company. Soon after, Linklater sent Hawke a script for *Before Sunrise*. Beginning in late 1993, Linklater spent the better part of nine months casting the movie. According to co-writer Kim Krizan, Linklater considered British actor David Thewlis and relative unknown Michael Vartan, who would later become familiar in the television series *Alias*, before the part went to Hawke. Robin Wright, Lili Taylor, and Sadie Frost auditioned for the role that eventually went to Delpy.[3] Because so much of the dialogue-heavy script relied on an easy chemistry between the two leads, the filmmaker budgeted even more time than usual for rehearsals. For two weeks, Linklater, Hawke, and Delpy rehearsed for sixteen hours at a stretch.

Linklater shared co-screenwriting credit with Krizan, who had appeared in *Slacker* and in *Dazed*. In the summer of 1991 Linklater had asked Krizan to write a movie with him after being impressed by her master's thesis about Anaïs Nin. He told Krizan he wanted their collaboration to be his next project after *Dazed*. Krizan was flattered but dubious since she had no screenwriting experience. In the spring of 1993 after completing the bulk of postproduction on *Dazed* in L.A., Linklater returned to Austin and called Krizan. Linklater offered her $1,000 to write the script with him, so she quit her job. Based on Linklater's idea of telling a "boy-girl story," together they hammered out a romance about two characters who meet on a train in San Antonio. The situations and dialogue in that first script came from lengthy discussions between Krizan and Linklater in brainstorming sessions at her North Austin duplex. "We each had our little notebooks and we would tell stories. It was sort of like relationship boot camp," recalls Krizan. Within about two weeks they had a first draft, and they decamped to Linklater's apartment and took turns, relay-style, typing the script into his computer. Linklater scripted the male dialogue and Krizan wrote lines for the female character. "Rick was ultimately in control of some stuff with that script. I remember being kind of frustrated with him because he'd have the guy talk, talk, talk and the girl going, 'Uh huh. Uh huh.' I would try to have the girl talk. But ultimately, it was his computer."[4]

The *Before Sunrise* crew included Linklater regulars Lee Daniel as cinematographer, Anne Walker-McBay as producer, and her husband, Clark Walker, as second assistant cameraman. During preproduction on the film, Walker received a magazine article from his and Linklater's friend Keith Fletcher. The engaging essay chronicled a family of Texas bank robbers, which Fletcher knew would appeal to the Texas history buff in Walker. "Someone should make a movie out of this," Fletcher told Walker as he gave him the article, which appeared in the January 1994 issue of *Smithsonian*. Writer Claude Stanush called the four Newton brothers, who grew up in Uvalde, southwest of San Antonio, "the most successful bank and train robbers in American history." They operated as a team during the 1920s, stealing from more than sixty banks and a handful of trains. Collaborating with a San Antonio English professor, Stanush recorded thirty-five audiotapes of conversations he had with two of the brothers, Willis and Joe, whom he first met in the 1970s. The Newtons' colorful anecdotes, woven together by Stanush's deft prose, leapt off the pages of the magazine.[5]

Says Walker of the story, "It was a fascinating blend of the gangster and western genres at a moment when the two were having some serious overlap." He immediately envisioned the Newtons' story as a feature film, and he grew more excited as he read the piece. "At the same time, almost from the first day, I had this sense of dread, like, we should have found this story when we were 50 years old," he recalls of the Detour production crew. "Because it was an epic. It was *Raging Bull*, and we'd barely made *Mean Streets* yet."[6]

Walker, Fletcher, and another friend, writer Paul Cullum, spent a weekend discussing possible directors to whom they could bring the idea. They tossed around names like Ron Shelton, Jim McBride, and Texas writer-director Robert Benton, who had written *Bonnie and Clyde* and more recently made *Places in the Heart*. Still, at the end of the weekend Walker had to face the fact that they didn't have the rights to the piece and any efforts they made on their own might be futile. The three friends even drove to San Antonio one day to try to meet Stanush, who was doing a reading at a local bookstore, but they arrived too late. Finally, Walker took it to Anne, his wife and Linklater's producer, who thought Linklater would relate to the story's Texas roots.

Busy with preproduction on *Before Sunrise*, Linklater seemed interested in the idea and encouraged them to pursue it. Although he wasn't entirely certain he wanted to make the movie, Linklater briefly toyed with the idea that perhaps Detour could package the project for another director. Says Fletcher, "I would have thought Rick might have executive produced or produced it. I didn't know him that well to know he might have wanted to do something more mainstream, an action story. I didn't understand Rick's ambition or ego enough to know that he would want to get involved in something big."[7]

Meanwhile Walker contacted the article's author, and Stanush somewhat reluctantly agreed to meet with him and Anne. In his mid-seventies at the time, Stanush had recently published an oral history of the Newton brothers with David Middleton, and the article Walker had fallen in love with was an excerpt from the new book. "There was a lot more than about crime in their stories. They were about sharecropper days. The 1920s were a time when we were passing from an agricultural, small-town society to a technological, industrial society, and the American dream changed from owning a piece of land to money. And that's what Willis wanted. He said, 'We're just businessmen, and our business is robbing banks.' He said, 'All we want is what everybody wants now: money,'" Stanush recalls.[8]

The Walkers spent the afternoon talking to Stanush about many things, including their desire to turn his article into a project for Detour. They also learned they weren't the first to contact the author about his piece. Says Stanush, "As soon as it came out in the *Smithsonian*, I got calls from a number of different Hollywood producers. Mostly they just wanted to buy the rights to it, but I wanted to be part of the scriptwriting." At one point there was talk of Dustin Hoffman being interested in a role. Stanush even fielded calls from executives at one of the television networks, who had visions of making the Newtons' story into a miniseries, an idea that Stanush admits might have been more suitable than a feature film given the episodic nature of the brothers' exploits.[9]

Walker and Stanush both shared a love of Texas history, and he told the Walkers about a 1946 article he had written for *Life* about Texas rodeo star Bob Crosby. Hollywood optioned the story and hired Stanush to develop it as a screenplay, which eventually became Nicholas Ray's 1952 movie *The Lusty Men*. Producer Jerry Wald initially courted Stanush to be a technical consultant on the project, but when Stanush saw an early draft of the script he realized that Wald had taken liberally from his own published article about Crosby. Stanush spent a good deal of time and energy battling with Wald for screen credit, and the matter eventually went to arbitration. "Claude was very cautious, and it took a while, and it took all of my people skills," says Walker-McBay.[10]

Walker suggested that Stanush watch *Slacker* and *Dazed and Confused* to see what he thought of Linklater's work. It seemed absurd to be telling a seventy-six-year-old former *Life* magazine correspondent to rent the offbeat movies, but Stanush liked Linklater's films. In July, on the eve of their departure for Vienna to shoot *Before Sunrise*, Linklater and the Walkers drove to San Antonio. Linklater and Stanush hit it off, talking about Texas history, Linklater's movies, and most important, adapting Stanush's book into a feature film. When they left after that second visit, the threesome had struck a verbal agreement with Stanush to write a first draft of the proposed screenplay while they went to Europe to shoot their next movie. "To be honest," says Walker, "it seemed like the best way to keep him from completely balking on us."[11]

### A Thorny Screenplay

In late July Stanush started work on the script while the Detour crew began their twenty-five-day shoot in Vienna. Although *Before Sunrise* originally had been set in San Antonio, the location was moved overseas, according to Krizan, when a European-based production company agreed to back the film. But producer Walker-McBay, who didn't think much of the original script, says she pushed to convince Linklater to move the setting. "I just felt like it was more of a quintessential experience set in Europe." Another reason the producer wanted to shoot the low-budget romance overseas was to distance the project from its co-writer, who Walker-McBay worried was becoming too involved. "We were thinking of shooting it in San Antonio, and Kim Krizan was part of the location scout. She was really part of everything. I didn't really respect Kim very much and I felt if we were to move it elsewhere, we could have more time to develop it and work on the cast and turn it into something that would work better than what we were working on."[12]

Linklater was preoccupied with his current project. Although *Before Sunrise* shared the same real-time setting as his first films, the intimate story differed radically from those movies. He had shaved his usual sprawling cast to just two main characters, and while it was as talky as his earlier projects, *Before Sunrise*'s romantic focus charted new territory for the director. Behind-the-scenes tensions also contributed to the director's stress. Old friend D. Montgomery, whom Linklater had hired as the production designer on *Before Sunrise,* had been diagnosed with Hodgkin's disease during the making of *Dazed and Confused.* She had undergone chemotherapy treatments and had told friends she was off alcohol. Once in Vienna, however, Montgomery resumed her drinking and, after one particularly destructive binge, passed out in the hallway of her hotel. The hotel staff managed to transport her to a local hospital, but Montgomery fled the building, an IV dangling from her arm. Walker-McBay, who had taken precautions against Montgomery's unpredictable behavior by going into therapy with her friend prior to the shoot, discussed the situation with Linklater. "Rick and I had to fire her and we sent her home," recalls Walker-McBay of the traumatic decision. Together she and her husband, Linklater, and Daniel paid to send Montgomery to the Hazelden Center in Minnesota.[13]

Despite Hawke and Delpy's wonderful on-screen chemistry in the finished film, some crew members noticed that the film's leads were less than friendly to one another off camera. Further complicating matters was the fact that Linklater was filming in another country and struggling to communicate American cultural nuances to European extras. Still, Linklater felt much more at ease during the production than he had on *Dazed and Confused* two summers before. As often happened with Linklater's actors, Hawke warmed to the collaborative nature of working with the filmmaker and the Detour crew. "Rick gave Julie and I a tremendous amount of freedom and it really made us collaborators in writing that movie. It was a huge transition in my life, realizing that you can take responsibility for your own career." For Hawke the experience would be a pivotal and inspiring moment in his career, second only to working on *Dead Poet's Society* as an eighteen-year-old actor surrounded by high-caliber talent like director Peter Weir and the movie's star, Robin Williams.[14]

At one point during the film's wrap party Walker-McBay pulled Hawke aside and told him, "There's this western, and there's a bunch of parts. And Rick's not sure who he's going to cast, but you're going to be getting a western in the mail."[15]

Stanush had finished a script of more than two hundred pages by the time the Detour crew returned from Vienna in late summer 1994. "I wanted to use the characters and set it in the setting of the times, and that was more interesting to me than the characterizations completely themselves. When Richard came back, I don't know what he thought, but he wanted to stick more closely to the facts of the story," says Stanush.[16]

"It needed a lot of work," says Walker, who read the script before Linklater and Walker-McBay. "I think in Rick's and Anne's minds, we were still making this *Smithsonian* magazine article and it was all going to work out."[17]

Walker appealed to his wife, who convinced Linklater to let him write a draft using Stanush's script as a jumping-off point. Consumed with postproduction decisions on *Before Sunrise*, Linklater agreed.

During the meeting between Stanush and Linklater a few months earlier, Stanush mentioned that he still had some of the audiotapes he had used to record Willis and Joe Newton in the 1970s. "Listening to that was electrifying," Walker recalls. "They had almost a biblical cadence to their voices and these extremely thick Texas accents that you don't hear any more. The character of Willis Newton came across on these tapes like electricity."[18]

But Stanush's script, according to Walker, hadn't sufficiently captured the Newtons' personalities. When Walker remembered that Linklater had suggested they incorporate the oral histories in the film, he thought he had found another way into the story. He envisioned the narrative told like *Little Big Man*, with a voiceover that both contradicts and enhances the on-screen story action. He also thought he had discovered the project's commercial "hook." The film *Forrest Gump* had recently come out, with director Robert Zemeckis using state-of-the-art digital technology to pair contemporary footage of Tom Hanks, the film's lead, with archival footage of John F. Kennedy and other historic figures. Walker wanted to use similar technology to incorporate Stanush's audiotapes into the Newton brothers film. "For me," recalls Walker, "that's what was going to take it beyond a film that had been made before."[19]

During the rewrite phase they also researched information through the National Archives and followed up with historians in the counties where the

Newtons robbed banks. They made use of local historical societies and were able, in some cases, to talk to a few of the people who were alive during the time of the various robberies. Says Linklater of their research, "We were even solving robberies in certain banks that no one ever knew who had robbed that bank, [but] we knew based on Willis's testimony."[20]

In November 1994 Linklater learned that *Before Sunrise* had been chosen as the opening night film for the 1995 Sundance Film Festival. Festival founder Robert Redford introduced the movie, recalls Krizan, who accompanied Linklater, Daniel, Hawke, and Delpy to the event. "I was told that Redford had not introduced a film in six years, and the reason he was introducing the film was because he believed in it so much." Redford also praised the movie at his annual press conference. Referring to Linklater's Sundance debut four years earlier with *Slacker*, Redford described the young director, in the words of one journalist, as "both a product and the future" of the Sundance Film Festival. Linklater was joined at the festival by the movie's co-stars, Ethan Hawke and Julie Delpy, and a phalanx of publicists promoting them and the film. The Sundance publicity push could not keep mixed reviews at bay, however. On January 19, the day of the movie's premiere at Sundance, *Variety* ran its review, which described the film as a "lovely" piece of work but criticized its "endless dialogue and repetitive settings."[21]

*Before Sunrise* fared better when it opened a week later. The $2.5 million romance, which screened in just over four hundred theaters, grossed $1.4 million during its first weekend. The *San Francisco Chronicle*'s Mick La Salle wrote, "*Before Sunrise* is so simple, successful and timeless that it's hard to imagine it not enduring." Roger Ebert liked it, and many other reviewers seemed at least charmed by, if not in love with, *Before Sunrise*.[22]

The movie had a more than solid domestic run, eventually grossing $5.5 million. As with Linklater's earlier films, *Before Sunrise* enjoyed a much better reception abroad. In February 1995 the film earned two nominations at the Berlin International Film Festival. Although the movie lost the Golden Berlin Bear award to Bertrand Tavernier's thriller *L'Appat*, Linklater won the Silver for Best Director. It was an award that seemed to carry a lot of weight with the filmmaker, who had first educated himself in film history by watching the European films of New Wave directors. By the end of its overseas run, *Before Sunrise* had earned more than $17 million abroad.[23]

Meanwhile script revisions continued on *The Newton Boys*, with more than twenty-seven drafts being worked on by Stanush, Walker, and Linklater or some combination of the three. With Walker and Linklater revising the thorny screenplay, and Walker-McBay overseeing the project as producer, the layers of involvement began to take a toll on all involved. "It was hard to be married to one of the writers. I think at the end of the day it's a director's medium," says Walker-McBay.[24]

"I was trying to make this perfect thing and they were just trying to get a movie made," says Walker. "I always feel like the movie is the most important thing, but Anne feels like the director is the most important thing. She sees this movie and the next movie and the next movie and the director's career and what he's trying to do as the big picture, and I see the individual film as the big picture."[25]

### Casting the Newtons

By the spring of 1995 Linklater had fulfilled half of his two-picture deal with Castle Rock. He hoped *The Newton Boys* would be his second film with the company, but instead Castle Rock executives gave into their reservations about the period piece and put the project in turnaround. Linklater began the process of shopping it to a number of other studios. Within days he and Walker-McBay were in Los Angeles meeting with Twentieth Century Fox chairman Bill Mechanic. From the start of his tenure in 1993 Mechanic sought to redefine Fox by hiring young filmmakers such as Baz Lurhmann, who updated *Romeo and Juliet* for the MTV generation, and Alfonso Cuarón, who did something similar with Charles Dickens's *Great Expectations*. Mechanic was a fan of *Dazed and Confused*—less so of Linklater's other films—and was very interested in working with the filmmaker. During the meeting at Fox they discussed casting (both Linklater and the studio were interested in Matthew McConaughey), budget, and the screenplay. "The script had a strong idea, but the idea was not perfectly realized," recalls Mechanic. "It sort of lingered in between a commercial movie and whatever the opposite of that would be. Clearly Rick wasn't going to make an action picture, but our desire was to make sure it was telling a good story." In the end, Mechanic thought the idea was decent enough, but the real draw for the studio was working with Linklater. In October, an item in *Daily Variety* officially announced the project would be made at Fox.[26]

Backing from an established studio like Fox would potentially provide Linklater with the resources to make the sweeping epic he envisioned. Over time the partnership would take its toll, however, and thrust the filmmaker and his company back into the restrictive world of studio production. Amy Lowrey, who began working at Detour in the summer of 1994 and eventually became Linklater's assistant, noticed a shift almost immediately. Her dealings with the studio on an administrative level were marked by seemingly arbitrary decisions and "lots of tricks," a working relationship that was quite different from the more straightforward collaboration she had experienced with Castle Rock on *Before Sunrise*.[27]

Linklater had at least two actors in mind almost from the start of discussions on *The Newton Boys*. He wanted to cast Hawke, and the actor expressed interest in playing the lead role. "Ethan was in and Ethan was out. He wanted to do Willis, and then he didn't want to be in the movie at all. It was a nightmare," recalls casting director Don Phillips, who had agreed to help cast the movie while it was still with Castle Rock. Linklater also wanted to work with Matthew McConaughey, whose breakout role in *Dazed and Confused* had earned the fledgling actor very good notices. "I wanted to play Willis," says Hawke, "but Rick wanted McConaughey to play that part. It was kind of a pivotal moment in our relationship: If I really wanted to be part of this band, I had to be willing to take a smaller position."[28]

Walker, still so enamored by the real-life Newtons, had trouble envisioning contemporary actors playing the brothers. He didn't think Hawke was right for the part of Willis, and he had reservations about McConaughey in the role, despite Linklater's enthusiasm for the actor. Walker-McBay shared her husband's reservations. "I never thought that Matthew was right. I really fought with Rick and resisted that idea for about a year and a half."[29]

McConaughey's star was rising quickly by the time Twentieth Century Fox signed on to the project in late 1995. After shooting *Dazed and Confused* in the summer of 1992, McConaughey returned to UT for his senior year. Unlike many of his fellow students, he now had real-world experience on a movie set and was itching to graduate. He began to wear a pager clipped to his belt in case he got a call about an audition.

After graduation in May 1993 McConaughey had his pickup truck and a U-Haul packed for Los Angeles, where a friend thought he could find the aspiring actor work as a production assistant. Instead, McConaughey unexpectedly found more work in Austin on *Return of the Texas Chainsaw Massacre*, a sequel of sorts to Tobe Hooper's 1974 horror film. After the month-long production wrapped, McConaughey once again packed up his pickup and drove out to California in mid-August, where he initially stayed with Don Phillips, who became something of a mentor to the aspiring actor.

The actor's next role was as Drew Barrymore's boyfriend in *Boys on the Side*, a small but juicy part that showcased McConaughey's easygoing charm.

John Sayles then cast McConaughey in *Lone Star*, and it was on the set of this movie in May 1995 that he learned he had been chosen to play the lead in the upcoming John Grisham adaptation *A Time to Kill*.

The news set Hollywood buzzing. Back in Austin, Walker worried about what McConaughey's newfound fame might do to *The Newton Boys*. "I saw him as this really powerful tool, but I didn't necessarily want to point that cannon in the direction of our movie."[30] By February 1996, when McConaughey signed with Creative Artists Agency (CAA), the word was out that he was "in talks" to appear in Linklater's next movie.

But nothing was finalized, and Linklater continued to meet with other actors. From a creative as well as a financial perspective, the most pressing issue was casting Willis. The studio considered most of the top box-office names at the time, including Alec Baldwin, Val Kilmer, and Tom Cruise. In March a small item in the *Boston Herald* announced that newcomer Viggo Mortensen was slated to appear in the movie. Linklater and Walker-McBay had met with Mortensen, and Linklater was intrigued by the idea of having Mortensen play Jess, although the actor wanted the role of Willis. Walker-McBay was very enthusiastic about Mortensen. "The studio," says Walker, "was completely cold." Linklater also talked to Sean Penn, who was Walker's first choice for the role of Willis. Penn also won support from Walker-McBay, who liked the idea of an "edgier" actor in the lead role. But given the actor's reputation for being temperamental, Linklater worried that Penn might agree to the project but then change his mind down the road. "Penn liked the fact that I was both a writer and a director, and it sounded like an interesting character to him," Linklater recalls, "but at that point the studio wouldn't have backed him. They didn't want him in the part."[31]

Casting decisions aside, it had become clear to all involved that *The Newton Boys* was not on the fast track into production. In the spring of 1996 and a few weeks into preproduction on the movie, Fox pulled the plug ostensibly for budgetary reasons. Says Walker-McBay, "One day we were making the movie, the next day it's like, 'Everybody go home. Close the office. You're not making the movie.'" Recalls Keith Fletcher, "So we all went out to dinner and got drunk, where Rick fired us."[32]

Not one to spin his wheels, Linklater turned his attention to a project that had first piqued his interest two years earlier while visiting New York. He had attended a performance of *SubUrbia*, a play by writer and actor Eric Bogosian, at Lincoln Center. Focused on a group of twenty-year-olds during one night of hanging out at a suburban convenience store, the play struck a chord with Linklater. "I saw it as a film, and I felt I knew the characters, or

I *was* the characters," he explained years later. "It really dredged up all this stuff in me that never went away." Although the two men had never met, they both admired one another's work, and after the performance Linklater stopped backstage to congratulate Bogosian. In the fall of 1995 when Bogosian brought his one-act play *Wake Up & Smell the Coffee* to Austin, Linklater interviewed the writer for the *Austin Chronicle*. Three months later, Castle Rock announced it had greenlighted a $3 million movie version of *SubUrbia*, to be scripted by Bogosian and directed by Linklater.[33]

The project came together quickly. Bogosian already had begun to adapt his play for the screen by the time Linklater got involved. They worked on the script together and cast some of the play's original actors, like Steve Zahn, in the movie version. As with *Before Sunrise*, principal photography took place during the summer and lasted less than twenty-five days. Cinematographer Lee Daniel worked behind the camera, and most of the movie was filmed at night on location at a convenience store in South Austin.

By January 1997, Linklater once again had a film in the coveted first-night slot at Sundance when *SubUrbia* was chosen to open the film festival. A month later Sony Pictures Classics, which reteamed Linklater with *Slacker* distributors Michael Barker and Tom Bernard, opened the movie theatrically in extremely limited release. Given that *SubUrbia* played in only sixteen theaters, its opening weekend gross of more than $69,000 was a respectable amount and earned the film the number-two spot at the box office behind *Dante's Peak*. Still, the movie barely made more than half a million dollars domestically, and the collaboration between Linklater and Bogosian failed to thrill the critics, although many reviews once again praised the director's steady hand with a young ensemble cast of mostly unknown actors. (Ajay Naidu, who played the Pakistani owner of the convenience store, was nominated for an Independent Spirit Award.) As for the film's exploration of aimless youth, a staple, by this point, of the Linklater oeuvre, the filmmaker admitted it was time to move on. "This one's the nail in the coffin. This was my final one in what I call my 'hangin' out quintet'—my first five films [including the unreleased *It's Impossible to Learn to Plow by Reading Books*]. This was a good one to end with because it's a good transition and I like the final kind of tragic elements. I think I've covered a pretty thorough bit of my own personal experience through these in a sort of realistic way."[34]

While finishing postproduction on *SubUrbia* during the fall of 1996, Linklater had also resumed preproduction for *The Newton Boys*. A few weeks before Christmas, McConaughey officially signed on to play Willis Newton. Says Walker-McBay, "It finally got down to where it didn't look like we could get the movie made without Matthew. We tried, although Claude thought that Matthew was great and was very similar to Willis. It really felt like, 'Fine. Give in and get this movie made with Matthew.'" But the genial actor's newfound celebrity would cause problems during production. Admits Walker, "His star was ascending so fast that he made a lot of people jealous."[35]

Securing McConaughey for the lead didn't necessarily seal the deal with Twentieth Century Fox. The studio wasn't happy with the latest draft of the script, so Linklater and the Walkers flew out to Los Angeles just before the holidays to meet with studio executives. For $27 million, the studio expected a big action movie, but they didn't see that in the script. "Even though the material was really exciting, really fun, they were afraid Rick was going to make an art movie," says Walker.[36]

There had been many times throughout the previous year when it seemed as if the studio were ready to pull out, but at this particular moment the project seemed especially fragile, even with McConaughey on board. The reality was that *The Newton Boys* was a period film with a budget four times larger than the director's most expensive movie to date. Its lead was a hot young actor who hadn't yet carried a film, and the story blended two genres—gangster and western—that weren't exactly in vogue at the time.

Walker-McBay suggested they hire a script doctor and mentioned writer-director John Sayles, who had recently done a polish on *Apollo 13*, written by Austin-based screenwriters Bill Broyles and Al Reinert. Sayles was available and interested, and he and Linklater spent a week together working on the screenplay's weakest parts. Although the writer-director left the story and structure essentially intact, he brought a much-needed energy to the script. Sayles honed the third act, beginning with a bungled train robbery in Rondout, Illinois, and telescoped the action so that the story zipped along toward the subsequent trial and conclusion. "He was the only one of us who could think that way. He condensed things and added a few clever moments that help you make a leap forward. I'll be forever grateful," says Linklater.[37]

By the time *SubUrbia* opened in February 1997, Linklater had finalized nearly all of the main roles for *The Newton Boys*. The lackluster reviews of his fourth produced film didn't seem to faze him as he shifted his focus to scouting locations for the 1920s period film, which would end up shooting in eighty different locales throughout Central Texas. By February, negotiations with Ethan Hawke, who originally wanted the lead role, were finally nailed down for the Linklater favorite to play Jess Newton. Julianna Margulies, who was a series regular on the popular television drama *ER*, had been cast opposite McConaughey as Louise Brown, the single mother romanced by his character. By March, with strong encouragement from the studio, Skeet Ulrich (*Scream*) had come on board to play Joe Newton. Vincent D'Onofrio (*Men in Black, The Whole Wide World*) signed on to play Dock. Country singer Dwight Yoakam, who had acted in a few small films and made-for-television movies, was cast as explosives expert Brentwood Glasscock. Yoakam had received very good notices six months earlier for his portrayal of a violent boyfriend in Billy Bob Thornton's *Sling Blade*.

As a group the four lead actors had interesting and fairly impressive resumes, and McConaughey's leading-man buzz certainly was a draw for the studio. Indeed, his potential bargaining power became evident when Steven Spielberg approached the young actor about co-starring in the historical slave narrative *Amistad*. "The films were scheduled as an either/or thing, and I didn't have the leverage or power to call my agent and say, 'Look, make them both work!'" says McConaughey, who was driving back to Texas when he got the call from Spielberg. The actor felt committed to Linklater and *The Newton Boys*, but he also wanted to work with Spielberg. It was, says McConaughey, a "high-class problem." At Detour, Walker-McBay understood that Linklater's next project, as far as Fox was concerned, needed McConaughey. He spoke with both directors, who then conferred with one another. The conflict was resolved in a matter of hours, and it was decided that *The Newton Boys*'s shooting schedule would be pushed back to accommodate McConaughey's working on the project.[38]

### We Still Need Their Money: AFS, *Pulp Fiction*, and Quentin Tarantino

In many ways, a lot was riding on *The Newton Boys* when production began in spring 1997. Not only was it Linklater's largest budget to date, but it also was the most expensive movie production ever to originate in Texas.

It made sense to shoot *The Newton Boys* locally given the story's Texas roots, and using Central Texas locations kept costs in check. Re-teaming with Phillips and with help from Austinite Lizzie Martinez, Linklater was able to cast most of the minor and extras roles regionally as well. Linklater was proud of the fact that a movie with such a large budget was being done locally. "People in L.A. think you just can't do anything outside of there," he said at the time. "Like, how would you edit? C'mon, man. We're *finishing* films here. We're doing everything. We're way ahead. Unfortunately, we still need their money. There are no real financing entities here in Texas that are going to give you a few million bucks to make a movie. It's kind of sad."[39]

To that end, Linklater had established in 1996 the Texas Filmmakers' Production Fund (TFPF), a program administered through the Austin Film Society that generated grants to regional independent filmmakers. During its first year, the TFPF awarded $30,000 to thirty filmmakers.[40] Most of the money for these grants was raised during AFS benefit premieres and other splashy events, whose precursor had been the 1994 premiere of Tarantino's *Pulp Fiction*. By then leadership at the Austin Film Society was about to be passed from Linklater's former girlfriend, Katie Cokinos, to Elizabeth Peters. Peters arrived in Austin in late summer 1992 to earn a master's degree in film production at the University of Texas. She had first met Linklater when he spoke to one of her film classes, and he approached her about running the film society when Cokinos decided to leave in 1995.

At their meeting Linklater explained his goals for the organization that he had co-founded ten years earlier with Lee Daniel. "Rick was really into this idea of free film for a year. He also was talking about more support for filmmakers—they needed to have help finding grants, fiscal sponsorship, and learning about other opportunities," says Peters. Linklater specifically wanted to provide funds to replace grant monies that until 1989 had been given by the National Endowment for the Arts (NEA) to nonprofits like Houston's SWAMP, which then administered grants regionally. Peters was skeptical about AFS's ability to raise sufficient funds but inspired by Linklater's energy and ongoing commitment to AFS despite his busy filmmaking schedule. She had brought her boyfriend, Jerry Johnson, to the interview in part because she wanted to make the case that AFS needed two staff members. She knew she had the skills to manage the organization, but she was less confident about her ability to program the film series. "Jerry was my boyfriend, but he was also a film geek in a way that I will never be, the way Rick is," says Peters of Johnson's tendency, like Linklater's, to keep journals about the films he watched. Linklater warmed to the idea, and the pair was hired to work about ten hours per week although they easily invested three times as many hours on a regular basis. Simultaneously, Peters was supervising the undergraduate advising program in the RTF department at UT.[41]

"That was a really important step for Rick and Katie to take, to risk going outside of their circle, but it was really important because that's when the film society started looking outward and also when more people became engaged with it," says Peters.[42]

During their first year at AFS, Peters and Johnson oversaw a number of events in recognition of the film society's tenth anniversary with a budget of approximately $10,000. They published a commemorative booklet and programmed forty-two free screenings that ran throughout 1996. Peters began holding regular meetings for AFS's board of directors, a group that had never attended formal meetings and included *Austin Chronicle* editor Louis Black, Linklater friend and ACC department head Chale Nafus, and UT RTF professor Charles Ramírez Berg, among others. The anniversary events, the free screenings, board meetings—it was, she thought, more than enough. "We're doing amazing things," she told Linklater. "Let's stop worrying about the filmmaker's fund."[43]

Although Linklater points to the 1991 Austin screening of *Slacker* as the first AFS benefit premiere, he credits the *Pulp Fiction* screening, which was held October 8, 1994, at the Hogg Auditorium on the UT campus, as the first one that made any significant money for the organization. Linklater had met Tarantino a year earlier in Los Angeles while he was in postproduction on *Dazed and Confused*. The two filmmakers had been at the same midnight screening in Santa Monica, and Linklater introduced himself to Tarantino as they were leaving the theater. As Tarantino says of their initial meeting, "Anybody who's going to be at a midnight screening of *Nashville*, or any movie for that matter, but in particular a three-hour movie from the Seventies, all right, is automatically kind of okay in my book. I was already prepared to like him."[44]

Tickets to the event, with Tarantino in attendance, were a mere $10, and they sold out within hours. Linklater squired Tarantino and his entourage around town, giving them a tour that included both Austin and *Slacker* landmarks. Tarantino gave a rousing, hyperbolic introduction to his second feature, the kind of introduction that would become very familiar to local film fans years later when Tarantino began hosting "QT Fests," week-long screenings of vintage genre films hand-picked from his personal collection.

Very quickly AFS board members realized from the tremendous response to the event that Austin's film-friendly audiences would gladly pay for similar opportunities. They also recognized they had essentially underpriced tickets to the screening, which pulled in less than $6,000 for the film society. "We could have made so much more," moans Linklater, and Peters agrees. "It was somehow tragic. It was the North American premiere of this film that had exploded at Cannes. It had been getting press all summer long. Quentin Tarantino was in town for it. It was probably the most seminally important film that AFS ever presented, and it was a huge deal. And they barely made enough to cover expenses. But it did cement Rick and Quentin's relationship."[45]

The *Pulp Fiction* screening also marked the beginning of Tarantino's love affair with Austin itself, a relationship that would help bring even more attention to the city's quietly expanding film community. On a return trip later that year, Linklater took Tarantino to an AFS screening of Rainer Werner Fassbinder's *The Bitter Tears of Petra von Kant* (1972), part of the Free Cinema series that had received support from the *Pulp Fiction* benefit. "You see this screening?" Linklater said to Tarantino. "You paid for it!" Already familiar with Eagle Pennell's work, Tarantino marveled at the Austin film scene, which reminded him of Australia's low-budget filmmaking explosion of the 1970s (an explosion that in actuality was funded with government support).[46]

### Keeping the Movie Light on Its Feet

In the spring of 1997 Linklater prepared for the first day of shooting on *The Newton Boys* with three weeks of rehearsal prior to the start of principal photography on April 21. He and Stanush had agreed early on that although the four Newtons had very different personalities, they shared a distinct sense of humor. The filmmaker wanted to keep the movie "light on its feet," and to that end the performances that came out of rehearsals infused the script with an upbeat energy.[47]

Part of McConaughey's prep included watching documentary footage of Willis Newton, who often spoke in a distinctive high-pitched voice and moved his hands in particular ways. The gestures were a habit, according to Stanush, cultivated during Willis's early days of picking cotton. In addition to doing his own research, the actor spent time with Stanush. "The conversation was about his character. For example, Willis was a man of action. He did things and thought about it afterwards. McConaughey seemed to understand that." Stanush liked the young actor and observed that despite his rising profile, he seemed to remain a good ol' boy at heart. Together in L.A. during one point in the production, Stanush watched in amusement as McConaughey ordered chili at an expensive eatery and continued to chew and spit tobacco while in the restaurant.[48]

Unlike McConaughey, Ulrich found the documentary footage of Joe Newton less helpful in crafting his character because it showed a man much older than the person he would be playing. Hawke, who was born in Texas but grew up in New Jersey, was obsessed with Texas mythology. "I did all this crazy stuff. I drove down to Uvalde and went to their house," says Hawke.[49]

Aside from Stanush's documentary and the audiotape recordings of Joe and Willis Newton, D'Onofrio had few resources for his character, but he did find a photograph of Dock that proved particularly helpful. Although

Yoakam didn't arrive on the set until a few weeks into production, he would call Linklater late at night with ideas for his character. For instance, it was Yoakam's idea, based on his research of Glasscock's violent tendencies, that the character carry a .32 caliber pistol at all times whether or not the scene required it. "He has a seriousness about him," says Stanush, who was impressed by Yoakam's acting skills.[50]

While Linklater rehearsed his actors in early April, Keith Fletcher worked with musician Mark Rubin to pre-record the movie's period music, which Linklater needed for playback once production began. After stumbling upon Stanush's *Smithsonian* article years earlier, Fletcher remained involved in the project's development by brainstorming ideas with the screenwriters and conducting research into the music of the 1920s. With a background in band promotion (he managed Austin's Poi Dog Pondering in the early 1990s) and years of record store retail experience, Fletcher instinctively gravitated toward this aspect of the project. After spending a year or so scouring available resources, Fletcher met Rubin, who was the bassist for popular Austin bluegrass band the Bad Livers and a music historian. Fletcher asked Rubin if he could help them find original music from the 1920s, and the musician eagerly began making tapes of songs from his collection of vintage 78s.[51]

Early in the process Rubin had described to Linklater two ways to go forward with the music: he could find and secure the rights to authentic material from the 1920s and create an archive, or he could hire contemporary songwriters to write songs in the style of that music. Linklater, who wanted to keep everything about the movie as authentic as possible, chose to be true to the period and use the original compositions.

One very big difference on *The Newton Boys* shoot involved who was *behind* the camera. For the first time in his career, Linklater was not working out shot setups with former roommate and cinematographer Lee Daniel. Instead, Australian director of photography Peter James had been hired to shoot the period film, having just finished the World War II-era *Paradise Road* for Fox. For *The Newton Boys*, Linklater wanted a visual look that was different from Daniel's documentary-like style and so chose James because of his ability to shoot pretty, stylized shots and capture a particular time period on film. He also wanted an experienced cinematographer who could help him with his own technical weaknesses. Linklater was the first "young" filmmaker with whom James had worked, and if he had any doubts about Linklater's confidence, these were put to rest during one of their initial conversations about the movie's anachronistic dialogue. James pointed out that the language in the script didn't really conform to the period, and Linklater explained that

that was intentional, to achieve a "modern sensibility" and appeal to younger viewers. Although James personally believed the contemporary dialogue would prove too distracting, he admired Linklater's decisiveness.[52]

In reality, Fox executives likely wouldn't have greenlighted the film with a less-experienced DP. But the decision created tension among the Detour group and fueled local gossip that Linklater had "gone Hollywood." At the time it was a disappointment for Daniel, but years later he was able to wax philosophical about Linklater's choice. "If you're doing a $30 million film with big movie stars you have to pick your battles. It's more of an insurance policy for the studio, which wants someone who's done 10 movies in that genre. They're more comfortable that way."[53]

The production filmed in and around Austin for approximately six weeks before the cast and crew headed south to San Antonio to re-create the Newtons' 1923 robbery of a bank in Toronto, Canada. Production designer (now director) Catherine Hardwicke had been hired on *The Newton Boys* prior to its first preproduction phase in 1996. When *SubUrbia* replaced *The Newton Boys* as Linklater's next project, Hardwicke stayed on. She was a bit of an eccentric and liked to wear decorative small faux birds in her hair. Once, after cinematographer James had suggested that they needed to strip the glossy paint from every piece of molding in order to be true to the period on *Newton Boys*, Hardwicke became agitated, concerned about her dwindling budget. "She burst into tears, and the little bird was flapping around in her hair," recalls James. (Hardwicke ultimately convinced the producers to increase her budget and the paint was removed, which, says James, "made the film look so much better.")[54]

Rain dogged the shoot, and bulldozers had to be brought in to scoop mud out of some of the sets. Roads were built across the "black gumbo" ground, whose swampy texture made constructing sets difficult. John Frick, who had been production designer on *Dazed and Confused*, worked as one of three art directors on *The Newton Boys*. Given the historical nature of the production, the art department ended up purchasing a number of older buildings and relocating them to the various sets around Central Texas. The pace was grueling, with crews building and dressing multiple sets, often spending less than a week on each location. "We had more locations than days on the film," observes James, a condition that was hard on the grips who seemed to spend more time packing up equipment than anything else.[55]

Hardwicke logged at least five hours in the car each day, driving from set to set to oversee the art direction. She had designed a separate color palette for each of the film's three acts to visualize the shifts in the brothers' fortunes: earth tones conveyed their humble beginnings, and a more vibrant palette in the second act revealed their growing infamy and newly acquired wealth, while the final third of the film, with its cool, monochromatic hues, illustrated the brothers' fortunes draining away. When Hardwicke arrived at a location an art director would be waiting, ready to show her samples of wallpaper, furniture, linens, whatever. Hardwicke would assess all of the choices, hop back in the car and finalize her decision while driving, calling back to the set en route to the next location.[56]

Weather and logistical problems aside, Linklater and his crew tried to keep the mood on the production purposeful but light. But while the four leading men often clowned around between takes, egos clashed behind the scenes. Some tension simmered between the laidback McConaughey and the more experienced actors like Hawke and D'Onofrio. "There were a lot of things artistically that Rick and I agreed on, but there were a lot of things that happened on set that we disagreed on," says D'Onofrio, who was troubled by some of the behavior taking place during the production and grew increasingly disappointed with the trajectory of the story. To him the film seemed to be moving away from an interesting exploration of the relationship among the brothers, of the ambiguities within the western genre, and toward a much more traditional action movie. "Rick comes from a kind of ensemble filmmaking. He tried to create an ensemble on *Newton Boys*, but what held us back were the sex and the action, which he definitely needed to get, according to the studio. Which means we didn't get the stuff he would have rather gotten."[57]

Nowhere was McConaughey's newfound fame more clearly on display than in San Antonio, where the company had headed during the last week of June for its final few weeks of filming. After shooting wrapped each day, the cast and crew would congregate in the hotel's bar, where business became so brisk that the management had to add another bartender just to keep up. McConaughey and other cast members partied as hard as the crew. More than a few times during preproduction, Hardwicke had used McConaughey's celebrity to her advantage when a business or homeowner seemed reluctant to let the production film at a particular location. "If it was a woman, I'd literally whip out a magazine with Matthew on the cover, looking really sexy, and I'd go, 'Well, Matthew McConaughey would be coming here and shooting in your place.' Three times that changed a no to a yes," says Hardwicke.[58]

## Postproduction: We Were All in Synch

Editor Sandra Adair had begun assembling the dailies in May at the Austin Film Center, a new postproduction facility co-owned by Linklater and businessman Don Craven, who had made his fortune by automating flood plain research. Located in the middle of downtown Austin, the space took up the second floor of a building that also housed a relatively new nightclub called The Speakeasy. *Before Sunrise* had been edited at Linklater's Detour offices using a KEM and editing benches purchased by the filmmaker, but by the late 1990s space had become tight in the facility just off the interstate, especially after the Austin Film Society moved its offices into the building. The Film Center offered more space and included an editorial area and a screening room. Adair had consulted on the design, and projectionist Stan Ginsel helped to remodel the screening room and add video capabilities. Ever the competitor, Linklater furnished the area with a ping pong table and the video game Asteroids, and he often passed time besting his scores while waiting for Adair to render footage on the Avid.

Although construction had begun on the Austin Film Center prior to production on *The Newton Boys*, the editorial space was not finished by the time Adair began work on the dailies. Adair's crew once again included Sheri Galloway, married to Texas Motion Picture Service's Ivan Bigley, and Eric Lewy, a second assistant editor. By 1997 when they began work on *Newton Boys*, Adair had edited all but one of Linklater's films.

Adair had a finished first cut by late July, a week after production wrapped. She had worked harder on this film, perhaps, than any other, because of its numerous story lines. Although *Dazed and Confused* had its fair share of characters, *The Newton Boys* had complicated action sequences in addition to an ensemble cast, and the train sequence in which D'Onofrio's character, Dock, is wounded proved to be particularly challenging. The first cut included a sequence featuring the real Willis Newton from Stanush and David Middleton's 1976 documentary. Also included in the rough cut was a very funny clip of Joe Newton's appearance on *The Tonight Show*, where his candid responses to Johnny Carson's questions about his criminal past earned big laughs from the audience and broke up the host. (Unlike other material Linklater had licensed in the past, the clip had been relatively easy to secure. Carson had agreed to the licensing, Linklater had heard, because he had always liked Joe Newton.) Initially Linklater wanted to include the footage at the beginning of the movie, to set the stage for the story to come. Adair and others objected, arguing that the documentary footage was too jarring in contrast to the stylized narrative images. They went back and forth over the footage, and eventually Linklater agreed that it should be removed.[59]

By September, with the editing in good shape, Linklater turned his attention back to the music. From the start Linklater, Walker-McBay, and others were hoping that Rubin and his Bad Livers partner Danny Barnes could do both the period songs and an original orchestral composition. But Barnes, like Rubin, was an unknown entity to Fox.[60]

Linklater and Walker-McBay managed to negotiate a deal with Fox to hire Barnes on a conditional basis. If he didn't work out, the filmmakers would come up with another composer. As a protective measure, Fox music supervisor Robert Kraft insisted they work with an arranger and brought in Scott Smalley, a Hollywood orchestrator who had worked on movies as varied as *Big Top Pee-Wee* (1988) and *Mission: Impossible* (1996). The studio's hired gun turned out to be a good fit. Smalley's experience helped Barnes learn how to "think cinematographically." With Barnes based in Seattle and Smalley in Los Angeles they spent most of September and October communicating via their computers, sharing ideas and sending sound files electronically. Like the making of the film itself, the production of the soundtrack certainly had its challenges, but as a process it flowed more smoothly. "We were all in synch and everybody was working really hard for the same thing. Everybody really cared, and it was great to be at that scale and still have everybody work really hard for it," says Walker-McBay. For the Detour group, the "horrible betrayals" that would later define relations with the studio over the movie itself were nonexistent during the production and post phases of the soundtrack.[61]

On September 15, in the midst of work on *The Newton Boys* soundtrack, came word that D. Montgomery had passed away. In remission from lymphoma cancer back in the summer of 1994, Montgomery had entered Hazelden for substance abuse treatment after being fired from the *Before Sunrise* crew. Montgomery began to flourish again after Hazelden, newly sober and working on her performance art pieces and other projects. When the cancer returned, Montgomery chose holistic practices over chemotherapy. Like the late Ed Lowry and George Morris before her, Montgomery was an extremely bright, creative, and perceptive individual whose untimely death deeply affected those in the Austin film scene whose work she inspired.

By early November, with a temporary score in place, *The Newton Boys* was ready for its first set of preview screenings. Fox tested the movie in Dallas and Phoenix during a two-week period, and Linklater was happy with the results. When the studio reps kept the audiences after the screening and asked them how many liked the movie, the filmmaker remembers, every hand in the theater went up. Audiences responded to the movie's upbeat energy and even seemed to love the ending despite the fact that it basically showed the heroes being sent to jail for their crimes. Still, Linklater sensed a lack of enthusiasm from Fox.

"It was strange," he says of the lukewarm reaction. "It tested well, just not through the roof. And they're looking for 'through the roof.' And the film has a lot of ambiguity in it. It's a total character piece. I mean, they get caught in the end. At the end they're going off to jail. Is that heroic? But the movie hit all the notes I was hoping it would hit artistically."[62]

Initially Linklater and others felt tremendous support from Peter Rice, who was Executive Vice President at Fox and spent a significant amount of time on *The Newton Boys* sets during production. As the project wore on, however, Walker-McBay and others began to sense a shift in Rice's feelings toward the film.

At Fox there had been concerns, going back to the dailies, that the film was playing too slow, that the frame was static and the camera wasn't moving enough. "In the action scenes it needed something more than an omniscient camera," says Mechanic. Eventually the studio told Linklater that they wanted him to shorten the film by cutting out the opening scene, a flashback of Willis Newton being wrongly accused and imprisoned for stealing cotton as a young boy. A lot of energy and time had been invested in the sequence, which was shot on the Gulf coast near Corpus Christi. According to Adair, the sequence seemed to delay the start of the movie. "You needed to get the brothers together. It just didn't work." Still, many people involved with the film thought the scene was essential, establishing as it did some motivation for the Newtons' later life of crime. Linklater resisted cutting the scene. Tensions between the filmmaker and the studio escalated, and despite some people advising Linklater that the back story was crucial and to stand his ground, he acquiesced.[63]

Don Phillips observed Linklater's struggles with Fox and empathized with the filmmaker. "I really believe Fox really hurt *Newton Boys*. If you look at Rick's script, and what Rick shot at the beginning of the movie, which was to build up the characters, you really get to know the characters so that you really have a feeling for them," says Phillips.[64]

Linklater received more bad news when he reviewed the studio's marketing campaign leading up to the movie's release, which was scheduled for late March 1998. He hated the poster, which featured medium shots of the four actors in period dress against a garish reddish-orange background. It was a nondescript image that conveyed very little detail about the movie itself, but it did reveal how much Fox was banking on its leading men. According to Mechanic, the studio planned to pitch the film to a younger demographic all along. They hoped that the hunky male cast would also attract female viewers although, years later, Mechanic admits that the genre wasn't exactly a proven favorite of female viewers. "It's not *Bonnie and Clyde*. It's *Clyde and Clyde and Clyde and Clyde*."[65]

Linklater had commissioned scenic artist Tim Dingle to design a hand-painted watercolor poster using period-specific graphics. The beautiful poster captured the vintage charm of the movie, but it featured illustrations of the lead actors rather than actual photographs. It was easy to understand how a studio, banking on the good looks and strong fan base of its actors, might react negatively to a marketing element that didn't take advantage of these factors.

Fox also made it clear that they didn't want anything associated with the marketing to draw attention to the fact that *The Newton Boys* was a period film. Indeed, the music accompanying the trailer was not a cut from the movie's lovingly produced soundtrack but a cover of Johnny Cash's "Ring of Fire" by punk band Social Distortion. "They made it look like a teen rock western romp or something," says Hawke of the trailer.[66]

A few months before the film's release, Linklater traveled to Skywalker Ranch outside San Francisco for the final sound mix. Finished in the late 1980s, Skywalker Sound was housed within a sprawling 140,000-square-foot facility on the ranch first built by George Lucas in 1980. They tested the sound mix and watched clips of *The Newton Boys* in the first-floor theater. "Rick had had such a bad experience with *Dazed*'s post production," recalls Fletcher, who accompanied the filmmaker and a small crew to Marin County. "A couple of people at Fox had recommended Skywalker, and I think Rick, Anne, and the others were a little leery, thinking 'Oh, it's too hoity toity,' but you get out there and they're really serious about what they do. There's a different vibe there than in L.A."[67] Being able to use the sound facilities at Lucas's Skywalker Ranch to put the finishing touches on their own movie was just another example of how far Linklater and the *Slacker* crew had come in less than ten years.

## What You Do Next Says Everything

Linklater worked with *Austin Chronicle* editor and SXSW Film Festival co-founder Louis Black to schedule the world premiere of *The Newton Boys* on the opening night of the March 1998 film festival. The screening, a benefit for

CHAINSAWS, SLACKERS, AND SPY KIDS

the Austin Film Society, was a splashy affair at Austin's historic Paramount Theatre, which had also served as one of the movie's many locations. McConaughey, Hawke, Ulrich, D'Onofrio, Yoakam, and Margulies were in attendance and arrived at the theater in vintage cars similar to the ones used in the film. (Actress Sandra Bullock, rumored at the time to be dating McConaughey, also attended the event.) The actors stepped out of the cars and onto a roped-off red carpet, and four roving searchlights illuminated the theater and the surrounding blocks of Congress Avenue. The glamorous scene was reminiscent of a 1920s Hollywood movie opening. A month earlier, *Premiere* magazine had published a six-page cover story that featured the four leading men and a sidebar article about filmmaking in the capital city entitled "Austin Power." Recalls Hawke, "The studio really wanted [the article] to be some kind of celebrity piece, and you know none of us were that big a celebrity."[68] Still, *The Newton Boys* had received some great buzz, and expectations were high and the mood electric when lines started forming outside the Paramount in the early evening of March 14.

The energy inside the theater, which was filled with 1,200 festival attendees, cast, and crew, remained upbeat as the movie began. "The audience was with Richard," remembers Stanush, whom Linklater acknowledged from the stage. "Whether they liked the movie or not, I think they loved Richard. And justly so. He's done a lot for Austin." The hometown crowd stayed with the film and received it warmly, but the scenes that earned the biggest laughs and most applause came during the closing credits. The documentary images of Willis and Joe Newton leapt off the screen and conveyed quite clearly the real charm of the original brothers. Unfortunately the brief scenes inadvertently upstaged the rest of the movie, an observation that more than a few critics would make two weeks later when *The Newton Boys* opened in theaters around the country. Says Linklater, "It's just one of those decisions you make, like, 'Yeah! It'll be the icing on the cake.' But maybe there's no cake there to ice."[69]

When the movie ended, the Paramount audience erupted into thunderous applause as Linklater and his leading actors took the stage. By 1998, four years after the *Pulp Fiction* screening, the film society had become more savvy about raising money. The glitzy *Newton Boys* screening and its exclusive after-party raised approximately $55,000 for AFS. Unfortunately, the movie did not generate nearly as much goodwill with most of the reviewers who wrote about Linklater's film when it opened on March 31. "Just because everyone wants to make a western doesn't mean everybody should," Kenneth Turan wrote at the end of his *Los Angeles Times* review. Like Turan, many of the critics commented on a certain blandness to the movie, from its attractive cast to its good-natured but lackluster storyline. And even those who praised the film did so in a qualified manner. As Thelma Adams wrote in the *New York Post*, "The script is witty and romantic and entirely lacking in narrative tension." Noting the story's inherent "mood shifts," *Time*'s Richard Schickel described the movie as "agreeable" but also lacking intensity. "Linklater is skillful at shooting and editing action for its comic potential, but his casting is way off the mark. It's the Bland Boys almost all the way, and who could give a fig about them?" wrote *Village Voice* critic Amy Taubin.[70]

*The Newton Boys*'s entertaining closing credit sequence proved to be the movie's undoing. If as a viewer you were satisfied with the movie up to that point, the spontaneity and high humor of the documentary footage made you rethink your take on the dramatized account. "The best part comes at the very end, when elderly members of the actual Newton gang reminisce briefly about their criminal careers," wrote the *Christian Science Monitor*. "They don't arrive until the final credits are rolling, though, and that's a long time to wait for a movie's payoff." More than a few others made similar observations. Mused Taubin, "Sure it sends us out laughing but also wondering why Linklater's Newtons lack the pizzazz they radiated in real life."[71]

Booked into more than 1,900 theaters around the country, *The Newton Boys* ranked ninth at the box office on its opening weekend and earned $4,010,245. (The studio had hoped for at least $10 million.) It remained in the top ten for its second weekend in release but had dropped to the eighteenth spot by the third weekend. When its domestic release came to an end in mid-May, the movie had grossed just over $10 million, less than half of its production budget. "Clearly, financially, the film didn't work," says Mechanic. Fox's international release of the film was spotty at best.[72]

The mood was grim around the offices of Detour. After laboring for nearly four years to bring Stanush's original magazine article to the screen, those closest to the project felt bewildered and even devastated by the movie's negative critical response and disappointing box office performance. "I don't think we thought it was going to be so successful as much as we thought it was going to be well-received," says Adair.[73]

For other crew members like art director Jeanette Scott, the shoot's incredible challenges had tested her limits but also pushed her to do some of her best work, which made the film's poor reception even more disappointing. "To this day I will say it was the hardest job I ever did in my life. I really felt like I should have just checked into a sanitarium at the end of it. I've never been so exhausted, but I also think I've never been more proud of the work, the way it looked, and what we accomplished for the money we had."[74]

But perhaps no one felt the bewilderment more keenly than Linklater himself. Having watched McConaughey's career explode over the previous two years, Linklater had assumed *The Newton Boys* would benefit from the actor's meteoric popularity. Instead he detected the beginnings of a media backlash against the actor. "In short order Matthew did *Amistad* and *Contact*. By the time *Newton Boys* came out, we were in Matthew-bashing mode. So no one could actually say they liked him or his performance even though I think he's really good in the movie," insists Linklater. Once the bad reviews started rolling in, grumblings also could be heard about the filmmaker's turning his back on his low-budget indie roots. "At that moment Rick was the crown prince of indie cinema, who all of a sudden seemed to be making a studio comedy. And I think people were disappointed in him about it," remembers Hawke.[75]

"It was weird the way that got flipped," says Linklater of the movie's $27 million budget, which by the studio's standards basically amounted to chump change. "When that came out, it was like I had sold out and did a big studio film. When actually that's a $60 or $70 million film we did for $27 million with very low-budget techniques."[76]

Continues Linklater, "It was a big step, working with a composer, etc. It was a great experience all the way through. I thought I matured a lot in the whole process. Won the big battle, but lost the war. The studio just never really got behind the movie."[77]

Stanush also was disappointed that the movie didn't fare better, and he wondered privately if its sprawling and action-oriented narrative hadn't supplanted the heart of the story. "I have no quarrel with Richard or what they did. It's just that I would have liked to have seen something more of the motivation," he says. "I thought Richard did the best he could. He was working with Fox and they had their idea of what a film was."[78]

While many who worked on *The Newton Boys* blamed the studio for its lack of support or vision, D'Onofrio's reaction to the finished film was more pointed. "I think we all screwed up. All of us. And I felt like an idiot to be working for a director like Rick and to fail miserably." But while the actor had had reservations about the project during production, he empathized with Linklater. "I know how hard people can try to do something right, and it can still come out wrong."[79]

To the industry, however, it looked as if Linklater's latest project—his most ambitious—had, quite simply, failed. He wouldn't realize exactly how pervasive this attitude was until a year later when he began to pitch other projects. He could still get meetings, but he couldn't secure financial backing.

"I had made other films that hadn't made much money, but they'd always gotten good reviews. I think that's the first time I made something that got neither box office nor good reviews," says Linklater.[80]

"That's almost a career-ending moment," observes John Pierson of *The Newton Boys*'s release. The producer's representative who sold *Slacker* remained over the years someone with whom Linklater would discuss potential film projects, and Pierson followed the filmmaker's career with interest. "There was conflict [*Dazed and Confused*] followed by commercial catastrophe and little or no critical support. That's three strikes."[81]

As was his style, Linklater pushed forward on another project. He had read Ben Hamper's 1992 book *Rivethead: Tales From the Assembly Line*, a series of essays about Hamper's experiences as an autoworker at a General Motors assembly plant in Flint, Michigan, during the 1970s and 1980s. A budget of around $10 million was drawn up, location scouts took place, and actor Matt Dillon became attached to the project. What was missing, however, was the financing. "We put a lot of energy into *Rivethead* and I think that would have been a fine film. If *Newton Boys* had done better, we could have gotten *Rivethead* made," says Walker-McBay.[82]

"It was just not a very commercial film so it was kind of a dumb strategy on my part, trying to follow up a failure with a thing that wasn't a $3 million and under film," adds Linklater, who had turned down many "packaged" projects in the years since *Slacker* and liked to give the impression of being a filmmaker who chose his projects carefully. Although Linklater still received offers to direct after *Newton Boys*, the projects were for scripts written by others, and the films were much more commercial in nature than his previous movies. As much as he wanted to work, he resisted saying yes to any of the offers. In his mind, his acceptance would signal acquiescence. Like Randall "Pink" Floyd in *Dazed and Confused*, who refused to give in to his coaches by signing the drug pledge, Linklater, the former competitive athlete, wanted to avoid what he saw as a potential "weak moment." He didn't want to give the appearance of atoning for his independent "sins" by making a Hollywood movie. "I remember Quentin [Tarantino] even talking about that as a theoretical possibility: what an artist does the moment he gets nothing. What you do next says everything."[83]

Linklater would admit years later that the months following *The Newton Boys* were indeed a dark time. "It sucked. Once films are out of your control, it's surprising and sometimes heart-breaking what happens to them." In addition to *Rivethead*, Linklater wanted to adapt for the screen the book *Friday Night Lights: A Town, a Team, and a Dream* by Pulitzer Prize winner

H. G. "Buzz" Bissinger. Like *Rivethead*, this project also would fall through in the year following *The Newton Boys*'s release. (The film eventually would be made by actor-turned-filmmaker Peter Berg. Released in 2004, *Friday Night Lights* included football sequences shot at Westlake High School in Austin. In 2006, it became a television series for NBC filmed in and around the city.) As the months dragged on without a viable project on the horizon, Linklater began to feel as if he was back to square one, back in Galveston a decade earlier, after finishing his first feature-length film but with zero prospects for its release.[84]

But *The Newton Boys* experience and what followed also reminded the filmmaker of the rules of the game. The flavor-of-the-month quality of high school that he so accurately captured on film in *Dazed and Confused* paralleled the hierarchical workings of the film industry. Yet Linklater compared the film business to a darker but equally well-established institution. "Being in film is like being in organized crime. Every now and again, you have to take a beating and keep your mouth shut. Then you get to do it again. You get to live."[85]

Linklater would indeed get to live again, not to mention flourish, as a filmmaker. But it would require some serious soul searching and, ultimately, a return to a less expensive mode of filmmaking that would allow him to experiment with cutting-edge digital technology in *Tape* (2001) and *Waking Life* (2001). He would also revisit a style of storytelling he favored earlier in his career.

### Hollywood, Texas

The late nineties may have been tough on Linklater, but the Austin film community in general was flourishing. The university's Radio-Television-Film department, which had helped to train so many of the city's earliest filmmakers, was entering into its third decade with renewed vigor. Linklater had sat in on UT film classes when he first arrived in Austin in 1983, but the university rejected his formal application because of low grades. After the success of *Slacker* a friend and UT RTF guest lecturer invited the filmmaker to talk about the movie. "I went and spoke to his class, which was great. He told me later, after he wasn't there anymore, that he had sort of got pulled into an office where someone asked, 'What are you doing? Why'd you bring that guy here?' They told him, 'We don't want that *Slacker* attitude around here,'" recalls Linklater.[86] Robert Rodriguez wasn't shy about voicing his ambivalence regarding institutionalized film programs, either. In general, both filmmakers promoted a DIY filmmaking aesthetic. In other words, Austin's hometown film heroes weren't exactly poster boys for the university's RTF program.

But by the late 1990s the department had beefed up its production program, hiring new faculty who injected much-needed energy into the curriculum, brought valuable industry experience, and boasted impressive credentials. In particular, the hiring of award-winning documentary filmmakers Paul Stekler, Ellen Spiro, and others did much to raise the RTF department's profile throughout the country and distinguish it from similar film programs. (In 2004 John Pierson would generate additional buzz for the department when he became a lecturer after he and his wife Janet relocated to Austin. In turn, Janet became producer of the South by Southwest Film Festival in 2008.) During production on *The Newton Boys* in 1997 Peter James was invited by the RTF department to give a talk about his work. "I thought we'd get about 20 to 30 people," recalls James, who was flabbergasted when a crowd of nearly 200 turned out for the event.[87]

In May 1998, *Texas Monthly* devoted nearly an entire issue to its "Hollywood, Texas" cover story. Deputy editor Evan Smith, himself an inveterate movie fan, began the feature with a recounting of the Hollywood-style premiere for *The Newton Boys*. Sandra Bullock graced the magazine's black-and-white cover. "At the time Sandra Bullock had just moved here, but it was emblematic of what was perceived by some people to be a good thing and others to be a bad thing—the appropriation of our community by these rascals from the West Coast," says Smith. But not only had Bullock starred in and co-executive-produced *Hope Floats*, a 1998 romantic comedy filmed southeast of Austin in nearby Smithville, the bankable actress had successfully lobbied to have the production moved to Texas from Arkansas, where the story originally was set. Perhaps most significant for Austin's rising national profile as a celebrity hotspot, Bullock was in the process of building a house on Lake Austin and had established an Austin office for her newly formed production company. McConaughey purportedly introduced Bullock to the city in 1996, and he himself kept a house in a neighborhood not far from downtown. Recalls Smith, "Historically, when we put non-Texans who happen to be here on the cover, the issue doesn't do well." In this case, however, the "Hollywood, Texas" special issue generated a lot of interest, selling close to 42,000 newsstand copies to become the fourth best-selling issue of the magazine in 1998 and the best-selling special issue for the next five years.[88]

Veteran Hollywood producer Lynda Obst, who at the time had a production deal with Twentieth Century Fox, produced *Hope Floats* and had herself become a resident of the Texas Hill Country around 1993. Obst penned a piece for *Texas Monthly*'s Hollywood issue that touted the strength of Texas women and the state's Teamsters. Another article highlighted the state film community's top crew people. Although the fact that more than half of those profiled hailed from Austin might have had something to do with the location of the magazine's editorial offices, it also reflected the fact that many Dallas- and Houston-based crew members had begun to migrate to Austin in the mid to late 1990s to take advantage of the city's thriving production opportunities. It was also around this time, recalls Smith's wife Julia, who worked at the Texas Film Commission, that production managers in Dallas and Houston began lobbying to be listed in the state's production manual under the Austin banner.[89]

That same issue of *Texas Monthly* also profiled a twenty-six-year-old film fan named Harry Knowles, who represented certainly the most interesting link between Austin and Hollywood at the time. After an accident in 1996 left Knowles with a debilitating back injury and confined to bed, he fought boredom by creating a web site devoted to his favorite subject. Knowles's Ain't It Cool News (AICN) Internet site featured chatty movie reviews and "cool news" about filmmakers and upcoming movie projects. What set his site apart from other fan sites were the veracity of his movie production scoops and the freshness of his information, not to mention Knowles's own unbridled enthusiasm. Thanks to a network of informants (initially fabricated to enhance the site's authenticity and mystery), Knowles was able to provide up-to-the-minute filmmaking news about top-secret productions and reviews of movies still being previewed by their studios.

In late 1997 Knowles posted positive advance reviews from AICN readers in Minneapolis about James Cameron's *Titanic,* which for months had been pummeled in the trade press for its escalating budget and delayed release date. But not everyone associated with *Titanic* appreciated the favorable scoops. In Hollywood there had always been something of a gentleman's agreement between the press and the studios regarding screenings of unfinished films, and here was some unknown movie geek in Texas, of all places, pontificating about work that in many cases was in a vulnerable state. Recalls then Fox chairman Bill Mechanic of the *Titanic* screening, "We went to Minnesota, the middle of nowhere, and by the time we got back to L.A., [the reviews] were posted on the Internet. This was a movie with tons of problems in terms of getting it made and ultimately we thought we had a good movie. It's the issue that you're not giving filmmakers the chance to do their work."[90]

Miramax's Bob Weinstein first met Knowles at a test screening of a Rodriguez film and had similar reservations. "At that time everybody feared Harry Knowles. They said, 'Harry's gonna fucking review the movie. Don't let him in.' And Robert's attitude was, 'Hey, I got Harry here and he's gonna see the movie.'"[91]

"In the beginning I was like everyone else," says *Dazed and Confused* producer Jim Jacks. "I was like, 'Fuck! What are they doing reviewing test screenings?'" But in 1998 when Knowles and his growing legion of fans wrote glowing advance reviews about *A Simple Plan*, a small film being shepherded by Jacks, the producer began to feel differently about the web site. "His people really liked the film, and it helped me keep the studio out of re-cutting it. So I kind of liked Harry and those guys. Here's a guy who's trying to break into the movie industry, and he finds a totally unique way of doing it. I kind of admired that."[92]

Years later during the first preview screenings for *The Newton Boys*, Linklater got a call from Fox VP Peter Rice. "Hey, we got a great review," Rice told Linklater. "On 'Ain't It Cool.' Somebody in the audience wrote a great review of the film." Although the movie would need more than a positive Internet review to earn the studio's full support, at the time Linklater was encouraged and grateful for the positive feedback.[93]

"Harry scared the shit out of Hollywood with the postings about test screenings," says Quentin Tarantino, who was introduced to Knowles by Linklater at a party following the *From Dusk Till Dawn* premiere in January 1996. Knowles had become a Tarantino fan after seeing *Reservoir Dogs* and *True Romance* (directed by Oliver Stone and written by Tarantino). But when he attended the AFS benefit screening of *Pulp Fiction* in 1994, he wasn't overly impressed by Tarantino. "I actually thought Quentin was a little arrogant," Knowles recalls. Still, at the *Dusk* premiere Knowles was eager to meet the filmmaker. "In a lot of ways that was the single most important conversation I've had in my life," says Knowles of his thirty-minute chat with both filmmakers. "Quentin was every bit as interested in what I had to say as I was in what he had to say. And Quentin was one of the most famous people at that time." For the first time, Knowles felt as if his immense knowledge of film history and arcania had cachet in the world beyond the Austin Citywide Garage Sale, where he and his father sold movie memorabilia. "That conversation told me that if Quentin and Rick wanted to hear what I had to say about film, then maybe others would as well."[94]

Ain't It Cool News boasted many scoops, such as details about the cast for George Lucas's upcoming *Star Wars* prequels. Knowles also had access to confidential scripts like the one for Stanley Kubrick's as-yet-unreleased *Eyes Wide Shut*. Buzz began building about Knowles's site relatively quickly, and by the fall of 1997 profiles began popping up everywhere: the front page of the *Wall Street Journal*, in the *New York Times Magazine*'s special filmmaking issue, and on *Entertainment Weekly*'s "Power 101" list (he earned a special final mention at the end of the list's 100 entries). In March 1998 at a party during the South by Southwest Film Festival, Knowles met filmmaker and longtime Austin film supporter Jonathan Demme. "I know you," Demme said when they were introduced. "Everyone in Hollywood is afraid of you."[95]

If Knowles's site and his budding industry connections amplified the hype about Austin's movie scene, the city's expanding production chart offered tangible evidence of a viable film community. In addition to its movie-star pedigree, *Hope Floats* also was one of eleven projects made in Austin in 1997 along with *The Newton Boys*, and by 1998 that number had risen to fifteen. Two years earlier in 1996, Austin had boasted twenty-five productions, which was the largest number of projects made in Texas's top four cities (including Dallas, Houston, and San Antonio) in the entire decade. As Smith wrote in his introduction, "Finally, it seems, we're living up to our billing as the Third Coast, a friendly alternative to the schmooze-'em-and-abuse-'em ways of Los Angeles and New York."[96]

More than two decades had passed since the term "third coast" was first used to describe the state's filmmaking aspirations. Now, as a new millennium approached, that phrase seemed almost justified. The successes—and even the failures—of individuals like Bud Shrake, Bill Wittliff, Tobe Hooper, Eagle Pennell, Bill Broyles, Richard Linklater, and Robert Rodriguez had fostered a creative community in Austin. Organizations and institutions like the Texas Film Commission, the *Austin Chronicle*, and the Austin Film Society helped to build an infrastructure for this community. Their collective support would encourage a new crop of filmmakers to bring projects to and settle in and around Austin in the late 1990s, and the talents and experiences of this next wave would expand the city's creative development in interesting ways.

I always had the myopia that the traditional way to break into Hollywood is you go out to Hollywood, you make it as a writer, and you work within that system. I knew about *The Texas Chainsaw Massacre,* but it never occurred to me [to do that]. It wasn't until Rick Linklater and Robert Rodriguez just made their damn movies that I realized, "Shoot! I could do that."

TIM MCCANLIES

# The Company Man

Tim McCanlies and *Dancer, Texas Pop. 81*

n the early afternoon hours of Sunday, April 27, 1997, two armed men and a woman forced their way into the home of Joe and Margaret Rowe in the Davis Mountains Resort subdivision about ten miles outside of Fort Davis, Texas. The three individuals were members of the Republic of Texas, a militia group that believed the state of Texas to be a sovereign nation. The militia targeted the retired couple because Mr. Rowe was head of a homeowners' group that had been battling against the Republic of Texas and its members, whose headquarters was located in the same subdivision. The militia group's leader, Richard McLaren, explained to a San Antonio radio station that the Rowes were being held in exchange for the release of two of its members who had recently been arrested. Additionally, McLaren wanted state and local authorities to "agree to a referendum to allow Texans to vote on the independence issue."[1]

More than four hundred miles away in Rosanky, just east of Austin, forty-four-year-old screenwriter Tim McCanlies and his wife, Suzanne, were in the midst of final preparations for a trip to Fort Davis the following day. McCanlies was four weeks out from making his directorial debut with a script about four high-school seniors stuck in a tiny West Texas town. Named for the fictional place his characters inhabited, the screenplay for *Dancer, Texas Pop. 81* was written in 1987 as a "fuck you" to his bosses at Disney when they placed McCanlies on probation for refusing to choose his next writing project from among three of the studio's ideas.

McCanlies had found the Fort Davis location a few months earlier with the help of the Texas Film Commission's Tom Copeland, who had become a good friend and ally in the years since McCanlies moved back to Texas from Los Angeles in 1988. Originally McCanlies hoped to film *Dancer* in Austin, but Richard Linklater had secured all of the best locations for *The Newton Boys*, which also was going into production that spring.

Tucked away in the Davis Mountains, Fort Davis in many ways would turn out to be a better fit for the *Dancer* script. A rugged town of about 1,200 people, it boasted the state's highest elevation and the prestigious McDonald Observatory, a University of Texas research facility. Adding to Fort Davis's rustic charm was the Overland Trail, the country's longest unpaved road, which ran through the town.

Within days of McLaren's seizure of the Rowe homestead, however, the tiny hamlet morphed into a three-ring circus. Correspondents from every network and cable outlet descended on Fort Davis and made it their base camp. Media trucks lined the streets, and satellite dishes sprang up throughout the town. Police patrolled the ordinarily quiet streets, now jammed with reporters, photographers, and curious onlookers. Los Angeles–based managers and agents of the *Dancer* cast saw the television reports and began calling McCanlies, nervous about sending their clients to the remote location. Because authorities had blocked off access to the resort itself, nearby Fort Davis became the de facto site from which news reports originated. Members of *Dancer*'s production team, who had arrived weeks earlier to secure the town's two hotels for the cast and crew, now had to show photo identification to the state troopers guarding the entrance into and out of the town.

Months earlier, when McCanlies had visited the area on a location scout, he had stopped at the first gas station he spotted. He picked up the local paper, and a front-page headline blared, "Hollywood Production Scouting Location." Oh my god, McCanlies thought. Somebody else is already here. "And then I read the article, and it was [about] us. Somebody knew we were coming and we were already in the paper."[2] Now, with all of the craziness surrounding the standoff and his isolated location caught in the middle, it was as if his initial fears had come true. Somebody else *had* gotten there first.

The idea that someone or something had beaten McCanlies to the punch seemed to be the defining theme of his career at one time. On the verge of receiving his first big break as a screenwriter in Hollywood, McCanlies lost the job—a rewrite of the sequel to *Beverly Hills Cop*—to fellow Texans Bud Shrake and Gary Cartwright. And his decision to risk his own money to make his directorial debut came only after he watched Richard Linklater and Robert Rodriguez—nearly a generation younger and less experienced than McCanlies—achieve overnight success with their own independently funded productions. In actuality the writer-director simply had approached his career in a different way, learning the craft by writing his own screenplays, then earning money for exploitation scripts featuring terrified Girl Scouts and backwoods zombies. By the late 1980s he was under contract at Disney and eventually wrote for all of the top studios. By then he had almost as much industry experience as the older generation of Austin screenwriters that included Shrake and Bill Wittliff. By the early 1990s McCanlies was known in Hollywood as a go-to guy to pump up characterization in action screenplays. McCanlies was the company man, but he was looking for a way out of Los Angeles.

Eventually he managed to break free of the system that he initially believed would offer the most direct route to success. By the early 1990s, however, the film industry had shifted once again, and McCanlies struggled to take advantage of new opportunities in independent financing and distribution. In the process, he would have to make the transition from writer to director and learn to be politically savvy about a rising union presence in Texas that would threaten the production of his feature film debut. By the late 1990s, when the fortysomething screenwriter finally became an "overnight" success with the combined critical achievements of *Dancer* and his script for the animated film *The Iron Giant*, McCanlies had been working in the business for more than fifteen years. Like Wittliff, McCanlies would become an experienced voice of reason within the Austin film community as its infrastructure gave way to more growth and development in the 2000s.

Back in the spring of 1997, however, McCanlies was still a first-time director struggling to make his low-budget movie. The April standoff between the Republic of Texas militia and the authorities that overshadowed the start of production on *Dancer, Texas* lasted just over a week. Most of the activity took place out on State Highway 166, the two-lane blacktop that ran between Fort Davis and the resort—the same two-lane road where McCanlies planned to shoot *Dancer*'s opening sequence. On May 3, the group surrendered peacefully, although two of its members managed to escape into the Davis Mountains. (One was shot and killed by authorities two days after fleeing the compound. After the third day, state troopers halted their search for the remaining fugitive.) The news crews and journalists cleared out, and the town returned to its normal rhythms, albeit with a small movie crew living in its midst.[3]

McCanlies continued to oversee preproduction on *Dancer*. He was meeting with Andrew Dintenfass, his cinematographer, and discussing shot lists and conducting walk-throughs of the various sets when he received a frantic phone call from *Iron Giant* director Brad Bird in Los Angeles. Warner Bros. had requested last-minute changes to the script, and Bird wanted McCanlies to fly out to L.A. "I'm three weeks out and I'm running back to *Iron Giant* to work on the script," recalls McCanlies. While he was gone, a representative from *Dancer*'s bond company (the corporation providing insurance for the film) called the production office to check in. The individual was incredulous when told that McCanlies had left Fort Davis for L.A.[4]

In all, it was an inauspicious beginning to a project that had taken nearly a decade to get off the ground.

### Breaking into the Business

McCanlies is a fifth-generation Texan and the product of a peripatetic upbringing, thanks to his father's career in the Air Force. He switched schools often, attending elementary school in Lubbock and high school in Bryan. Summers were spent in Cisco with his grandparents. He was a precocious reader, and by the second grade he was writing novels that were influenced as much by the Hardy Boys detective series as the Tom Swift adventure novels. He also passed the time by fooling around with his dad's 8mm movie camera.

The discipline and pragmatic confidence that would mark the adult McCanlies as a screenwriter was present from an early age. In his early teens, for instance, McCanlies developed an interest in stage acting and behind-the-scenes technical work, but he dismissed his high school's theater program as amateurish. "I hung out at the local movie theater just so I could learn to run the projector. That was as close as I could get to the film business in Bryan, Texas."[5]

His bookishness and good grades allowed him to take college-level courses at nearby Texas A&M University while still in high school. He enrolled in a 16mm film production class and fine-tuned the primitive filmmaking techniques he had taught himself years earlier.

In 1971 McCanlies moved to Austin to attend the University of Texas. He chose to major in Radio-Television-Film but had trouble getting the classes he wanted because demand was so high. He realized he would probably be a senior before he was able to take all of the necessary film classes. With his student films in tow, he met one-on-one with the professors in order to gain admittance into UT's production courses.

For two years McCanlies took as many film classes as he could. (Fellow Bryan classmate Eagle Pennell was in one of his courses.) In late April 1973

*Kid Blue* opened in Austin at the State Theater downtown. McCanlies recalls going to a special screening of the film with Bud Shrake in attendance and being stunned that a local writer had Hollywood connections. "I'd never seen an actual writer of any sort before in the flesh."[6]

But by 1973 McCanlies had grown frustrated in Austin and with UT. He began to think that the movies he and his fellow students were making had very little to say. By the end of the school year McCanlies had dropped out of UT and moved back to Bryan, where he spent the next couple of semesters taking classes at Texas A&M. Eager for the life experience that he found missing from his and his classmates' first films, the twenty-one-year-old McCanlies decided to become a police officer. He was attracted to the idea because of its Hemingwayesque quality. He applied to and was accepted into the Dallas police academy, which, unlike Austin's academy, allowed younger officers to join the force.

McCanlies moved to Dallas in 1975 and for the next few years would live a split existence as he served on the force and took graduate film classes at Southern Methodist University. Barely out of his teens, he worked in some of the seediest sections of the city and was assigned to patrol the projects and break up fights in biker bars. McCanlies never planned to be a career officer, but he knew that his experiences as a rookie cop might provide valuable insight into human behavior and, perhaps, inspiration for future screenplays.

McCanlies enjoyed being at SMU, where he learned proper screenplay format and continued to make short films that impressed his teachers and colleagues. These shorts also fared well in national competitions, which boosted his confidence.

His films caught the attention of Dallas-based agents, who offered to help him find local work directing commercials and corporate training films. Recalls McCanlies, "It was like nobody had known anybody who had ever gone west of the Rockies to make it in L.A. The whole orientation was to stay in Dallas and work in industrials or do commercials. That's what everybody thought to do, and I never wanted to do that." Dr. G. William Jones was one of McCanlies's SMU professors and the founder of the well-regarded USA Film Festival, which had over the years screened first films by Austinites Tobe Hooper and Eagle Pennell. Years before McCanlies enrolled at the university, Jones had gone to L.A. to make his mark in the film industry. "He had the best contacts in the business, having been at the USA Film Festival. He came back several years later, back to teach. He was sort of a cautionary tale for everyone," says McCanlies.[7]

In 1978, after completing his master's degree at SMU, the aspiring screenwriter, who by now had several completed scripts under his belt, headed for L.A. Ostensibly he was planning to enroll in the American Film Institute's screenwriting program. But when he finally sat down with the three instructors who made up the core program, they pressed him about his aspirations. "We know that you already know how to write a screenplay," one of the teachers told him, and they explained that the program's first year was devoted to what were essentially writing exercises. They encouraged him to really think about his decision, to talk to other students currently enrolled. McCanlies argued that he was there to learn, but in reality he simply wanted to make contacts within the industry.[8]

McCanlies arrived in L.A. in the summer of 1978 and planned to begin the AFI program the following fall. In the meantime, however, he needed a job. He found script work writing "really, really low-budget stuff."[9] His first project was for a guy who made soft-core films and wanted to branch out into the horror genre, which was still going strong after the success of movies like *The Exorcist* and *The Texas Chainsaw Massacre* years earlier. McCanlies's script chronicled the terror of a group of young girls bunking at a Girl Scout camp and trapped between a raging forest fire and man-eating zombies. It was called *Crazies*, and it earned him a few thousand dollars. When the fall finally rolled around, McCanlies decided against going to AFI. Money was tight, and he reasoned that—technically—he already was getting paid for his writing.

He continued to work on his own screenplays and supported himself by writing computer programs, a skill that grew out of a lifelong interest in computers. By the early 1980s he had written six scripts, but he felt only two to be worth showing to agents. *Harlem* was a period piece that riffed on another of McCanlies's passions, a love of jazz. "That was the first one that anyone read. It was kind of Chandleresque, set in the Thirties, about a black musician who has to turn detective to find out who killed his mentor, another jazz musician," says McCanlies.[10] He had sent the script to Creative Artists Agency (CAA), where it had caught the attention of a few representatives.

He met with Rosalie Swedlin, Jack Radkey, and Tina Neuys, three of CAA's top agents. They spent a good chunk of the conversation extolling the virtues of their company, and after about twenty minutes an eager McCanlies interrupted them. "Are you going to ask me to be a client? If so, yeah! Don't sell me."[11]

Like *Harlem*, McCanlies's script for *Louisiana Run* showcased the writer's facility for action and character development, but it was a contemporary story inspired by McCanlies's experiences as a Dallas cop. On the strength of this script McCanlies got a meeting with an executive at Paramount who talked to him about writing a sequel to *Beverly Hills Cop* (1984), a fish-out-of-water story pairing Eddie Murphy with Judge Reinhold that was about to open in theaters. McCanlies was passed over for the project.

## Mouschwitz

Although McCanlies didn't work on the screenplay for *Beverly Hills Cop II*, he did collaborate with Dan Petrie, Jr., who created the original characters and wrote the script for the first film. At the time Petrie was under contract to Walt Disney, and McCanlies pitched a movie featuring three brothers, all of whom were Texas cops. One of the brothers worked as a county sheriff, another was a Dallas lieutenant, and the third was a member of the military police. When one brother finds himself involved in a gun-running incident in Monte Carlo, he summons his siblings to help. McCanlies pitched it as "three Texas cops in Monte Carlo, like *Beverly Hills Cop* with three guys." Although various studios came close to producing the script, it never got made. Still, it brought McCanlies to the attention of the Disney brass, who then signed him to a two-year deal.

In 1984 when Michael Eisner left Paramount Pictures to become CEO of the Walt Disney Company, he brought along protégé Jeffrey Katzenberg to head up motion picture development and resuscitate the studio's catatonic feature animation department. Part of their strategy involved cultivating talented actors and writers and convincing them to sign contracts with the studio. McCanlies joined the studio's ranks of promising young writers like Chris Carter (*The X-Files*), Chuck Pogue (*D.O.A.*), and Jim Mangold (*Heavy*, *Cop Land*). All of them kept tiny offices on the Disney lot, where the studio, according to McCanlies, concentrated on "keeping their salaries low and keeping them working." Still, McCanlies was thrilled to be working within the Hollywood system.[12]

Soon after McCanlies finished the script about the Texas cops he had lunch with Ricardo Mestres, one of Disney's top production executives. Mestres explained to the newly hired writer that the studio would pitch him three ideas, and from those he would select his next writing project. His choices included a story about an invisible teenager in high school, a movie about a talking dog, and the third installment in the *Ernest* comedies starring comedian Jim Varney. McCanlies hated all of them but took particular exception to the *Ernest* series, which he deemed "morally reprehensible. It's one thing to do slapstick and a guy gets his fingers caught in the window. But these movies enjoy Ernest's pain. They go in for a close-up while he's screaming for a full minute. It ceases to be humor and becomes sadistic."[13]

When McCanlies expressed his objections, Mestres reminded him of how profitable the *Ernest* series had been for the studio. By 1987, surprise hits like the *Ernest* comedy had boosted Disney's industry standing to third place in box office totals. But McCanlies wanted to write movies like the ones that he had grown up with. Live-action Disney classics like *Zorro* and *The Lovebug* had shaped McCanlies's sense of screen comedy and action. "At the time," he recalls, "I didn't think the Disney guys really got Disney movies."

Finally, McCanlies told Mestres that he didn't want to script any of the pitches offered to him.

"Well, tough," responded Mestres. "Pick one."

McCanlies was dumbstruck. "I was just outraged that I should be forced to write something that I didn't want to write. So I just pitched a fit there in the executive dining room at Disney."

Mestres was nonplussed. "Well, you just go home and sit for a month," he told McCanlies, essentially placing the writer in a studio-enforced time-out.[14]

McCanlies, of course, wasn't the first Disney writer under contract to be told what he could and couldn't write. "They called it Mouschwitz. There were a lot of other writers who weren't happy for whatever reason. Chris Carter's deal ended and they threw him off the lot."[15]

After his meeting with Mestres, McCanlies spent the following month channeling his frustration and anger into a script of his own entitled "Ties That Bind." The story centered on four graduating high school seniors who had spent all of their lives in the fictional West Texas town of Dancer. They daydreamed about moving to Los Angeles upon graduation, but when the moment finally arrives, all but one have cold feet. McCanlies drew upon his own experiences of growing up in Bryan as well as conversations about leaving Texas that he had had over the years with his friends.

As he wrote, McCanlies thought about Disney and its restrictive regime. A meticulously organized and controlling personality, Katzenberg had circulated a set of rules among the studio's writers that dictated what could and could not appear in a Disney production. He and Eisner had come up with the list while still at Paramount, and it included directives like, "Nothing rural. No dust. No snow. No quaint New England Village. No saddles." Explains McCanlies, "So basically with the script I set out to break every one of those rules. It wasn't a deliberate thing, but it was sort of like 'Okay, screw you.'"[16]

It was also during this time in late 1987 that McCanlies met his future wife, Suzanne. He was in his mid-thirties, quiet, a bit rumpled. The writer's friends, some of whom were also transplanted Texans, hounded him about meeting another native because, as McCanlies observes dryly, "Dating California girls wasn't working that well."[17]

McCanlies's best friend, who also knew Suzanne's sister and her husband, an aspiring actor, introduced the couple. "The arrangement was if Tim could get him an agent, he would get Tim a wife," recalls Suzanne.[18]

"It really wasn't love at first sight," she remembers. The thirty-five-year-old writer was still working on the script for "Ties That Bind," and he would eventually return to Disney to finish out his contract. Explains Suzanne, "I was very intimidated when we first started dating because he's almost eleven years older than I am. I was just out of college. He was a grown up."[19]

Still, the pair continued to spend time together, and they eventually hit a comfortable groove. Their Texas backgrounds no doubt offered a familiarity and groundedness that neither had really found since arriving on the West Coast. Suzanne's anxiety gradually gave way to an innate silliness, and Tim began to trust the relationship enough to let her read his work. The first script she read was "Ties That Bind." Tim told her he wanted someone from Texas to weigh in on it. She loved the story and its characters, who were very much like the boys she had grown up with.

McCanlies returned to Disney, script in hand. He gave it to Mestres, who read it and told the writer that he didn't think he "got it."

In April 1988, Tim proposed to Suzanne. Members of the Writers Guild of America, West, had recently gone on strike against the studios, and McCanlies, a member, was in a holding pattern. The couple waited a bit to see what would happen with the strike, and when it looked as if there were no immediate end in sight, they decided to get married two months later. (The strike ended after twenty-two weeks.)

Given their shared dislike of L.A., they decided to return to Texas. Suzanne and Tim found a house overlooking Austin's Lake Travis and moved there at the end of 1988. Tim had gotten out of his contract with Disney, which made the move a little easier. Still, says Suzanne, "Back then, people didn't live somewhere else and work in L.A."[20] Writers like Bill Wittliff and Bill Broyles had made Texas their home base, but they also were more successful and established than McCanlies.

## If They Can Do It, I Can Do It

McCanlies didn't have a lot of time to hang out in Texas. In a relatively short period he began working with many of the major studios as a script doctor and writer for hire. McCanlies's uncredited rewrites included Touchstone's action-adventure movie *Shoot to Kill* (1988). He also worked on a few scripts for Columbia and was involved with a handful of projects at Warner Bros. including the family comedy *Little Giants* (1994). "I would sort of write the draft that would have character moments in them so they could then go out and get the actors," recalls McCanlies. With the script for *My Fellow Americans* (1996), for instance, he toned down the story's original thriller elements and massaged it into a comedy that eventually starred Jack Lemmon and James Garner as two former presidents forced to team up in order to expose a political scandal. With each project, McCanlies attempted to navigate that particular studio's politics. He also received screenplay and story credit for his work on Warner's sequel to *Dennis the Menace*. In his original version of the script, McCanlies teased out the underlying affection between the curmudgeonly Mr. Wilson and his annoying young neighbor, but the movie ultimately privileged sight gags over characterization. McCanlies was bitterly disappointed when the movie went straight to video. Despite the ups and downs of working with the studios, McCanlies was relieved to be out of his contract with Disney and relished his "free agent" status. "I was still at an age where I was trying to figure out what my voice was, what it was I wanted to do."[21]

As the years passed McCanlies's reputation grew, but he describes his rise in the business as "workmanlike." By the mid-1990s he had become known for his ability to resuscitate weak action scripts. Gradually his increased clout allowed him to pick better people with whom to collaborate, and his experiences taught him how to be savvier about working with the studios.

The McCanlieses were glad to be based in Texas, and they enjoyed living in Austin. Marlene Saritzky, then executive director of the Texas Film Commission, invited Tim to lunch with a number of other local writers. McCanlies also was asked to speak at the first Austin Heart of Texas Film Festival and Screenwriters Conference in the fall of 1994. With a mixture of curiosity and envy Tim took note of Richard Linklater's success with *Slacker*, and he and Suzanne were equally interested in *El Mariachi* when it was released in 1992. "When Robert's movie first came out, we went to see it and to several things where he spoke about it and told how he did it. It was such a great story," recalls Suzanne.[22]

But for Tim, who had just turned forty and was nearly two decades older than Rodriguez, his and Linklater's seemingly overnight success felt almost like an affront to his own years of toiling for and kowtowing to the studios in Hollywood. "At first I was sort of outraged. 'Wait a minute! They're cheating! They took a shortcut.'" But their successes also galvanized him. "Once he heard them," says Suzanne, "he said, 'You know what? If they can do it, I can do it.'" He took note of shifts in the industry, too, and observed in the mid-1990s that the market was widening for independently made films, especially first features, which seemed to be displacing foreign films. Gradually and over the next couple of years, McCanlies began to make plans to produce his coming-of-age movie himself.[23]

By the mid-1990s the couple had moved from their house on the lake to a 250-acre ranch in Rosanky, a small town southeast of Austin. Together they turned the property into a working cattle ranch with around 60 cows. Not long after, Warner Bros. approached McCanlies about adapting Ted Hughes's *The Iron Man* into a screenplay for an animated musical to be directed by Brad Bird. (The musical component was dropped during preproduction.) Bird was known for his work on the Fox television series *The Simpsons*, and the animated adaptation of Hughes's book would mark his feature filmmaking debut. After receiving a copy of the book and a cassette tape of songs, McCanlies set to work on the project.[24]

Between 1996 and 1997, McCanlies spent a good deal of time in L.A. working with Bird on the script, which would be called *The Iron Giant*. Initially Bird and McCanlies got along well even though they disagreed about certain plot points. According to McCanlies, Bird wanted to kill off the giant at the end of the movie, but he preferred Hughes's original ending, in which the fallen giant reassembles himself. McCanlies was impressed by Bird's handling of the studio brass although he also privately thought that the first-time director created many of his own problems. McCanlies suggested to Bird that he pick his battles, but Bird saw no reason to back down. "He would go toe to toe with the head of the studio over the littlest things," recalls McCanlies, who began to notice that after Bird would storm out of a meeting, those left behind would speak almost reverentially about Bird's talent. "And I realized, you can get away with a lot more than you think if you really act like you know what you're doing. Because in [the executives'] heart of hearts, I think *they* really don't know."[25]

### I Could Say Red or Green

During this time McCanlies also began moving forward with plans to make his own movie. He had changed the title of his script to *Dancer, Texas Pop. 81* after a thriller called *The Tie That Binds* opened in theaters in 1995. After talking to various individuals about how they had produced their first low-budget films, he decided he could shoot *Dancer* on Super 16mm for about $100,000 of his own money. He also began meeting interested parties through his contacts in the industry. He was introduced to Chase Foster, an L.A. producer with ties to a group of Alabama-based investors made up of family friends, dentists, and the like. After hearing McCanlies's pitch, Foster told him he thought he could raise $200,000, maybe even $300,000. As Foster began to shop the idea around, more money was added to the proposed budget while the list of "producers" multiplied. Eventually Foster brought the project to Leanna Creel and Michael Burns of Ignite Entertainment, an independent production company that focused on small-budget films. Burns had overseen the Los Angeles office of Prudential Securities and had recently created the Hollywood Stock Exchange, an Internet site that allowed players to buy and sell entertainment companies, actors, and film properties in a virtual world, much like they would stocks and bonds. From that Burns spun off HSX Films, which eventually became Ignite. But as McCanlies soon found out, Burns was more than a wannabe producer. He had successfully raised budgets of $1 million and secured additional financing from various banks. (In 2000 Burns became vice chairman of Lionsgate.) He was impressed by McCanlies's script and the writer's strong point of view. And after meeting McCanlies, he had no doubts about his commitment to the project.[26]

For McCanlies's film, Burns was willing to invest around $300,000 and thought he could secure an additional $500,000 from Imperial Bank, which had provided him with a line of credit for the Hollywood Stock Exchange. By the time McCanlies went into production in the spring of 1997, the budget had swelled to $1.1 million.

McCanlies was determined to shoot his film in Texas. Texas Film Commission executive director Tom Copeland (who replaced Marlene Saritzky after Governor Ann Richards left office) had introduced himself to McCanlies at an Austin film function a few years back. Before he even met McCanlies he had been knocked out by his script for *Secondhand Lions*, a touching comedy about two crusty old Texans. Many in the industry loved the script but few were willing to take a chance on it partly because of the advanced age of its protagonists. At one point Warner Bros. did consider shooting the script and scouted Texas for possible locations, which is when Copeland got a hold of the screenplay. A McCanlies fan ever since, Copeland helped him find the Fort Davis location.

With his budget more or less in place, McCanlies began to assemble a crew. They were a typical mix of department heads from Los Angeles overseeing Texas-based electricians and grips. Veteran Austin sound recordist

Wayne Bell brought his low-budget experience from movies like *The Texas Chainsaw Massacre* and *Red Headed Stranger*. McCanlies knew he needed a cinematographer who could work fast given the movie's tight, three-week shooting schedule. Through contacts in L.A. he found Andrew Dintenfass, who had experience shooting commercials and television and was used to working on deadline.

Still spending the majority of his time in L.A. because of *Iron Giant*, McCanlies also began to read actors for *Dancer*. "There weren't that many great parts for guys of that age," recalls McCanlies, who met with nearly 60 young actors to cast the four teenagers in the movie. Joey Lawrence (of television's *Blossom*) auditioned for the part of Terrell Lee, and David Faustino (*Married With Children*) and Seth Green (*Austin Powers*) also read for lead roles. The parts eventually went to four up-and-coming actors. Breckin Meyer originally read for the part of Squirrel, the most socially challenged of the four characters, but McCanlies asked him back to read for the slightly larger role of Keller Coleman. With his open, amiable face, Meyer seemed like a good fit for the sensitive Keller, and he had recently played a similar part in Amy Heckerling's hit comedy *Clueless*. For the role of rich boy Terrell Lee, McCanlies cast Peter Facinelli, a classically handsome actor who had appeared in a handful of small films and television movies. The part of Squirrel went to Ethan Embry, who had perhaps the most film experience of the four young actors. He had also appeared as part of the young male ensemble in Tom Hanks's directorial debut *That Thing You Do!* Relative newcomer Eddie Mills rounded out the foursome as John.[27]

Principal photography on *Dancer* began on May 31, 1997. The Republic of Texas standoff had blown over although the subsequent trial of the militia members had yet to begin. Meyer, Facinelli, Embry, and Mills all flew together from Los Angeles to Texas. They arrived in El Paso, where they boarded a van and made the fairly desolate three-hour drive into the mountains surrounding Fort Davis. "We finally got to the little motel in Fort Davis. We're all in the van and we're like, 'Good grief. What have we gotten ourselves into?'" recalls Mills. As they disembarked from the van and gathered their luggage, they spotted a tarantula moving slowly across the parking lot. "The four of us were like, 'No way! Where *are* we?'"[28]

Because McCanlies eventually cast a number of Fort Davis locals as extras, the entire town began to resemble a film set. "It sort of made everybody feel like they were part of the movie," recalls Suzanne, who signed on as her husband's unpaid assistant after the bond company demanded that he hire one. Fort Davis really was like the fictional Dancer in many respects. Everything, including the gas station, shut down around five o'clock each day. Cell phones didn't function in the mountainous area, so if someone needed to talk to a cast or crew member, they drove around until they found that person.[29]

McCanlies had spent a week rehearsing with the four actors prior to shooting. "That week of rehearsal was probably the most important thing that film had going for it," says Mills, who had a friendship with Meyer that predated the film. "It gave the four of us time to bond as if we were growing up in this town." McCanlies also encouraged the actors to hang out together and explore the area. Like the old men in the movie, they passed the time sitting in chairs on the front porch of their hotel and playing cards or exploring the surrounding mountains and small towns.[30]

For McCanlies, it was a strange experience being on the set and surrounded by so many people dependent on him for information and guidance. "Tim got overwhelmed with people asking him questions a million times a day. He's used to working by himself in a room, not talking to anybody. People just bombarded him every time he turned around," says Suzanne.[31]

But perhaps the biggest adjustment for the soft-spoken McCanlies was thinking of himself as a director instead of a writer. "I had spent most of my life in Hollywood being politic and really learning how to never be demanding, to always be a writer—to be obsequious, to be sneaky—to get my way in a roundabout way, to never get in anyone's face." Friends in L.A. offered advice, encouraging him to fire someone on the set in full view of cast and crew on the very first day of production "to set the mood." McCanlies had observed two types of directors in Hollywood: the asshole who's a little bit paranoid and the "gracious host of the party." He tried to be the latter, but he also had to overcome people's assumptions about filmmakers. With his burly build and no-nonsense attitude, McCanlies still looked and acted like the Dallas cop he had once been. He dressed casually on the set, occasionally wearing overalls that made him look more like a farmer than a filmmaker.[32]

Early on in preproduction the make-up artist chewed out McCanlies for lounging in the director's trailer before he realized that the laidback guy with the thinning hair was indeed the filmmaker. After shooting began, McCanlies made the mistake of plopping down at the grips' table for lunch one day. It was an uncomfortable meal—"They were just quaking," recalls Suzanne—and McCanlies realized that he too had things to learn. When the wardrobe department asked him to choose between a red and a green dress for one character's costume, McCanlies, used to appeasing heads of production and other studio executives, solicited the opinion of the wardrobe person. "And it would just confuse them by trying to include them in the process like I would a studio guy. Finally I realized that it was just this amazing thing as a director: I could say what I wanted, and I didn't even have to give a reason. I could say red *or* green," remembers McCanlies. "From that point on, it really changed me."[33]

## We Bought You

At the beginning of the second week of principal photography the *Dancer* production office began receiving calls from the Accounts Payable office of Sony Pictures. The person on the other end of the phone was requesting paperwork and social security numbers for tax purposes, but no one in the *Dancer* office knew why. "We bought you," the Accounts Payable clerk explained matter-of-factly. This was news to everyone, and a big surprise to McCanlies, who immediately got on the phone to Burns in Los Angeles.[34]

Unbeknownst to McCanlies, sometime during preproduction Burns had shown the *Dancer* script to his good friend Jon Feltheimer, who headed up TriStar Television, the broadcast arm of Sony Pictures. "He loved the script and gave it to John Calley," says Burns of Feltheimer's decision to pass it to the chairman of Sony Pictures. Although Feltheimer thought *Dancer* had potential as a television series, "it was really a feature film that we were selling," says Burns. Calley read the script, liked it, and gave the go-ahead to buy it. He didn't seem to mind that *Dancer* already was in production, shooting on location in Texas. According to Burns, Calley liked the authenticity of McCanlies's screenplay.[35]

But McCanlies was less than thrilled to hear the news. "I wanted to go to Sundance. I wanted to do the whole indie thing. I was joking about how I was an independent filmmaker for a whole week, then I was back in the studio system again." He also worried that representatives from the studio would bear down on the set, giving him notes on the script, and possibly worse.[36]

"All hell broke loose, basically," recalls Suzanne, who watched her husband shift into panic mode as he made numerous phone calls to his manager and agent. "He thought, 'Sony Pictures bought this. The first thing they're gonna do is come in and fire me.'"[37]

For the next few days the mood on the set was tinged with anxiety. Crew members worried about their own jobs, and some began to suspect that the Sony call was a ruse, that McCanlies had lied about *Dancer*'s being an independent production in order to hire people for less money. A couple of individuals even lobbied for higher salaries. "It was still in the first week, and people still didn't really know Tim," recalls Suzanne. Additionally, the scenario seemed a little far-fetched, that a major studio would suddenly decide to pick up a low-budget film already in production.[38]

The studio did not send executives to the set, however, and no one pulled the plug on McCanlies or the production. "Once the panic wore off and we realized they weren't going to fire anybody, then everyone settled down," says Suzanne. It didn't hurt that they were working on location more than 150 miles from the largest city. "[Sony] couldn't find us on a map."[39]

In reality the sale of the movie to Sony meant an infusion of $1 million earmarked for postproduction. *Dancer* would be released through TriStar Pictures, an entity originally created in 1982 when Columbia Pictures, HBO, and CBS merged their resources. TriStar became a division of Sony Entertainment when the company purchased Columbia in 1989. Now that *Dancer* had a distributor, the extra money from Sony would be spent on the film's "deliverables," or the materials required for a theatrical release. The deliverables included things like a more expensive sound mix, which would be done on the Sony lot. It also meant that McCanlies could cut the film using the studio's editing facilities.

### Right to Work for Less: State of the Union in Texas

The downside of the deal, if there was one, was that it drew attention to the production, something McCanlies and his producers had been trying to avoid in order to keep the film non-union and shoot it as quickly and as cheaply as possible. (In the end McCanlies did hire a couple of Teamsters who handled most of the union details.) Thanks in part to the film commission's Copeland, *Dancer* never appeared on the Film Production Hotline, the listing of productions shooting in the state at any given time. It also remained absent from *Variety*'s Film Production Chart, the official industry listing of projects currently in production. "We were like this big secret because the unions were just then really getting strong and we were probably one of the last [shows] not to get organized. We were completely off the radar," says McCanlies.[40]

By the mid-1990s, Texas's status as a right-to-work state had come under fire. By definition, the phrase "right to work" means that a production cannot refuse someone the right to work on a film simply because they do not belong to the union. Unit production manager Bill Scott had worked on *The Newton Boys* with Richard Linklater, and he had had to negotiate some of the union issues at stake on that film and had heard about many others on projects going into production around the same time. "There were productions coming in—and even some local shows—that were exploiting people, working them sixteen hours per day without overtime, just abusing people. So they started to get Texas unionized," recalls Scott. Before 1996, says Copeland, the union generally left alone projects with budgets of less than $3 million. But as the pressure to organize increased, the union dropped this figure to $1 million, and they began looking specifically at Texas, which attracted mostly low-budget features and television movies.[41]

Around this time, Copeland decided to hold a powwow of sorts with approximately forty union representatives, producers, vendors (caterers, equipment owners, etc.), and state-wide crew members in order to address the situation. Says Scott, "We all met at the State Capitol and just had a half-day long bitch session. Tom moderated it beautifully. From that point on, it was smooth." Observes Copeland, "Producers and production managers thought it was great. If you represented the IATSE [International Alliance of Theatrical Stage Employees], it was a public lynching. They got hammered pretty hard, but what could they expect? They had thrown down a gauntlet and it was affecting a lot of people's lives who weren't a part of the IATSE."[42]

Copeland's opinion of the unions began to change as he and his contemporaries grew older and had to worry about things like insurance and college tuition for their families. Also, by the mid-1990s, as more and more studio films—unionized by California law—began coming to the state, Austin crew members found it necessary to join the union if they wanted to keep working—not to mention living—in their hometown.

Ken Rector had started in the business as a prop master at the Paramount Theatre, which like many Austin theaters had been unionized for decades. (Local 205, whose majority members were projectionists, had been chartered in 1911.) So when Rector segued from theater to feature films in the 1980s, he was already a union employee. He shared the commonly held view among union members about Texas's right-to-work status: "We called it 'right to work for less' because it usually equates with a businessperson wanting to pay a below-scale wage. And for the most part that's always how it's been interpreted from a labor standpoint."[43]

In 1991 Local 484 was established in Austin to represent individuals in stagecrafts such as set design, wardrobe, electricians, and the like. (Cinematographers were considered a separate group and represented by Local 600.) The local enjoyed relative freedom apart from the IATSE and was able to negotiate its own contracts with Los Angeles-based producers and studios. "Back then," says Rector, who would become IATSE's regional business manager in 2001, "we had full autonomy to write our own agreements." But as film and television projects began migrating to Canada so producers could take advantage of the country's generous tax incentives, it became clear to the union's chief officers that something needed to be done to keep work within the borders of the United States. In 1993 the president of the IATSE, in an effort to bring order to the "patchwork quilt" of regional and local contracts throughout the country, announced the union's desire to establish a national film contract. By January of 1999, the union would reach a three-year agreement for productions in the southern states, including Texas. The agreement would take effect retroactively on October 1, 1998, five months after the release of *Dancer*.[44]

But in April 1997, when McCanlies was about to start production, the union tensions were still somewhat unresolved. The brouhaha over the Republic of Texas standoff during *Dancer*'s preproduction had threatened to draw attention to the project. Members of the media, who had descended on the town to cover the incident, began to suspect something else was happening in Fort Davis when they heard the hotels were booked and saw members of the crew moving purposefully around the town. Restricted in their access to the standoff taking place on the highway outside of Fort Davis, some reporters began to nose around for another story. The hotel staff, none of who wanted the media attention, agreed to keep mum about the upcoming film shoot, as did business owners and other locals.

In the week after *Dancer*'s sale to Sony TriStar in June 1997, producer Chase Foster gave an interview to the *Odessa American* newspaper and mentioned that the film had been picked up by Sony. The article, which ran on June 14, caught the attention of union representatives in Texas. "I think they were content to leave us alone until they found out we were a Sony movie," says McCanlies. "Suddenly the full scale of the union started looking around Fort Davis. And I'm told that Tom [Copeland] went to the head of the IATSE and said, 'Look, he doesn't have any money. He's from Texas, just let him get his movie made. The next one, he'll hire union guys. Just don't kill him.'" Although Copeland never told McCanlies that he did this, the filmmaker heard from a number of other people that the head of the Texas Film Commission indeed had gone to bat for him. "I'd like to take all the credit, but I can't," says Copeland, who remembers that under the union's guidelines at the time, *Dancer*'s budget was "right on the line" of films they were trying to organize. Copeland credits McCanlies's L.A. producer Tina Brawner (a Houston transplant) and production manager Tim Swan for putting together a crew that included a couple of union technicians, which alleviated some of the pressure.[45]

## Wrapping Up

McCanlies and Dintenfass had scheduled the shooting of *Dancer*'s poignant finale during the second full week of production. The scene had the four friends saying their goodbyes at the local bus stop as the Dancer townsfolk sent them on their way to California. It required a kind of bonding that had yet to occur among the four actors, who had arrived on set less than two weeks earlier. "Nobody was emotionally invested in the scene," recalls Suzanne. "My guys were just not ready for that," agrees McCanlies, who wanted to be supportive of his actors but didn't want to be seen as an ass-kisser.[46]

Mills, who was twenty-eight at the time, was the oldest of the four actors. He and McCanlies shared similar backgrounds: both were raised in small towns, and Mills, who grew up raising cattle, could appreciate McCanlies's "other" life as a Texas rancher. Meyer, Facinelli, and Embry, however, were less enamored of Fort Davis's picturesque community and its slow-paced lifestyle. "The other guys were a bit more on the city side of things," explains Mills. "They were bored stiff, so it was constantly like looking for trouble." According to Mills, his castmates also didn't seem to respond to McCanlies's quiet personality and were less willing to cooperate with the first-time director. "They gave Tim respect when respect was due, but they didn't go out of their way to make his life a little easier."[47]

Despite McCanlies's hopes that the director of photography would work quickly given his experience in commercials and television, the first-time director felt they were wasting time on shots they wouldn't use in the final cut. Dintenfass didn't think McCanlies quite understood what it took to translate a written scene for the screen. "You don't realize that when you write a particular scene it takes an effort to put it on film," he says.[48]

"He got a good look, but he took a lot of time to do stuff," recalls McCanlies. The two would often disagree about how to shoot certain scenes, and against his better judgment McCanlies found himself acquiescing. "The DP would say, 'No, you want this [shot] instead,' and I would go, 'Uh, I don't think so, but okay,' and I would let him have his shot too." The rest of the crew picked up on the tension and tended to side with McCanlies. At one point the production's lone Teamsters, who disparagingly referred to the cinematographer as "Dental Floss," offered to "take care of" him for McCanlies. (He declined.)[49]

The *Dancer* crew was shooting six-day weeks, but for McCanlies Sundays were spent working on the *Iron Giant* script. "Brad was sending me drafts. I was giving him notes on my one day off," says McCanlies. After being in charge of his own movie, McCanlies's confidence had increased and his overall attitude had changed. Now when he dealt with Bird, he didn't feel the need to mince words. If he disliked Bird's choice of dialogue, he told him so. Recalls McCanlies, "I don't know that Brad and I got along as well at that point. And I've sort of been that way ever since."[50]

The remoteness of the Fort Davis location meant that McCanlies had to wait at least seventy-two hours to review a particular day's footage. At the end of each shooting day a crew member would drive six hours roundtrip to El Paso to send the footage to the lab and pick up the previous day's dailies. In some cases, the actors already had finished their scenes and left Texas before their footage arrived back from processing. McCanlies reviewed the dailies on a videocassette recorder in one of the hotel's common areas, which turned the event into an open house of sorts. "Everybody went because there wasn't anything else to do," recalls Suzanne.[51]

Fort Davis and its residents, many of whom were in the movie as extras, were eager to assist the production in whatever ways they could. "A lot of that had to do with Tim's knowledge of the place and his sort of empathy with the small-town sensibilities," says Dintenfass, whose own assumptions about small-town Texas life were challenged by the "worldly" attitudes of the amiable locals.[52]

A week later McCanlies and his cast and crew gathered on Highway 166 to shoot the movie's opening scene, which features the four boys lounging in lawn chairs as Keller reads his letter to the Rand McNally publishing company requesting that their remote hometown be added to the map of Texas. By late June, the *Dancer* production had entered its fourth week and the four young actors had finally relaxed into their characters. They were all excited to be filming the scene, whose remote location and minimalist framing offered a simple and effective visual joke to start the movie. In the original shooting script the scene began with an establishing shot of the four boys, sitting four abreast across the blacktop outside an old filling station, and then cut to a montage of insert shots of things referenced in Keller's letter. "The guys had worked on that scene so much. I did just one take of them doing the whole scene, and then I did the pickups, got the coverage for before and after the reading of the letter," says McCanlies, who liked the single shot greatly and decided to open the movie with just the long take, which lasts nearly two minutes. During filming crew members were stationed ten miles out in both directions to hold traffic once the cameras rolled, but in a case of life imitating art, not a single car passed during the two hours it took to shoot the scene.[53]

Filming wrapped at the end of June, and McCanlies and his producers threw a Texas-themed party for the cast and crew on June 29. After a couple of days back in Rosanky, McCanlies headed out to Los Angeles to oversee postproduction on the film. On July 1, an article appeared in *Variety* officially announcing TriStar's acquisition of *Dancer*.[54]

### A Different Mindset

Once out in L.A., McCanlies and editor Rob Kobrin began to sift through the footage and assemble a rough cut of the movie. Kobrin had gotten his start as an assistant editor on Robert Altman's political miniseries *Tanner '88*. He had a string of forgettable films to his credit, but he worked fast. At the time of the sale to TriStar, McCanlies was adamant that the rough cut shown to Sony chairman John Calley be screened on film rather than video, a technical expense that would eat up $150,000 of the approximate $1 million postproduction budget. McCanlies knew that the other films in the Sony pipeline would be screened as work prints, or fully edited film prints (as opposed to videotape) from which the final negative would be pulled. McCanlies also knew that *Dancer*, with its endless West Texas landscapes, would look its most spectacular on film. So he and Kobrin edited on the Avid and then pulled a work print only for the shots that they needed. (Typically, a work print contains the best three or four takes of a scene, taken from the projected dailies, and the final cut of the movie comes out of that work print.) Although McCanlies feared that working on the Sony lot might invite meddling from studio executives, the opposite was true, and the writer-director found himself enjoying the postproduction process. The editing went quickly if only because the budget hadn't allowed time to shoot much additional footage.

After a favorable screening for his producers in Los Angeles later that fall, McCanlies was ready to show the film to Calley and other executives at Sony and TriStar. Many of his friends in the business had advised McCanlies not to attend the studio screening, telling him it "wasn't done," but the stubborn first-time director wasn't about to miss the opportunity to gauge Calley's reaction in person.

McCanlies arrived early for the noon screening, which took place on the Culver City lot in one of the studio's screening rooms. "It was really intimidating because all of these executives came screaming in on their cell phones," recalls McCanlies, who immediately began to worry that the distracted "suits" wouldn't be able to appreciate *Dancer*'s relaxed pace.[55]

When the movie ended and the lights came up ninety minutes later, most of the executives scurried back out the door. A few remained behind—"a handful of Young Turks"—and told McCanlies that they'd get their notes together and call him the following day. But Calley, who was one of the first to stand after the closing credits, said simply, "Oh, it was just lovely."[56]

McCanlies appreciated Calley's kind words, but he still waited anxiously for the obligatory phone call the following day telling him how the studio wanted him to change the movie. Burns, who was not at the screening, had spoken with some of the executives by phone afterward and learned that in actuality they had few notes to pass on to Calley. McCanlies and Kobrin were in the editing room when the studio call finally came. On the other end of the phone an assistant told him, "Mr. Calley says your movie's lovely, don't change a thing. Finish your movie." McCanlies thanked the assistant and hung up. He turned to Kobrin and said, "It'll never be this way ever again."[57]

Sony had scheduled *Dancer* for a May 1 release, sandwiching it between bigger TriStar releases like *My Giant*, a comedy starring Billy Crystal, and the hotly anticipated re-make of *Godzilla*. The studio told McCanlies they'd open his film in New York and Los Angeles, the same way they opened all of their other small movies.

"Well, this is not a New York or L.A. movie," McCanlies argued. "It's for everyone *except* the people in New York or L.A. You're really doing it a disservice."

TriStar was unmoved by McCanlies's protests. When he complained to friends in the business, other filmmakers who'd had their movies released by the studios, they all pretty much told him the same thing: They stayed out of it "because they're just going to do what they do."[58]

Like Linklater and Rodriguez, McCanlies couldn't imagine *not* being involved in the marketing and release of his first movie. Instead, he scoured the trades for relevant articles that backed up his suggestions. He wrote letters to Jeff Blake, president of Sony Pictures Releasing, which handled distribution for all of the company's divisions, and included the articles. Recalls McCanlies, "I was sort of used to dealing with studio guys in development who were generally pretty well-read, loved movies, etc. So now I'm dealing with guys who are salesmen. It was just a different mindset than what I was used to."[59]

What McCanlies didn't know at the time was that the studio had decided to cut its losses, spending as little as possible to advertise and release the movie in only two markets in order to secure an output deal, a common business practice in Hollywood. The terms of these deals vary, but essentially the studio enters into a contract with, for instance, a video or cable company to purchase the movie once it's been released in a certain number of theaters in a minimum number of markets. The studio makes a few million dollars on the deal, recouping its initial investment without having gambled significant revenue on an uncertain theatrical release. In turn a sale to cable could also trigger foreign deals.

Impressed, perhaps, by McCanlies's persistence on behalf of his movie (or simply weary of the filmmaker's badgering), Blake sat him down and explained the studio's strategy. "He showed me how they were going to make much more money on my movie than *Godzilla*," recalls McCanlies, referring to the outsized Prints and Advertising budget spent to generate buzz for the monster movie, a film estimated to cost $125 million. While he might have understood the practice from a business perspective, McCanlies was disappointed the marketing and distribution people didn't "think outside that box."[60]

### Going Gently Against the Grain

Meanwhile McCanlies was pushing the film on his own, submitting a rough cut to the Sundance Film Festival that ultimately was rejected. He had better luck closer to home when he received word that *Dancer* would have its first public screening at the South by Southwest Film Festival in March 1998, where it would play in one of the coveted opening night slots at the 1,200-seat Paramount Theatre.

On Friday, March 13, the historic theater in downtown Austin was filled to capacity for the screening. The festival audience included many of McCanlies's friends and family as well as local crew who had worked on the film. Tim and Suzanne had arranged to fly in Mills, who had maintained a close friendship with the couple after the movie wrapped.[61]

The audience embraced the film warmly despite a minor technical problem that sent Rob Kobrin, McCanlies's editor, scurrying into the projection booth. A few days before the Paramount screening, technicians had been running tests with *The Newton Boys*, which was having its world premiere at the festival the day after *Dancer*'s first screening. Unbeknownst to McCanlies, during these tests someone had disconnected the bell that signals the projectionist to change reels. It had never been reconnected, so when the first reel of *Dancer* finished, the celluloid flew right off the reel and the screen went black for a few minutes while the projectionist and Kobrin scrambled to start the second reel.

Favorable buzz began to build around the film, which was scheduled to screen again at the Paramount on Thursday, March 19. Although the full *Variety* review wouldn't run until after the festival, critic Emanuel Levy spotlighted *Dancer* in a piece filed from Austin on March 16, calling McCanlies's film "one of the highlights" of SXSW's opening weekend. McCanlies phoned the studio, crowing, "Look, I'm the hit of the festival! Look at my *Variety* review!" The studio seemed unimpressed with the film's positive reception in what was essentially McCanlies's hometown but nevertheless sent a public relations person to oversee the film's second screening. Local festival reviews in the *Austin Chronicle* and the *Austin American-Statesman* were also flattering, with a favorable piece running in the *Statesman* the same day as *Dancer*'s final screening.[62]

The *Variety* review, which ran a week after SXSW ended, called *Dancer* "an impressive directorial feature debut" and favorably compared its energy to that of Frank Capra's Depression-era comedies. "Perhaps not since the eccentric early comedies of Jonathan Demme ("Citizens Band," aka "Handle With Care," and "Melvin and Howard") has there been an American comedy that captures the unique texture of small-town life without condescending to its characters," wrote Levy.[63]

"The *Variety* review helped reignite Sony's interest and their attempts to get the movie out there theatrically. And they spent some money to release it," says Burns, who attended the SXSW screening. "At that point," recalls McCanlies, "TriStar decided they'd give me a Texas release."[64]

After enjoying a fairly favorable reception at the USA Film Festival in Dallas a month later—no small feat given that local writers were taking the festival to task for its "flabby, mediocre, and slapdash" programming—*Dancer, Texas Pop. 81* had its premiere at a small theater in Santa Monica. It was an unimpressive affair with a handful of no-name reporters on hand for the event.[65]

Sony's marketing of the film prior to its May 1 release included a smattering of television commercials that ran at off-peak hours and a couple of full-page advertisements in the *New York Times* and the *Los Angeles Times*. The print ads featured a well-chosen group photograph of the four leads, arms slung around each other's shoulders, and a few favorable press blurbs, two of which were from Texas critics. (Levy's highly quotable *Variety* review was not sampled for the ad, says Burns, probably because the studio assumed the trade paper was not as well known outside of New York and Los Angeles.)

*Dancer, Texas Pop. 81* opened on May 1 in fewer than thirty theaters around the country. The movie had "exclusive" engagements at the AMC Century 14 in Los Angeles and the Sony Theater in New York's Lincoln Square. In Texas *Dancer* played at two theaters in Fort Worth, eight in Dallas and Houston, and on four screens in Austin. It also opened in Chicago and Toronto on one screen each, with play dates in Vancouver and Ottawa added a week later.[66]

Not surprisingly the Texas reviews were quite positive, vindicating McCanlies's push for a Lone Star state release. The filmmaker's hometown paper praised *Dancer's* timeless qualities: "For the price of admission, you visit a fully-realized world for a near-picture-perfect slice of small-town life that is charming and poignant in the classic tradition of American cinema." Louis B. Parks, who in the *Houston Chronicle* described *Dancer* as a "warm, likable film," clearly "got" the film in a way that few other critics did: "The film is small in budget and reach. McCanlies isn't trying to make a powerful statement here, just a small one."[67]

*Dancer's* sweetness met with varying degrees of success elsewhere in the country. Nearly all of the critics praised the movie's acting whether or not they seemed to like the film overall. "The best thing about the movie is the easygoing camaraderie that its four young leading actors establish in the opening scene and effortlessly sustain for the rest of the film," wrote the *New York Times*. The *Hollywood Reporter* also singled out the "quietly effective performances from its young cast." Likewise, the *Chicago Tribune* credited the film's believable characters to *Dancer's* "talented, fairly unknown actors."[68]

Most of the reviews discussed *Dancer's* sentimental story, which worked better for some critics than others and perhaps reflected a bit of regional bias. On the West Coast, critic Kenneth Turan wrote in the *Los Angeles Times*, "Likable, affectionate and unashamedly warm-hearted, *Dancer, Texas* is a sentimental little picture that goes gently against the grain." Turan also credited McCanlies for keeping the film believable. Although the *Tribune* noted that the movie "strikes a lot of the right chords," the critic took issue with a level of nostalgia that "occasionally drifts into Country Time lemonade land, complete with an old-timer sitting on the porch ruminating about comforts of small-town living." But perhaps the least positive review appeared in the *Village Voice*, where critic Amy Taubin found fault with the story's dismissal of a promising female character (Vivian, the fifth graduate among the group) and griped that the four lead actors—"indistinguishable from one another"— appeared to be much older than their eighteen-year-old characters. Taubin also took a swipe at McCanlies when she condemned the film for being "so mediated by TV clichés that even when it's autobiographical it's still unlifelike."[69]

It came as no surprise, then, that *Dancer* was off the screens in New York after only one week. And although the *Hollywood Reporter* had praised the film's "nice character touches" and McCanlies's "gentle humor," the trade paper hadn't predicted big business, observing that "TriStar should anticipate audience levels in the vicinity of *Dancer*'s dwindling populace."[70]

That prediction wasn't too far off. *Dancer* opened in twenty-six theaters around the country and earned $87,983 its first weekend. After adding two more theaters, the movie pulled in just over half that amount in its second week of release. All told, the movie's domestic gross amounted to just under $700,000. Burns, who was understandably disappointed in the way the movie was released, says the studio would have been happy with a box office of about $2 million.[71]

*Dancer* fared best, of course, in Texas. After it had left all of the other theaters in Austin it opened at the Village Cinema Art, a popular art-house theater north of the UT campus, where it played for five months straight.

As the months passed *Dancer* began to take on a life of its own. While back in L.A. for another project, McCanlies noticed that the film was enjoying a long run as a midnight movie at a local gay theater. Curious, McCanlies went to a screening to gauge the audience's reaction and observed "boys in leather eyeing the four guys." The movie began popping up at small theaters in random states like Ohio, and Tim and Suzanne began to get calls from friends around the country who had seen the film.[72]

In the fall Tim and Suzanne accompanied *Dancer* to the London Film Festival, where they were pleasantly surprised to discover overseas audiences identifying with the characters and relating to the movie's small-town feel. The film received a similar reception when it opened in Australia in late October.

Sony Pictures released the film on video and DVD in October. McCanlies was once again disappointed when the studio declined to spend extra money to add a commentary track or other extra features to the DVD. Months later he heard through word of mouth that high school teachers were successfully using *Dancer* as a teaching tool, screening the movie on video as a way to spark discussion with their soon-to-be graduating seniors.

### Not Driven to Direct

By the end of 1998 McCanlies had begun to think about his next move. He had spent almost the entire year focused on *Dancer*, and now it was time to return to paying work. Nickelodeon had acquired the rights to the very successful *Hank the Cowdog* children's books by Texas writer John R. Erickson, and McCanlies was hired to adapt the stories for the screen.

"I always figured I'd direct again, but I wasn't ready for a year or two," says McCanlies. "When guys are just directors, they have to look for another job right away." *Dancer's* negligible box office didn't exactly have Hollywood studios pounding down his door, either, offering money to make another film. And unlike fellow Austin filmmakers Richard Linklater and Robert Rodriguez, McCanlies wasn't driven to direct. He still considered himself a writer first and foremost.[73]

If McCanlies were to direct again, he preferred to make a film from his own script. He still had *Secondhand Lions*, which he had written a few years earlier as an antidote to all of the action films he was being hired to script in the early 1990s. Like *Dancer* this other script was set in Texas, but the story was even less commercial. Although it had garnered a lot of attention, no studio had wanted to take a chance on the story, which, in addition to featuring older actors, also included ambitious flashback sequences inspired by the *Arabian Nights* tales. Finally, around the time he began shooting *Dancer*, McCanlies had taken it off the market and hoped one day to make it himself.

In August 1999 Warner Bros. released *The Iron Giant*, whose script McCanlies had fine-tuned while shooting *Dancer* two years earlier. The animated film was overshadowed at the box office by the sleeper hit *The Sixth Sense*, but critics loved the clever tale of a nine-year-old boy who befriends a towering robot amidst the Cold War paranoia of the 1950s. Writing in the *Chicago Sun-Times*, Roger Ebert described the film as "not just a cute romp but an involving story that has something to say." Critic David Edelstein gushed about the film in the on-line magazine *Slate* and later predicted that it would become a classic that viewers would return to decades later. That November *The Iron Giant* swept the Annies, the industry's most prestigious awards for recognition in the field of animation. The film won nine of its thirteen nominations, including a writing award for McCanlies and Brad Bird. And by year's end, the film was regularly popping up on "Ten Best" lists. In *Premiere* magazine's January 2000 issue, which summarized critics' year-end picks in a list of the top 100 films, *The Iron Giant* ranked seventh.[74]

The critical success of *The Iron Giant* translated into more and better writing opportunities for McCanlies. And, says Burns, although *Dancer* didn't do particularly well at the box office, the fact that McCanlies's directorial debut was critically well received eventually helped to boost his image in the industry. At the age of forty-six, he was finally at a point in his career where he could be choosier about his projects.

Although McCanlies talked about the possibility of directing another movie, perhaps from someone else's screenplay, his wife privately believed this would never happen. "He always said if the right script came along, he would direct it. I don't think he ever will. I think he won't ever find anything he is as passionate about as his own movie."[75]

At least for the time being, Suzanne McCanlies was right. Four years would pass between *Dancer* and *Secondhand Lions,* which would be released by New Line in 2003.

9

*Office Space* is a revenge
tragedy, like *The Killing*.
AJAY NAIDU

# Office Space

## The Making of a Cult Classic

- - - - - - - - - - - - - - - - - - - - - - - - - - - - - - - - - - - - - - - - - - - - - - -

**B**raker Lane in North Austin was clogged with idling cars stacked four abreast. The automobiles' exhaust fumes only made the late spring afternoon that much steamier for the extras who sat inside each of the two hundred cars. A film camera dollied in on the face of actor Ron Livingston, who sat in the driver's seat of an immobile Corolla. A soft-spoken thirty-five-year-old clad in gray shorts and wearing black sunglasses stood just off screen and studied the monitor as Livingston began to fidget on cue. Mike Judge, his receding hairline obscured by the obligatory director's baseball cap, called for the camera to cut. All around the staged traffic jam various crew members sprang into action.[1]

By late May 1998, Judge was three weeks into production on *Office Space*, a comedy partly inspired by an animated short film that he'd created seven years earlier. Livingston's shot was part of an elaborate set piece for a visual joke in which his character, stuck in traffic, realizes that an aging pedestrian using a walker is moving faster than he is. The forty-day shoot, which marked Judge's live-action directorial debut, had been proceeding relatively smoothly. But on this particular day, everything that could go wrong, did.

Judge had been disappointed in the initial storyboards commissioned for the scene, and as the crew set up the shot he discovered that he would need additional reaction shots and other inserts for the joke to play effectively on-screen. "I realized on the set that I hadn't planned it out enough to really make it work," recalls Judge. City of Austin police had been brought in to control traffic on the busy thoroughfare. A crane maneuvered Tim Suhrstedt, the director of photography, and his camera operator into position, but a persistent haze that hovered over the city delayed actual filming. Tensions were also high because the first assistant director had just fired a production assistant who had failed, among other infractions, to have a supporting actor's paperwork delivered in time for him to shoot his scene. A number of crew members had donned black arm bands in protest—a "minor soap opera rebellion," recalls Suhrstedt. And, in the middle of the day's shoot, a local newspaper critic arrived for a scheduled interview with the harried filmmaker. Says Judge, "That was the baptism of fire for me."[2]

Tim McCanlies's directorial debut, *Dancer, Texas Pop. 81*, had opened a few days before *Office Space* went into production. *The Newton Boys* had been released two months earlier. Robert Rodriguez was filming *The Faculty* less than ten miles from Judge's set. Everyone in Austin, it seemed, was making a movie.

In fact, it was this level of creative energy and artistic activity that had attracted Mike Judge to Austin in the first place. While Linklater, Rodriguez, and others had been carving out a regional cinema in the early 1990s, Judge, a former musician, had become well known for the wildly popular *Beavis and Butt-head* animated series on MTV, which spawned a top-grossing animated feature film and a host of ancillary products. By the time he relocated to Austin in 1994, Judge was established enough in his career that he didn't need to rely on his friends to cobble together his feature film debut (although Linklater and Rodriguez would become pals and offer valuable advice on *Office Space*). Simultaneously, the Austin film community had matured enough so that it had the resources to support someone like Judge, who worked in both film and television. And as with Linklater and Rodriguez, Judge enjoyed the fact that Texas was thousands of miles from New York and Los Angeles, offering a buffer from the studios and television networks.

In 1996 Judge launched *King of the Hill*, another successful animated series on the Fox television network. Two years later Judge wrote and directed *Office Space*. Budgeted at $10 million and shot in Austin, *Office Space* was loosely based on Judge's short-lived career as an engineer. The comedy featured a cast of relatively unknown character actors and Jennifer Aniston. She was the film's most recognizable face, but Aniston had little screen time as Ron Livingston's love interest and seemed to be causing more of a stir off camera with her new boyfriend, actor Brad Pitt. *Office Space* stalled at the box office, and the fictional characters' fates foreshadowed the downturn in

Austin's own high-tech economy just a few years later. But *Office Space* would eventually develop a cult following after its release to video, and Judge's successful crossover from television to film demonstrated the increasing flexibility of Austin's artistic community.

### I Was Just Figuring It All Out

Years earlier, while Linklater was shooting *Slacker* in the summer of 1989, Mike Judge lived in Dallas and was earning a living by touring the United States and Europe playing bass guitar with blues musician Anson Funderburgh. One night he and his wife, Francesca Morocco, drove to Dallas's Inwood Theater to attend an animation film festival. Judge had always drawn, but it wasn't something he ever took seriously. That night, his interest was rekindled while watching *Scaredy Cat,* a one-minute animated short film by Dallasite Paul Claerhout. Although Claerhout wasn't at the screening, select *Scaredy Cat* cels (illustrated transparencies used in animation) were on display in the theater lobby. What impressed Judge most about the animated short was that it had all been done in Dallas. "I had always thought that animation takes tons of money and a studio, but here was this guy in the town where I lived who had done it," says Judge.[3] The next day, Judge flipped through the phone book to try to find a place that would rent animation cameras. He found one at Bill Stokes Associates, a production company that had gotten its start in the mid-1960s by providing services and a soundstage for the filming of *Bonnie and Clyde.* Then Judge went to the local library and checked out a few animation books. Next he purchased a $200 Bolex film camera, and then he began to teach himself how to make animated shorts.

He took some test film, shot with the Bolex, to a Dallas lab that developed 16mm football films. Judge was thrilled when he viewed the animated moving images—a man walking, another making a face at the camera. He felt the way he did when he discovered that *Scaredy Cat* was animated locally. "It actually looked like a cartoon. I was like, 'This is it. I can now make a film.' I didn't know how to thread the film. I was just figuring it all out and hoping it would work, so it was really exciting that it actually did."[4]

Between playing music and the demands of graduate school—where Judge was taking math courses in a half-hearted attempt to become a community college instructor—Judge didn't have time to complete his first animated sound film until the end of 1990. The two-minute short featured two characters, a frustrated office worker named Milton and his boss, Lumbergh. "I figured it was a little embarrassing. I mean, you have no reason to think you're going to be successful at something like this," said Judge years later. He recorded voices, sound effects, and music for his animated characters on a four-track cassette player, using a stopwatch to synch the dialogue and sound effects to the characters' movements. "But I knew that when I played the track for my wife and for somebody else, it made them laugh, so I thought, 'Well, my track's funny even if my animation is bad.'" He called the story *Office Space*.[5]

Judge's interest in drawing began in childhood, and his love of animals inspired attractive renderings of deer and other wildlife. By junior high, however, a budding interest in cartooning took his drawing skills down another path. "I drew really sick cartoons. I'd go through phases where I'd try to learn to draw better, and it would always turn into a sick joke. I have this urge to deface my own art," Judge told an interviewer in 1993.[6]

### Beavis and Butt-head and MTV

Judge was born in Ecuador on October 17, 1962, the second of three children. His father was working at the time as an organizer for the Cooperative League of the United States, but the family would soon move to Albuquerque, where Judge's father took a position as an archaeology professor at the University of New Mexico. Judge's mother worked as a high school librarian. Although their son expressed interest in art, music, and comedy—early influences included Jerry Lewis, Cheech & Chong, and *Animal House* (1978)—he also had an aptitude for math and science.

After high school Judge enrolled at the University of California at San Diego, where he studied physics. When he graduated in 1985, he accepted a job working for a military contractor in California. By the late 1980s, however, he had grown tired of his engineering position and decided to pursue a career in music. He moved to Texas, where he began playing and touring the country with Funderburgh and, later, Doyle Bramhall.

By the summer of 1991, Judge had been experimenting with his newfound animation skills for about two years. He was still playing music regularly and taking graduate math courses. Judge's wife, a full-time engineer, was expecting their first child, a daughter, in October. At the very least, Judge figured, he now had an interesting hobby that would take the edge off of even the worst "cubicle" job. He transferred two of his cartoons, the *Office Space* short and another one called *Huh?*, onto a videocassette, made copies, and mailed the tapes to Comedy Central, MTV, and about eighteen other companies and cable television programs. Years later, Judge would see parallels between his own early efforts and those of Richard Linklater. "In a sense, I feel we've both done the same thing," said Judge. "He raised his own money. He had no connections. And he made *Slacker*. And that's pretty much what I did, on a smaller scale."[7]

But just as Linklater had schooled himself at the Independent Feature Film Market and researched people with industry connections like John Pierson, Judge realized that outlets like the fledgling cable channel Comedy Central were ripe for new talent. Comedy Central was created in April 1991 when Time Warner's cable network, the Comedy Channel, merged with Viacom's Ha!, and its new 24-hour format increased the demand for original programming.

One of the first calls Judge received was from Scott Thompson and Bruce McCullough. The Canadian comedians had a relatively new sketch comedy show called *Kids in the Hall*, which by early 1991 was being broadcast on the Comedy Channel, and they liked Judge's short films. *Huh?* was accepted into a new festival called Spike and Mike's Sick and Twisted Festival of Animation, for which Judge received $2,000. ("So already I was profitable," laughs Judge.) He also received a call from Allan Havey, a comedian who had a late-night talk show on Comedy Central. Havey told Judge he loved his animation and wanted to use *Office Space* on the show. Judge was flown to New York, where he met with Havey's staff. "How fast can you do these?" they asked, and soon Judge was making more animated short films.[8]

One of the characters that followed was based on a neighbor of Judge's who was friends with his brother. Judge attempted to sketch him from memory, but like his junior high "hybrid" drawings of deer and other animals, the image of this childhood acquaintance began to warp into something else. Eventually the drawing depicted a character holding a cigarette lighter and a locust. "Every time I'd see these sketches," Judge later recalled, "they'd make me laugh."[9]

The cartoon developed into a pair of similar-looking adolescent boys. One character had blond hair and a prominent lower jaw, but it was his sidekick who seemed to have the more dominant personality of the pair. This character had brown hair and wore braces. Both had unfortunate haircuts. Judge named the light-haired character Beavis, after Bobby Beavis, his brother's friend. The name for the second character came less easily. Judge considered a number of different options, then put the storyboard aside for a couple of weeks. When he looked at it again, he noticed that he had scribbled the word "Butt-head" next to the image.

Judge did the voices for both characters, whose (limited) dialogue was punctuated by distinctive, grunting nervous laughter. Judge's animation style was equally crude and primitive. "I wanted it to look like it was drawn with contempt, like the guy doing it was deranged also. That came a little more easily than drawing nicely," said Judge.[10]

Planning to enter a short film in the by-now annual Spike and Mike's Sick and Twisted Festival of Animation, Judge created storyboards for "Frog Baseball" around the Beavis and Butt-head characters. In the two-minute short the boys detonate a firecracker inside a locust and use a live frog for batting practice. "I liked that it felt just completely messed up and crazy and wrong. There was just really something kind of liberating about it," says Judge.[11] But when he originally proposed the idea to Craig "Spike" Decker and Mike Gribble, co-founders of the Spike and Mike festival, they weren't interested. But Judge insisted on drawing "Frog Baseball," and eventually Decker advanced him the money to finish the cartoon in time for the January 1992 festival.

"Frog Baseball" received raves when it played at the first festival screening in California. A few days later, Judge received a call about showing the cartoon on MTV's *Liquid Television* animation series.[12] At the time, Judge said, "I wasn't even going to put my name on it because I thought, 'What if this is what I get remembered for.'" Within a week of the short's first appearance in the 1992 festival, and just days after the initial call from *Liquid Television*, Judge was in talks with MTV to sell the rights to the two characters. "I hadn't been to New York and met anyone at MTV. I hadn't met Spike [Decker]," he recalls.[13]

The flurry of activity was cut short, however, when Decker "freaked out" about the deal. According to Judge, Decker told producers for *Liquid Television* that not only would he refuse to license the Beavis and Butt-head short, but he also would block their use of any other animation featured in the Spike and Mike festival. (Most of the festival's material had been licensed to Decker for a period of two years, which included television rights.) *Liquid Television* decided not to pursue the matter. "So suddenly I had no career because of this guy," says Judge, who reluctantly agreed to create another Beavis and Butt-head short for the Spike and Mike festival in exchange for retaining limited broadcast control over the material.[14] Judge labored over the second Beavis and Butt-head "adventure," in which the pair wreak havoc at a monster truck show.

Judge spent a good part of the spring of 1992 going back and forth with Decker and executives at *Liquid Television*. By the time he finalized a deal with MTV later that summer, Judge was worn down by all of the negotiations. "I never really thought making little short films for festivals would turn into such an ugly, vicious business." Beavis and Butt-head made their first appearance on MTV during the 1992 Video Music Awards. Judge, who still had not met any of the MTV executives, watched the broadcast from his home in Richardson. "They get to Best Hard Rock Video, and there's Beavis and Butt-head," Judge remembers. In the end, MTV ordered thirty-five episodes featuring the two characters. At the time Judge told himself, "I can't even think of one more thing these guys could do."[15]

Originally the cable network thought Beavis and Butt-head could act as veejays, introducing and commenting on the music videos that aired on MTV, but the idea quickly shifted into an episodic series that would allow the fictional characters to inhabit their own juvenile universe. The episodes, which aired every weeknight, consisted of two fifteen-minute "stories" interspersed with several music videos. (In creating the episodes, Judge had access to the music channel's entire library.) For the most part Beavis and Butt-head sit on a couch, watching and commenting on the videos, "sort of like Siskel and Ebert on airplane glue," observed one magazine writer.[16] Occasionally Judge would create scenarios that would require them to leave their lair and venture into their suburban neighborhood.

By January of 1993, Judge, Francesca, and their two-year-old daughter had left Texas and moved just outside of New York City to suburban Westchester County to be closer to MTV's animation studio in White Plains, New York, and the cable network's headquarters in midtown Manhattan. The March 8 premiere of the series was fast approaching, and Judge was unhappy with the animation. "They were supposed to have 20 episodes. I think they had two. And they looked horrible. And I still didn't have a signed contract."[17]

From the moment MTV expressed interest in "Frog Baseball" for *Liquid Television* and then premiered the *Beavis and Butt-head* series a year later in March 1993, Judge's life had changed dramatically. As he told one reporter, "The *L.A. Times* wrote an article about *Beavis and Butt-head* on a Wednesday or a Thursday on the week it debuted—and by Friday every major movie studio except Paramount and Warner Bros. called to make a movie offer."[18] David Letterman became a fan, and when *Rolling Stone* made Beavis and Butt-head its cover models in March 1994, it became *Rolling Stone*'s bestselling issue of that year. Programmed into a primetime slot on MTV, *Beavis and Butt-head* quickly became a hit.

### *King of the Hill* and Twentieth Century Fox

The following year, in 1994, Judge renegotiated his contract with MTV. The terms of the new deal gave him a healthy percentage of the licensing of *Beavis and Butt-head* t-shirts, posters, and other ancillary products. Equally important, the arrangement allowed Judge and his family to leave New York. Within eighteen months of relocating to the East Coast, they moved back to Texas in the summer of 1994, but this time they settled in Austin. Ever since Judge began visiting the laid-back state capital while touring with Doyle Bramhall's band, he had thought about moving there. Since Judge oversaw *Beavis and Butt-head*'s animation, worked on story ideas with a team of writers, and provided the voices for both characters, his living in close proximity to MTV headquarters and its animation and recording studios made sense on a number of levels. But being in Austin made more sense, he soon discovered. "I got way into writing memos and faxing drawings. It almost made it an easier way to run things. I actually think the show got better."[19]

He also began to branch out in his career. By the end of 1994, Judge had signed an exclusive two-year deal with Twentieth Century Fox that was worth nearly $2 million. The arrangement would allow Judge to continue to work in television and develop another animated series while also giving him the opportunity to write, direct, and produce live-action feature films. "I wanted to do a live-action movie, even when I was doing my animated shorts with my Bolex. My next plan was to shoot some little comedy short, but *Beavis and Butt-head* just took over my life," says Judge, whose contract with MTV committed him to doing six seasons of the animated series.[20]

Judge was a big fan of *Dazed and Confused*, and he arranged to meet Richard Linklater prior to moving to Austin in 1994. The filmmaker took Judge on a tour of Detour's production offices, where Judge ended up renting space for nearly a year before finding an office just west of the University of Texas campus. Linklater's friendship and support, and Austin's thriving arts community in general, helped to ease Judge's professional transition back to Texas. It was at a premiere of one of Linklater's films that Judge also met Robert Rodriguez. Both equally quiet, especially around new people, the two men became absorbed in conversation almost immediately, much to the surprise of their respective wives. On the drive home, Elizabeth Avellán turned to Rodriguez.

"What were you and Mike talking about?"

"Our sugar mommas."

Avellán was puzzled. "Who's that?"

"You and Francesca!"[21]

Like Avellán, who held a full-time job while Rodriguez worked on *El Mariachi*, Judge's wife had worked as an engineer while Judge played bass and taught himself animation. At one point before moving to New York, Morocco and some of her friends helped Judge finish painting the animation cels for the second Beavis and Butt-head short. "It was almost like a quilting bee," recalls Judge.[22]

Judge continued to work on *Beavis and Butt-head* throughout 1995, and by the end of the year he also was collaborating with series writer Joe Stillman on a full-length *Beavis and Butt-head* feature. *Beavis and Butt-head Do America* (1996) propelled the characters on a cross-country trip to recover their stolen television. The trip took the clueless pair far afield of their usual sedentary perch, depicting them at various national landmarks such as the Grand Canyon, Yellowstone National Park, and even the White House. While some critics bemoaned the fact that Beavis and Butt-head's prolonged adventure couldn't sustain interest for the duration of a feature-length film, others praised the movie's ability to retain the series' original "double vision": "It views the world simultaneously through the porcine eyes of its characters," wrote the *New York Times*, "and through the cooler perspective of their creator and cartoon voice, Mike Judge."[23]

The movie opened five days before Christmas in 1996 and grossed more than $20 million its first weekend in theaters. By the end of its domestic run, Judge's first feature, which he co-directed with animator Yvette Kaplan, had earned more than $63 million, at the time making it the highest-grossing non-Disney animated feature.[24] Judge had resisted film studios' arguments that a live-action version of the series would fare better as a feature, and the movie's astonishing financial performance eventually proved him right.

While in development and production on the feature, Judge also began work on *King of the Hill*, a new animated series for the Fox television network. Whereas the *Beavis and Butt-head* characters were inspired in part by kids with whom Judge had grown up, the adult characters in his new series drew upon his Richardson, Texas, neighbors, whom he once described as "guys sitting around with beers in an alley." When he first pitched the idea to Fox television executives as Texas bubbas who were partly inspired by Foghorn Leghorn, one of Judge's favorite cartoon characters, they were thrilled. Recalls Judge, "Fox television president Peter Roth just slams his hands down on the table and goes, 'Yes! Foghorn Leghorn. That's what we want!' I think they were afraid of me because I was the *Beavis and Butt-head* guy, and when I came in and pitched something that was just regular guys with beers, they were like, 'Oh my god! We're getting the best of everything. He's edgy, *and* he wants to do something about a family.'"[25]

Judge submitted the pilot script and drawings to Fox in the summer of 1995, and the studio executives weighed in with their suggestions. For starters, they wanted the main character's pudgy adolescent son to be "cuter." And they also took issue with the proposed age of Hank Hill, the main character, whom Judge had described as forty-nine years old. He received a phone message from a "lower-placed female executive" who explained that the network's average viewer was thirty-two years old and Fox would prefer that Hank were also thirty-two. Says Judge, "I got all angry, and then I was like, 'Well, wait. It's just a drawing.' So I just went back with the same drawing and said, 'Okay, he's 34.'"[26]

Executives also introduced Judge to Greg Daniels, a former co-executive producer, or showrunner, of *The Simpsons*. Judge was about to go into production on the *Beavis and Butt-head* feature, so he told the studio he was pretty much done with development on the proposed series. They suggested bringing in Daniels, to which Judge agreed. Daniels pared down the pilot, suggesting that Judge save some of the plotlines for future episodes. "He was a little more savvy [than I was]. He knew that they don't just pick up one episode. He actually hadn't changed all that much, and I was relieved," says Judge, who collaborated with Daniels to write treatments for twelve additional episodes.[27]

By the end of the year, Fox had given the go-ahead on the project. *King of the Hill* was, like *Beavis and Butt-head* before it, a different kind of show compared with much of what was on television at the time. The animated series focused on Hank Hill, voiced by Judge, who sold propane tanks and lived with his wife, Peggy, and their son, Bobby, in Arlen, a fictional Texas suburb. Even though Judge and his own family had relocated to Austin, he had only good memories about the time they spent living in suburban Richardson. And after seeing Spike Lee's *Do the Right Thing* (1989), in which the heat of a New York summer inflames simmering racial tensions, Judge thought that a suburban white neighborhood would be an equally inspired, if very different, setting. "You wouldn't have trash cans going through windows, but a lot of interesting, funny stuff goes on."[28] It was this affection for Richardson that inspired Judge to create Hill, his family, and their North Texas neighbors, an affection that eventually would transcend the characters' regionalism and help the show capture a much wider audience.

Judge's animation style for *King of the Hill* didn't have the edgy, "deranged" quality that had distinguished *Beavis and Butt-head* from other cartoons of the time, but it did retain the homemade look that Judge favored. The animated series also was unusual in that it featured a large ensemble cast of characters, and the casting process was extensive. Character actor Stephen Root, who had found success playing boss Jimmy James on the popular sitcom *Newsradio*, "met" Judge over the phone to discuss the characters. Like a lot of people meeting Judge for the first time, Root was surprised that the creator of a show about 14-year-old juvenile delinquents was so shy and unassuming. Initially, Root read for the voice of Hank Hill's paranoid neighbor, Dale. Recalls Root, "Then we tried [the character of] Bill, and that was a much better fit." With a surname identical to that of series writer and native Texan Jim Dauterive, Bill is an army barber and an all-around lovable loser. After Root's final audition, also over the phone, Judge responded in his best Hank Hill voice, "Well, that's as funny as that can be."[29]

Actress Kathy Najimy gave voice to Hank's wife Peggy, a homemaker and substitute Spanish teacher, and longtime voice actress Pamela Segall played the Hills' son, Bobby, a plump and somewhat underachieving middle school student.

As with most animated series, *King of the Hill*'s production schedule was a lengthy process of about nine months per episode. Throughout 1996, while Judge was overseeing the production and release of the *Beavis and Butt-head* movie, he was also working with Daniels and director Wes Archer to ready thirteen episodes of *King of the Hill* as a mid-season replacement for Fox. The show scored a coveted timeslot between Fox's animated stalwart *The Simpsons* and the equally popular live-action science fiction series *The X Files*.

*King of the Hill*'s pilot episode premiered on January 12, 1997. The initial program introduced the Hills in a topical story that featured the unathletic Bobby getting a black eye during a baseball game, which fuels a rumor around town that Hank Hill beats his son and leads to a visit from an overzealous caseworker. The program gently poked fun at everything from politically correct social service practices to Hank's awkward attempts to bond with his son. Initial critical reception was mixed, and some reviewers didn't think much of Judge's realistic animation style and observational humor. "Maybe *King of the Hill* is trying a tricky balancing act, hoping to please people who look down on the Hills and people who can identify their neighbors on the show," mused the *New York Times*. Judge himself later admitted to worrying about the first few episodes, which he called "a little shaky."[30]

But by mid-April, *King of the Hill* had finished ahead of *The Simpsons* in the ratings and had been picked up for a second season. "Even though it's set in Texas it's really about suburban, working-class people," Judge explained in one interview.[31] Still, even he admitted to being surprised that the show caught on so quickly and with such a wide audience. By the end of its second season, *King of the Hill* had received numerous Annie nominations (the top award in the field of animation) and two Emmy nods for Outstanding Animated Program (the series eventually won in 1999).

### A Character Study of Cubicle People

On November 28, 1997, in the midst of the second season of his new series, Judge bid goodbye to Beavis and Butt-head. After a successful four-and-a-half-year run, the once-controversial animated series on MTV finally came to the end of its first-run episodes. Judge had great affection for the adolescent characters with whom he had made his mark creatively, but he was ready to move on.

The deal that he had signed with Fox in 1994 had been the best way to become "unowned" by MTV, and the success of the Beavis and Butt-head movie gave Judge leverage with the network and Paramount, its parent company, in collecting fees owed him from the series and various licensing arrangements. Even though Paramount eagerly sought a sequel to *Beavis and Butt-head Do America*, Judge was more interested in directing a live-action feature. According to the terms of his deal with Fox, the studio wanted a live-action film based on Milton, the put-upon office worker from Judge's first animated short, *Office Space*. Judge originally created the character as a composite of a number of work colleagues he had met over the years.

Making the character the focal point of a feature-length comedy wasn't easy. Recalled Judge, "I tried to come up with a story, and the more I tried the more I realized that Milton's a character you really don't want to know that much about. He works better as a guy you just sort of wonder about." Peter Chernin, then president of Fox Entertainment, suggested that Judge incorporate the character into a larger story. As an example of a workplace ensemble, he pointed to the 1976 Universal comedy *Car Wash*, written by Joel Schumacher. Instead of a car wash, suggested Chernin, Judge's film could be set among cubicles. "And that's what I had wanted to do when I first started animating, a character study of cubicle people. I had worked in cubicles before and just thought it was a wealth of material, but you didn't really see it that often. Movies that were about office jobs seemed more like the 1950s, like *9 to 5*. And no one works nine to five. They work 8 am to 6 pm if they're lucky," says Judge, who wrote the treatment very quickly in January 1996, during the middle of production on the Beavis and Butt-head feature and preproduction on *King of the Hill*.[32]

Gradually *Office Space* morphed into a comedy about an employee at a high-tech company who rebels against the threat of corporate downsizing and nine-to-five conformity. Milton became an eccentric supporting character within the larger ensemble. The characters' various work problems reflected some of Judge's own on-the-job experiences.

Fox responded favorably to Judge's treatment, but he didn't return to the project until a year later, after he had finished *Beavis and Butt-head Do America* and gotten the first episodes of *King of the Hill* on the air. He took some time off, and then, in the spring of 1997, turned his attention back to the *Office Space* project. He worked on the script throughout the summer and solicited feedback from friends like Robert Rodriguez. "He gave me a lot of very practical suggestions, some really smart ideas about cutting."[33] In one conference room scene, for instance, Rodriguez suggested using photographs instead of names on the file folders, a minor but effective visual joke that earned laughs at preview screenings.

At the end of January 1998, *Daily Variety* officially announced the project in the trades, putting its budget at around $10 million.[34] Shooting was scheduled to begin in April, and Judge had been adamant that the production be based in Austin so he could be with his family and continue to oversee production on *King of the Hill*.

Fox's suggestions to Judge about casting ranged from the interesting to the absurd. One of the first names they recommended for Milton was Bill Murray. Although Judge was a big fan of Murray's comedy, he worried that the character would be "like him being Mr. Lupner on *SNL* or something." And, he didn't think Murray would accept the role. Another suggestion, rather unbelievably, was Mel Gibson. "They would suggest people who were just ludicrously off the mark," recalls Tim Suhrstedt, the cinematographer. "But from their standpoint, that would be somebody they could use for marketing."[35]

But Judge had his own ideas. In fact, up until a few minutes before he and an assembled group of actors did a table read of the script for Fox in the fall of 1997, Judge himself was considering playing Milton. The group included actors with whom Judge worked on *King of the Hill* as well as others, like Heather Graham, whom the studio thought might be right for the film.

About a dozen Fox executives attended the reading, which in Judge's mind was a complete disaster. "Some of it got some laughs, but boy, it was grueling. After it was over, I said, 'Ugh. Not going to make that one.'" But the studio responded with encouragement. ("It's funny," observes Judge. "Those people are in such combat/negotiation mode all the time. I think if I had said, 'That went really well,' they would have said, 'Uh, I don't know.'")[36]

Disastrous or not, Fox was still interested in *Office Space*, and they asked Judge to audition "name" actors for the project. For the main character of Peter they suggested Ben Affleck, who was riding a tidal wave of success thanks to *Good Will Hunting* (1997), *Shakespeare in Love* (1998), and the blockbuster *Armageddon* (1998). Affleck's agent said his client would do the movie for $6 million. Fox executives told Judge they were trying to negotiate for $4 million, which represented 40 percent of the movie's entire budget. But Judge thought the actor Ron Livingston, who had appeared in the sleeper hit *Swingers,* would be well cast as Peter. Although Livingston was a virtual unknown, his comedic timing and Everyman quality convinced Judge that he would be right for the role.

"It was the first time the character had worked at all," says Judge of Livingston's audition. Instead of the strong-jawed, overly aggressive performances Judge had seen up to that point from actors like Steve Zahn and Noah Wylie, Livingston approached the material from another perspective. "Ron was very much like the way Charles Grodin would have played the character in the 1970s, very kind of internal," Judge remembers.[37]

Recalls Livingston, who first auditioned in late January 1998, "I was about two levels below where you want to be to get cast in a studio film. Mike and the studio had fundamentally different views of how they wanted to cast the movie. Mike wanted to do it with a bunch of unknown faces, and they wanted Ben Affleck. And I think Mike's response to that was, 'Who really wants to see Tom Cruise's terrible day at work?'" One day while getting his hair cut, Judge listened as his stylist raved about the movie *Good Will Hunting,* which she had seen twice. When Judge mentioned that the studio was eager for him to cast Affleck in *Office Space,* the stylist paused and then asked, "Now, which one was he?" Later Judge told the studio, "Look, you guys. My hairdresser wouldn't know from Ron Livingston or Ben Affleck."[38]

Judge wanted to use "unknowns" in the other roles as well, and he knew he would have to defend his choices to the studio. "Mike wanted me to do the role but we had to officially go through Fox channels and do the full-on audition for them and him," says Stephen Root of being cast as Milton. Judge worked closely with the actor prior to the audition, "honing exactly what he wanted. So it wasn't as much an audition as, 'I want you to show them this so they'll give me the go-ahead to give you the job.'"[39] The rehearsals worked, and Fox eventually went with Root. But still the studio leaned on Judge to "replace" at least one of the actors with a bigger name.

By April of 1998 Root and Livingston had signed on to the project. Dave Herman was cast as Michael Bolton, Peter's unfortunately named work colleague. Ajay Naidu, who had received an Independent Spirit Award nomination for his role in Linklater's *SubUrbia,* would play Peter and Michael's Jordanian colleague, Samir Nagheenanajar. Character actor Gary Cole signed on to play Peter's smarmy boss, Bill Lumbergh. Recalled Judge of the protracted negotiations, "I really believed in the casting. They wanted bigger names, but

I fought tooth and nail to get Ron Livingston, Gary Cole, Diedrich Bader [who played Peter's neighbor, Lawrence]. The only reason I won all those battles, probably, was because *King of the Hill* was being done by the same company and they didn't want it to get all the way to the top that I was angry."[40]

Judge wasn't too far off. As Fox's Bill Mechanic recalls, "Mike didn't want to make it with stars. I didn't care. As far as I was concerned, he had earned his freedom. He had created two TV shows that were very different, very idiosyncratic. This is a guy who clearly has a voice."[41]

In the end, the only "name" actor in the movie was Jennifer Aniston, whose wildly popular *Friends* television series had led to some crossover success in romantic comedy features like *She's the One* (1996), *Picture Perfect* (1997), and *The Object of My Affection* (1998). "Casting her was a little risky because I hadn't heard her read for the part, but I had a feeling she would be good," says Judge. Although Aniston's role was of little consequence to the overall plot—she played Joanna, Peter's love interest—Judge did realize the value of having "one bankable person" in the cast, and it seemed to put the studio at ease. Additionally, he knew that Aniston had the comedic chops to develop her own small part. "She was actually in a sketch comedy show called *The Edge* that Julie Brown had on Fox. I had seen her in that and thought she was really good," says Judge.[42]

### Wait Till We Get to Act Three

Production on *Office Space* began in early May 1998, just weeks after details for Aniston and a few other cast members had been finalized with the studio. Late spring in Austin is typically a pleasant time of year, with relatively mild temperatures and little rain. By the first week of May when the *Office Space* cast assembled, however, the local weather forecasters already were trumpeting record-setting temps for what eventually would become the hottest May on record in years. A thick blanket of haze drifting up from grass fires in Mexico compounded the stifling conditions.

Although *Office Space* marked Judge's live-action directorial debut, he was relieved to discover that his animation experience helped him get the hang of staging scenes and setting up camera shots. He also armed himself with a capable director of photography. Tim Suhrstedt had nearly twenty years of experience shooting feature films and television episodes, having worked on movies like *Bill & Ted's Excellent Adventure* (1989) and *The Wedding Singer* (1998), which had recently opened and was doing well for Fox. Suhrstedt also had collaborated successfully with a number of first-time directors.

Judge was especially impressed during their first meeting when Suhrstedt began suggesting ways to set up and frame specific shots that would make the material even funnier. Before principal photography began, Suhrstedt gave Judge a quick lesson in cinematography that, according to Judge, "demystified the whole process." In turn Judge shared with Suhrstedt his collection of actual employee training tapes, "all this motivational stuff that Mike had a particularly weird fascination with," says Suhrstedt.[43]

The tapes may have also provided inspiration for the look of the film, which more than a few reviewers would praise once *Office Space* opened the following year. Judge and Suhrstedt color-tested different shades of grey to convey a mood of surrealistic boredom. "He didn't want to style it up," says Suhrstedt of the set design, and Livingston remembers Judge going to every cubicle and making each one look as bland as possible. Recalls Suhrstedt, "He wanted it to feel like you were at work. He wanted you to feel that quality of light and quality of bored that would make you think, 'Oh god, how am I going to get through this day?'"[44]

Judge worked hard to create a laid-back and easygoing on-set vibe despite the fact that he was feeling daily pressure from the studio. "The mood wasn't good for Mike because Fox was up his ass," recalls Root. "They saw early stuff where he was doing very slow, long scenes that were his vision of the film, and they were going, 'Where are the jokes? Where's the comedy?' They were down there ready to pull the plug a couple of times because they weren't happy with what they were seeing."[45]

Editor Dave Rennie cut the *Office Space* footage at Richard Linklater's Austin Film Center postproduction facility while the production filmed in Texas. In late 1997 when he first heard about the project, Rennie was trying to make the transition from assistant to lead editor on feature films, and *Office Space* gave him that opportunity. He had worked most recently for Fox on *Volcano* and *Titanic*. "The pacing of *Office Space* is very odd, and I knew that the studio was going to panic. Comedies have to be fast-paced, laugh-a-minute. And this wasn't that kind of movie. You can't tell that story with zany, quick cuts. That was the big concern of dailies," says Rennie.[46]

Recalls Livingston, "The studio's looking at dailies, they didn't know what the hell was going on. If you're seeing *Harold and Maude,* and all you see is a kid in a black suit sitting on a sofa staring at the camera, and you're sitting in a room watching dailies and you see eight takes of that, you really have to trust the director, trust that at that point in the movie, that scene's going to be hysterical." In one of *Office Space*'s earliest scenes, Peter is put under hypnosis during a therapy session when suddenly the therapist drops dead from a heart attack. After some discussion in rehearsals, Livingston and Judge had agreed that he would play the second third of the movie as if Peter were still hypnotized. Recalls the actor, "We started shooting the Act Two stuff with Lumbergh, and they didn't understand why Peter wasn't getting in his face and saying, 'Hey, back off, Lumbergh!' At one point our studio executive sidestepped Mike and came and said something to the order of, 'Have more fun with it.' I tried as best I could to tell him, 'Just hang on. Wait till we get to Act Three.' But it was a little tough."[47]

That summer Fox enjoyed a surprise success with the Farrelly brothers' gross-out comedy *There's Something about Mary*, which also seemed to shape executives' reactions to the *Office Space* footage. "Everything didn't seem exaggerated and big enough to them," recalls Judge. "They're used to seeing big fat faces screaming into a wide angle lens. That's comedy, normally."[48]

But occasionally Judge's dry sense of humor was almost too subtle. He and Suhrstedt planned a scene in which a minor character, after reconsidering a suicide attempt by carbon monoxide poisoning, backs his car out of his garage, down his driveway, and into the path of a speeding truck. Judge wanted the car crash to happen instantaneously, in a single flash as with a cartoon, before cutting to the next shot of the character in a full body cast. Typically in live-action movies, car crashes are filmed from a multitude of angles and edited to draw out the action. "We've all seen those car crashes, the biggest, most expensive car crashes in the world," says Livingston. "Mike wanted the opposite of that. He wanted it completely two-dimensional and flat."[49]

The sequence was shot on a quiet residential street in one of Austin's unassuming suburban neighborhoods. "There were people from the studio wanting us to set up about six cameras and a slow-motion camera," recalls Suhrstedt, who photographed the scene instead with a single camera "locked" on a tripod and used identical Ford Tauruses, one with its gas tank removed. During the actual crash, which was done in a single take, a truck plowed into the car going about fifty miles per hour down the street. In the finished film one sees the crash as the garage door is closing on the action, making it appear almost as an afterthought. "They shot it exactly right, so it just came together perfectly in the editing," remembers Rennie. During previews, Judge and his editors were disappointed to discover the effect was almost too much for the audience, many of whom were shocked by the shot. ("There was just a gasp and then silence," recalls second assistant editor Eric Lewy.) Says Rennie of the scene's unconventional placement, "You don't show a car crash like that in a long shot, and you don't show it with the garage door shutting. The crash happens all in the background. Typically, this is a breath [during the film]. This is a moment for the audience, a transitional moment. You don't put a car crash like that in the middle of it!" Eventually the sequence was re-edited with voice-over narration that informs the audience up front that the character indeed survives the crash.[50]

Despite the pressure Judge was feeling from the studio, he managed to create a casual, open feeling on the set that encouraged some of the actors to improvise their scenes. Root and Herman, who had worked with Judge on *King of the Hill*, noticed little change in Judge as he transitioned into the role of filmmaker. "[The issue] was whether or not he could control the set in terms of the producers and do what he wanted to do, which he ultimately did, but it was, I think, a rough struggle for him," recalls Root. "With the actors, we were all on the same page. We all wanted to do what Mike wanted to do. That's why we were there."[51]

Judge's background in animation made him especially wary of the temptation to exaggerate some of the more eccentric characters, like Milton or Cole's Lumbergh, into caricatures. Says Root, "Milton was an extreme character that had to be done very small for film, so it was a dichotomy."[52] Ultimately, Root's ability to make Milton a sympathetic but funny oddball, someone with work frustrations that audiences could relate to, would earn the movie a loyal following.

Cole, who had received a videotape of Judge's *Office Space* short prior to his audition, took inspiration for his character from conversations he and Judge had about the filmmaker's engineering career. "He talked about the office where he worked, and he described this guy who would just kind of drift in and out with a coffee cup and kind of peek over cubicles. He was very, very passive-aggressive. He didn't confront anybody and he never raised his voice but he was annoyingly always around and making sure that people were doing what they were supposed to be doing but always in that kind of lounge lizard way of not being direct about anything." Perhaps because he had "heard" Lumbergh and Milton in his head for years, says Cole, Judge was very specific about his performance, which Cole did not ad lib. "It was really laid out, down to the number of 'yeahs,'" recalls the actor.[53]

As the shoot progressed throughout the month of May and into June, Judge continued to oversee the year-round production of *King of the Hill*. The *Office Space* production schedule left room for midday telephone calls to Los Angeles, when he would often participate in table readings via conference calls from his trailer.

## It Looked Like an Ad for Office Depot

After the film's production wrapped in June, Judge spent the remainder of the summer and fall commuting between Austin and an editing room in West Los Angeles near the Fox studio. Head of Production Tom Rothman watched a rough cut of the film sometime in October. Judge wasn't present at the screening, but Eric Lewy, Rennie's second assistant editor, told him, "Rothman laughed once during the whole thing, and then he looked sick to his stomach afterwards."[54]

Rennie received a call from Ted Galliano, Fox's head of postproduction, who explained that the studio had some concerns with the film. In particular they were unhappy with the character of Milton—in effect, the initial inspiration for the entire movie—and asked Rennie to "minimize" the character as much as possible. "They wanted to get rid of the basement stuff," says Rennie, referring to the scenes in which Lumbergh relocates the hapless employee so many times that he eventually ends up in the company's below-ground storage area. "They were just going to have him sent down there and you'd never see him again."[55]

Says Rennie, "I was a first-time editor, and Tom Rothman didn't know me, and he felt like I had not served the movie well. But Ted really went to bat for me." Galliano brought in a more established editor, who watched the cut and offered some notes but essentially assured the studio that the editing was in good shape. To Judge, Rothman was candid and matter of fact after his first viewing, saying, "I can't tell. We really just need to get it in front of an audience."[56]

By early fall of 1998, the studio began testing the movie at a number of preview screenings around the country. The first screening took place at a theater in a San Fernando Valley mall. Judge began to panic as he took in the line of mallrats at the ticket counter. The audience was all wrong for the film. "But it got big laughs through a lot of it," he recalls. Viewers even applauded after a scene in which Peter meets two characters nicknamed "the Bobs," who have been sent to the company from its corporate headquarters to downsize the staff. The scene had been the source of a lot of tension between Fox and the filmmaker. The studio thought Judge hadn't played up the humor, telling him it was a "completely missed opportunity for comedy." They asked him to reshoot it, and he threatened to quit the production. When the audience burst into applause after the scene, says Judge, "that was a huge load off my mind." The studio did ask for other, minor reshoots, however, which Judge and Suhrstedt did in Los Angeles in November.[57]

By the third screening Judge felt as if the movie had finally found its audience. The studio executives also seemed pleased with the film's reception, milling around afterwards and discussing, with some surprise, how well it had done. "Who knew?" joked one executive. "Well, I'm not surprised," thought Judge, more than a little annoyed. "Me and 250 people from a mall aren't surprised."[58]

After overseeing a final mix at George Lucas's Skywalker Ranch in January 1999, Judge continued to struggle with the studio in the weeks leading up to the movie's February release. Judge was dumbstruck during one marketing meeting when a young guy entered the room wearing a suit covered in yellow plastic tags. "The executives all had on these kind of 'You're gonna love this' faces. And I just looked at the poor guy, sweating inside this outfit, and thought, 'What is it?' I couldn't even give them a courtesy laugh." Continues Judge, "They wanted the 'crazy guy covered in Post-its.' Because that says comedy. But nobody knew what it was." The image eventually materialized on the movie's poster, depicting a figure holding a briefcase whose face and entire body are obscured by hundreds of yellow Post-it notes. "The first time I saw it," says Judge, "it looked like an ad for Office Depot."[59]

One day Richard Linklater dropped by Judge's office for a visit. As the filmmakers chatted casually, Judge's assistant interrupted him for a phone call from the Fox marketing executive overseeing the project. Recalls Linklater, "Mike was dealing with all the same crap—a lackluster release and marketing campaign—that I had had to deal with on *Newton Boys*." Linklater, who at the time had more experience in dealing with studio politics—and perhaps took some grim enjoyment in the competitive nature of such negotiations—encouraged Judge to exercise his power with Fox. "I'm like, 'Mike, you've made that studio a lot of money from your television stuff alone. You don't have to listen to some shit from some junior executive. Get him fired!'" Explains Suhrstedt, "If Mike were a different kind of personality, and he could go into meetings and yell or throw tantrums or make demands, he probably could have some success with that. But that's not who he is."[60]

The studio was equally frustrated. "We were having a hell of a time trying to market the movie," recalls Bill Mechanic, who advised Judge at the final *Office Space* preview screening that, for his *next* movie, he needed to "do more short gags or something that we could 'pop.'" Says Mechanic, "The funniest stuff in *Office Space* wouldn't 'lift.' It wouldn't work in the half-minute you might give it in a trailer, and it certainly wasn't working in the ten seconds that you need for a commercial."[61]

Root was privy to Judge's struggles with the studio over *Office Space* because of his ongoing involvement with *King of the Hill*. "Fox didn't know how to market it because it wasn't really Jennifer Aniston's movie. In the best of all possible worlds, in my opinion, they should have used Mike's name in the title—*Mike Judge's Office Space*, which would have immediately defined the audience. But they didn't because they didn't know how to market it. They didn't spend any money on the marketing, and they didn't know how to present it—as a romantic comedy or as what it is, which is a kind of farce."[62]

What the studio did spend money on was a rather bizarre gimmick that featured an anonymous young office worker (in reality, an unknown actor) toiling away in a glass-encased cubicle on the roof of a thirteen-story building in New York City's Times Square. "As publicity stunts go, it's a pretty elaborate one," observed one reporter. In the days leading up to the movie's release on February 19, 1999, the man known only as "The Office Guy" took phone calls and answered e-mail questions from "disgruntled employees." A Web link allowed online users to monitor his activity, or lack thereof. He also did press, ostensibly to publicize the movie, but the resultant interviews barely touched on Judge's film. At one point Ron Livingston visited the actor in an effort to help publicize *Office Space*. "Of course it illustrated the fundamental problem with the movie," says the actor. "The reporters who were there, none of them were interested in talking to me about the movie at all. They talked to the guy about what it was like to be alone in Times Square for a month. And he hadn't seen the movie, either."[63]

### This Is Like a Coen Brothers Movie That Didn't Do Well

Judge was depressed going into the movie's opening weekend despite a call from Rothman, who assured him that no matter how the movie fared, the studio wanted to work with him again. On the first day of its release, the *Hollywood Reporter* noted that "prerelease patron polls" indicated "subdued" interest in *Office Space*, which opened in 1,740 theaters around the country. By the end of its first weekend, the film had earned $4.2 million at the box office.[64]

Reviews of *Office Space* were mostly positive. Unlike the Fox executives who originally took issue with the movie's slower pacing and quieter observational humor, some critics already familiar with Judge's work clearly "got" and appreciated the film's sly comedy. "This is minimalist filmmaking; the smaller the movie becomes, the funnier it gets," wrote the *Houston Chronicle*. The *L.A. Times* praised its "inspired humor and all-around smarts" and even singled out the performance of "William King" as Joanna's annoying boss— in actuality a role played by a heavily made-up Judge. One reviewer even compared the movie's effectively flat look and corporate sets to the films of French comedy actor-director Jacques Tati. "Judge may not be fully aware of how wildly talented he is, which, in a Hollywood culture swarming with relentless blowhards, makes him something of an anomaly," wrote Peter Rainer in *New York*. "He has it in him to make classic comedies."[65]

But for some reviewers *Office Space*'s particular brand of comedy was more of an acquired taste. Critics of the film often complained about a meandering plot and a sense of inactivity among the characters. As Stephen Holden observed in the *New York Times*, "It has the loose-jointed feel of a bunch of sketches packed together in a narrative that doesn't gather much momentum." Texas film critic Joe Leydon, who by the late 1990s was writing for *Daily Variety*, overlooked the movie's "slapdash plot" in favor of Judge's "sharply satirical barbs." Leydon also correctly predicted the film's eventual cult status: "Indeed, it's easy to imagine a new trend: Friday happy-hour get-togethers topped off with visits to multiplexes for repeat viewings of *Office Space*."[66]

But if this trend indeed occurred during the movie's initial run, it barely registered at the box office. Dave Herman saw the film on opening day in Santa Monica in a theater that was at best half full. "I loved the movie and I wrote Mike right away saying how much I loved it. And then I went straight to the movie review query engine and read every review." Herman took issue with criticisms about the film's predictable ending. "What were they expecting? Ron Livingston to turn out to be a double agent? What movie were they watching that they were expecting a surprise twist ending? I thought, 'Oh my god, this thing's going to go away forever and it really doesn't deserve to.'"[67]

"It was a disappointment," recalls Root of the movie's lackluster release. "I think we all felt like we were making a really, really good comedy at the time and nobody's going to see it." Certainly the film's characters, office workers stuck in dead-end jobs, had the potential for universal appeal. As one reviewer wrote of *Office Space*'s target audience, "Wage slaves convinced that the people they work for are meaner and stupider than they are. Are we talking big numbers here or what?"[68]

In the end the numbers weren't all that big. *Office Space* earned a domestic gross of only $10.8 million, which meant that Judge's live-action debut barely earned back its production costs for Fox.[69]

In the week after the movie opened, Judge got a call from actor Jim Carey, who had loved the movie. More congratulatory calls poured in from filmmakers John Landis and David Zucker as well as from other actors who hoped to work with Judge. "That counts for a lot in Hollywood. When actors want to meet with you, that's like a big deal," explains Judge, whose disappointment was also eased somewhat by a call from Fox executive Sanford Panitch. "Look, this isn't like a bad movie that fails. This thing got some good reviews. This is like a Coen brothers movie that didn't do well," said Panitch encouragingly. Muses Judge, "They have this term in Hollywood, 'movie jail.' When a director does this horrible movie that fails, he's in movie jail, where they're not letting him make another movie again. It definitely wasn't movie jail. But I was in no rush to do anything again."[70]

### Sometimes History Judges Movies a Different Way

Six months after its first-run theatrical release, in August 1999, *Office Space* debuted on video. Two years later, the movie was released on DVD. And gradually, *Office Space* began to find its audience. Gary Cole was living in Chicago while performing in a play in the summer of 2000. "People started coming up to me 'doing' Lumbergh's dialogue," he recalls. "They didn't even stop me. They'd just come up to me and do his lines. I thought, once, that's a fluke. But it happened multiple times and seemingly like every day. I thought, 'What the hell's going on? I thought this movie tanked?'"[71]

About six months after *Office Space*'s DVD release in 2001, Root also began to sense the movie's cult status. "People would just come up all the time and say, 'I didn't know this movie existed. I couldn't believe it was you in this role.'" Root was being asked to autograph red Swingline staplers, the prop symbolically coveted by his perpetually displaced character. "It was a word-of-mouth movie," says Root. "By 2002, it was raging through the underground that you had to see this movie."[72]

"The reason I think it hit a nerve is because it's coming from real things," muses Cole. "People in office culture identified with whatever character they saw, whether it be themselves or people they worked with or bosses of theirs or just the culture itself."[73]

By 2003, when *Entertainment Weekly* named *Office Space* to its list of Top 50 Cult Classic films, more than 2.6 million VHS and DVD copies of the movie had been sold. Says Mechanic, "In my mind it's one of the more frustrating pictures that we had because we just never found a real way to sell it. Sometimes history judges movies a different way."[74]

In retrospect, Judge realizes he had gotten a glimpse of *Office Space*'s potential cult status during postproduction. In phone conversations with the administrative assistants and accountants in Fox's Accounts Payable department, who handled the cast and crew's rental car reimbursements and the like, the editors noticed that the Fox employees began mimicking Lumbergh's smarmy speech patterns.[75]

**271**

Suhrstedt recalls attending an early evening screening of the movie about two weeks after it opened, just before it left the theaters in Los Angeles. "Here's a movie that you know is almost out of the theaters. They've stopped advertising it. But the theater was almost full. The place was going crazy, and there were clearly people in that theater who had seen it before. And I was thinking to myself, 'This doesn't feel like a movie that should be closing,'" says Suhrstedt. "It had already started to happen. Word of mouth had already built."[76]

Livingston, for one, relished the movie's stealth status. "I would much rather have it have the kind of legacy it has got now than if it had made $20 million in the opening weekend and nobody went and saw it after that. There is something kind of special about it being a[n] underdog movie. It's about underdog people." And years later Judge told Suhrstedt, "Look, in many ways I'm in better shape this way because now I've got a cult movie that's doing well rather than a movie that did just okay."[77]

Unlike Richard Linklater and Robert Rodriguez, Judge didn't feel compelled to direct movies. And by 1999 he felt that the animated series *King of the Hill* was hitting its stride creatively. It was, he said, "a nice part-time job that I don't have to stay up until 3 a.m. and agonize over." Judge had no illusions about filmmaking, and after *Office Space*, he wasn't in a race to make another movie. "You get up at six in the morning and you work sixteen-hour days for ten weeks. It's brutal. I wanted to take it easy and watch my kids grow up for a while."[78]

Five years would pass before Judge stepped behind the camera again.

Robert doesn't believe in doing anything for longer than 15 minutes.
HARRY KNOWLES

# Rebel With or Without a Crew

### Robert Rodriguez and *Spy Kids*

- - - - - - - - - - - - - - - - - - - - - - - - - - - - - - - - - - - - - -

**B**y June 1997 Elizabeth Avellán and Robert Rodriguez had made two films together and had two young sons. Their first child, Rocket Valentino Rodriguez Avellán, was born in 1995, shortly after Rodriguez wrapped production on the Quentin Tarantino–scripted genre bender *From Dusk Till Dawn*. Throughout 1995 and into early 1996, Rodriguez traveled between the couple's rented house in Los Angeles and their new house under construction in Austin. Meanwhile, Avellán was flying between Los Angeles and Houston with the infant Rocket, juggling producing duties and caring for her ailing mother. Ever the multitaskers, the couple managed to conceive their second son later that same year. In April 1997, Avellán gave birth to Racer Maximiliano Rodriguez Avellán in Los Angeles. Two months later, the family was back in Austin for good.

Family, says Avellán, was "one of the themes of our life," and it had clearly inspired Rodriguez in his earliest short films like *Bedhead*, which exaggerated the rivalry that he knew so well growing up in a family of ten siblings. By the mid-1990s, the arrival of his own children and work on films like *Four Rooms* would inspire *Spy Kids* (2001), Rodriguez's most ambitious project to date. A new deal with Miramax's Harvey and Bob Weinstein made the project possible, and it also allowed Rodriguez and Avellán to create Troublemaker Studios, a full-service film facility in Austin.

The production of *Spy Kids*, a $36 million family-oriented action movie, was plagued with setbacks. Principal photography was delayed for 15 months, and its digital effects required labor-intensive postproduction, but the surprise blockbuster grossed more than $100 million domestically in just the first month of its release. It injected approximately $17.5 million back into the state's economy by way of salaries and expenses. *Spy Kids* shot in and around Central Texas and employed nearly three hundred crew members and more than 1,500 extras from around the state. A few of these extras even included friends Richard Linklater and Mike Judge, who made brief cameos. Austin Film Society board members and longtime Rodriguez champions like the *Austin Chronicle*'s Louis Black and UT Radio-Television-Film professor Charles Ramírez Berg also appeared in the film.[1]

Like Rodriguez, the Austin Film Society in the late 1990s was undergoing its own transformation that included a board of directors, the hiring of an executive director, and the realization that the nonprofit needed a source of revenue more dependable than the semi-annual benefit premieres of films by Linklater, Rodriguez, and Judge. As big-budget Hollywood productions continued to leave the United States to take advantage of Canada's tax-free locations, Austin began to feel the effects of a nationwide filmmaking dry spell. This situation, and the ongoing search for a reliable revenue source, prompted AFS to create Austin Studios, the city's first multimedia production facility, on the site of the old airport. It also sparked the idea for the first Texas Film Hall of Fame, an annual celebrity-studded awards ceremony sponsored by AFS. The creation of both the studios and the awards event caused many observers of the local film scene to question if Austin would be able to sustain local, independent productions even as it embraced more ambitious film projects. In what was fast becoming a global digital age, what would become of Austin's regional cinema? And how would this affect the already uneasy tension between art and commerce that resulted from the ongoing maturation of Austin's filmmakers and film scene?

## A Dive Picture

By 1997 Robert Rodriguez found himself face to face with this tension. He and Avellán spent the year settling into their new home, which featured an impressive editing studio. One day Bob Weinstein called Rodriguez to talk about a horror script he wanted to put into production. Written by *Scream* screenwriter Kevin Williamson, the story centered on a group of high school misfits who suspect their teachers are turning into aliens. It was called *The*

*Faculty.* Says Avellán, "Bob knew that that genre was dying out, and he had this very expensive script from Kevin Williamson that he wanted to get out there. Bob was like, 'You know what? I just need to make some money off of it because I paid too much for it.'"[2]

Weinstein asked Rodriguez to direct the script. In return, Miramax would give the filmmaker a five-picture deal in addition to the overall deal Rodriguez had first made with the company in May 1995. Rodriguez didn't really want to direct the movie. As he would reveal later, "*The Faculty* was a dive picture in order to do four other films. But it was a good trial run to try out the Austin crews and try out the effects company. But it was like I had to do it. I enjoyed doing it, but I couldn't wait to do [*Spy Kids*]." The Miramax deal would allow him to stay in Austin. In 1995, when he and Avellán purchased the land for their house, they also bought another parcel of land about 11 miles from the main property in the Texas Hill Country. "We had this great plan for stages we were going to build close to our house," recalls Avellán.[3]

Rodriguez deliberated over the Weinsteins' latest offer. He knew that his friend Quentin Tarantino seemed happy with the company, and he felt confident that he had already established a career on his own terms. "They know that they didn't make me, which is good," says Rodriguez of the relationship. "It's not like with Quentin or Kevin Smith or those guys that they kind of discovered and helped make their first movies. I had already made *Mariachi*, I had already made *Desperado*, and then I came to them fully formed. I always allude to the fact that I'm very unloyal, just so they're always on their toes. Always make them think that I have one foot out the door."[4]

After the deal was signed but before Rodriguez started production on *The Faculty* in the spring of 1998, Rodriguez pitched Weinstein an idea he had been mulling over since making his segment of *Four Rooms* three and a half years earlier. Rodriguez's vignette, "The Misbehavers," features a husband and wife (played by Antonio Banderas and Tamlyn Tomita) who leave their two young children (Lana McKissack and Danny Verduzco) in the care of a harried hotel clerk (Tim Roth) on New Year's Eve. As the segment begins, the children's parents are trying to dress them in party clothes for the evening. When Rodriguez saw the young actors in their costumes—particularly Verduzco, who was wearing a tuxedo—he immediately thought of the James Bond movies and imagined the children as pint-sized spies. According to Tarantino, who also worked on the project, many people were encouraging Rodriguez to do more projects with children, and Banderas liked his character and wanted to expand the role beyond *Four Rooms*. Rodriguez hinted that he was considering a future project that could include all of the characters.

The idea and the positive feedback, in fact, inspired Rodriguez to begin work on a new script. "It was based on my experiences growing up in a large family," he recalls, "memories I had of when I was nine or ten."[5]

Rodriguez tinkered with the idea, working on the script off and on for nearly three years before he pitched it to Bob Weinstein at the Venice Film Festival in September 1997, where he and Rodriguez were feeling like the odd men out at the elegant after-party for Miramax's *The Wings of the Dove*. Rodriguez described it as *Bedhead* meets James Bond, a family film with two children who realize their parents are spies. "When the parents are captured," explained Rodriguez, "the only two people that can save them from the villains are the kids, who have to become spies in their own right."[6]

Unit production manager Bill Scott, who had worked on *The Newton Boys*, received a call from Avellán in the fall of 1997. Based on Richard Linklater's recommendation, Avellán asked Scott to work as a UPM and line producer on *The Faculty*. Recalls Scott, "Robert was very quiet. Elizabeth would state the policy and that's who I'd be doing my talking to [on the film], but Robert would be the one who would be making the decisions."[7]

Script re-writes delayed the start of production on the $20 million horror movie, which finally began shooting in the spring of 1998, at the same time as Mike Judge's production of *Office Space* and soon after *The Newton Boys* opened in theaters. Rodriguez and Avellán were able to convince the Weinsteins that it would make better financial sense to shoot the feature in Austin as opposed to Canada, and they employed a crew that was 80 percent Texan, 70 percent of whom lived in Austin. Jeanette Scott, who had worked as an art director on Linklater's film, was hired by production designer Cary White on *The Faculty*. By 1998 Scott had worked in the industry for more than a decade, but after watching Rodriguez on set she quickly realized that she had never worked with a director quite like him before. "Robert sees his own world in his head. You just get little glimpses of it and then see the movie and see what it was."[8]

Just across the river from downtown Austin, Rodriguez and his crew transformed an abandoned building on the grounds of the Texas School for the Deaf into Herrington High School. Rodriguez and Avellán also leased an empty warehouse as studio space from John "Shampoo King" McCall, an entrepreneur who had made his fortune in beauty supplies. Football game scenes were shot at a high school in nearby Lockhart. Up-and-coming young actors including Elijah Wood, Jordana Brewster, and Josh Hartnett were cast in the various student roles, while stage and screen veterans Piper Laurie and Bebe Neuwirth signed on to play the school's top administrators. Rodriguez regular Salma Hayek joined Robert Patrick, Famke Janssen, and Jon Stewart to round out the adult cast.

Production began in mid-April and ran through July. The movie's relatively low budget and rigorous shooting schedule made it a tough show. According to line producer Bill Scott, the relative inexperience of cinematographer Enrique Chediak also caused problems. "We had a very green director of photography, and Robert does not like to wait." Rodriguez also worked with a visual effects supervisor to achieve some of the movie's scarier scenes, an experience that convinced him it was yet another crew position that was expendable. "Visual effects supervisor is the biggest bullshit job there is," insists Rodriguez. "They just sit around figuring out how to make an effect, and they don't know anything about photography or editing or other things they could do. They kind of go off into their own world and make their own movie and bring you the effect and it sucks and they have to start over."[9]

If the Miramax deal and *The Faculty* indirectly cemented Rodriguez's plans to create a moviemaking foundation in Austin, it also marked Avellán's coming of age as a producer. Although she had earned some type of producing credit on every Rodriguez film since *El Mariachi*, Avellán had yet to produce a movie herself. She worked with a line producer on *Desperado* and with Tarantino partner Lawrence Bender on *From Dusk Till Dawn*. But on *The Faculty*, she came into her own. Given that the movie was being shot in and around the couple's hometown, *The Faculty* also gave Rodriguez and Avellán a chance to cultivate an Austin crew base. "It was something we were building instead of [working in] L.A. where it was like picking and choosing. *The Faculty* was something we were building together, so that's really the first time I felt like I was master of my domain," says Avellán.[10]

On set Avellán was a warm, calming presence, which was especially helpful on *The Faculty*, with its rising stars and scores of youthful and occasionally jittery extras. "I think she makes people feel loyal," says Jeanette Scott, who after *The Faculty* continued to work with the couple on successive films. "I think she sees her job as to facilitate whatever Robert wants to happen. She wants to see that he gets to make the movie he wants to make, and she runs interference and pretty much leaves him free to create."[11]

On *The Faculty*, as with future productions, Weinstein relied on Avellán to keep Rodriguez on track. "She tells it like it is. She says, 'This is what we could do, here's what we *have* to do,' and then I say, 'Excuse me. There's a [release] date. It's been on the chart, the advertising's running. I know he wants 7,000 more special effects. Please do whatever you like, but I have to have the film.' Somehow that print arrives and the movie's in the theater. I don't want to know how she does it, but she does it. And I know it's [because of] her."[12]

Production on *The Faculty* wrapped in mid-summer. Rodriguez spent the fall editing and overseeing other aspects of the film's postproduction. Miramax pressed to release *The Faculty* on Christmas Day, which mimicked the holiday release pattern for their hyper-successful *Scream* series, also written by Williamson. Buzz increased throughout the fall of 1998, and on Christmas Eve, the day before its release, the *Hollywood Reporter* predicted box office to rival the *Scream* franchise.[13]

*The Faculty* debuted in the fifth spot on its opening weekend and earned a very respectable $11.8 million at the box office. It would eventually gross $40.2 million domestically, less than half of *Scream*'s domestic total and a far cry from the $100 million predicted for Rodriguez's second horror movie. "Results may not be Nobel Prize material, but they're zesty and cogent," wrote *Variety*, but critics generally weren't kind to the film. Rodriguez took a few hits for his flashy camerawork and limited storytelling skills, but many reviewers blamed Williamson and the script.[14]

### Casting *Spy Kids*, Building a Studio

Bill Scott had first heard about *Spy Kids* while making *The Faculty*. When Scott read the script, he immediately began to worry. It featured multiple locations, stunts and props, and he wasn't sure how they could afford to shoot it for a budget that would satisfy the cost-conscious filmmaker.

Recalls Rodriguez, "It was challenging to get everybody to think in this direction, which was, I was going to shoot the movie very inexpensively compared to what it could cost. I remember Bill Scott looked at the script and goes, 'Well, you want us to make this guerilla-style, but you didn't give us a guerilla script.' I said, 'I should send you the script for *Mariachi*. That didn't look like a $7,000 movie, either.'" Rodriguez assured his crew that with visual "tricks" and computer-generated effects, they could make the movie look pricier than it was. "They hadn't really produced something like that with me before," he says.[15]

Although Rodriguez had been tinkering with the *Spy Kids* idea for years, actual production on the film wasn't slated to begin until October 1999. Says Bill Scott, "Robert's not real good at long-range planning and timing because he's doing so many things at once." When the start date pushed into early spring 2000, Harry Knowles addressed swirling rumors of script and casting problems in a report on his *AICN* Web site. "Rodriguez, being the smart filmmaker he is, decided to try and get an advertising partner for his *KID* movie." McDonald's agreed to partner on a *Spy Kids* Happy Meal, but the fast-food giant didn't have available promotional time until March 2001.[16]

"We had talked to McDonald's about going after that tie-in," recalls Weinstein, but he claims the movie's release date—an untested time of year to open a family-friendly film, a genre typically released during the summer— had more to do with box office. "There's business to be had out there in any particular time and place. I learned with *Scream* that the best playing time is the best playing time for your particular movie. One of the things I think Robert and Elizabeth trust me with is looking at the schedule and knowing where to put a movie and how to market it. I consider Robert a marketing partner, but I know he leaves it up to me to sort of say what's the best date."[17]

In the downtime between the original 1999 start date and the new production start of March 2000, Rodriguez traveled to Chile and the Bahamas to shoot second unit photography for the movie.

Around this time Rodriguez and Avellán were also working on a long-term plan that would have tremendous reverberations for the Austin film community. When the couple returned to Austin for good in 1997, one of their goals was to build and invest in a studio of their own. They had purchased suitable land, and the couple also paid to send family friend and local architect Robert Steinbomer to Los Angeles to learn about the nuts and bolts of creating sound stages.

In the mid-1990s as Austin's population swelled thanks in part to the area's high-tech boom, the city proposed a plan to replace its existing airport in East Austin with a new larger facility southeast of the downtown area. Rodriguez and Avellán had seen the facilities at the State Aircraft Pooling Board, a site adjacent to the old airport that housed then-Governor George W. Bush's official plane.

Although the original plan was to build sound stages closer to the Rodriguez home, the existing raw space offered by one of the hangars at the site adjacent to the old airport was equally tempting. To make it work for their present needs as well as their future plans, however, Rodriguez and Avellán would have to convince the state to enter into a long-term lease.

Eric Williams, who had trained as an editor on Bill Wittliff's *Red Headed Stranger,* had begun working with Rodriguez and Avellán as a locations manager on *The Faculty* and also signed on for *Spy Kids.* Williams's step-father was a member of the Texas legislature and good friends with then Speaker of the House James "Pete" Laney. Laney had created the Pooling Board and appointed former Speaker of the House William Clayton as chairman, and in

July 1999 Williams introduced Rodriguez and Avellán to Laney and Clayton. The husband and wife impressed the two men—"She's a take-charge person," says Laney of Avellán—but the Texas Department of Transportation (TX DoT) also was interested in utilizing the same site. "At that time TX DoT wanted it for storage," recalls Bill Scott. Although *The Faculty* hadn't done the box office that many in the industry projected, on paper the movie still made back its production budget and then some. The couple's use of local crew, locations, and businesses also suggested they were committed to shooting and staying in Austin. Rodriguez's earlier movies earned impressive profits, and with another film on the way—budgeted at $36 million, it would be his most expensive to date—Rodriguez and Avellán's Los Hooligans production company looked to be a good risk. "We thought it was a good investment for the state, so we pushed that," recalls Laney. "I think the fact that *Spy Kids* was a kid's movie made it a lot easier to sell to anybody. If it had been another *Texas Chainsaw Massacre* or even an R-rated film, it might have raised some hackles around [the Capitol]."[18]

Simultaneously, one of the vacant hangars at the old airport, which had closed on May 1, 1999, was being used to shoot the Sandra Bullock comedy *Miss Congeniality*. Around the same time an idea was being floated over at the Austin Film Society to convert the former airport into a studio complex as well. Says Scott, "I think all of that went to impress Speaker Laney and former Speaker Clayton. Plus, they liked to come out and schmooze with the stars. So they really went to bat and basically got us that property."[19]

In the end Avellán and Rodriguez negotiated a multi-year lease through August 2001 to use the tarmac as a parking lot and two hangars for special effects shots and to construct temporary sets for *Spy Kids*.

To find many of the supporting roles for *Spy Kids*, Rodriguez collaborated with veteran casting director Mary Vernieu, whose credits included a number of Oliver Stone films and with whom Rodriguez had worked on *The Faculty*. Longtime Rodriguez favorite Danny Trejo, who played numerous villains in the director's earlier films, was on board by September 1999.

From the start the filmmaker had planned to offer the role of Gregorio Cortez to Antonio Banderas, with whom he had first worked in *Desperado*. The Spanish actor had also played the dashing father in "The Misbehavers." Although sets were being built at the rented South Austin warehouse and the newly acquired studio, and Rodriguez hoped to begin production around November, Banderas still had not committed to the project by the end of 1999.

By the time *Spy Kids* was in preproduction, the young actors who had appeared with Banderas in *Four Rooms* were too old to play the roles of Juni and Carmen Cortez in *Spy Kids,* but Rodriguez was adamant that he wanted actors who were at least half Latin in background. By late September he had narrowed down his choices to Daryl Sabara and Alexa Vega.

Only six years old when he was cast—he turned seven by the time production began—Sabara already was a veteran actor. He and his twin brother Evan, who would have a small part in *Spy Kids* as Juni's evil robot clone, had been acting in television since the age of six weeks, when they both played Candice Bergen's infant son on *Murphy Brown.*

The eleven-year-old Vega was also an experienced actor with credits in both television and film, and she was especially eager to be cast in *Spy Kids.* "Back then I never really read scripts. It was more about, you go and audition, and you just kind of do whatever role comes next. But this one was definitely a new experience altogether," recalls Vega. She was impressed by the thirty-one-year-old Rodriguez, whose boyish enthusiasm and trademark bandanas and cowboy hats only added to the project's novelty. "I was like, 'No way! Directors do *not* wear that stuff.' So right away I knew I wanted to work with him just because he was a cool guy."[20]

For the role of Ingrid Cortez, Gregorio's wife and spy partner, Rodriguez decided on Kelly Preston, an actress who had most recently appeared in *For the Love of the Game* and who was married to John Travolta. Preston was eight months pregnant with her second child when her official involvement in the film was announced in late March 2000. (Rodriguez had begun shooting scenes with other cast members that same month.) Rodriguez couldn't have been happier about the casting of Preston. "Kelly was perfect because she was warm and she was already a mother yet sexy. All the things that she had to be—tough, spy-like."[21]

Preston gave birth in early April 2000, mere weeks before her scheduled start date on *Spy Kids.* It soon became clear that Preston wouldn't be able to recover in time, and Rodriguez didn't want to push back production any longer.

"We were two weeks into filming and Robert couldn't find a mom," says Sabara. "My brother Evan had just worked with Carla Gugino on a Hallmark movie called *A Season for Miracles,* so we both went to Elizabeth, and we gave the tape to Elizabeth and said, 'She's perfect.' Elizabeth gave the tape to Robert and Robert actually watched the entire movie the whole way through."[22]

A petite dark-haired beauty, Gugino had most recently co-starred in Brian DePalma's thriller *Snake Eyes* (1998) and had worked with Banderas years earlier in *Miami Rhapsody* (1995). She originally hadn't appeared on any of the casting lists because, at twenty-eight, she was considered too young for the role. "Age-wise, there was no way I literally could have been a spy and had these kids," laughs Gugino. Anxious to cast the part, Rodriguez was thrilled to discover that Gugino loved the character of Ingrid and could bring to the role many of the same qualities as Preston. "Carla also felt warm and sophisticated yet sexy enough and dangerous enough to be a spy," he recalls.[23]

Gugino flew to Austin, colored her hair for the role, and was in front of the cameras all within forty-eight hours of meeting Rodriguez.

When the original 1999 start date for *Spy Kids* was pushed back to spring of 2000, the art department took advantage of the extra time. Rodriguez had hired veteran production designer Cary White, with whom he had first worked on *The Faculty*, to oversee the look of the film. Like Bill Scott, who had never worked on a project quite like *Spy Kids*, White wanted the chance to collaborate on a fictional world unlike any he had ever designed. "We had a difficult time at first," remembers White. "We kept experimenting with different things, and Robert wasn't finding anything that he really liked."[24]

### It's Such an Un-Hollywood Place

*Spy Kids* shot on location in and around Austin and Central Texas. (In addition to the location footage Rodriguez had shot in Chile and the Bahamas, a small amount of miniature model work was done in California.) A local parochial school near the University of Texas campus became the setting for Juni and Carmen's school. A home on Lake Travis stood in for the remote safe house where Juni and Carmen discover their parents' true identities. Some scenes and exteriors were also shot at the State Capitol in downtown Austin, and the Capitol's rotunda was then re-created on an interior stage for longer sequences featuring many young extras. The hangar at Troublemaker's new home adjacent to the former airport site housed the green screen. The shoot even traveled to San Antonio, where the city's public library doubled as another *Spy Kids* set.

For the young actors, the production felt like summer camp. Sabara was just a few years older than Rodriguez and Avellán's oldest son, Rocket. Along with Rocket's brothers Racer and Rebel (born in 1999), the Rodriguez children and the couple's extended family were a constant presence on the set. Avellán, who was "Miss Elizabeth" to the younger actors, worked hard to create a family-friendly environment, hiring a mariachi band for special occasion lunches and instituting "Silly String Day" and sanctioning cake fights. Sabara and Vega would hang out in the director's trailer, where Rodriguez would give them tips for making their own short films. Observes Gugino, "It felt like Robert was very at home making this movie. I think it connected the fantastical, comic book elements of things that he really loves with something that meant so much to him, which was his family."[25]

The script's family focus affected the set in a positive way. Crew members tended to watch their language, especially around the young actors and other children, and the general mood was upbeat. There was also a sense among those working on the production that *Spy Kids* could be a significant film for Rodriguez's career, and they wanted to help the "hometown boy" do well. Many also felt that the movie's potential success would only reflect well on Austin and its film community.

Bob and Harvey Weinstein were an occasional presence on the *Spy Kids* set, flying into Austin to enjoy family-style dinners with Avellán, Rodriguez, and their cast during the two-month shoot. The Weinsteins' set visits, at least for the actors, didn't incite the typical panic on a production in progress. "It's such an un-Hollywood place," says Gugino of Troublemaker. "There aren't studio executives there all the time. People aren't second-guessing other people." Says Vega, who had made six studio films by the time she was cast in *Spy Kids*, "There are usually so many bosses, you never really get a final answer, so you end up doing things all these different ways. You're free to do whatever you want on a Rodriguez film. You don't have to worry about impressing the studio. Robert's the guy. If he's comfortable with something, then you don't have to worry about asking somebody else."[26]

Bill Scott, who had worked both with Rodriguez and Richard Linklater, saw similarities in how the two filmmakers bonded with talent. "They're both very, very good in their involvement with actors. They know clearly what they want in a performance and they're able to let an actor know that without making him a puppet." The budget-conscious Rodriguez, however, would cut production costs by shooting around actors. "For instance, Antonio Banderas may be in an awful lot of the movie, but we'll shoot him out in six to 10 days. Robert does not believe that one actor has to have the other actor there to do a scene," says Scott.[27]

"It was definitely unique," says Gugino of her first experience shooting with Rodriguez. "But if there was a point at which Antonio had to be finished before me and we had a couple of scenes left, Robert literally was operating the camera and reading Antonio's lines off-screen."[28]

### A Franchise Is Born

Production on *Spy Kids* ran sixty-seven days and wrapped in late July 2000. Rodriguez spent the next few months working on a rough cut and tinkering with the movie's effects. As excited as he was about the movie taking shape, he tried to keep details about the project under wraps. "It was a very simple idea that no one had really done before. And no one was doing family films at that time."[29]

By November, Rodriguez had a finished trailer ready to run in theaters. As with nearly every other aspect of his films, Rodriguez had a hand in cutting his own previews. He loved the process and, ever since *El Mariachi,* he had approached the task in part as a way to get fired up about editing the entire feature. He knew his footage better than anyone else, he reasoned, and he couldn't understand why other filmmakers didn't cut their own trailers, especially if they had access to their own editing equipment.

"You give your movie that you've worked on all this time to a studio, they give it to an agency. The agency does a bunch of trailers, but if you go into the back room and see who's actually cutting the trailers, it's film-school rejects, people who can't even get a job in the movie business," Rodriguez insists. "They just kind of cookie-cutter them out, and the trailers all look the same."[30]

The *Spy Kids* trailer hit theaters in November and immediately began to generate buzz. Knowles, who had groused on his Web site about the initial design and offerings of the *Spy Kids* site that went live on the Internet in late October, had nothing but enthusiastic praise for the action-packed teaser. Rodriguez was thrilled but not surprised by the overall positive response. "I always felt that would be my most successful film," he says years later.[31]

Agent Robert Newman loved the idea but says that the prerelease data on *Spy Kids* was telling a different story. "The tracking wasn't looking that great. And it made no sense to me. The materials that I saw that were out there looked great. Robert did a great job, and this was a great idea for a movie. And it just made no sense to me why [the forecasted numbers] weren't bigger." (At the time Miramax executive David Kaminow was quoted in the trades as saying just the opposite: "Our family tracking looks great, and we're looking forward to the weekend.")[32]

*Spy Kids* screened in Las Vegas at the annual ShoWest convention held for exhibitors in March 2001. An Internet movie reviewer described the movie's "through the roof" reception on Knowles's Web site, while *Daily Variety* interpreted the exhibitors' responses as "curiously ho-hum."[33] But *Spy Kids* buzz continued to build over the next few weeks before its March 30 release. Rodriguez and Avellán arranged to have the movie premiere in Austin a week earlier as part of a special screening at the Paramount Theatre that benefited the Austin Film Society and Austin's Ronald McDonald House. City officials closed off a couple of blocks of Congress Avenue in front of the theater for a street carnival complete with rides and games. After the screening, *Spy Kids*'s youngest actors joined Rodriguez on stage for a lively Q & A.

Released in just over 3,100 theaters around the country, *Spy Kids* debuted in the number-one spot at the box office.[34] For the first time in his career, Rodriguez had made a mainstream movie that showcased his strengths as a director and storyteller. *Spy Kids*'s characters were immensely appealing, and its storyline felt fresh and exuberant. The fact that *Spy Kids*'s protagonists were a Latino family was groundbreaking for a family movie. Instead of trumpeting the fact, however, Rodriguez treated his characters as nothing out of the ordinary, which encouraged audiences to do the same. The movie successfully and smartly targeted multiple generations of moviegoers.

It earned $26.5 million on its opening weekend, roughly three-quarters of its $36 million budget. Rodriguez and Weinstein were on the phone to each other, rejoicing over their mutual good fortune. "He was calling every hour for the grosses," remembers Weinstein. "And we knew we were heading into Easter so we knew we'd have some legs." The following Monday, *Daily Variety* reported that Weinstein had already approved a script for a *Spy Kids* sequel, which meant that Dimension would expand its franchises from the horror genre into the family film arena. "The decision to do *Spy Kids 2* came out of the nature of, 'Hey, we have this little hit. Might as well just keep it going.' And [Vega and Sabara] were young so we knew that you can't wait and sit around," says Weinstein.[35]

Recalls the filmmaker, "We were number one for three weeks. There was nothing out. Now [March] is a big date, but at the time no one was putting movies out in March like that. Now it's a family spot."[36] *Spy Kids*'s phenomenal performance at the box office earned it the distinction of having the most successful opening for a family film ever in that particular calendar slot.

Reviews of the movie were interesting. Many critics observed that on first glance the family-oriented film seemed like an odd departure for a filmmaker normally associated with action and violence. But those familiar with his short film *Bedhead* (and, to a lesser degree, *Four Rooms*'s "The Misbehavers") noted Rodriguez's skill with stories about children. "Considering that Rodriguez's previous movies include gore fests like *From Dusk Till Dawn*, *Spy Kids*'s sweetness comes as a surprise. In some ways, though, it is a return to his roots," observed the *Houston Chronicle*. Others noted that Rodriguez's penchant for manic action and quick cuts served him well in this particular genre. The *San Francisco Chronicle* favorably compared *Spy Kids* to a video game. The Minneapolis, Minnesota *Star Tribune* observed that the movie was "vintage Rodriguez": "The maker of *El Mariachi, Desperado, From Dusk Till*

*Dawn* and *The Faculty* has taken his action-driven formula and converted it to a PG format. There's lots of slapstick fighting, but no one ever gets hurt."[37]

Most of the reviews were positive, if somewhat qualified. "*Spy Kids* is an enjoyable and charming if overactive fantasy that bulldozes much and sacrifices the chemistry between the two young stars that they need to develop," wrote the *New York Times*. Writing about Rodriguez for the *Washington Times*, Gary Arnold called *Spy Kids* "an uneven but likable attempt to merge the spy-thriller genre with family comedy."[38] Others focused on the movie's technological advances, observing that Rodriguez utilized a fairly new technology to create impressive special effects on a relatively low budget.

But perhaps no critic was as effusive as Roger Ebert, who called it a "treasure": "*Spy Kids* is an intelligent, upbeat, happy movie that is not about the comedy of embarrassment, that does not have anybody rolling around in dog poop, that would rather find out what it can accomplish than what it can get away with."[39]

After only a month in theaters, *Spy Kids* had grossed about $67 million and was moving quickly toward $100 million and blockbuster status. Before the end of May, it would easily surpass that figure. Even Michael Bay's *Pearl Harbor*, released over Memorial Day and expected to earn $100 million in its first weekend (it grossed $75 million), couldn't stop the *Spy Kids* juggernaut. In mid-May Dimension capitalized on the movie's success by announcing plans to release into theaters a "special edition" *Spy Kids* in August. The new version would include an additional sequence with footage Rodriguez filmed in the Bahamas early on during the movie's production. He had planned to use the footage behind an action scene featuring Juni and Carmen, but it was eventually scrapped from the original release because its special effects proved too costly.[40]

In early August, Rodriguez and Avellán celebrated their movie's success by taking out a full-page advertisement in the *Austin Chronicle*. Designed in the style of a *Spy Kids*-type mission report and signed by Rodriguez and Avellán, the ad featured a photograph of the entire cast and crew and thanked the Troublemaker crew, fellow Austinites, the city, and the Texas Film Commission. Recalls old friend Carlos Gallardo, "Robert was frustrated when Miramax made him do *The Faculty*. He had to prove himself until he did *Spy Kids*. Then he made $100,000,000, and things became easier."[41]

### I'm Following Obi-Wan

With *Spy Kids* still in theaters, Rodriguez already had turned his attention to his next two projects, both of which would also mark significant turning points in his career. With *Spy Kids 2* Rodriguez would be building a franchise in another genre. With *Once Upon a Time in Mexico*, he would be concluding the *Mariachi* trilogy with a long-awaited follow-up to *Desperado*. Rodriguez was aware of the negotiating power *Spy Kids*'s success afforded him and he employed it in discussions with Sony executives, who were interested in working with him on *Once Upon a Time in Mexico*. Explained Rodriguez, "When I made the kinds of movies I used to make—the *Dusk Till Dawns*—I knew what they were. I made them for a price, I knew there was a specific audience, and I was okay with that. But now, having done *Spy Kids,* that's what interests me. Doing films that reach that level of audience. For a price."[42]

Both *Spy Kids 2* and *Once Upon a Time* also would mark Rodriguez's conversion to digital moviemaking. George Lucas, himself a pioneer of film technology, showed Rodriguez footage from his *Star Wars* prequel *Episode II: Attack of the Clones* at Skywalker Ranch when Rodriguez was mixing *Spy Kids* in early 2000. Lucas had shot his movie using the Sony 24P camera, which utilized new digital technology. "We got into long conversations about digital and regional filmmaking and the difficulties of negotiating through the business without getting swamped by the Hollywood aesthetic," recalls Lucas of their first meeting. "Robert is an independent regional filmmaker, so he isn't wedded to doing it through the system the way the system has always done it. He looks at digital and says, 'Hey, this looks great! It's cheaper, it's better.'"[43] Rodriguez was intrigued by the new technology and conducted some tests of his own to compare film to high-definition digital video. Over the years he had grown dissatisfied with the quality and cost of shooting on film.

"I'm following Obi-Wan," Rodriguez said of his decision to mimic Lucas's shift away from celluloid. "I'm not waiting 10 years for everyone else to catch on."[44]

After a mere two weeks of prep, Rodriguez traveled to Mexico in late May 2001 to shoot *Once Upon a Time*, which continued the Mariachi's story with an all-star lineup that reunited *Desperado* alums Antonio Banderas, Salma Hayek, and even Quentin Tarantino. Rodriguez later described the movie as loosely based on Sergio Leone's spaghetti western *The Good, the Bad and the Ugly.* Johnny Depp, Mickey Rourke, and newcomer Eva Mendes rounded out the cast. The movie re-teamed Rodriguez and Avellán with Sony Corporation's Columbia Pictures. By 2001, the entertainment conglomerate was struggling financially. The studio was essentially broke, so they agreed to a deal in which Dimension would put up half of the $29 million budget, with Sony covering the other half in exchange for domestic distribution rights. Dimension would own the international rights. Says Avellán, who had not forgotten the tensions between her and Rodriguez and Columbia executive

Gary Martin on *Desperado*, "I was very leery of Gary Martin. [Sony] wanted *Once Upon a Time*, and we held out until some respect was given us."[45]

The *Once Upon a Time* shoot lasted only seven weeks, a blur of activity and long days. Says production designer Cary White, who was prepping *Spy Kids 2* at the time so that Rodriguez could begin shooting in the fall, "*Once Upon a Time* was a show they were trying to slip in before a de facto actor's strike. There was no prep time, and it burned up a lot of people that went down there. It just chewed them up and spit them out."[46]

Rodriguez described the summer shoot as "down and dirty," a return to the exhilarating hardscrabble filmmaking of his first feature. Avellán shared producing credit on *Once Upon a Time* with Carlos Gallardo. Tony Mark came on board as one of the movie's co-producers. Mark had first worked with Avellán on *Desperado* when he served as that film's unit production manager, and he and Avellán had established a good working relationship. She was much less enthusiastic about working with the studio again. "It's like molasses around that place. Not oil, molasses."[47]

In late September 2001, one month after the release of the *Spy Kids* "special edition" in theaters, the *Spy Kids* video debuted in the number-one spot.[48] About five weeks later, *Spy Kids 2: Island of Lost Dreams* began production in Rodriguez's original hometown of San Antonio, where the filmmaker shot a number of scenes in the main branch of the city's public library. Banderas, Gugino, Vega, and Sabara all reprised their roles from the first *Spy Kids*. They were joined by actors Ricardo Montalban and Holland Taylor, who played the children's grandparents.

Whereas *Spy Kids* filmed on a number of sets, most of its locations were confined to the Central Texas region. The *Spy Kids* sequel involved more exterior scenes shot around the state in locations like Dallas, San Antonio, and West Texas, as well as a shoot in Costa Rica that quickly inflated the budget. Originally budgeted to be filmed on the fly using a handheld camera and a crew of about five people, the location work mushroomed into two weeks of production with a full cast of young actors. And because Costa Rica lacked the necessary film infrastructure, seventeen tons of equipment had to be flown in for the shoot. Recalls production manager Bill Scott, "None of that was in the original plans. That's why that's the only one of the films I've done since working with Robert that we've gone over budget. Basically, the cost of Costa Rica."[49]

The location work made the sequel a more physically demanding shoot than the first *Spy Kids*. Pleased with the performance of Sony's digital camera, Rodriguez continued to work on video as he had done with *Once Upon a*

*Time.* For production designer Cary White, the sequel had greater ramifications. Midway through production on *Spy Kids 2*, the filmmaker fired White. "Prior to that, there was a good esprit de corps and a good sort of feeling," says White. "Over the course of the period I spent with Robert, there was a shift, a change in the whole feel of the thing. It kind of got mean, I think, when they went down to shoot *Once Upon a Time in Mexico.*" While still on the project, White and Bill Scott traveled to Costa Rica to scout locations for *Spy Kids 2*, then moved on to San Miguel de Allende, Mexico, to meet up with Rodriguez. Recalls White, "From that point on there was sort of a different atmosphere that, it seemed to me, had changed somehow."[50]

"The problems began when *Spy Kids* happened," says Avellán. "Cary didn't write that script. They weren't getting what Robert wanted. But what Robert wasn't understanding was that they can't read his mind. It was exhausting because poor Cary would give him his vision of what *he* read, but it wasn't the vision of the guy that wrote it."[51]

Rodriguez decided to stop working with a production designer and instead to rely on an art director (Jeanette Scott) who would work from his own drawings. Continues Avellán, "Robert has learned that he needs to just do it. As he's written these things, he's already worked out a lot of what it looks like in his mind."[52]

But White's firing caused rumblings within the local film community, and it only exacerbated some criticisms of the notoriously multi-talented Rodriguez. The cost-conscious filmmaker's embracing of computer-generated effects work and his impressive ability to assume more of the key positions on his own productions allowed him to pare down his crew, which further reduced overhead at Troublemaker. But it also meant he was employing fewer local technicians. The way he preferred to work—shooting for a few weeks at a time and then taking a week-long hiatus to edit—also made some crew members feel as if they were being "dayplayed," a situation where they are employed (and paid) for a short amount of time but are still tethered to the production, making it impossible to collect unemployment or seek other work during the breaks.[53]

As Troublemaker Studios expanded, security was increased and visitors had to enter and exit past a guard booth, an arrangement that was quite different, for instance, than Richard Linklater's and Mike Judge's nondescript production offices or even Richard Kooris's 501 Studios complex east of downtown. Says Gugino of working at Troublemaker, "It's this feeling that you're doing something under the radar, and in truth you kind of are because nobody really knows what's going on, in terms of Hollywood. It's so removed."[54] The protected facilities certainly provided Rodriguez with the privacy he valued. (As did the confidentiality agreements he required of everyone involved with each of his productions.) But while Rodriguez and Avellán were most definitely a part of and tremendous boosters of Austin's expanding film community, the foundation that they had both worked so hard to create was beginning to seem, at least to some observers, less a part of—literally and figuratively—the very community it claimed to serve.

### The Studio That Miramax Built

Dimension planned an August 2002 release for *Spy Kids 2*. By this time Rodriguez and Avellán had renegotiated and extended their initial lease of the facilities at the State Aircraft Pooling Board and moved the bulk of their production and postproduction facilities to the site. For *Spy Kids 2* they had expanded into a third hangar. *Spy Kids 2* marked the first time that Troublemaker was able, with its new facilities, to complete a movie's postproduction entirely in Austin. Rodriguez had consulted with George Lucas as he expanded the facilities, and Lucas advised the younger filmmaker to consider overhead issues and whether or not he wanted to start—and maintain—his own special effects company. As Lucas would observe a few years later, with Troublemaker Rodriguez had become more than just a filmmaker. He was a studio.[55]

*Spy Kids 2* pulled in $16.7 million on its first weekend, nearly $10 million less than its predecessor. Still, the movie recouped its $38 million budget within its first two weeks. Says Avellán, "You have to make money for your partners. That's the secret to being successful. You always have to think about what the break-even point is on your film, and that should be the top part of the budget. I feel so happy when my movies make their budgets back in 10 days, because then it's a moneymaker." *Spy Kids 2: Island of Lost Dreams* eventually grossed $85.8 million, nearly $40 million less domestically than the first *Spy Kids*. ("Usually sequels drop 50%," says Weinstein. "We dropped about 14% from *Spy Kids*, but we went up 40% on *Spy Kids 3*, which is very, very rare.")[56]

After completing postproduction on *Spy Kids 2*, Rodriguez turned his attention back to *Once Upon a Time*, which opened in September 2003. It took the number-one spot at the box office and grossed $23.4 million—nearly the entire domestic gross of *Desperado*—during its first weekend in theaters. *Once Upon a Time* received mixed reviews. Although many critics were impressed by Rodriguez's growing list of talents and his ability to make digital video virtually indistinguishable from film, they were less enamored of his narrative abilities. Wrote the *New York Times*, "Mr. Rodriguez, while he gluts the audience's appetite for blood, fire and music, starves us for character, feeling and story."[57] But audiences didn't seem to mind.

The success of the *Spy Kids* franchise produced a third and final movie in July 2003. Rodriguez had worked at a fever pitch during this period, perhaps the most frenetic since shooting and editing *Mariachi* more than a decade earlier. The *Spy Kids 3D* cast worked without a script for the first three months of the film's six-month production schedule. Instead, Rodriguez would hand the actors new pages every morning as they came on the set. Recalls Sabara, "Robert would come to work every day, he would shoot *Spy Kids*, he would go home and watch dailies, he was editing *Once Upon a Time in Mexico*, he was trying to finish *Spy Kids 3D* and he was starting to write *Sin City*. It was crazy, but he pulled it off."[58]

The fruits of their labor also allowed Rodriguez and Avellán to expand their facilities at Troublemaker Studios to include an additional sound stage, production offices, equipment, editing and sound mixing facilities, and a digital effects house. The Weinsteins and Rodriguez himself referred to Dimension as "the house that Rodriguez built," while locals within the Austin film community dubbed Troublemaker "the house that Miramax built." But Tarantino compares the facilities to Francis Ford Coppola's earliest attempts, with friend George Lucas, to create American Zoetrope in 1970. "The thing that I kind of realized at a certain point, that made me so incredibly proud of Robert, was the fact that Coppola's dream that he had had with American Zoetrope is Robert's reality. What Coppola wanted to do with Zoetrope—have a studio and a crew more or less on call, actors more or less on call, where you can just make movie after movie, follow your own artistic impulses, that's Robert's reality. Robert has done that."[59] With *Spy Kids*, Rodriguez and Avellán felt they had achieved a certain amount of respect and power within Hollywood even as they worked outside of the system.

### Growing Pains: The Austin Film Society and Austin Studios

Around the time that Rodriguez and Avellán began filming *The Faculty* in the spring of 1998, a recent University of Texas RTF graduate named Rebecca Campbell succeeded Elizabeth Peters in overseeing the Austin Film Society. Under Peters's three-year tenure, AFS had begun the transition from being "just" a local arts organization that screened films, brought visiting filmmakers to Austin, and held the occasional premiere to becoming an organization

**291**

with a national reputation that provided badly needed financial assistance to young filmmakers with the creation of the Texas Filmmakers' Production Fund. In 1997 alone, AFS held four benefit premieres that allowed the fund, established one year earlier, to nearly double its grant amounts (from $30,000 to $50,000) and the number of recipients (from 30 to 50).[60]

In 1997 as Peters prepared to leave her post at the film society, she approached Campbell about taking over her "part-time" position as managing director. Campbell began training in March of 1998 and took over on May 1. "What was so interesting was to discover that which films we were going to show was really a very macho topic that people would get into deep, passionate arguments about."[61] Linklater still served as artistic director, a position he had segued into after the establishment of a board of directors and a small paid staff to handle the day-to-day details of running the organization. Many of the individuals who made up the board, like Louis Black, Charles Ramírez Berg, and Chale Nafus, had supported the film society from its inception and did not take their positions lightly.

AFS board member Judith Sims, who had offered the art museum to Linklater and Lee Daniel as a programming venue in the organization's early years, was one of the first people to suggest that the film society needed to involve itself more with the local community. She also said AFS should revamp its image and shore up its fundraising efforts, which at the time were essentially limited to the premieres of films by Linklater, Rodriguez, and friends like Quentin Tarantino. At one meeting a professional fundraiser took the board through a variety of group exercises designed to tease out a vision for the organization. Anne del Castillo had moved to Austin in 1997 after working for PBS, and in the summer of 1998 she was hired as the Director of Artists Services for AFS. "Talk about a culture clash," she says of the early meetings to professionalize the organization. "[The fundraiser] created this plan that sort of looked like a map for a treasure hunt. She kept trying to get people to talk about vision." Skeptical board members found themselves putting dots on pieces of paper and wondering how it all related to AFS's original mission of programming movies. When they were asked, "Where do you see AFS in five years?" their response was, "Showing more movies." The board said they envisioned their audience as the same, only bigger. Recalls del Castillo, "She was trying to get us to think big, but strategically."[62]

"But still," says Campbell, "a vision got drawn out of that group. We want to be a sustainable engine of film culture, making Austin the best place to be and watch movies." Among other changes, the board voted to revise the film society's bylaws and appoint a president who would serve for two years.

*Austin Chronicle* editor Louis Black was the obvious first choice. A tiered ticket system was also implemented for premieres in order to raise more money for the TFPF. AFS members protested the change, arguing that they were being blocked out of the better seats, which were given to those who could afford or were willing to pay higher ticket prices. "Rick and Louis were on the side of the members," says del Castillo, but the change eventually went through. One thing that Linklater stood firm on, however, was the process by which TFPF funds were given to recipients. Del Castillo pointed out to Linklater that some recipients were using their grant monies on other projects or, in one particular case, to purchase a bicycle, and that perhaps stricter guidelines should be implemented to track the funds. "We just want to support filmmakers," Linklater told her. "We don't want to make them go through all that red tape. This is not public money. It's money we're raising ourselves."[63]

The film society began formulating a strategic plan in the summer of 1999. One of its primary components involved the leasing of the site of Robert Mueller Municipal Airport for film production purposes, an idea that was fueled, at least in part, by Rodriguez and Avellán's interest in and eventual leasing of the space at the adjacent State Pooling Board site.

In fact, it was at the December 1998 premiere of *The Faculty* when then Mayor Kirk Watson heard Rodriguez mention how difficult it was for filmmakers to find available production space in town. As Rodriguez took final questions at the premiere, Watson thought that maybe the empty hangars at the former airport might work as temporary soundstages and production spaces. After Rodriguez left the stage, Watson approached Louis Black. "I mentioned it to Louis, and he didn't immediately indicate that it was a great idea," recalls Watson. "Several weeks, a month, maybe six weeks later, he called me and apparently he and some others had been talking about that. And whether he recalled the conversation or not, the idea of those hangars being used was something people were talking about."[64]

Plans to build a film studio in Austin had been batted around at least since the 1980s, when projectionist Stan Ginsel worked at Texas Motion Picture Service with Ivan Bigley. It was Bigley's idea, says Ginsel, to build a facility in Austin that could house production under one roof and attract more business to the area and its growing film community. Initially they scouted possible existing locations but soon realized that they'd need to build the facility from scratch.

Investors were resistant to the rather intangible and extremely risky idea. "It was very, very difficult to convince anybody to fork over that kind of money where there was no track record or existing facility," recalls Ginsel.[65]

By the early 1990s, Bigley had tried again to generate interest in the idea. He approached producer Lynda Obst, who was working with Twentieth Century Fox at the time and was eager to shoot in Austin, and she offered her support to the project. Dwight Adair, married to editor Sandra and owner of a production company in town, also proposed plans to build a studio in the 1990s.

In 1995 five state senators sponsored a bill to authorize a feasibility study to determine if the state should construct a soundstage in Central Texas based on the fact that both Houston and Dallas already had soundstages and, in 1994, more than half of the feature films made in the state had been shot in the Central Texas area. In 1997, the Texas legislature considered a bill whose purpose was to secure state funds to build a film studio. The bill did not pass, in part because of the testimony given by a gentleman from Houston who had owned and operated a studio for more than two decades and objected to the state's essentially making a gift of money to other citizens to compete with his business.[66]

In the summer of 1999, Ginsel proposed the idea of turning the abandoned airport hangars into soundstages to Gary Bond, head of the Austin Film Office. From there, says Ginsel, Bond contacted Mayor Watson and determined that he was interested in and supportive of the idea. Ginsel's next step was to approach Linklater and take him out to the vacant airport site. Initially Linklater didn't seem interested in the proposal, but within a few days he had changed his mind.[67]

Watson remembers meeting with Black and Linklater and a few others to discuss the idea and to determine the steps they needed to take to present a proposal to the Austin City Council. "It became clear to me that Richard was going to become the 'get it done' guy. He was going to become the guy who talked to everybody and worked it through the process," says Watson, who put the group in touch with Jim Walker, the head of a coalition of fourteen neighborhoods that surrounded the airport land.[68]

Watson and other city representatives felt strongly that the proposed facility needed to be part of a not-for-profit organization. Linklater and others knew from previous experience that it took time and effort to establish a nonprofit, so Linklater approached Campbell about designating AFS as the facility's managing organization. But Ginsel had serious doubts about the organization's ability to manage a fully functioning soundstage.

Although Linklater may have been the group's de facto leader, the actual nuts and bolts of drafting the proposal fell to Ginsel and Cathy Crane, who had begun working at Detour with Linklater in 1997. Ginsel and Crane worked through the end of 1999 and into the holidays to draft a proposal that incorporated, among other details, data from feasibility studies gathered by Avellán and her assistants when she and Rodriguez initially were planning to build their own studio. The proposal also included a plan to establish paid internships that would be available only to the young people from the surrounding neighborhoods, a population of kids who typically wouldn't have access to such opportunities.

In the midst of meetings about the proposed studio, AFS heard from the Directors Guild of America that it had been selected to receive the organization's first DGA Honors Award in recognition of the film society's efforts to create and sustain regional film culture and production. Linklater and Campbell traveled to New York for the ceremony in December 1999, where John Sayles presented the award and Martin Scorsese was on hand to offer his congratulations.[69] The recognition was particularly appropriate given the organization's current efforts to create a soundstage, which seemed to many like the next logical step for Austin's burgeoning film scene.

By January of 2000, Ginsel and Crane submitted the AFS proposal to the Austin City Council. On February 3, Mayor Watson and the six-member City Council gave the proposal their unanimous approval.

What followed were nine months of detailed negotiations to hammer out a management contract with the city of Austin. The city's main concerns, according to Watson and Campbell, involved the length of the lease and designating a location for the facility that would not hinder future development of the area. "What we ended up doing was selecting what we thought would be the most profitable spaces," says Campbell. Members of an AFS studio committee negotiated a ten-year lease (with a five-year renewal option), with the most valuable parts of the facility covered under a separate clause, or "lockout period," that "protected" them from being rescinded by the city for future development before the end of the lease. For an annual rent of $100, AFS became the tenants of a 20-acre facility they called Austin Studios. The complex included a two-story office building, which would serve as production offices, and several hangars, which would be used as soundstages, all available for rent on a sliding scale to local and out-of-town productions. Although the two-story building was in good shape, the hangars required electricity and interior and exterior soundproofing before they could function adequately as soundstages.[70]

Ever since Ginsel first approached Linklater about the studio idea, Ginsel was under the impression that he would manage the facility. "Then the rest of the folks [at AFS] started having meetings without me. And they said, 'Well,

**295**

we're just having meetings with the attorney to hammer out the wording of the lease.'" In late spring 2000 Ginsel left town to work on a film production. He returned weeks later to find a letter inviting him to meet with Suzanne Quinn, the new head of Austin Studios.[71] Quinn had earned an MBA from the University of Texas and had since 1997 handled sales and media relations for the South by Southwest Film Festival.

Crane also had been told by Linklater that she would be involved in running the new facility, so she was as surprised as Ginsel to learn about Quinn's hiring. "I went to Rebecca [Campbell] and said, 'Who's Suzanne?' And she said, 'Oh, Rick hasn't talked to you about this?' So she told me the whole story, and obviously, I was devastated," recalls Crane.[72]

Explains Linklater, "All along it was like, Stan could run the studio when it was small. But as it got bigger and bigger, it was really apparent that it was basically a political administration position, filing reports with the city and keeping up with the money. And that's not Stan's skill set."[73] Linklater and Campbell assumed Ginsel could work alongside Quinn by handling the technical operations of the facility, making repairs and screening dailies as he had at Linklater's Austin Film Center, which Linklater had closed that year.

"They basically asked me to do a janitor's job," says Ginsel. "At the time it was offensive. I had worked for years and years to create a studio in Austin and finally brought it to the table."[74]

"I told him, 'We've got this woman Suzanne, who's going to be great, to run this with you. She'll do this, and you'll do that,'" says Linklater. "Stan was kind of hurt that he wasn't the absolute figurehead. Even when asked, 'Do you want to administrate?' He said, 'No, I hate that shit.' So I said, 'Okay. So you're saying you can't do it. So what are you pissed off about?'"[75]

Crane eventually discussed the situation with Linklater, who told her, "I fucked up. It was moving quickly, and I was someplace else." In retrospect, says Crane, "I think Rick tried to handle it as well as he could. I think a lot of it had to do with the film society coming in as the nonprofit [for the studio], and some things moved very quickly at a time when Rick was very busy. And he just didn't pay enough attention."[76]

By November 1, 2000, after nine months of negotiations with the city and a team of lawyers, AFS and Quinn moved into their new offices—a double-wide trailer for AFS, a single-wide for Quinn—on the site of the new Austin Studios at the former Robert Mueller Airport.

Quinn immediately began putting in fourteen-hour days and working weekends to transform the hangars. Upon vacating the facilities, the city had removed air conditioning units from offices within the hangars to use in other city buildings, and the cost of replacing them averaged about $5,000 per unit. Repairs also were needed almost immediately when the electricity went out and one of the hangar's water pipes broke, creating a sewage flood.

During the nine-month negotiation period, the studio had accrued debt in the form of Quinn's salary and the various legal costs associated with the endeavor. AFS had covered these costs. "At the time there was this fear among the AFS board members that the film studios might pull the film society under if something happened," says Quinn. "And it was a legitimate fear."[77]

### A Million-Dollar Gala: The Texas Film Hall of Fame

The acquisition of Austin Studios, while certainly a huge undertaking, was only one component of the Austin Film Society's overall strategic plan. A separate but equally important element was the decision to "diversify" the AFS board. Shortly after *Texas Monthly* deputy editor Evan Smith took over as editor of the magazine in early 2000, Campbell and Judith Sims approached him about joining the AFS board. In some ways Smith exemplified the kind of person some of the longtime AFS board members feared would pollute the organization. A native New Yorker, Smith had moved to Austin in late 1992 to join the staff of *Texas Monthly* after a stint at *Self* magazine and writing for *Mother Jones*.

Ramírez Berg, who had been one of the organization's first board members and would become its third president, represented the old guard of AFS. "I just realized, it used to be friends of Rick's who were on the board. Then it's like these strategic kind of board member appointments."[78]

Says Smith, "The tension between the few of us who came on the board who were more on the commerce side and the masses on the board who were on the art side was palpable."[79]

And yet even within the ranks of the "masses," changes had occurred over the years that also became more visible around this time. Explains Ramírez Berg, "The people we started off as in 1985—we've changed too. Louis Black is now wealthy and influential. Rick is a wealthy filmmaker. Robert Rodriguez is a wealthy filmmaker. When we started in 1985, we were all the same. We were probably making under $30,000 a year, and $30,000 was a lot."[80]

Of course this tension within the AFS boardroom exemplified a larger shift that had begun taking place throughout Austin in the late 1990s. Technology start-up companies founded by CEOs barely out of college were booming, and suddenly a new class of creative individuals was taking up residence in the city.

During the course of a few AFS meetings with an outside fundraising consultant, the phrase "million-dollar gala" began to be thrown around. The discussions around this term, from Smith's point of view, essentially were about AFS "trying to figure out how they would transition as an organization and a board from a bunch of people watching Rick's home movies sitting on the edge of his bed to something larger."[81]

In addition to the concept of a new kind of fundraising model, the consultant suggested that AFS begin to think about attracting another demographic. "It was to some degree chasing this tech ephemera," recalls Smith of the idea that Austin suddenly had a new, untapped market of creative individuals. "But it was also this idea—not incorrect, it turns out—that there was a community larger than the film geeks who thought [an AFS premiere] is interesting, this is fun and this is cool and we would like to associate with this even if it meant paying. And so I took this to heart."[82]

As Smith recalls, he and friend Jan Baskett were having lunch in early January 2001 at Las Manitas on Congress Avenue. Austin's movers and shakers—politicians, writers, musicians, etc.—regularly packed the storefront Mexican restaurant's crowded booths, tables, and lunch counter to make deals and to see and be seen. Baskett had once worked at *Texas Monthly* and was by 2001 working for SXSW in marketing. They discussed the kind of person the organization was trying to reach. They were, says Smith, "people who don't care about the Latvian New Wave series, and people who don't care about the movies in Quentin Tarantino's collection, and people who wouldn't know Harry Knowles if they ran into him on the street. What they like is being able to see and feel and smell and touch movie stars. In the most crude and calculating way, that's what they care about."[83]

"So let's do an event," he began, "in which we bring a whole bunch of stars here so in turn a whole bunch of people who don't give a shit about the art of film or the craft of film will pay to be associated with them."[84]

"Evan already had been floating the idea of some kind of hall of fame-ish, one thing, maybe a film at SXSW or something," recalls Black, who was then president of AFS. "So he called me up and said, 'Look, why don't we do the Hall of Fame. And we'll honor people, and if you honor people, they'll come. And we'll ask them to pick their presenters so we'll have celebrities, so we'll make money.'"[85]

The idea met resistance when it was pitched to the AFS board of directors and staff soon after. "Intellectually, we understood that the Hall of Fame would bring more money to the organization and allow us to continue doing what we were doing," says del Castillo. "But there was a real fear that it was going to change the culture of the film society."[86]

**298**

"The hesitation was, 'Well, is there enough depth of talent?' That was Rick's [concern]," recalls Black. Others said, "We're going to run out of famous people in three years."[87]

Black responded to the naysayers with a lengthy list of potential Texans. The plan moved forward.

### All Side Dishes and No Entrée

Because the event piggybacked onto the SXSW festival, Black essentially had an army of helpers at his disposal. At AFS, Campbell and Melissa Nathan, a fundraiser who worked at the film society, commandeered their resources. And Smith pulled out his Rolodex.

One of the first people Smith called was Mike Simpson, Warren Skaaren's longtime agent at the William Morris Agency, which represented *Texas Monthly*. The Hall of Fame would honor the agent and UT graduate with a lifetime achievement award named after Skaaren, who died in 1990. As he would with all of the other honorees, Smith asked Simpson to choose his presenter, and Simpson chose client Quentin Tarantino.

Next he called *New York Newsday* gossip columnist Liz Smith, a Fort Worth native and an old friend from his days in New York. Another pick was writer-director Robert Benton, who left Waxahachie for Hollywood and first achieved recognition with his script for *Bonnie and Clyde*. In 1979 Benton wrote and directed *Kramer vs. Kramer*, which earned him an Academy Award for Best Director. But by 2001, recalls Smith, "Benton wasn't working really, so Benton was an easy phone call. And then Bill Wittliff was here."[88] Giving a writing award to Wittliff, whose admirable career by then spanned nearly three decades, was a no-brainer. In 2000 his adaptation of *The Perfect Storm*, starring George Clooney, had raised his profile yet again.

Wittliff had been a longtime supporter of the Austin Film Festival, and he chose AFF co-founder Barbara Morgan as his presenter. The planners were hoping he'd select one of the stars who had appeared in his movies, maybe Clooney or even Brad Pitt (*Legends of the Fall*). But Wittliff's decision was especially diplomatic given that he was being honored at an event co-founded by Black, who also established the SXSW Film Festival. Six years had passed since Black and Morgan first clashed over their respective festivals, but tensions still simmered. "Wittliff went for Barbara Morgan to induct him because he was worried about the bad feelings," says Black.[89]

Explains Smith, "Getting Barbara Morgan to introduce Wittliff was easy. Getting people who were at war with the [AFF] film festival to understand that this had to be a 'Why-can't-we-all-get-along?' Rodney King moment, that was a little harder."[90]

The biggest draw for the event would be Sissy Spacek, a native of Quitman who first came to Hollywood's attention as the naively romantic Holly Sargis in *Badlands,* Terrence Malick's hauntingly beautiful account of the Starkweather-Fugate killings in the 1950s. Spacek also had worked with Wittliff on *Raggedy Man.*

But sometime in February Smith received a disquieting phone call. Spacek's father had died suddenly, and she would be unable to attend the Hall of Fame event. Smith was in a panic. "We have all side dishes and no entrée. The whole fucking thing is gonna fall apart."[91] He made phone call after phone call to Spacek's agent and manager and anyone else he could think of, all to no avail. Less than a month out from the event, they were losing the evening's top attraction.

"And then, Sissy called and said, 'No, I want to come. I *need* to come. I need to distract myself.'"[92] Smith couldn't believe their good luck. For her presenter Spacek chose actor Rip Torn, who also happened to be her first cousin. Things were back on track.

Although individual tickets were sold for the event, the organizers hoped to make their money back by selling tables, which could be purchased for $1,500, $3,000 or $5,000. In late February, two weeks before the event, Campbell received a FedEx envelope from Quentin Tarantino's office in Los Angeles. Inside was a check for $5,000. "He bought a table, just like Hollywood people are really well-trained to do and usually do," says Campbell. But honoree Simpson was the only other invitee to purchase a table that year. (By 2005, when the event was in its fifth year, honoree Marcia Gay Harden was the only other Hollywood celebrity to purchase a table, according to Campbell.)[93]

For the invitation AFS borrowed an image of the hangar's exterior from the Texas Film Commission. The photograph was mounted in the layered style of a David Hockney image, which created an impressive panorama of the hangar and its surrounding land. The invitation was stunning, but its design was also pragmatic. "It basically showed the facility available for rent," explains Campbell.[94] Texas artist Bob Wade and Austin-based designer Marc English collaborated on the award itself. They designed an oversized film reel and adorned it with a rustic metal star. A thick braid of rope lay coiled inside the reel.

## Terry Malick's Here

On the night of the ceremony, the VIP tents overflowed with people like Lyle Lovett, Tim McCanlies, and Harry Knowles, who observed honoree Sissy Spacek spritzing her palms with antibiotic spray after every handshake.[95] Elizabeth Avellán chatted with honoree Bill Wittliff. Because the Hall of Fame piggybacked with the start of the annual SXSW Film Festival, visiting filmmakers such as Ron Mann and Penelope Spheeris and actors Jeffrey Tambor and Jill Clayburgh dropped by to check out the scene.

"Welcome to the Austin Studios and the first Texas Film Hall of Fame Awards," emcee Turk Pipkin began in his deep West Texas baritone.[96] Pipkin had published a couple of novels as well as books about magic with friend and magician Harry Dean Anderson, whom he had met when he wrote for the television series *Night Court* in the 1980s. He also did occasional acting work and most recently had shot a few episodes for *The Sopranos*, a gritty new dramatic series on HBO. Pipkin played the narcoleptic boyfriend of New Jersey crime boss Tony Soprano's scheming sister (Aida Turturro). Although the show had quickly become a critical success, by 2001 *The Sopranos* had yet to really explode in Texas.

Ann Richards was the first presenter to take the stage, and the mix of hometown guests and Los Angeles visitors greeted the popular former governor with affectionate applause and even cheers. Richards surveyed the crowd as she prepared to introduce friend and honoree Liz Smith. "I remember when I came in office, we could get all of the supporters of Texas film in a phone booth," she drawled.[97]

At one point in the evening Smith stood near the entrance to the hangar, a huge smile on his face. "Look what we were able to put together in five weeks," he boasted to a local journalist as he gestured toward the raucous crowd.[98] Sixteen hundred people crammed into Hangar Four, but many of them, it seemed, were stuck in long lines at either the bar or the portable toilets parked outside the venue.

Privately, Smith was freaking out. Up on the stage between presenters, Pipkin kept making jokes about Big Pussy, a reference to a *Sopranos* character played by actor Vincent Pastore. Pastore happened to be in Dallas shooting a movie, and Pipkin had suggested he come to Austin for the awards show. Pastore sat in the audience laughing at Pipkin's jokes, while Smith stole nervous glances at Richards and Spacek. "Turk's making Big Pussy jokes and Ann and Sissy are sitting there. I remember just thinking, 'Ugh, we look like such idiots,'" Smith recalls.[99]

But perhaps the night's biggest hiccup belonged to Tarantino, who appeared on stage to introduce agent Mike Simpson after a video tribute to Simpson from director and client Tim Burton. "Quentin started talking and clearly hadn't prepared anything," recalls Black. "He got a few laughs and thought [the audience was] with him, and so he kept going and going and going."[100]

Recalls Tarantino, "I'm so comfortable in Austin, so I was used to doing introductions for the QT Fests [ten-day programs of genre films from his personal collection] so I just did it like that. It hadn't hit me that it was going to be a whole bunch of people who never go to the QT Fest. I was in QT Fest mode, and they were all in $200-a-plate-blue-haired-lady mode." Tarantino ad libbed his monologue, according to Black, "the gist of which was, 'Mike Simpson deserves an award for recognizing what a genius I was before anybody else.'" According to another onlooker, when Tarantino finally signaled the end of his meandering introduction with the words, "without further ado," the crowd broke into grateful applause. Says Tarantino, "Whatever ribbing I got, I was thankfully saved because Rip Torn proceeded to do performance art a la Jean-Paul Sartre. Now, I didn't see it, I only heard about it. But I was glad somebody else could take the heat along with me."[101]

Rip Torn was the last presenter to take the stage. For whatever reason, he avoided the microphone and instead roamed the stage as he talked inaudibly about Spacek. "People were at the bars, drinking and yelling and screaming, and Rip Torn refused to use his microphone and you couldn't hear," says Campbell.[102]

Spacek lightened the mood when she walked onstage and deadpanned, "I'm sorry I didn't prepare anything to say tonight. I didn't think I was going to win." With her lilting Texas drawl the actress offered an eloquent tribute to her roots: "When I was a little girl living in northeast Texas, I remember thinking, 'I'm so lucky. I was born into this family in this house on this street in this town in this great state of Texas.' It was the center of the universe for me." For perhaps the first time that evening the rowdy crowd hushed itself, charmed by Spacek's quavering voice as she delivered what was clearly a sincere speech made more emotional, perhaps, by her father's recent death.[103]

Spacek was the last honoree of the evening, and her speech gave the slapdash event an unexpectedly poignant polish. "The place just went crazy," recalls Smith. "Half of the people knew that her father had died and she had come under very difficult circumstances and came despite those circumstances, and they loved her more. And half didn't know, and they still loved her."[104]

Richard Linklater took the stage at the end of the evening. Linklater had never enjoyed speaking in public, and this night was no different. He looked slightly uncomfortable as he gazed out over the crowd even though he knew many of the people in the audience. He shifted nervously and spoke quickly as he read from his prepared notes. "As artistic director of the Austin Film Society, all I can say is what an honor it is to be here tonight with so many great film people."[105] Linklater initially had been skeptical of Smith and Black's idea to host the Hall of Fame, but publicly, at least, he was willing to acknowledge the significance of the event and its impact on the film society's ability to continue offering money to Texas filmmakers.

"Everything the film society is about came together tonight," said Linklater, and he was right.[106] For better or worse, the old guard of the Austin Film Society—film lovers like Chale Nafus and Charles Ramírez Berg—and members of the first generation of Austin's film community—writers like Bud Shrake, Gary Cartwright, and Bill Wittliff—rubbed shoulders with the film society's future, which included Smith and other well-connected board members with perhaps only a cursory interest in film history.

In the end, the first Texas Film Hall of Fame made $35,000 dollars. The event was successful enough that plans began almost immediately to host a second awards show in 2002.[107] But even before the award show's profits were tallied—in fact, even before the event was over—Smith had an inkling that things were going to be all right.

One of the night's biggest surprises came courtesy of filmmaker Terrence Malick, perhaps Austin's most reclusive and revered celebrity. The notoriously shy director had come to the event to support Spacek. Malick managed to slip into the hangar undetected and stood in a corner toward the back. After spotting Malick in the crowd, Smith says, "We all stood around most of the night, not watching the stage but staring at Terry Malick, pointing and whispering to each other and saying, 'Shit. Terry Malick's here.'"[108] The highly regarded filmmaker's presence shocked the Austin film community and impressed the jaded Los Angelenos and other out-of-town movie people. It was like the filmic equivalent of the *Good Housekeeping* Seal of Approval for the first Texas Film Hall of Fame Awards.

And it was then that Smith thought, "Maybe this is actually gonna work."[109]

The point of regional filmmaking is
to get filmmakers to stay where they
are and not move to Hollywood.

GEORGE LUCAS

# Conclusion

## Outside the System, Inside the System

-----------------------------------------------------------------

**W**hen the list of top-grossing films for the first weekend in October 2003 was released, it was the first time in Austin's history that three of the city's filmmakers all had films in the Top Ten. Richard Linklater's *School of Rock*, made for $35 million and distributed by Paramount, grossed an impressive $19.6 million on its opening weekend and landed in the number-one slot. Tim McCanlies's *Secondhand Lions*, budgeted at $30 million and distributed by New Line, had opened on September 19 and was still in fifth place at the box office two weeks later. Robert Rodriguez's *Once Upon a Time in Mexico*, released by Sony on September 12 and made for $29 million, took the ninth spot.[1]

For Linklater, the success of *School of Rock* was especially sweet. Five years had passed since the disappointing release and reception of *The Newton Boys*. In 2001 Linklater had rebounded with the back-to-back releases of two smaller films, *Waking Life* and *Tape*. Linklater and a few other crew members shot *Waking Life* over twenty-three days in August 1999, and he spent six days making *Tape* that same year. Both productions marked Linklater's first foray into digital filmmaking. "Rick is so not Robert Rodriguez. He was a luddite. He didn't even use e-mail. But I think he very much waited until he had a project that could use the technology and was appropriate for the technology," recalls Cathy Crane, Linklater's assistant at the time and the sound assistant on *Waking Life*.[2] That film's multiple locations and large ensemble cast featured many sites and actors from Linklater's previous films, including *Slacker*. *Waking Life* used rotoscope animation, a conventional mode of animation made modern through local filmmaker and computer programmer Bob Sabiston's Rotoshop software, which digitally animated Linklater's live-action footage. The film also employed 30 Austin-area graphic artists who each designed sequences in the movie.

*Tape*, an intimate character study co-starring Ethan Hawke, Uma Thurman, and Robert Sean Leonard, was based on a Stephen Belber play about three friends in a Michigan motel room who reminisce about their high school days. Hawke and Linklater, friends and frequent collaborators, had talked for years about experimenting with the new digital video technology and were also inspired by Lars von Trier's *Celebration*. Hawke sent Linklater Belber's play with a note that read, "This might be the perfect thing for us to play around with on DV."[3]

With the critical success of both movies, Linklater's confidence had returned, but he also was keenly aware of how difficult the previous few years had been. In 2002 he wrote in a memo, "In the last four years I've been in production 30 days. That's not how I see myself. I'm a filmmaker. I want to be making films." By the time producer Scott Rudin approached Linklater with the script for *School of Rock*, written by *Chuck and Buck*'s Mike White, the filmmaker was in a better place. "I'd had two independent successes—not big moneymakers, but they both got great reviews. I was really confident. And they came kind of begging me to do *School of Rock*," says Linklater.[4]

The success of *Secondhand Lions* was a similar triumph for Tim McCanlies. Written in the mid-1990s, the script about the unexpected friendship between two eccentric elderly brothers and their ten-year-old nephew had floated around Hollywood for years. As with *Dancer, Texas*, McCanlies had written *Secondhand Lions* as an antidote to the unsatisfying action screenplays he was being paid to write at the time. He had also scripted the story because he wanted to work with older actors, and he finally got his wish when the project went into production with Michael Caine and Robert Duvall in the lead roles. Months before principal photography began in and around Austin, the forty-nine-year-old McCanlies had dinner with filmmakers John Sayles and Guillermo del Toro during the 2002 SXSW Film Festival. The *Austin Chronicle*'s Louis Black was present at the dinner: "Tim is nervous; it's his second film and first with name actors. Sayles and del Toro launch into the best directing seminar I've ever heard, dispensing advice and wisdom on everything from working with actors to directing a scene to placing cameras." Although McCanlies had been a part of the Austin film community since the early 1990s, participating on festival panels and teaching writing classes at the University of Texas while pursuing his career in Hollywood, it wasn't until he transitioned into the role of filmmaker that he really began to feel as if he were a part of the local film scene. McCanlies's dinner with Sayles and del Toro reminded him that he did indeed belong to such a community, and the success of *Secondhand Lions* only confirmed this. "I didn't get a sense of the community so much as I have since I've been a director," he says.[5]

The tremendous popularity and blockbuster payday of the *Spy Kids* franchise helped Robert Rodriguez to achieve a certain level of power within Hollywood. With the box office success of *Once Upon a Time in Mexico*, which earned $53 million in its first four weeks, says Avellán, "I think we proved it. No one else can make these movies for less than $100 million." *Once Upon a Time in Mexico* reunited Rodriguez and Avellán with Sony Pictures and studio executive Gary Martin who, during a meeting with Avellán while making *Desperado*, had condescendingly explained a film crew's division of labor by comparing it to the workings of a beauty parlor. "Gary Martin is an incredibly talented man in his own area. It's just that he was dealing with a different kind of animal that he had never dealt with," says Avellán, who held her tongue at the time because she believed Martin and others would eventually come to understand Rodriguez's mode of filmmaking. "I was patient, and it bore out that way," she says. With *Once Upon a Time in Mexico* still in theaters, Rodriguez was already busy in preproduction on his next project, a live-action adaptation of Frank Miller's graphic novels entitled *Sin City* (2005).[6]

On April 7, 2006, Rodriguez announced that he and Avellán were separating after sixteen years of marriage but that the pair would remain business partners. (They later divorced.) Less than two weeks after the separation, Troublemaker Studios announced that they had renegotiated a ten-year lease at the former Aircraft Pooling Board site.

By the fall of 2003 Mike Judge was also moving forward with his next film, a live-action comedy for Twentieth Century Fox set in the future and starring Luke Wilson. Originally called *3001*, the feature shot in and around Austin in the spring of 2004 and eventually was re-titled *Idiocracy*. Postproduction on the film would drag on for months, however, and the studio delayed *Idiocracy*'s release for nearly a year until the fall of 2006. The financial success of *Beavis and Butt-head* and *King of the Hill*, Judge admits, allowed him to consider *not* directing another feature film after *Office Space*. Judge was optimistic that his second feature for Fox would result in a better working relationship, but it didn't. "I wasn't going to make a movie that way again, with the studio in control. And yet, I went and did it. Now I'm saying I'll only do it if I own the film or have complete control over cast and crew [decisions] and director's cut," says Judge.[7]

Bill Wittliff chose not to direct another feature after *Red Headed Stranger*. He continued to write scripts for television and film, which led to the enormously popular *Lonesome Dove* miniseries, the critically acclaimed but short-lived *Ned Blessing* television series and screenplays for *Legends of the Fall* (1994) and *The Perfect Storm* (2000). Like so many other talented writers, Wittliff had countless scripts that for one reason or another had never been made into movies. *A Night in Old Mexico* was one such screenplay, and by the late 1990s the script had achieved almost mythic status among writers in the industry. Tim McCanlies first heard about the script from producer David Valdes, who began working with Clint Eastwood in the mid-1980s and had produced many movies in Texas including *Secondhand Lions*. "*A Night in Old Mexico*'s got this character in his 60s, a real feisty old guy. Valdes gave it to Clint Eastwood, who at the time was in his mid-60s. Clint said, 'Boy, that's a great script. You'd need to find a great old guy for that.' These actors," says McCanlies, "they don't think of themselves as we see them."[8] By 2006, Robert Duvall had become attached to the project with Dennis Hopper as director, and *A Night in Old Mexico* was back in development. Still, however, the screenplay remains unproduced.

Eagle Pennell continued to make films throughout the 1980s and into the 1990s, but he never achieved the success he had with *The Whole Shootin' Match* or even *Last Night at the Alamo*. By the late 1980s, to make ends meet, Pennell shot second-unit camera on *RoboCop 2*, which filmed in Houston. *Heart Full of Soul*, which Pennell made in 1989 with funding from SWAMP, was well-liked overseas where it played at the Berlin International Film Festival in 1990, but the movie went nowhere in the United States. In 1993 *Doc's Full Service* re-teamed him with cinematographer Brian Huberman but the film, like his other later projects, came and went. By the mid-1990s, Pennell was still bitter about *The King of Texas*, an unproduced script that he and Henkel had written for Warner Bros. a decade earlier. Said Pennell in 1994, "It's the best thing I've ever done, and now it sits in a vault at Warner Bros. We've been told we can buy it back for $300,000." But things began to look up in 1996 when Pennell received an unexpected check in the mail. The filmmaker who had inspired Linklater and Quentin Tarantino was now the recipient of their largesse in the form of a $1,500 Texas Filmmakers' Production Fund grant. He planned to use it to write a screenplay about homelessness entitled *The Jumping Off Place*. He "researched" the idea by panhandling, sleeping in a Houston park, and engaging in other behaviors that eventually led to a stint in an Austin rehabilitation center. As Pennell told a reporter friend in 1999, "My research turned into a lifestyle."[9]

Pennell visited many old friends and acquaintances in Austin over the years, often down on his luck and asking to borrow money. Almost no one refused him. Much as Pennell had entrusted Lin Sutherland with the print of *The Whole Shootin' Match*, he kept a small box of treasured possessions at his parents' house as his drinking once again escalated, his health declined, and his lifestyle became more peripatetic as the 1990s drew to a close. The box contained reviews of his films, letters, and other artifacts from his life, including a check stub from Warner Bros. for $2,500—partial payment for *The King of Texas* script. "If *The King of Texas* development deal hadn't gone sour, Eagle may have been able to evolve from that point into a real film-maker, a real person," says his brother Chuck Pinnell. "He was headed in the direction he ultimately went, but with the failure of *King of Texas*, it was written in stone." Pennell died in Houston on July 20, 2002, eight days shy of his fiftieth birthday.[10]

After the release of *The Texas Chainsaw Massacre 2* in 1986, Tobe Hooper continued to work in the horror genre, directing and writing films like *The Mangler* (1995) and the re-make of *Toolbox Murders* (2004) and television programs such as *Tales From the Crypt*. Hooper's television work fared better than his features, but in many ways he seemed always to be working in the shadow of his best-known film. Makeup artist Dorothy Pearl, grateful to Hooper for her start on *The Texas Chainsaw Massacre*, introduced him to *Chainsaw* fan Steven Spielberg in the 1980s. Pearl had left Texas for Hollywood soon after the release of *Chainsaw* and very quickly parlayed the movie's success into a thriving career in feature films. In the early 1980s when Spielberg had to abandon plans to direct *Poltergeist* for MGM in order to focus on *ET*, he called Pearl and asked if she thought Hooper might want to direct *Poltergeist*. Although the subject matter was a good fit, says Pearl, the project was difficult for Hooper, and Spielberg, who retained control as writer-producer, was on set every day. "I think it couldn't have been more apples and oranges for Tobe. I think as experiences go, he will always think *The Texas Chainsaw Massacre* was a more interesting, more fun experience."[11] Although Hooper and Kim Henkel would never work together after *Chainsaw*, they did receive credit as co-producers of the 2003 re-make of their film, which shot in and around Austin. Harry Knowles's cameo as a disembodied head provided an interesting bridge, of sorts, between the Austin film scene of the 1970s and the city's contemporary film culture.

That film culture has been shaped in part by a proliferation of filmmaking organizations and outlets that sprang up in the mid-1990s as a response to local film activity but also as a result of the rise of independent low-budget films and more accessible equipment. If the University of Texas's campus film series inspired the Austin Film Society, then AFS certainly influenced the creation of organizations like Reel Women, a nonprofit established by Cyndy Kirkland and Dawn Cooper in 1996 to offer support, services, and production skills to women working in the film and television industries. Steve Mims, who was one of Robert Rodriguez's earliest supporters at the University of Texas, left UT in 1993 and started his own college-level film production program called Austin FilmWorks. At a time when the university's increasingly competitive RTF program was becoming less of an option for many aspiring filmmakers, Mims's courses offered a viable alternative. In the late 1990s Barna Kantor and Kris DeForest filled a similar void when they established Cinemaker Co-op as a nonprofit filmmaking collective that offered Super 8 equipment rental and workshops. The organization's Make a Film in a Weekend (MAFIA) workshops helped to demystify the filmmaking process and championed the DIY aesthetic made popular years earlier by filmmakers like Linklater and Rodriguez.

The late 1990s also saw an increase in the number of Austin film festivals. As with other campus film programs throughout the country, CinemaTexas struggled through the late 1980s and early 1990s as it lost more and more of its audience to the video rental market. In 1995 the program sponsored a showcase of student films, and within a couple of years artistic director and co-founder Rachel Tsangari transformed the showcase into the Cinematexas International Short Film Festival. The festival very quickly grew into a highly regarded short-format showcase that attracted filmmakers like Todd Haynes and Chantal Akerman. Sadly, the Cinematexas festival lost financial support and went into "semi-permanent hibernation" in the fall of 2007.[12]

In 1997 the University of Texas announced that it would be closing the economically challenged Texas Union film series, which was still being programmed by Steve Bearden. Although some protested the closing, generally the news was greeted with apathy by the UT student body. Matt Dentler was an RTF undergraduate at the time as well as a volunteer for the student-run Cinematexas festival, and he was somewhat surprised that more of his fellow RTF classmates didn't protest the Union's closing. "I think that might have a lot to do with the 'Hollywoodization' of what it means to be a student filmmaker. People were like, 'Oh, this film program's closing? Well, how does that affect companies like Miramax?' Because those were the words we knew. 'Film series' was not in our vocabulary."[13]

By 1997 both SXSW Film and the Austin Film Festival (AFF) were beginning to find their identities, and that year in particular marked a turning
point for each of the festivals. At the time, says Suzanne Quinn, who worked
in sales and marketing for SXSW, "No one knew who the festival was outside of Texas, so the first couple of years was an education process: getting
the word out, telling people what it was." In an effort to build its brand the
festival decided to expand its conference, and in 1997 organizers planned
a "monster" panel called "Outside the System, Inside the System" with filmmakers Quentin Tarantino, Richard Linklater, Robert Rodriguez, Kevin Smith,
George Huang, and Mike Judge. "That was a huge deal," recalls Dentler, who
attended the panel and began volunteering for the festival soon after. "No one
was really sure if those guys were the real thing, so that panel was really great
timing. Here are these guys who have been this huge overnight sensation,
they do this panel, and they all went on to do bigger things." Halfway through
the 1997 festival, *Daily Variety* wrote that SXSW was "rapidly becoming one
of the most important film forums in the country."[14]

AFF's lineup that year was equally impressive. Oliver Stone previewed
his latest film, *U-Turn*; Buck Henry introduced a restored print of *The Graduate*; and Dennis Hopper screened *Easy Rider*. Stone and Hopper also participated in a freewheeling panel moderated by Bud Shrake, who had made his
first film with Hopper. "The festival became so big, it was like the *Chronicle*
couldn't ignore it. They just ignored us for the first three years," says AFF co-
founder Marsha Milam.[15] In reality, the *Austin Chronicle* began covering the
festival in some depth a year earlier, but its 1997 coverage (multiple articles
and interviews with visiting filmmakers and screenwriters) would mark a
turning point, on paper at least, in the newsweekly's response to AFF's rising profile.

Around the same time, Austin's film festival offerings broadened somewhat with the creation of the Cine Las Americas International Film Festival in
1998. The festival, which focused on films and filmmakers from the Americas, grew out of a well-received program of Cuban films organized by Lara
Coger. Other smaller festivals sprang up during this time as well.

This influx of festivals in the late 1990s also increased the need for more
theatrical venues in Austin. In 1996 Tim and Karrie League moved to town
from Bakersfield, California. They rented a rundown building in the downtown Warehouse District and began to renovate it into a 213-seat movie
theater that would serve a full menu as well as beer and wine. They were set
to open the Alamo Drafthouse in May 1997 when representatives from SXSW
convinced them to screen movies during that year's festival in mid-March.

The theater was so far from being finished that during the ten-day festival, instead of locking the front door at the end of the evening, Tim would have to nail a piece of plywood to the doorframe.

The intimate theater's combination of eclectic programming and casual movie-going atmosphere almost immediately won over Austin's energetic and supportive community of movie lovers. After hosting his first two QT Fests at the Dobie Theatre, Tarantino moved the event to the Alamo Drafthouse in 1999, a decision that essentially anointed the theater as a hip hangout. That same year at the Alamo, Harry Knowles began hosting Butt-Numb-a-Thon (BNAT), his annual December birthday party that masquerades as a 24-hour film festival. Knowles invites people to "apply" to the event by writing essays, and he personally selects its attendees. In 2003, *The Lord of the Rings* director Peter Jackson and his wife, screenwriter Fran Walsh, surprised the crowd with a sneak-peek screening of *Return of the King*, the third film in the *Rings* trilogy. During the final hours of the event, Mel Gibson also made a surprise appearance to preview and answer questions about his movie, *The Passion of the Christ*. The programming coup said as much about Knowles's reputation in certain industry circles as it did about the Alamo's international appeal among filmmakers and cinephiles.

Along with Knowles, Tim League, Matt Dentler, Tim McCanlies, and producer Paul Alvarado-Dykstra co-founded the genre film festival Fantastic Fest, which since 2005 has steadily grown in size and reputation and is held at the Alamo Drafthouse. In 2005, *Entertainment Weekly* chose the Drafthouse as its top pick in a listing of the ten best theaters in the country, describing its exhibition as "one of America's most fanatically unique moviegoing experiences."[16]

If people like the Leagues exemplify Austin's next generation of behind-the-scenes talent, those who are following in the footsteps of Louis Black and others who have helped to create the infrastructure of Austin's film community, then people like Kat Candler (*cicadas, Jumping Off Bridges*), Kyle Henry (*Room*), and Bryan Poyser and Jacob Vaughn (*Dear Pillow, The Cassidy Kids*) represent a small sampling of the next wave of Austin filmmakers. Candler moved to Austin in 1997 after earning a degree in creative writing from Florida State University. She made short films while taking classes at Austin FilmWorks and became involved with Reel Women. Henry, Poyser, and Vaughn all went through the UT RTF program as either undergraduate or graduate students, and all three have affiliations with AFS, SXSW, or the Cinematexas festival. Henry's first short film, *University Inc.*, documented the closing of the Texas Union film series, and in 2005 his first feature, *Room*, premiered at the Sundance Film Festival and screened at the Cannes Film Festival. Vaughn and Poyser began collaborating on short films in the late 1990s, and in 2004 their first feature, *Dear Pillow*, did well on the festival circuit and earned Poyser a 2005 Independent Spirit Award nomination. That same year Poyser and Vaughn signed on to write and direct *The Cassidy Kids* for Burnt Orange Productions, a for-profit production company that operated under the auspices of the university and was run by former Alive Films executive and producer Carolyn Pfeiffer. Burnt Orange was the brainchild of UT RTF professor Thomas Schatz, who began teaching at the university in 1976 and in 2003 became the executive director of the University of Texas Film Institute (UTFI), the educational partner of Burnt Orange. Although Burnt Orange closed its doors in 2008, UTFI continues to exist and has expanded into production.[17]

The Duplass Brothers could also be considered part of this next wave. Although no longer based in Austin, Mark and Jay Duplass took film classes at the University of Texas in the 1990s and in 2002 made *This is John*, a short film featuring Mark that played at the 2003 Sundance Film Festival. The Austin-made short also earned them representation with the William Morris Agency. More short films led to the feature *The Puffy Chair*, which premiered at Sundance in 2005, received two Independent Spirit Award nominations (the Duplasses joined fellow nominee Brian Poyser at the ceremony) and landed a distribution deal with Netflix in 2006. The hallmarks of their filmmaking style—low budgets, dry humor, an ensemble of non-professional actors, and stories centered on relationship dramas specific to twentysomethings—earned them a place in a relatively new movement of young independent filmmakers dubbed "Mumblecore," a term coined during a SXSW event. Currently based on the West Coast, the brothers chose Austin over New York and Los Angeles to open their second feature, *Baghead*, in June 2008. Their decision bucked conventional industry wisdom, but to them it acknowledged the city's commercially viable film culture. "For us, Austin is the quintessential movie-watching town," explained Mark. "People there will go to the movies without even knowing what they're going to see, just to see something new."[18]

There are also filmmakers like Luke Savisky, whose career developed in tandem with those of Linklater and Rodriguez. Savisky was an art major at the University of Texas who studied with installation artist Bill Lundberg in the early 1980s and began to incorporate 16mm film loops and found footage into his work. He was inspired by bands like the Butthole Surfers, who projected film images during their live shows, and eventually staged similar film installations for Austin-based bands like Poi Dog Pondering. Working with 16mm and 35mm film and video, Savisky staged "Film Actions" beginning in the mid-1990s that combined performance with projections of found footage, original film, and video images. In 2001 at the *Slacker* reunion screening, Savisky—who appeared in the film as the "Video Cameraman"—received the first-ever D. Montgomery Award from the Austin Film Society.

The film society has continued to oversee the development of Austin Studios, which generated much excitement and optimism—and, of course, some criticism—upon its opening in November 2000. More than six years later, the hangars still had yet to be adequately insulated for noise nor did they have the necessary equipment (lighting grids, etc.) to be considered true soundstages. Some improvements have been made, including the addition of an on-site screening room that can show dailies and be rented out for small theatrical events to provide ongoing revenue between productions. On-site vendors like Chapman/Leonard also ensure that visiting productions can quickly secure last-minute equipment needs. "We're not trying to be a state-of-the-art facility," said Quinn in response to complaints about the studios' lack of upgrades. Variables outside the film society's control—a lack of tax incentives to attract out-of-state productions, the "vagaries" of the industry in general—forced Quinn to adjust her marketing strategy early on. "The studios didn't have that much to sell themselves—a big space, an office, parking, which was very necessary, but the facility was not that fancy. So it became about marketing Austin. 'Come to Austin, we have this great crew.'" By its fifth anniversary, the studio had provided space and facilities to more than thirty feature films and numerous television productions, music videos, commercials, and photo shoots. A month later, in December 2005, Quinn resigned from her position at Austin Studios. Catherine Parrington, who previously worked for Sony Pictures Entertainment as its manager of production services, became director of operations in 2007. Simultaneously, the studio received $5 million in city bonds and an additional $1 million from Austin Energy and Austin Water Utility to help fund its much-needed renovations, which were completed in 2008.[19] A year later, in April 2009, Governor Rick Perry signed into law a statewide film incentives program after an aggressive lobbying effort by members of the state's film industry. With tiered incentive payments that allow productions to recoup between 5 and 15 percent of eligible spending in Texas, the incentives program was designed to replace a less-competitive plan approved—but not funded—by the Texas legislature in 2007. As of this writing the 2009 program, with a budget of just over $60 million, was awaiting funding by the House Appropriations Committee.[20]

It remains to be seen, however, if these improvements can stop the flow of production work going to states like New Mexico and Louisiana, which have more competitive incentives plans. And, while these states initially did not have the crew base that Texas boasted, they have since been able to remedy that. In 2006, thirty-seven films shot in Texas. A year later, only nine productions had chosen to film in the state. By 2008, Shreveport, Louisiana, had replaced Austin as the top film production center behind New York and Los Angeles.[21]

Still, Austin's film scene retains its reputation, exemplified, for instance, by the Duplass Brothers' 2008 decision to open *Baghead* there. "You don't buy [film] culture. It comes from the ground up. That's the indigenous thing Austin has," explains AFS executive director Rebecca Campbell.[22] Tim McCanlies's *The Two Bobs* offered an example of this culture when it premiered at the 2009 SXSW Film Festival. A locally funded, low-budget comedy set in the gaming industry, the movie represents a synergy of Austin's top film talent. Produced by Anne Walker-McBay, Richard Linklater's longtime producer, and written and directed by McCanlies, *The Two Bobs* lensed in and around Austin with cameras on loan from Robert Rodriguez's Troublemaker Studios. Another Linklater veteran, editor Sandra Adair, assisted in postproduction.

"This is the Austin that I thought I was moving to in 1996, but it wasn't quite there yet," insisted Matt Dentler in 2004, the year he began a four-year stint as the SXSW Conference and Festival producer. "This is the Austin that people thought they were moving to in 1992 after *Slacker*. This really is the wonderful, frustrating, exciting, productive, lazy town that everyone thought they were moving to. That's kind of what it's become. The promise was kept."[23]

# Notes

This book is based on more than 150 interviews with the people involved in the creation and development of the Austin film scene. Biographical details and other background information have been taken from interviews (and, when necessary, verified with other sources) unless otherwise noted. When thoughts are attributed to an individual, they are also drawn from interviews. The research for this story also includes primary materials from personal collections and public archives as well as secondary materials such as newspaper articles and books. The following abbreviations appear throughout the notes to distinguish the source of quotations or specific information.

AI  Author's Interview
AHC  Austin History Center, Austin Public Library, Austin, Texas
CAH  The Center for American History, University of Texas at Austin
THC  The Tobe Hooper Collection, Harry Ransom Humanities Research Center, University of Texas at Austin
WSC  The Warren Skaaren Collection, Harry Ransom Humanities Research Center, University of Texas at Austin

INTRODUCTION

1. Chale Nafus, AI, August 12, 2001.
2. Peter Biskind, *Easy Riders, Raging Bulls: How the Sex-Drugs-and-Rock `n' Roll Generation Saved Hollywood* (New York: Simon & Schuster, 1998), 14; Austin City Council, "Austin Tomorrow: Interim Report," September 1973, 13, CAH.
3. Tom Copeland, AI, June 2001.

4. Burnes St. Patrick Hollyman, "The First Picture Shows: 1894–1913," in *Film Before Griffith*, ed. John L. Fell (Berkeley: University of California Press, 1983), 188–195, AHC.

5. W. Hope Tilley letter to Mrs. Katherine Hart, November 20, 1970, AHC.

6. Ruth Lewis, "Movies, After Place in Sun, Chose Fair Austin," *Austin American-Statesman*, ca. 1941, AHC.

7. See *Austin American-Statesman*, November 28–December 16, 1915, CAH and Katherine Hart, "Flicks Had Day of Glory Here," *Austin American-Statesman*, October 31, 1970, AHC; Paramount Fact Sheet, AHC; "New Face Nears for Theaters," *Austin American-Statesman*, November 24, 1963, B11, AHC.

8. John Hayes, *Wide Screen Movies Magazine*, Issue 2; Robert Wilonsky, "Reel Challenge," *Dallas Observer*, October 14, 1999, n.p.

9. Marc Savlov, "Thirty Years on Location," *Austin Chronicle*, June 15, 2001, 57.

10. Rick Ferguson, AI, July 7, 2006; Mary Lee Grant, "Wanted: Moviemakers," *Houston Chronicle*, January 22, 2004, 1, CAH.

11. "UT Adds One School, 2 Departments," *Daily Texan*, August 20, 1965, 12A, CAH; Richard Kooris, AI, February 6, 2004.

12. Bill Scott, AI, June 29, 2005; Ron Policy, AI, May 18, 2004; Kooris, AI, February 6, 2004.

13. Thomas Schatz, AI, October 29, 2003; Marjorie Baumgarten, AI, January 10, 2004.

14. Elaine Pinckard, *Alternative Film Organizations in Austin: A Historical Examination of Their Roles and Functions within the Community* (unpub. Master's thesis, University of Texas at Austin, 1990), 48–75.

15. "French Director Postpones Visit," *Daily Texan*, October 14, 1966, 8, CAH; *Austin Rag*, November 18, 1968; Pinckard, *Alternative Film Organizations in Austin*, 55; "Cinema 40 Society Gives Second Season," *Daily Texan*, August 19, 1966, CAH.

16. Pinckard, *Alternative Film Organizations in Austin*, 75–78.

17. George Lellis, AI, April 7, 2004.

18. Anton Riecher, "CinemaTexas takes the bite out of bad films like 'Count Yorga, Vampire,'" *Daily Texan*, September 6, 1977, 15, CAH.

19. Cathy Crane, AI, January 5, 2005.

20. Larry Carroll, AI, November 23, 2003; Lee Daniel, AI, October 12, 2004.

21. Stefan Jaworzyn, *The Texas Chain Saw Massacre Companion* (London: Titan Books, 2003), 14.

22. Ibid., 30; ibid., 18.

23. Copeland, AI, September 20, 2002; Sandra Adair, AI, February 25, 2006.

24. Austin City Council, "Austin Tomorrow: Interim Report," September 1973, 13, CAH.

25. Bud Shrake, AI, January 7, 2004.

26. Ibid.

27. Jerry Hall, AI, December 12, 2003.

28. Mike Simpson, AI, October 28, 2004.

29. Ron Bozman, AI, January 8, 2003.

30. Hall, AI, December 12, 2003.
31. Ibid.
32. Bozman, AI, January 8, 2003.
33. Other reports say the figure was $100,000; see Savlov, "Thirty Years on Location." Smith appointed Skaaren in December 1970 although Skaaren didn't take office until May 24, 1971; see Natasha Waxman, *Warren Skaaren: Screenwriter: His life, films, and letters*, Harry Ransom Humanities Research Center, University of Texas at Austin, 17, 41.
34. David Foster, AI, July 28, 2003.
35. Bill Broyles, AI, June 13, 2006.
36. Typed document, May 29, 1973, WSC.
37. Robert Kuhn, AI, February 4, 2003.

## ONE

1. *The Texas Chainsaw Massacre* Outtakes, THC.
2. "The Top 50 Cult Movies," *Entertainment Weekly*, May 23, 2003.
3. Ann Bordelon, "The Big Time," *Austin American-Statesman*, 1965, AHC.
4. *Eggshells* Press Kit (courtesy of Bob Burns).
5. Wayne Bell, AI, April 29, 2002.
6. Kim Henkel, AI, February 28, 2003.
7. Kim Henkel and Tobe Hooper, *Leatherface* (courtesy of Julie Hall).
8. Henkel, AI, February 28, 2003.
9. Ellen Farley and William K. Knoedelseder Jr., "The Real Texas Chain Saw Massacre," *Los Angeles Times*, September 5, 1982, 4.
10. Farley and Knoedelseder Jr., "The Real Texas Chain Saw Massacre," 4; B. Burns, AI, January 23, 2004; Daniel Pearl, AI, March 16, 2003.
11. Ron Bozman, AI, January 8, 2003.
12. B. Burns, AI, August 22, 2002.
13. Dorothy Pearl, AI, March 14, 2006.
14. B. Burns, AI, August 22, 2002.
15. B. Burns, AI, August 22, 2002; MM Pack, "The Killing Fields, Kind Of," *Austin Chronicle*, October 31, 2003, 48.
16. Marilyn Burns, AI, February 23, 2003.
17. Allen Danziger, AI, January 28, 2003.
18. Paul Partain, AI, April 4, 2003.
19. Gunnar Hansen, AI, September 19, 2003.
20. *The Texas Chainsaw Massacre* Outtakes, THC.
21. Ted Nicolaou, AI, June 28, 2003; Dr. W. E. Barnes, AI, December 6, 2002.
22. Daniel Pearl, AI, March 16, 2003.
23. Ed Neal, AI, April 17, 2003.
24. Daniel Pearl, AI, March 16, 2003; Henkel, AI, February 28, 2003.
25. Bill Vail, AI, July 31, 2003.
26. Hansen, AI, September 19, 2003.

27. B. Burns, AI, August 22, 2002.

28. Hansen, AI, September 19, 2003.

29. B. Burns, AI, January 26, 2004; Farley and Knoedelseder Jr., "The Real Texas Chain Saw Massacre," 6.

30. In the documentary *The Texas Chainsaw Massacre: A Family Portrait*, Dugan says that Barnes had made only two masks, the second of which they cut apart, so the dinner scene had to be his final scene since there were no more masks available to transform him into the character.

31. Stefan Jaworzyn, *The Texas Chain Saw Massacre Companion* (London: Titan Books, 2003), 62.

32. Neal, AI, April 17, 2003.

33. Lou Perryman, AI, March 2004.

34. Dorothy Pearl, AI, March 14, 2006.

35. Ted Nicolaou, AI, June 28, 2003; Alex Lewin, "Adventures in the Scream Trade," *Premiere*, February 2001, 84; Bozman, AI, January 8, 2003.

36. B. Burns, AI, January 26, 2004; Sally Nicolaou, AI, January 4, 2003; Hansen, AI, September 13, 2003, and others.

37. *The Texas Chainsaw Massacre* Outtakes, THC.

38. Henkel letter, October 9, 1973, WSC.

39. Carroll, AI, November 23, 2003.

40. Ibid.

41. Bell, AI, April 29, 2002.

42. Carroll, AI, November 23, 2003. Carroll suggests that the poker game may have been a guise for Skaaren and Bozman to convince Hooper to go with the new title. Robert Burns tells a similar story in *The Texas Chain Saw Massacre Companion* (34).

43. Jaworzyn, *The Texas Chain Saw Massacre Companion*, 72.

44. Henkel, AI, May 2, 2003; Farley and Knoedelseder Jr., "The Real Texas Chain Saw Massacre," 6; Kuhn, AI, February 4, 2003.

45. Bill Wittliff, AI, November 10, 2003; Joe K. Longley, AI, October 22, 2003; PITS Investors List (courtesy of J. Longley).

46. "Skaaren Resigns as TFC Director," *FilmTexas!*, March 1974, 1; untitled document, WSC.

47. Memo, March 26, 1974, and document, April 1, 1974, WSC.

48. Jaworzyn, *The Texas Chain Saw Massacre Companion*, 77; letter, April 18, 1974 (courtesy of J. Longley); letter, July 13, 1974 (courtesy of J. Longley).

49. Stephen H. Smith letter, July 6, 1973, WSC; David Foster, AI, July 28, 2003; Farley and Knoedelseder Jr., "The Real Texas Chain Saw Massacre," September 12, 1982, 3.

50. Dun & Bradstreet report, November 18, 1976, WSC.

51. Fred Beiersdorf, AI, January 8, 2004.

52. Letter, July 19, 1974, WSC.

53. Typed document, WSC.

54. Bozman, AI, January 8, 2003; contracts and memos, WSC.

55. Hooper letter, September 4, 1974, WSC; Thomas Glass, AI, September 23, 2003.

56. Henkel letter, September 3, 1974 (courtesy of J. Longley).

57. Richard Logan letter, September 4, 1974, WSC.

58. B. Burns, AI, January 23, 2004.

59. Beiersdorf, AI, January 8, 2004; Philip Wuntch, *Dallas Morning News*, October 12, 1974, 5D.

60. Mike Simpson, "The Horror Genre: Texas Chainsaw Massacre," *Filmmakers Newsletter*, August 1975, 28; Patrick Taggart, "'Chainsaw Rivals 'Living Dead',"* *Austin American-Statesman*, October 11, 1974, 48; Mack, "The Texas Chain Saw Massacre," *Variety*, November 6, 1974.

61. Longley, AI, October 22, 2003.

62. Linda Gross, "'Texas Massacre' Grovels in Gore," *Los Angeles Times*, October 30, 1974, IV:14; Michael Wolff, "What Do You Do at Midnight? You See a Trashy Movie," *New York Times*, September 7, 1975, II:17:3.

63. Various documents, ca. 1976 and 1977, WSC.

64. *FilmTexas!*, January 1975, 2; letter and report, March 17, 1975 (courtesy of J. Longley); letter to Henkel, April 16, 1975, WSC.

65. B. Burns, AI, January 23, 2004.

66. Reports and memos, WSC.

67. Neal, AI, April 17, 2003.

68. B. Burns, AI, January 23, 2004.

69. Bozman, AI, January 8, 2003.

70. Memo and notes, ca. October 1976, WSC.

71. Henkel letter, September 4, 1975, WSC.

72. Nicholas Gage, *New York Times*, October 12, 1975, 1; see also WSC.

73. Farley and Knoedelseder Jr., "The Real Texas Chain Saw Massacre," September 5, 1982, 7; see also Kuhn, AI, February 4, 2003, and March 4, 2003; Clint Parsley, AI, September 18, 2003.

74. Kuhn, AI, March 4, 2003.

75. Ibid.; agreements and memos, May 12, 1976, WSC.

76. Letter, March 9, 1976, WSC; Ellen Farley and William Knoedelseder Jr., "Family Business: Episode 3 'The Fall,'" *Los Angeles Times*, June 27, 1982, "Calendar," 7.

77. Farley and Knoedelseder Jr., "Family Business: Episode 3: 'The Fall,'" 3.

78. Henkel, AI, May 2, 2003.

79. *Variety*, December 29, 1976, 9.

80. Documents, WSC; also see legal documents concerning suits (courtesy of J. Longley); Farley and Knoedelseder Jr., "The Real Texas Chain Saw Massacre," September 12, 1982, 4.

81. David Foster, AI, July 28, 2003; Glass, AI, September 23, 2003.

82. Kuhn, AI, March 4, 2003; Farley and Knoedelseder Jr., "The Real Texas Chain Saw Massacre," September 12, 1982, 5.

83. *Austin American-Statesman*, April 10, 1981, WSC.

84. Documents, WSC; also Charles Grigson, AI, September 30, 2003.

85. *Austin American-Statesman,* April 10, 1981, WSC.
86. Farley and Knoedelseder Jr., "The Real Texas Chain Saw Massacre," September 12, 1982, 3; Document, WSC.
87. Farley and Knoedelseder Jr., "The Real Texas Chain Saw Massacre," September 12, 1982, 3; booklet, "Texas Chainsaw Massacre: November 1, 1980 to July 31, 1982," Solomon, Finger & Newman, WSC; Kuhn, AI, March 4, 2003.
88. Advertisement, *Variety,* November 2, 1982, WSC.
89. Matthew McConaughey, AI, May 10, 2006.
90. Chris Garcia, "Fire Up the Texas Chainsaws Again," *Austin American-Statesman XLent,* September 25, 2003, 40.
91. Henkel, AI, May 2, 2003.

TWO

1. Lou Perryman, "In Memoriam," *Austin Chronicle,* August 30, 2002, 44; Sonny Carl Davis, AI, July 13, 2004.
2. Lin Sutherland, AI, November 19, 2003.
3. Quentin Tarantino, AI, November 30, 2005.
4. Brian Huberman, AI, November 14, 2003; Chuck Pinnell, AI, August 23, 2004.
5. Eagle Pennell, quoted in Steve McVicker, "Fade to Black: The Wasted Life of Texas Filmmaker Eagle Pennell," *Houston Press,* October 14, 1999, 3; Mark Pritchard, "Animation, features close USA Festival," *Daily Texan,* March 27, 1978, 29, CAH.
6. Elaine Pinckard, *Alternative Film Organizations in Austin: A Historical Examination of Their Roles and Functions within the Community* (unpublished Master's thesis, University of Texas at Austin, 1990), 84–87; also, *FilmTexas!,* January 1975.
7. Davis, AI, July 13, 2004.
8. Ibid.; Lou Perryman, AI, March 2004; Davis, AI, July 13, 2004.
9. Pinnell, AI, August 2, 2004.
10. "Doing It the Way They Used to Do," *FilmTexas!,* April 1977, 5 (courtesy of C. Pinnell).
11. Sutherland, AI, November 19, 2003.
12. Ibid.
13. Kim Henkel, AI, May 2, 2003.
14. Untitled document dated February 27, 1974, WSC.
15. Undated letter ca. Fall 1977, written by Eagle Pennell (courtesy of C. Pinnell); Pinnell, AI, August 2, 2004.
16. George Wead, "Where Eagle Dares," *American Film,* September 1984, 55.
17. The finished film adheres fairly closely to the original script.
18. Perryman, AI, March 2004; Doris Hargrave, AI, November 28, 2004; Wead, "Where Eagle Dares," 54.
19. Perryman, "In Memoriam," *Austin Chronicle,* August 30, 2002, 44.
20. Hargrave, AI, November 28, 2004; Davis, AI, July 13, 2004.
21. Hargrave, AI, November 28, 2004; Eric Henshaw, AI, April 14, 2006; Davis, AI, July 13, 2004; Sutherland, AI, November 19, 2003.

22. Sutherland, AI, November 19, 2003.
23. Ibid.
24. "Rain Check," *FilmTexas!*, February–March 1978, 7, CAH; Hargrave, AI, November 28, 2004.
25. Knight, "Good Words," *FilmTexas!*, 2.
26. Sutherland, AI, November 19, 2003; "What's Happening," *FilmTexas!*, February–March 1978, 10, CAH; Sutherland, AI, November 19, 2003; Wead, "Where Eagle Dares," 55.
27. Sutherland, AI, November 19, 2003.
28. Lory Smith, *Party in a Box: The Story of the Sundance Film Festival* (Salt Lake City: Gibbs Smith Publisher, 1999), 6; "Hollywood or Bust," *FilmTexas!* October 1978, 6, CAH.
29. Smith, *Party in a Box*, 23-24.
30. Smith, *Party in a Box*, 24; Pinnell, AI, August 23, 2004.
31. Patrick Taggart, "Stargazing," *Austin American-Statesman*, August 28, 1983, 4; "Hollywood or Bust," *FilmTexas!*, October 1978, 6, CAH.
32. Henkel, AI, May 2, 2003.
33. Vincent Canby, "Get-Rich-Quick Duo," *New York Times*, April 21, 1979, 18:1; Sutherland, AI, November 19, 2003.
34. Sutherland, AI, November 19, 2003.
35. Pinnell, AI, August 23, 2004; Henkel, AI, May 2, 2003.
36. "Memorandum to Shareholders," April 24, 1981, written by Lin Sutherland (courtesy of C. Pinnell).
37. Ibid.
38. Thomas Schatz, AI, October 29, 2003.
39. Wead, "Where Eagle Dares," 53.
40. Henkel, AI, May 2, 2003.
41. Davis, AI, July 13, 2004; Hargrave, AI, November 28, 2004.
42. Henkel, AI, May 2, 2003.
43. McVicker, "Fade to Black," 7.
44. Carlos Clarens, "Mavericks Anonymous," *Village Voice*, October 11, 1983, n.p.; Charles Ryweck, "Last Night at the Alamo," *Hollywood Reporter*, October 7, 1983, n.p.; Lor., "Last Night at the Alamo," *Variety*, October 12, 1983, 16; Davis, AI, July 13, 2004.
45. Vincent Canby, "'The Alamo' is an offbeat American barroom ballad," *New York Times*, July 15, 1984, 15.
46. Pinnell, AI, August 23, 2004.

## THREE

1. Joe Dishner, AI, August 25, 2003.
2. George Dolis and Ingrid Weigand, "Making *Red Headed Stranger*," *Austin Chronicle*, February 27, 1987, 20, AHC.
3. Thomas Schatz, AI, October 29, 2003; Steve Bearden, AI, November 17, 2003.

4. George Lellis, AI, April 7, 2004.

5. Louis Black, AI, December 13, 2004.

6. Lellis, AI, April 7, 2004.

7. Charles Ramírez Berg, AI, October 24, 2003.

8. Schatz, AI, October 29, 2003; Ed Lowry, "CinemaTexas Looks at . . . *Jaws*," *Cin-emaTexas Program Notes*, vol. 10, no.1 (Feb. 12, 1976), Department of Radio-Television-Film, University of Texas at Austin, 91.

9. Dishner, AI, August 25, 2003.

10. Black, AI, December 13, 2004.

11. Dishner, AI, August 25, 2003; Nick Barbaro, AI, September 27, 2004.

12. Marjorie Baumgarten, AI, January 10, 2004.

13. "Chapter 1: Before the Beginning," *Austin Chronicle*, September 7, 2001.

14. *Austin Chronicle*, September 4, 1981, 2, AHC; Baumgarten, AI, January 10, 2004.

15. Ed Lowry, "A Long-Time Tradition," *Austin Chronicle*, September 18, 1981, 12, AHC; Robert Sternberg, "On the Set of Raggedy Man," *Austin Chronicle*, September 18, 1981, 13, AHC.

16. Louis Black, "'Made in Texas' makes it in New York," *Austin Chronicle*, October 30, 1981, 8, AHC; Louis Black, "Page Two," *Austin Chronicle*, August 3, 2001; See Black, "'Made in Texas,'" for excerpts from other New York papers and magazines.

17. Sternberg, "On the Set of Raggedy Man," 13.

18. Willie Nelson with Edwin Shrake, *Willie: An Autobiography* (New York: Simon & Schuster, 1988), 211.

19. Bill Wittliff, AI, November 10, 2003.

20. Ibid.

21. Bill Broyles, AI, June 13, 2006.

22. Wittliff, AI, November 10, 2003.

23. Natasha Waxman, *Warren Skaaren: Screenwriter: His life, films, and letters*, Harry Ransom Humanities Research Center, University of Texas at Austin, 21; Warren Skaaren, undated letter ca. 1975, WSC; also Wittliff, AI, November 10, 2003.

24. Wittliff, AI, November 10, 2003.

25. Neil Roach, AI, October 5, 2004.

26. Wittliff, AI, November 10, 2003.

27. Nelson with Edwin Shrake, *Willie: An Autobiography*, 169.

28. "What's Cookin,'" *FilmTexas*, January 1979, 2, CAH.

29. Nelson with Edwin Shrake, *Willie: An Autobiography*, 212.

30. Nelson with Edwin Shrake, *Willie: An Autobiography*, 212, 213.

31. Wittliff, AI, November 10, 2003.

32. Ibid.

33. The woman's name is being withheld at her request. Bud Shrake, AI, January 17, 2004.

34. Wittliff, AI, November 10, 2003.

35. Ibid.; Cary White, AI, June 30, 2004.

36. Ibid.
37. Roach, AI, October 5, 2004.
38. Ibid.; Cate Hardman, AI, July 14, 2004.
39. Connie Todd, AI, November 24, 2003.
40. Ibid.
41. Morgan Fairchild, AI, April 13, 2006.
42. Katharine Ross, AI, May 2, 2006.
43. Roach, AI, October 5, 2004.
44. Ibid.; Hardman, AI, July 14, 2004.
45. Wittliff, AI, November 10, 2003.
46. Roach, AI, October 5, 2004.
47. Fairchild, AI, April 13, 2006.
48. Roach, AI, October 5, 2004; Fairchild, AI, April 13, 2006.
49. Fairchild, AI, April 13, 2006.
50. Hardman, AI, July 14, 2004.
51. Roach, AI, October 5, 2004.
52. George Dolis and Ingrid Weigand, "Independent Images," *Austin Chronicle*, November 29, 1985, 18–19, CAH.
53. Shrake, AI, January 17, 2004.
54. *Austin Chronicle*, October 18, 1985, 21, AHC; Baumgarten, AI, January 10, 2004.
55. Eric Williams, AI, July 19, 2004.
56. "One on One," VH-1, 1986, The Films of Bill Wittliff, Southwestern Writers Collection, Texas State University–San Marcos.
57. Michael Healy, *Denver Post*, October 18 1986, 6F; Alyo, "Feeble Willie Nelson vehicle," *Variety*, October 29, 1986.
58. John T. Davis, "No stranger to these parts," *Austin American-Statesman*, February 20, 1987, A1, A6.
59. Louis Black, "Red Headed Stranger," *Austin Chronicle*, February 27, 1987, 22, AHC.
60. "50 Top-Grossing Films," *Variety*, March 18, 1987, 11. See also Maggie Brown, "'Elm 3' Sprouting 112G, Sea-Tac; 'Widow' Elegant; 'Platoon' 104G," *Variety*, March 4, 1987, 34; and Bob Rees, "'Weapon' Fiery at $40,500 in Mpls," *Variety*, March 11, 1987, 32.
61. Savlov, "Thirty Years on Location," *Austin Chronicle*, June 15, 2001, 57, 58; also Tom Copeland, AI, September 30, 2002.

FOUR

1. Austin Film Society, *Tenth Anniversary Retrospective*, 6.
2. Scott Dinger, AI, July 6, 2004.
3. Richard Linklater, AI, October 6, 2003; Clark Walker, AI, October 4, 2004.
4. John Pierson, *Spike, Mike Reloaded: A Guided Tour across a Decade of American Independent Cinema* (New York: Hyperion/Miramax, 2003), 185.

5. *Slacker* Ten Year Reunion Program, Austin Film Society, July 1, 2001, 5; Peter Biskind, *Down and Dirty Pictures: Miramax, Sundance, and the Rise of Independent Film* (New York: Simon & Schuster, 2004), 21; Linklater, AI, October 6, 2003.

6. Linklater, AI, October 6, 2003.

7. Ibid.

8. Lee Daniel, AI, October 12, 2004.

9. Gary Price, AI, March 30, 2006.

10. Linklater, AI, October 6, 2003.

11. Price, AI, March 30, 2006; Linklater, AI, October 6, 2003.

12. Daniel, AI, October 12, 2004.

13. Linklater, AI, October 6, 2003.

14. Walker, AI, October 4, 2004.

15. Linklater, AI, October 6, 2003.

16. Linklater, AI, October 6, 2003; Denise Montgomery, Austin Film Society, *Tenth Anniversary Retrospective*, 11.

17. Linklater, AI, October 6, 2003.

18. Ibid.

19. Ibid.

20. Linklater, AI, October 6, 2003; "Early Treatment," *Slacker*, Criterion Collection, September 14, 2004.

21. Walker, AI, October 4, 2004.

22. Richard Linklater, *Slacker* (New York: St. Martin's Press, 1992), 118.

23. Linklater, AI, October 6, 2003; Daniel, AI, October 12, 2004.

24. Walker, AI, October 4, 2004.

25. Linklater, *Slacker*, 11–13; *Slacker*, Criterion Collection, Program Notes; ibid., 13.

26. Linklater, *Slacker*, 15.

27. Chris Garcia, Alison Macor, John DeFore, and Jody Seaborn, "'Slacker': An oral history," *Austin American-Statesman XLent*, June 28, 2001, 18.

28. Teresa Taylor, AI, July 2001.

29. Grant application reprinted in Linklater, *Slacker*; Garcia, et al., "'Slacker': An oral history," 18.

30. Katie Cokinos, AI, May 18, 2005.

31. Linklater, *Slacker*, 11; Price, AI, March 30, 2006.

32. Kim Krizan, AI, January 28, 2006; Linklater commentary, *Slacker*, Criterion Collection, September 14, 2004.

33. Walker, AI, October 4, 2004.

34. Scott Rhodes, AI, June 1, 2004.

35. Linklater, AI, October 6, 2003.

36. Linklater, *Slacker*, 12.

37. Linklater, AI, September 8, 2005.

38. Rhodes, AI, June 1, 2004; Walker, AI, October 4, 2004; Rhodes, AI, June 1, 2004.

39. Cokinos, AI, May 18, 2005.

40. Ibid.

41. Linklater, *Slacker*, 20.

42. *Dallas Times Herald,* April 21, 1991, n.p.
43. Linklater, AI, September 8, 2005.
44. Cokinos, AI, May 18, 2005.
45. Robert Horton, "Stranger Than Texas," *Film Comment* (July–August 1990: 78).
46. Pierson, *Spike, Mike Reloaded,* 186-187; Pierson, AI, September 20, 2004.
47. Dinger, AI, July 6, 2004.
48. Ibid.
49. Chris Walters, AI, January 24, 2005; Patrick Taggart, "Slacking off in Austin," *Austin American-Statesman,* July 27, 1990, Weekend Supplement, 9.
50. Undated letter (courtesy of John Pierson); Pierson, *Spike, Mike Reloaded,* 189.
51. Linklater letter (courtesy of John Pierson).
52. Pierson, AI, September 20, 2004.
53. Michael Barker, AI, October 15, 2003.
54. Barker, AI, October 15, 2003; Pierson, AI, September 20, 2004.
55. Cokinos, AI, May 23, 2005.
56. Pierson, *Spike, Mike Reloaded,* 188; Walker, AI, October 18, 2004.
57. Pierson, *Spike, Mike Reloaded,* 179; Pierson, AI, September 20, 2004.
58. Dinger, AI, July 6, 2004.
59. Walker, AI, October 18, 2004; Price, AI, March 30, 2006.
60. Rhodes, AI, June 1, 2004.
61. Daniel, AI, October 12, 2004; Amy Lowrey, AI, January 31, 2006.
62. Linklater, AI, October 6, 2003.
63. Daniel, AI, October 12, 2004.
64. Ibid.
65. Barker, AI, October 15, 2003; Cart., "Slacker," *Variety,* January 28, 1991, 71.
66. Vincent Canby, "Some Texas Eccentrics and Aunt Hallie," *New York Times,* March 22, 1991, C8.
67. Linklater letter (courtesy of John Pierson).
68. Pierson, AI, September 20, 2004.
69. Barker, AI, October 15, 2003.
70. Barker, AI, October 15, 2003; Pierson, AI, September 20, 2004; ibid.
71. Peter Travers, "Slacker," *Rolling Stone;* Jack Kroll, "Zonking Out in Austin," *Newsweek,* July 22, 1991, 57; Stuart Klawans, "Slacker," *Nation,* July 8, 1991, 65; Stanley Kauffman, "Slacker," *New Republic,* July 8, 1991, 27.
72. Cokinos, AI, May 23, 2005.
73. Cokinos, AI, May 23, 2005; Rhodes, AI, June 1, 2004.
74. Price, AI, March 30, 2006.
75. Daniel, AI, October 12, 2004.
76. "A $23,000 Film Is Turning into a Hit," *New York Times,* August 7, 1991, C13; Barker, AI, October 15, 2003; *Dallas Morning News,* September 8, 1991, E1; Doris Toumarkine, "Shoestring Slacker," *Hollywood Reporter,* August 9, 1991; Barker, AI, October 15, 2003.
77. Pierson, *Spike, Mike Reloaded,* 194.
78. *Associated Press,* December 6, 1990.

79. Pierson, *Spike, Mike Reloaded*, 194; Linklater, AI, August 31, 2004.
80. Linklater, AI, August 31, 2004; Pierson, *Spike, Mike Reloaded*, 195; Linklater, AI, August 31, 2004.
81. Linklater, AI, August 31, 2004.
82. Pierson, AI, September 20, 2004.
83. Ibid.
84. Steve Weinstein, "Making a Winner out of Losers," *Los Angeles Times*, July 24, 1991, F7.

## FIVE

1. Robert Rodriguez, *Rebel Without a Crew: Or How a 23-Year-Old Filmmaker With $7,000 Became a Hollywood Player* (New York: Dutton, 1995), 120.
2. Anita M. Busch, "Young Director Rodriguez Wins Col Film Deal," *Hollywood Reporter*, April 23, 1992.
3. John Evan Frook, "ColPix Signs Rodriguez to 2-Year Pact," *Daily Variety*, April 23, 1992, 1.
4. Stephanie Allain, AI, March 6, 2006.
5. Carlos Gallardo, AI, November 15, 2005.
6. Rodriguez, *Rebel Without a Crew*, 2; Ibid.
7. Rodriguez, AI, August 11, 2005; Avellán, AI, April 28, 2005; Rodriguez, AI, August 11, 2005.
8. Steve Mims, AI, July 7, 2004.
9. See *Daily Texan*, June 1, 1988, 15; May 31, 1988, 14, CAH.
10. Mims, AI, July 7, 2004.
11. Rodriguez, AI, August 11, 2005.
12. Rodriguez, *Rebel Without a Crew*, 11.
13. Rodriguez, AI, August 11, 2005.
14. Gallardo, AI, November 15, 2005.
15. Rodriguez, *Rebel Without a Crew*, 12–15.
16. Ibid., 23.
17. Gallardo, AI, November 15, 2005.
18. Ibid.
19. Rodriguez, *Rebel Without a Crew*, 56–58.
20. Rodriguez, AI, August 11, 2005.
21. Rodriguez, *Rebel Without a Crew*, 64.
22. Ibid., 67–68.
23. Ann Richards, AI, December 4, 2003.
24. Marlene Saritzky, AI, October 26, 2003.
25. Tom Copeland, AI, September 30, 2002.
26. Saritzky, AI, October 26, 2003.
27. Ibid.
28. Michael MacCambridge, *XLent, Austin American-Statesman*, December 1, 1994, 52, CAH; Summary of Film/Television Production 1980–1995, Texas Film Commission; Julia Null Smith, AI, August 25, 2005.

29. *Austin American-Statesman*, November 8, 1991, A1, CAH.

30. Rodriguez, AI, August 11, 2005.

31. Rodriguez, *Rebel Without a Crew*, 80-81.

32. Robert Newman, AI, February 24, 2006.

33. Rodriguez, *Rebel Without a Crew*, 88-89.

34. Gallardo, AI, November 15, 2005.

35. Rodriguez, *Rebel Without a Crew*, 92.

36. Rob Patterson, "Steve Mims: Practice What You Teach," *Austin Chronicle*, February 21, 1992, 22, CAH.

37. Louis Black, "Bedhead Rising," *Austin Chronicle*, February 21, 1992, 22, CAH; Rodriguez, *Rebel Without a Crew*, 94.

38. Avellán, AI, April 28, 2005.

39. Newman, AI, February 24, 2006.

40. Rodriguez, *Rebel Without a Crew*, 106; Allain, AI, March 6, 2006.

41. Allain, AI, March 6, 2006; Rodriguez, *Rebel Without a Crew*, 113.

42. Rodriguez, AI, August 11, 2005.

43. Allain, AI, March 6, 2006.

44. Gallardo, AI, November 15, 2005.

45. Rodriguez, AI, August 11, 2005; Avellán, AI, April 28, 2005.

46. Newman, AI, February 24, 2006; Bob Weinstein, AI, September 21, 2005.

47. Allain, AI, March 6, 2006.

48. Rodriguez, *Rebel Without a Crew*, 127; Avellán, AI, April 28, 2005.

49. Rodriguez, *Rebel Without a Crew*, 132.

50. Rodriguez, *Rebel Without a Crew*, 150; Avellán, AI, April 28, 2005; Rodriguez, AI, August 11, 2005.

51. Allain, AI, March 6, 2006.

52. Rodriguez, AI, August 11, 2005.

53. Roger Ebert, "'El Mariachi': The Ballad of Unknown Filmmaker," *Chicago Sun-Times*, September 13, 1992, 12; Todd McCarthy, "Telluride Fest," *Variety*, September 14, 1992.

54. Tarantino, AI, November 30, 2005.

55. Rodriguez, *Rebel Without a Crew*, 155.

56. "$7,000 feature wins Col release," *Hollywood Reporter*, January 4, 1993; Rodriguez, *Rebel Without a Crew*, 171.

57. Tarantino, AI, November 30, 2005.

58. Allain, AI, March 6, 2006.

59. Ibid.

60. Allain, AI, March 6, 2006; Tarantino, AI, November 30, 2005.

61. Peter Travers, "El Mariachi and the Sundance Kid," *Rolling Stone*, March 18, 1993, 49; John Pierson, *Spike, Mike Reloaded: A Guided Tour across a Decade of American Independent Cinema* (New York: Hyperion/Miramax, 2003), 262; Rodriguez, AI, August 11, 2005.

62. Pierson, *Spike, Mike Reloaded* 263; Bernard Weinraub, "The Talk of Sundance," *New York Times*, February 1, 1993, C15; Travers, *Rolling Stone*, March 18, 1993, 46.

63. Rodriguez, *Rebel Without a Crew*, 183.

64. John Horn, "'Falling Down' No. 1," *Associated Press*, March 1, 1993.

65. Eleanor Ringel, "Comic timing boosts budget 'El Mariachi,'" *Atlanta Journal and Constitution*, May 14, 1993, C2; Janet Maslin, "El Mariachi," *New York Times*, February 26, 1993, C6; Jay Carr, "Rodriguez's $7,000 Wonder," *Boston Globe*, April 30, 1993, 54.

66. Caryn James, "Poverty Becomes Oh So Chic," *New York Times*, February 28, 1993, II:13.

67. Gary Arnold, "Mariachi," *Washington Times*, April 6, 1993, E4.

68. Rodriguez, *Rebel Without a Crew*, 192-193.

69. Peter Travers, "On the Move with Robert Rodriguez," *Rolling Stone*, March 18, 1993, 47; Rodriguez, AI, August 11, 2005; Office of the Registrar, University of Texas at Austin.

70. Allain, AI, March 6, 2006; Gallardo, AI, November 11, 2005.

71. John Evan Frook, "Fleiss Courts Hollywood Attention," *Daily Variety*, August 19, 1993, 1; Bill Borden, AI, June 8, 2006.

72. Rodriguez, AI, August 11, 2005.

73. Allain, AI, March 6, 2006.

74. Louis B. Parks, "Action Man," *Houston Chronicle*, August 24, 1995, 1; Allain, AI, March 6, 2006.

75. Gallardo, AI, May 26, 2006.

76. Allain, AI, March 6, 2006.

77. Avellán, AI, April 28, 2005.

78. Rodriguez, AI, August 11, 2005.

79. Avellán, AI, April 28, 2005.

80. Gallardo, AI, November 15, 2005.

81. Parks, "Action Man," 1; Borden, AI, June 8, 2006.

82. Avellán, AI, April 28, 2005.

83. Gallardo, AI, November 15, 2005.

84. Avellán, AI, April 28, 2005.

85. Gallardo, AI, May 26, 2006.

86. Borden, AI, June 8, 2006.

87. Gary Martin, AI, February 17, 2006; Avellán, AI, April 28, 2005.

88. Avellán, AI, April 28, 2005.

89. Ibid.

90. Ibid.

91. Martin, AI, February 17, 2006.

92. John Pierson, AI, September 20, 2004; Tarantino, AI, November 30, 2005; Peter Biskind, *Down and Dirty Pictures: Miramax, Sundance, and the Rise of Independent Film* (New York: Simon & Schuster, 2004), 218-221; Tarantino, AI, November 30, 2005.

93. Rodriguez, AI, August 11, 2005; Martin, AI, February 17, 2006.

94. Rodriguez, AI, August 11, 2005; Martin, AI, February 17, 2006.

95. Rodriguez, *Rebel Without a Crew*, 195.

96. Avellán, AI, April 28, 2005.

97. Ibid.

98. Martin, AI, February 17, 2006.

99. Rodriguez, AI, August 11, 2005.

100. Rodriguez, AI, August 11, 2005; Weinstein, AI, September 21, 2005; John Brodie, "Miramax Pacts with Rodriguez," *Daily Variety*, May 24, 1995, 14.

101. Avellán, AI, April 28, 2005.

102. Biskind, *Down and Dirty Pictures*, 15.

103. Avellán, AI, April 28, 2005.

104. Weinstein, AI, September 21, 2005.

105. Avellán, AI, April 28, 2005; Rodriguez, AI, August 11, 2005.

106. Avellán, AI, April 28, 2005.

SIX

1. Manohla Dargis, "In the Loop," *Village Voice*, December 29, 1992, 70.

2. Matthew McConaughey, AI, May 10, 2006; John Spong, "The Spirit of 76," *Texas Monthly*, October 2003, 159.

3. John Frick, AI, March 11, 2005; John Cameron, AI, April 18, 2006; Richard Linklater, "*Dazed* by Days," *Austin Chronicle*, September 24, 1993, 39.

4. Linklater, AI, June 15, 2001.

5. Lee Daniel, AI, October 12, 2004.

6. Linklater, "*Dazed* by Days," 38.

7. Jim Jacks, AI, February 7, 2005.

8. Daniel, AI, October 12, 2004.

9. Linklater, AI, September 8, 2005.

10. Clark Walker, AI, October 4, 2004.

11. Daniel, AI, October 12, 2004.

12. Anne Walker-McBay, AI, January 26, 2006.

13. Wiley Wiggins, AI, January 14, 2005.

14. Keith Fletcher, AI, March 1, 2005; Scott Rhodes, AI, June 1, 2004.

15. Alma Kuttruff, AI, September 10, 2003.

16. Don Phillips, AI, March 10, 2006.

17. Jacks, AI, February 7, 2005.

18. Daniel, AI, October 12, 2004; Cameron, AI, April 18, 2006; Daniel, AI, October 12, 2004; Jacks, AI, February 7, 2005.

19. Linklater, "*Dazed* by Days," 39; Jacks, AI, February 7, 2005; Dargis, "In the Loop," 70.

20. Kuttruff, AI, September 10, 2003; Jacks, AI, February 7, 2005; Richard Klein, "H'wood's backyard sets '83 b.o. record," *Daily Variety*, January 4, 1984, 28.

21. Walker, AI, October 18, 2004.

22. Phillips, AI, March 10, 2006.

23. Adam Goldberg, AI, April 25, 2006.

24. Peter Biskind, *Down and Dirty Pictures: Miramax, Sundance, and the Rise of Independent Film* (New York: Simon & Schuster, 2004), 279.

25. Walker-McBay, AI, January 26, 2006; Linklater, *"Dazed* by Days," 39.

26. Linklater, AI, August 31, 2004; Linklater, letter to *Dazed and Confused* cast and crew, June 16, 1992 (courtesy of J. Frick).

27. Goldberg, AI, April 25, 2006; Phillips, AI, March 10, 2006; Kim Krizan, AI, January 28, 2006.

28. Jason London, AI, March 28, 2006.

29. Phillips, AI, March 10, 2006.

30. London, AI, March 28, 2006; Biskind, *Down and Dirty Pictures,* 279.

31. Linklater, AI, August 31, 2004; Walker, AI, October 18, 2004.

32. Spong, "The Spirit of 76," 123; Linklater, letter to *Dazed and Confused* cast and crew, June 16, 1992 (courtesy of J. Frick); McConaughey, AI, May 10, 2006; Phillips, AI, March 10, 2006.

33. Linklater, *"Dazed* by Days," 39; Walker-McBay, AI, January 26, 2006; Linklater, *"Dazed* by Days," 39.

34. Walker-McBay, AI, January 26, 2006.

35. Cameron, AI, April 18, 2006; Walker-McBay, AI, January 26, 2006; Cameron, AI, April 18, 2006.

36. From memo included in Kahane Corn, *Making Dazed,* Actual Reality Pictures, © 2005 AMC; Jacks, AI, Feburary 7, 2005.

37. Cameron, AI, April 18, 2006; Daniel, AI, October 12, 2004.

38. McConaughey, AI, May 10, 2006; Wiggins, AI, January 14, 2005.

39. Kuttruff, AI, September 10, 2003; Cameron, AI, April 18, 2006.

40. Jacks, AI, February 7, 2005.

41. Ibid.; Walker, AI, October 18, 2004; Goldberg, AI, April 25, 2006; Jacks, AI, February 7, 2005.

42. Goldberg, AI, April 25, 2006.

43. Spong, "The Spirit of 76," 160; Fletcher, AI, March 1, 2005.

44. Spong, "The Spirit of 76," 160.

45. Linklater, AI, June 15, 2001; Alison Macor, "Editor's Cut," *Tribeza,* July–August 2001, 16.

46. Sandra Adair, AI, February 25, 2006.

47. Linklater, *"Dazed* by Days," 40.

48. Adair, AI, 2001.

49. Walker-McBay, AI, January 26, 2006.

50. Jacks, AI, February 7, 2005; Linklater, AI, August 31, 2004.

51. Linklater, *"Dazed* by Days," 40; Adair, AI, February 25, 2006.

52. Adair, AI, February 25, 2006.

53. Russell Schwartz, AI, May 25, 2006.

54. Jacks, AI, February 7, 2005.

55. Adair, AI, February 25, 2006; Jacks, AI, February 7, 2005; Linklater, *"Dazed* by Days," 41.

56. Linklater, *"Dazed* by Days," 41.

57. Linklater, AI, August, 31, 2004.

58. Linklater, AI, September 8, 2005; Krizan, AI, January 28, 2006.

59. Linklater, AI, September 8, 2005; Walker-McBay, AI, January 26, 2006. Kathy Nelson declined to be interviewed.
60. Goldberg, AI, April 25, 2006.
61. Linklater, "*Dazed* by Days," 42.
62. Schwartz, AI, May 25, 2006; Cameron, AI, April 18, 2006.
63. Linklater, AI September 8, 2005.
64. Jacks, AI, February 7, 2005.
65. Ken Eisner, "Dazed and Confused," *Daily Variety*, June 9, 1993, 41-42.
66. Walker-McBay, AI, January 26, 2006; Jacks, AI, February 7, 2005; Linklater, AI, September 8, 2005.
67. Linklater, "*Dazed* by Days," 42.
68. Larry Jacobson, AI, February 8, 2005.
69. Ibid.
70. Jacobson, AI, February 8, 2005; Schwartz, AI, May 25, 2006.
71. Linklater, "*Dazed* by Days," 43.
72. Walker-McBay, AI, January 26, 2006; Linklater, AI, August 31, 2004; Schwartz, AI, May 25, 2006.
73. Schwartz, AI, May 25, 2006.
74. Judy Stone, "Richard Linklater 'Slacker' Director Still in State of Confusion," *San Francisco Chronicle*, September 19, 1993, 31.
75. Claudia Eller, "MPAA Just Says 'No' to Film Ad," *Los Angeles Times*, September 22, 1993, B8, B11.
76. Linklater, "*Dazed* by Days," 43; Jacks, AI, February 7, 2005.
77. John Pierson, AI, September 20, 2004.
78. Duane Byrge, "'Good Son' does great with $12 million debut," *Hollywood Reporter*, September 27, 1993; Anthony Lane, "American High," *New Yorker*, October 4, 1993, 215; advertisement in *Village Voice*, October 5, 1993, 59.
79. Joe Levy, *Village Voice*, September 28, 1993, 58; "Dazed and Confused," *Rolling Stone*, October 4, 1993, 128; Jay Carr, "Dazed and Confused," *Boston Globe*, September 24, 1993, 52.
80. Goldberg, AI, April 25, 2006.
81. Jacks, AI, February 7, 2005.
82. Schwartz, AI, May 25, 2006.
83. Louis B. Parks, "Unfazed and hangin' loose," *Houston Chronicle*, October 3, 1993, 11.
84. Biskind, *Down and Dirty Pictures*, 280.
85. Walker-McBay, AI, January 26, 2006; London, AI, March 28, 2006.
86. Peter Travers, "The Year in Movies," *Rolling Stone*, December 23, 1993-January 6, 1994, 174; Jacks, AI, February 7, 2005.
87. Jacobson, AI, February 8, 2005.
88. Linklater, AI, August 31, 2004; Jacks, AI, February 7, 2005.
89. Jon Pareles, "Celestial Romance and the Darker Side," *New York Times*, October 25, 1993.
90. Scott Dinger, AI, July 6, 2004.

91. Ibid.
92. Diane West, "New Texas film festival healthy, despite snags," *Dallas Morning News*, March 19, 1978, AHC; Elaine Pinckard, *Alternative Film Organizations in Austin: A Historical Examination of Their Roles and Functions Within the Community* (unpublished Master's thesis, University of Texas at Austin, 1990), 107.
93. Barbara Morgan, AI, June 2, 2004.
94. Marlene Saritzky, AI, November 9, 2003.
95. Louis Black, AI, December 13, 2004.
96. Michael MacCambridge, "Coming Soon: 'Clash of the Film Fests,'" *Austin American-Statesman*, October 22, 1993, "Weekend," 6.
97. Morgan, AI, June 2, 2004.
98. Black, AI, December 13, 2004.
99. Morgan, AI, June 2, 2004.
100. Bill Broyles, AI, June 13, 2006.
101. Marsha Milam, AI, July 2, 2004; Morgan, AI, June 2, 2004.
102. Katie Cokinos, AI, May 23, 2005.
103. Michael MacCambridge, "A Film Festival is Born," *Austin American-Statesman*, March 11, 1994; Nancy Schafer, AI, July 15, 2004.
104. Morgan, AI, June 2, 2004; Milam, AI, July 2, 2004.
105. Suzanne McCanlies, AI, October 3, 2005.
106. Nick Barbaro, "Page Two," *Austin Chronicle*, September 30, 1984, 2; MacCambridge, "A Film Festival is Born," *Austin American-Statesman*, March 11, 1994; Black, AI, December 13, 2004.
107. Tom Shales, "'Blessing': Top-Drawer Quick Draw," *Washington Post*, August 18, 1993, B3.
108. Letter, Ann Richards (ca. 1994), The Films of Bill Wittliff, Southwestern Writers Collection, Texas State University–San Marcos.


SEVEN

1. Michael MacCambridge, "Linklater takes Vienna by Night," *Austin American-Statesman*, September 8, 1994, CAH; Vance Muse, "The Eyes of Hollywood Are on the Hill Country," *New York Times*, February 20, 1995.
2. Ethan Hawke, AI, March 30, 2006.
3. Kim Krizan, AI, January 28, 2006.
4. Ibid.
5. Clark Walker, AI, October 18, 2004; Claude Stanush, "Robbing banks and trains was our business," *Smithsonian*, January 1994, 75.
6. Walker, AI, October 18, 2004.
7. Keith Fletcher, AI, March 1, 2005.
8. Claude Stanush, AI, March 7, 2005.
9. Ibid.
10. Anne Walker-McBay, AI, January 26, 2006.
11. Walker, AI, October 18, 2004.

12. Walker-McBay, AI, January 26, 2006.

13. Ibid.

14. Hawke, AI, March 30, 2006.

15. Ibid.

16. Stanush, AI, March 7, 2005.

17. Walker, AI, October 18, 2004.

18. Ibid.

19. Ibid.

20. Linklater, AI, August 31, 2004.

21. Kim Krizan, AI, January 28, 2006; "Sundance's Hollywood Horizon," *Washington Post*, January 28, 1995, D01; "Before Sunrise," *Daily Variety*, January 19, 1995.

22. *Daily Variety*, June 17, 2003; see also John Brodie, "Distribs' Marketing Debate Becomes Tale of 3 Cities," *Variety*, February 13, 1995–February 19, 1995, 9; Mick LaSalle, *San Francisco Chronicle*, January 27, 1995, E3; Matt Zoller Seitz, "Before Sunrise," *Dallas Observer*, January 26, 1995.

23. *Daily Variety*, June 17, 2003. See also Box Office Mojo, "Before Sunrise," http://www.boxofficemojo.com/movies/?id=beforesunrise.htm.

24. Walker-McBay, AI, January 26, 2006.

25. Walker, AI, October 18, 2004.

26. Bill Mechanic, AI, June 20, 2006; John Brodie, "Fox lands Linklater's 'Newton,'" *Daily Variety*, October 24, 1995, 3.

27. Amy Lowrey, AI, January 31, 2006.

28. Don Phillips, AI, March 10, 2006; Hawke, AI, March 30, 2006.

29. Walker, AI, October 18, 2004; Walker-McBay, AI, January 26, 2006.

30. Walker, AI, October 18, 2004.

31. Walker, AI, October 18, 2004; Linklater, AI, September 8, 2005.

32. Walker-McBay, AI, January 26, 2006; Fletcher, AI, March 1, 2005.

33. Marjorie Baumgarten, "Subdividing subUrbia," *Austin Chronicle*, February 21, 1997.

34. Monica Roman, "'Shine' Gleams on Top of Exclusive B.O.," *Variety*, February 11, 1997, 17; Baumgarten, "Subdividing subUrbia."

35. Walker-McBay, AI, January 26, 2006; Walker, AI, October 18, 2004.

36. Walker, AI, October 18, 2004.

37. Linklater, AI, September 8, 2005.

38. Matthew McConaughey, AI, May 10, 2006.

39. Baumgarten, "Subdividing subUrbia."

40. Austin Film Society, *20th Anniversary Retrospective*, 26.

41. Elizabeth Peters, AI, October 16, 2003.

42. Ibid.

43. Ibid.

44. Quentin Tarantino, AI, November 11, 2005.

45. Linklater, AI, October 6, 2003; Peters, AI, October 16, 2003.

46. Tarantino, AI, November 30, 2005; Marjorie Baumgarten, "Austin on the Q.T.," *Austin Chronicle*, August 8, 1996, 39.

47. Linklater, AI, August 31, 2004.
48. Stanush, AI, March 7, 2005.
49. Hawke, AI, March 30, 2006; Lowrey, AI, January 31, 2006.
50. Linklater, AI, August 31, 2004; Stanush, AI, March 7, 2005.
51. Fletcher, AI, March 1, 2005.
52. Linklater, AI, August 31, 2004; Peter James, AI, February 13, 2006.
53. Chris Garcia, ""The right place at the right time," *Austin American-Statesman,* June 29, 2001, E3.
54. James, AI, February 13, 2006.
55. Ibid.
56. Catherine Hardwicke, AI, August 18, 2005.
57. Vincent D'Onofrio, AI, April 12, 2006.
58. Jeanette Scott, AI, May 11, 2005; Hardwicke, AI, August 18, 2005.
59. Sandra Adair, AI, February 25, 2006; Linklater, AI, August 31, 2004.
60. "How the West Was Sung," *Austin Chronicle,* March 20, 1998, 8.
61. Ibid., 9; Walker-McBay, AI, January 26, 2006.
62. Linklater, AI, August 31, 2004.
63. Mechanic, AI, June 20, 2006; Adair, AI, February 25, 2006.
64. Phillips, AI, March 10, 2006.
65. Mechanic, AI, June 20, 2006.
66. Hawke, AI, March 30, 2006.
67. Fletcher, AI, March 1, 2005.
68. Hawke, AI, March 30, 2006.
69. Stanush, AI, March 7, 2005; Linklater, AI, September 8, 2005.
70. Kenneth Turan, "The Newton Boys," *Los Angeles Times,* March 27, 1998, 6; Thelma Adams, "The Newton Boys," *New York Post,* March 27, 1998, 45; Richard Schickel, "The Newton Boys," *Time,* April 6, 1998, 70; Amy Taubin, "The Newton Boys," *Village Voice,* March 31, 1998, 68.
71. David Sterritt, "The Newton Boys," *Christian Science Monitor,* April 3, 1998, B3; Taubin, *Village Voice,* 68.
72. "Top 10 US," *The Guardian,* April 3, 1998, 25; "Top Ten Films," *Washington Post,* April 7, 1998, D12; "Box Office," *Variety,* April 20–April 26, 1998, 8; see also Box Office Mojo, "The Newton Boys," http://www.boxofficemojo.com/movies /?id=newtonboys.htm; Mechanic, AI, June 20, 2006.
73. Adair, AI, February 25, 2006.
74. J. Scott, AI, May 11, 2005.
75. Linklater, AI, September 8, 2005; Hawke, AI, March 30, 2006.
76. Linklater, AI, August 31, 2004.
77. Ibid.
78. Stanush, AI, March 7, 2005.
79. D'Onofrio, AI, April 12, 2006.
80. Linklater, AI, September 8, 2005.
81. John Pierson, AI, September 20, 2004.
82. Walker-McBay, AI, January 26, 2006.

83. Linklater, AI, September 8, 2005.
84. Geoffrey Macnab, "Pop: Life, Death, Love, Whatever," *The Independent*, April 19, 2002, 14; Linklater, AI, September 8, 2005.
85. Macnab, "Pop: Life, Death, Love, Whatever," 15.
86. Linklater, AI, October 6, 2003.
87. James, AI, February 13, 2006.
88. Evan Smith, AI, July 14, 2005; Texas Monthly Consumer Marketing, July 2006.
89. Rick Ferguson, AI, July 7, 2006; Julia Null Smith, AI, August 25, 2005.
90. Mechanic, AI, June 20, 2006.
91. Bob Weinstein, AI, September 21, 2005.
92. Jim Jacks, AI, February 7, 2005.
93. Linklater, AI, September 8, 2005.
94. Tarantino, AI, November 30, 2005; Harry Knowles, AI, December 14, 2005.
95. Louis Black, "The Fan," *Texas Monthly*, May 1998, 134; Ibid., 108.
96. Summary of Film/Television Production 1996-November 2003, Texas Film Commission; Evan Smith, "Hooray for Hollywood, Texas," *Texas Monthly*, May 1998, 104-105.

EIGHT

1. Douglas Holt, "Armed militia takes captives in West Texas," *Dallas Morning News*, April 28, 1997, 1A, 8A.
2. Tim McCanlies, AI, August 29, 2005.
3. *Dallas Morning News*, May 7, 1997, 1A.
4. Tim McCanlies, AI, August 29, 2005.
5. Ibid.
6. Ibid.
7. Ibid.
8. Ibid.
9. Ibid.
10. Ibid.
11. Ibid.
12. Joe Flower, *Prince of the Magic Kingdom: Michael Eisner and the Re-Making of Disney* (New York: John Wiley & Sons, 1991), 171; Tim McCanlies, AI, August 29, 2005.
13. Tim McCanlies, AI, August 29, 2005.
14. Ibid.
15. Ibid.
16. Stephen Schiff, "Dizzyland," *Vanity Fair*, November 1985, 121; Tim McCanlies, AI, August 29, 2005.
17. Tim McCanlies, AI, August 29, 2005.
18. Suzanne McCanlies, AI, October 3, 2005.
19. Ibid.
20. Ibid.

21. Tim McCanlies, AI, August 29, 2005.
22. Suzanne McCanlies, AI, October 3, 2005.
23. Tim McCanlies, AI, August 29, 2005; Suzanne McCanlies, AI, October 3, 2005.
24. Tim McCanlies, AI, January 6, 2000.
25. Tim McCanlies, AI, August 29, 2005.
26. Tim McCanlies, AI, August 29, 2005; Michael Burns, AI, January 17, 2006.
27. Tim McCanlies, AI, August 29, 2005; Eddie Mills, AI, May 25, 2006.
28. Mills, AI, May 25, 2006.
29. Suzanne McCanlies, AI, October 3, 2005.
30. Mills, AI, May 25, 2006.
31. Suzanne McCanlies, AI, October 3, 2005.
32. Tim McCanlies, AI, August 29, 2005; Burns, AI, January 17, 2006.
33. Suzanne McCanlies, AI, October 3, 2005; Tim McCanlies, AI, August 29, 2005.
34. Tim McCanlies, AI August 29, 2005; Burns, AI, January 17, 2006.
35. Burns, AI, January 17, 2006.
36. Tim McCanlies, AI, August 29, 2005.
37. Suzanne McCanlies, AI, October 3, 2005.
38. Ibid.
39. Ibid.
40. Tim McCanlies, AI, August 29, 2005.
41. Bill Scott, AI, June 29, 2005; Tom Copeland, AI, July 16, 2006.
42. Scott, AI, June 29, 2005; Copeland, AI, July 16, 2006.
43. Ken Rector, AI, April 25, 2006.
44. Rector, AI, April 25, 2006; David Robb, "D. Tolla Seeks National Film Pact," *Hollywood Reporter*, November 9, 1993; Nick Madigan, "IATSE Reaches Agreement in South," *Daily Variety*, January 5, 1999, 6.
45. Benjamin Cheng, "Hollywood actors descend on Texas town for movie," *Odessa American*, June 14, 1997; Tim McCanlies, AI August 29, 2005; Copeland, AI, July 16, 2006.
46. Suzanne McCanlies, AI, October 3, 2005; Tim McCanlies, AI, August 29, 2005.
47. Mills, AI, May 25, 2006. Embry and Meyer declined to be interviewed. Facinelli did not respond to multiple interview requests.
48. Andrew Dintenfass, AI, March 2, 2006.
49. Tim McCanlies, AI, August 29, 2005.
50. Ibid.
51. Suzanne McCanlies, AI, October 3, 2005.
52. Dintenfass, AI, March 2, 2006.
53. Tim McCanlies, AI, August 29, 2005.
54. Dan Cox, "Stock Pic Hot Buy," *Daily Variety*, July 1, 1997, n.p.
55. Tim McCanlies, AI, August 29, 2005.
56. Ibid.
57. Ibid.
58. Ibid.
59. Ibid.

60. Ibid.

61. Mills, AI, May 25, 2006.

62. Emanuel Levy, "SXSW taps local flavor," *Variety*, March 23–March 29, 1998, 12.

63. Emanuel Levy, "Dancer, TX," *Variety*, March 23–March 29, 1998, 87, 88.

64. Burns, AI, January 17, 2006; Tim McCanlies, AI, August 29, 2005.

65. Jimmy Fowler, "That sinking feeling," *Dallas Observer*, April 9, 1998.

66. Box office reports (courtesy of Suzanne McCanlies).

67. Rob Patterson, "In small Texas town, staying and leaving are equally hard," *Austin American-Statesman*, May 1, 1998, E3; Louis B. Parks, "Dancer, an ode to small-town life," *Houston Chronicle*, May 1, 1998, F1 and F6.

68. Stephen Holden, "Change Ripples Through a Tiny Town," *New York Times*, May 1, 1998, E14; Michael Rechtshaffen, "'Dancer, Texas Pop. 81' is the motion picture equivalent of the town it portrays," *Hollywood Reporter*, May 1, 1998; Monica Eng, "Believable 'Dancer, Texas' gives a glimpse into small-town life," *Chicago Tribune*, May 1, 1998, M.

69. Kenneth Turan, "A Warm-Hearted Visit to Small Town of 'Dancer, Texas,'" *Los Angeles Times*, May 1, 1998, F6; Eng, *Chicago Tribune*, M; Amy Taubin, "Dancer, Texas Pop. 81," *Village Voice*, May 5, 1998, 119.

70. Rechtshaffen, *Hollywood Reporter*.

71. Box office reports (courtesy of Suzanne McCanlies); Burns, AI, January 17, 2006.

72. Tim McCanlies, AI, August 29, 2005.

73. Ibid.

74. Roger Ebert, "The Iron Giant," *Chicago Sun-Times*, August 6, 1999; Alison Macor, "Easy Writer," *Texas Monthly*, July 2000, 94; "Less Than '00," *Premiere*, January 2000, 75.

75. Suzanne McCanlies, AI, October 3, 2005.

## NINE

1. Chris Garcia, "Workaday world provides model for Judge's satire," *Austin-American Statesman*, February 19, 1999, E1.

2. Mike Judge, AI, November 8, 2005; Tim Suhrstedt, AI, November 29, 2005; Judge, AI, November 8, 2005.

3. Judge, AI, August 31, 2005.

4. Ibid.

5. Evan Smith, "Mike Judge," *Texas Monthly*, October 2004, 114.

6. Charles M. Young, "Meet the Beavis! The Last Word From America's Phenomenal Pop Combo," *Rolling Stone*, March 24, 1994, 38–40.

7. Brad Bucholz, "Judge Rules," *Austin American-Statesman*, January 5, 1995.

8. Judge, AI, August 31, 2005.

9. Smith, "Mike Judge," 116.

10. Ibid., 114.

11. Judge, AI, August 31, 2005.

12. Although the timing of the call coincided with the festival screening, *Liquid Television* had actually seen the short courtesy of Dallas animator Paul Claerhout. In 1991 Judge had finally met Claerhout, whose short film *Scaredy Cat* had first inspired Judge. It was Claerhout who sent "Frog Baseball" to a contact at MTV.

13. Terry Kattleman, "A Boy's Life," *Advertising Age*, July 5, 1993, 19; Judge, AI, August 31, 2005.

14. Judge, AI, August 31, 2005.

15. Judge, AI, August 31, 2005; Elizabeth Kolbert, "Keeping Beavis and Butt-head Just Stupid Enough," *New York Times*, October 17, 1993, 33.

16. Kattleman, "A Boy's Life," 19.

17. Judge, AI, August 31, 2005.

18. Bucholz, "Judge Rules," January 5, 1995.

19. Judge, AI, August 31, 2005.

20. *Daily Variety*, December 13, 1994, 1; Judge, AI, August 31, 2005.

21. Elizabeth Avellán, AI, April 28, 2005.

22. Judge, AI, August 31, 2005.

23. Stephen Holden, "Hormones Coursing O'er the Land," *New York Times*, December 20, 1996, C18.

24. Chris Petrikin, "Judge to helm Fox's 'Office,'" *Daily Variety*, January 26, 1998, 1; see also Box Office Mojo, "Beavis and Butt-head Do America," http://www.boxofficemojo.com/movies/?id=beavisandbuttheaddoamerica.htm.

25. Smith, "Mike Judge," 118; Judge, AI, August 31, 2005.

26. Judge, AI, August 31, 2005.

27. Ibid.

28. Smith, "Mike Judge," 118.

29. Stephen Root, AI, August 5, 2005.

30. Caryn James, "Like Life, Somewhat, Yet Quite Unlike It," *New York Times*, January 11, 1997, 23; Marc Savlov, "Work Release," *Austin Chronicle*, February 19, 1999.

31. Savlov, "Work Release," February 19, 1999.

32. Garcia, "Workaday World," February 19, 1999, E1; Judge, AI, August 31, 2005; Ibid.

33. Judge, AI, August 31, 2005.

34. Petrikin, "Judge to helm Fox's 'Office,'" 1.

35. Savlov, "Work Release," February 19, 1999; Suhrstedt, AI, November 29, 2005.

36. Judge, AI, August 31, 2005.

37. Ibid.

38. Ron Livingston, AI, April 5, 2006; Judge, AI, August 31, 2005.

39. Root, AI, August 5, 2005.

40. Smith, "Mike Judge," 122.

41. Bill Mechanic, AI, June 20, 2006.

42. Judge, AI, August 31, 2005.

43. Savlov, "Work Release," February 19, 1999; Suhrstedt, AI, November 29, 2005.

44. Suhrstedt, AI, November 29, 2005.

45. Root, AI, August 5, 2005.

46. Dave Rennie, AI, January 11, 2006.
47. Livingston, AI, April 5, 2006.
48. Judge, AI, November 8, 2005.
49. Livingston, AI, April 5, 2006.
50. Suhrstedt, AI, November 29, 2005; Rennie, AI, January 11, 2006; Eric Lewy, AI, February 7, 2006; Rennie, AI, January 11, 2006.
51. Root, AI, August 5, 2005.
52. Ibid.
53. Gary Cole, AI, April 25, 2006.
54. Judge, AI, November 8, 2005.
55. Rennie, AI, January 11, 2006.
56. Rennie, AI, January 11, 2006; Judge, AI, November 8, 2005.
57. Judge, AI, November 8, 2005.
58. Ibid.
59. Judge, AI, August 31, 2005.
60. Richard Linklater, AI, September 8, 2005; Suhrstedt, AI, November 29, 2005.
61. Mechanic, AI, June 20, 2006.
62. Root, AI, August 5, 2005.
63. Bob Ivry, "Workaday World," *Record*, February 18, 1999, Y03; Livingston, AI, April 5, 2006.
64. Roger Cels, "New Three May Be Crowded," *Hollywood Reporter*, February 19, 1999; "Weekend Analysis," *Hollywood Reporter*, February 23, 1999.
65. Jeff Millar, "Office Space," *Houston Chronicle*, February 19, 1999, 1; Kevin Thomas, "Office Space," *Los Angeles Times* Calendar, February 19, 1999, 6; Peter Rainer, "Office Space," *New York*, March 1, 1999, 92.
66. Stephen Holden, "One Big Happy Family?" *New York Times*, February 19, 1999, E14; Joe Leydon, "Office Space," *Daily Variety*, February 16, 1999, 2.
67. Dave Herman, AI, May 1, 2006.
68. Root, AI, August 5, 2005; Gene Seymour, "Office Space," *Newsday*, February 19, 1999, II:B7.
69. Box Office Mojo, "Office Space," http://www.boxofficemojo.com/movies/?id=officespace.htm.
70. Judge, AI, August 31, 2005; Judge, AI, November 8, 2005.
71. Cole, AI, April 25, 2006.
72. Root, AI, August 5, 2005.
73. Cole, AI, April 25, 2006.
74. "The Fax of Live," *Entertainment Weekly*, May 23, 2003; Mechanic, AI, June 20, 2006.
75. Judge, AI, November 8, 2005.
76. Suhrstedt, AI, November 29, 2005.
77. Nick Powilss, "Livingston's Acting Ability Drives Success," *Lumino*, March 2004, http://www.luminomagazine.com/2004.03/spotlight/officespace/livingstont.html; Suhrstedt, AI, November 29, 2005.
78. Savlov, "Work Release," February 19, 1999; Smith, "Mike Judge," 122.

TEN

1. Elizabeth Avellán, AI, April 28, 2005; production overview, Troublemaker Studios.
2. Avellán, AI, April 28, 2005.
3. Chris Garcia, "The Tao of Rodriguez," *Austin American-Statesman, XLent,* March 29, 2001, 14; Avellán, AI, April 28, 2005.
4. Robert Rodriguez, AI, August 11, 2005.
5. Quentin Tarantino, AI, November 30, 2005; Rodriguez, AI, August 11, 2005.
6. Bob Weinstein, AI, September 21, 2005.
7. Bill Scott, AI, June 29, 2005.
8. Production overview, Troublemaker Studios; Jeanette Scott, AI, May 11, 2005.
9. B. Scott, AI, June 29, 2005; Rodriguez, AI, August 11, 2005.
10. Avellán, AI, April 28, 2005.
11. J. Scott, AI, May 11, 2005.
12. Weinstein, AI, September 21, 2005.
13. Thom Geier, *Hollywood Reporter,* October 16, 1998; Roger Cels, *Hollywood Reporter,* December 24, 1998.
14. Brian Fuson, "Williams starrer earns $25.3 mil.," *Hollywood Reporter,* December 28, 1998; Dennis Harvey, "The Faculty," *Daily Variety,* December 28, 1998, 2.
15. Rodriguez, AI, August 11, 2005.
16. B. Scott, AI, June 29, 2005; Knowles, "Harry Adds Comments," Ain't It Cool News, April 4, 2000, http://www.aintitcool.com/node/5567.
17. Weinstein, AI, September 21, 2005.
18. Pete Laney, AI, January 26, 2006.
19. B. Scott, AI, June 29, 2005.
20. Alexa Vega, AI, May 26, 2006.
21. Rodriguez, AI, August 11, 2005.
22. Daryl Sabara, AI, March 29, 2006.
23. Carla Gugino, AI, May 25, 2006; Rodriguez, AI, August 11, 2005.
24. Cary White, AI, June 30, 2004.
25. Gugino, AI, May 25, 2006; Anonymous.
26. Gugino, AI, May 25, 2006; Vega, AI, May 26, 2006.
27. B. Scott, AI, June 29, 2005.
28. Gugino, AI, May 25, 2006.
29. Rodriguez, AI, August 11, 2005.
30. Ibid.
31. Knowles, "SPY KIDS Site Goes Live," Ain't It Cool News, October 26, 2000, http://www.aintitcool.com/node/7294; Rodriguez, AI, August 11, 2005.
32. Robert Newman, AI, February 24, 2006; Carl DiOrio, "B.O. Swordfight," *Daily Variety,* March 30, 2001, 1.
33. Knowles, "Zboneman Reports," Ain't It Cool News, March 8, 2001, http://www.aintitcool.com/?q=node/8348; DiOrio, "B.O Swordfight," 1.

34. Carl DiOrio, "'Spy' Steals B.O. Kitty," *Daily Variety*, April 2, 2001, 1.
35. Weinstein, AI, September 21, 2005; DiOrio, "'Spy' Steals B.O. Kitty," 1; Weinstein, AI, September 21, 2005.
36. Rodriguez, AI, August 11, 2005.
37. Eric Harrison, "Spy Kids," *Houston Chronicle*, March 30, 2001, 1; Mick LaSalle, "Spy Kids," *San Francisco Chronicle*, March 30, 2001; Jeff Strickler, "'Spy' High," *Star Tribune*, March 30, 2001, 26.
38. Elvis Mitchell, "Espionage Is the Family Business," *New York Times*, March 30, 2001, E12; Gary Arnold, "No Secret to Film Director's Success," *Washington Times*, March 30, 2001, C5.
39. Roger Ebert, "Spy Kids," *Chicago Sun-Times*, March 30, 2001.
40. Andy Seiler, Bill Keveney, Edna Gundersen, "Special-edition 'Spy Kids' adds sharks for more bite," *USA Today*, May 11, 2001, 1E.
41. *Austin Chronicle*, August 3, 2001; Carlos Gallardo, AI, May 26, 2006.
42. Newman, AI, February 24, 2006.
43. George Lucas, AI, June 13, 2006.
44. Mike Snider, "The digital force is with big-time directors," *USA Today*, August 5, 2002, 4D.
45. Avellán, AI, April 28, 2005.
46. White, AI, June 30, 2004.
47. Marla Matzer Rose and Zorianna Kit, "'Spy Kids' duo reteaming for 'Mexico' entry," *Hollywood Reporter*, May 9, 2001, n.p.; Avellán, AI, April 28, 2005.
48. *Video Business*, October 1, 2001, 27.
49. B. Scott, AI, June 29, 2005.
50. White, AI, June 30, 2004.
51. Avellán, AI, April 28, 2005.
52. Ibid.
53. Anonymous.
54. Gugino, AI, May 25, 2006.
55. Production documents, Troublemaker Studios; Lucas, AI, June 13, 2006.
56. Documents, Troublemaker Studios; Avellán, AI, April 28, 2005; Weinstein, AI, September 21, 2005.
57. Brian Fuson, "September to remember at b.o.," *Hollywood Reporter Online*, September 30, 2003, http://web.lexis-nexis.com.content.lib.utexas.edu:2048 /universe; A. O. Scott, "Once Upon a Time in Mexico," *New York Times*, September 12, 2003, E12.
58. Sabara, AI, March 29, 2006.
59. Tarantino, AI, November 30, 2005.
60. Austin Film Society, *20th Anniversary Retrospective*, 2006, 26.
61. Rebecca Campbell, AI, April 25, 2005.
62. Anne del Castillo, AI, March 15, 2006.
63. Campbell, AI, April 25, 2005; del Castillo, AI, March 15, 2006.
64. Kirk Watson, AI, July 6, 2006.

65. Stan Ginsel, AI, December 14, 2005.
66. David Elliott, "Senate bill could have Texas going Hollywood," *Austin American-Statesman*, May 5, 1995, B3; Carol Pirie, AI, December 9, 2003.
67. Richard Linklater, AI, September 8, 2005.
68. Watson, AI, July 6, 2006.
69. Campbell, AI, April 25, 2005.
70. Campbell, AI, June 16, 2005; Shermakaye Bass, "Boosting films and the community," *Austin American-Statesman*, February 19, 2000, D8.
71. Ginsel, AI, December 14, 2005.
72. Cathy Crane, AI, June 5, 2005.
73. Linklater, AI, September 8, 2005.
74. Ginsel, AI, December 14, 2005.
75. Linklater, AI, September 8, 2005.
76. Crane, AI, January 5, 2005.
77. Suzanne Quinn, AI, January 19, 2006.
78. Charles Ramírez Berg, AI, October 24, 2003.
79. Evan Smith, AI, June 17, 2005.
80. Ramírez Berg, AI, October 24, 2003.
81. Smith, AI, June 17, 2005.
82. Ibid.
83. Ibid.
84. Ibid.
85. Louis Black, AI, December 13, 2004.
86. del Castillo, AI, March 15, 2006.
87. Black, AI, December 13, 2004.
88. Smith, AI, June 17, 2005.
89. Black, AI, December 13, 2004.
90. Smith, AI, June 17, 2005.
91. Ibid.
92. Ibid.
93. Campbell, AI, April 25, 2005.
94. Ibid.
95. Harry Knowles, AI, December 14, 2005.
96. *Texas Film Hall of Fame Awards*, VHS, 2001, Austin Film Society.
97. Ibid.
98. Michael Corcoran, *Austin American-Statesman*, March 10, 2001, B1.
99. Smith, AI, June 17, 2005.
100. Black, AI, December 13, 2004.
101. Tarantino, AI, November 30, 2005; Black, AI, December 13, 2004; Corcoran, March 10, 2001, B1; Tarantino, AI, November 30, 2005.
102. Campbell, AI, April 25, 2005.
103. "Lone Stars," *Austin Chronicle*, March 16, 2001; *Texas Film Hall of Fame Awards*, VHS, 2001, Austin Film Society.
104. Smith, AI, July 14, 2005.

105. *Texas Film Hall of Fame Awards*, VHS, 2001, Austin Film Society.
106. *Texas Film Hall of Fame Awards*, VHS, 2001, Austin Film Society.
107. Campbell, AI, April 25, 2005.
108. Smith, AI, June 17, 2005.
109. Ibid.


CONCLUSION

1. "Film Box Office Wrap," *Daily Variety*, October 7, 2003, 12.
2. Cathy Crane, AI, January 5, 2005.
3. Ethan Hawke, AI, March 20, 2006.
4. Richard Linklater, AI, September 8, 2005.
5. Louis Black, "Page Two," *Austin Chronicle*, March 22, 2002; Tim McCanlies, AI, August 29, 2005.
6. Elizabeth Avellán, AI, April 28, 2005; "Film Box Office Wrap," 12.
7. Mike Judge, AI, November 8, 2005.
8. McCanlies, AI, January 6, 2000.
9. Patrick Taggart, "Focusing in Eaglevision," *Austin Chronicle*, March 11, 1994, 48; Steve McVicker, "Fade to Black: The Wasted Life of Texas Filmmaker Eagle Pennell," *Houston Press*, October 14, 1999, 3.
10. E. Pennell documents (courtesy of Chuck Pinnell); Chuck Pinnell, AI, August 23, 2004.
11. Dorothy Pearl, AI, March 14, 2006.
12. Chris Garcia, *Austin American-Statesman*, August 23, 2007, E1.
13. Matt Dentler, AI, November 22, 2004.
14. Suzanne Quinn, AI, January 19, 2006; Dentler, AI, November 22, 2004; *Daily Variety*, March 12, 1997.
15. Marsha Milam, AI, July 2, 2004.
16. "The Ten Best Theaters in America," *Entertainment Weekly*, August 12, 2005.
17. Joe O'Connell, "Changes in the Weather," *Austin Chronicle*, January 18, 2008; Chris Garcia, "Unable to Turn Profit, UT Rethinks Film Venture," *Austin American-Statesman*, July 5, 2008, A1.
18. Josh Rosenblatt, "Building Buzz, One 'Bag' at a Time," *Austin Chronicle*, June 6, 2008, 61.
19. Quinn, AI, January 19, 2006; Joe O'Connell, "Studio Involvement," *Austin Chronicle*, July 6, 2007.
20. Richard Whittaker, "Gov. Perry signs film incentives bill into law," *Austin Chronicle*, May 1, 2009, 53; see also "Gov. Perry signs HB 873 to Provide Incentives for Entertainment Industries," Texas Film Commission Web site, April 23, 2009, http:// governor.state.tx.us/film/news-detail/12279.
21. Joe O'Connell, "Abandoning the Nest," *Austin Chronicle*, May 23, 2008, 54, 55.
22. Chris Garcia, "Slow Dissolve," *Austin American-Statesman*, October 31, 2008, D4.
23. Dentler, AI, November 22, 2004.

# Selected Bibliography

Abramowitz, Rachel. *Is That a Gun in Your Pocket? Women's Experience of Power in Hollywood*. New York: Random House, 2000.

Biskind, Peter. *Down and Dirty Pictures: Miramax, Sundance, and the Rise of Independent Film*. New York: Simon & Schuster, 2004.

———. *Easy Riders, Raging Bulls: How the Sex-Drugs-and-Rock 'n' Roll Generation Saved Hollywood*. New York: Simon & Schuster, 1998.

Dunne, John Gregory. *The Studio*. New York: Farrar, Straus & Giroux, 1969.

Flower, Joe. *Prince of the Magic Kingdom: Michael Eisner and the Re-Making of Disney*. New York: John Wiley & Sons, 1991.

Harden, Tim. "The Texas Chainsaw Massacre: A Visit to the Film Locations." http://www.texaschainsawmassacre.net/.

Hoberman, J., and Jonathan Rosenbaum. *Midnight Movies*. New York: Da Capo Press, 1983/1991.

Hollyman, Burnes St. Patrick. "The First Picture Shows: 1894–1913." In *Film Before Griffith*, edited by John L. Fell, 188–195. Berkeley: University of California Press, 1983.

Horton, Robert. "Stranger Than Texas." *Film Comment* (July–August 1990): 77–78.

Jaworzyn, Stefan. *The Texas Chain Saw Massacre Companion*. London: Titan Books, 2003.

Knowles, Harry, Paul Cullum, and Mark Ebner. *Ain't It Cool?: Hollywood's Redheaded Stepchild Speaks Out*. New York: Warner Books, 2002.

Levy, Emanuel. *Cinema of Outsiders: The Rise of American Independent Film*. New York: New York University Press, 1999.

Linklater, Richard. *Slacker*. New York: St. Martin's Press, 1992.

Milner, Jay Dunston. *Confessions of a Maddog: A Romp through the High-flying Texas Music and Literary Era of the Fifties to the Seventies.* Denton, Texas: University of North Texas Press, 1998.

Mottram, James. *The Sundance Kids: How the Mavericks Took Back Hollywood.* New York: Faber and Faber, 2006.

Nelson, Willie, and Edwin Shrake. *Willie: An Autobiography.* New York: Simon & Schuster, 1988.

Pierson, John. *Spike, Mike Reloaded: A Guided Tour across a Decade of American Independent Cinema.* New York: Hyperion/Miramax, 2003.

Pinckard, Elaine. *Alternative Film Organizations in Austin: A Historical Examination of Their Roles and Functions within the Community.* Unpublished Master's thesis, University of Texas at Austin, 1990.

Reid, Jan. *The Improbable Rise of Redneck Rock: New Edition.* Austin: University of Texas Press, 2004.

Rodriguez, Robert. *Rebel Without a Crew: Or How a 23-Year-Old Filmmaker with $7,000 Became a Hollywood Player.* New York: Dutton, 1995.

Smith, Lory. *Party in a Box: The Story of the Sundance Film Festival.* Salt Lake City: Gibbs Smith Publisher, 1999.

Waxman, Natasha. *Warren Skaaren: Screenwriter: His life, films, and letters.* Austin: Harry Ransom Humanities Research Center, University of Texas at Austin.

Wheeler, Kenneth W. *To Wear a City's Crown: The Beginnings of Urban Growth in Texas, 1836-1865.* Cambridge: Harvard University Press, 1968.

# Index

Academy of Motion Picture Arts and Sciences, 19, 77

Adair, Dwight, 167, 294

Adair, Sandra, 11, 47, 294, 314; *Dazed and Confused,* 167-170; *The Newton Boys,* 208, 210, 213

Affleck, Ben, 152, 159, 161-162, 179, 261-262

Ain't It Cool News (AICN), 218, 219-220

Alamo Drafthouse Theater, 47, 309-311

Allain, Stephanie, 116, 131-132, 133, 135, 137, 141-145

Alvarado-Dykstra, Paul, 311

Anders, Allison, 89, 145-146

Anger, Kenneth, 8, 153

*Animal House* (1978), 153, 156, 252

Aniston, Jennifer, 250, 263, 269

Arau, Alfonso, 118

Armadillo World Headquarters, 11, 51, 69, 70, 75

Armstrong, R. G., 84

*Austin Chronicle,* The, 87, 91, 177, 199, 310; creation of, 64, 68-70; and Linklater, 91; and Rodriguez, 129-130, 286

Austin City Limits, 51

Austin Community College, 90, 92

Austin Fantasy Film Festival, 181

Austin Film Center, 208, 264, 296

Austin Film Festival, 180, 181, 182-187, 310

Austin Film Office, 294

Austin Film Society (AFS): and Austin Studios, 293-297, 313; creation of, 87-88, 91; and DGA Honors Award, 88, 295; early years of, 92-94, 108-109; *Pulp Fiction* screening, 203; strategic plan for, 291-293; Texas Film Hall of Fame, 298-299, 303; Texas Filmmakers' Production Fund (TFPF), 202, 203, 292

Austin Film & Video Society, 182

Austin FilmWorks, 309, 311

Austin Gay and Lesbian International Film Festival (AGLIFF), 181

Austin Heart of Film Festival. *See* Austin Film Festival

Austin Studios, 2, 274, 291, 293, 294-297, 313

Avellán, Elizabeth: background of, 118; *Desperado,* 142-145; *El Mariachi,* 123, 127, 130, 132, 134-135, 138;

*The Faculty*, 276-278; family of, 147, 273, 282; on Harvey and Bob Weinstein, 148; *Once Upon a Time in Mexico*, 287-288, 306; and Rodriguez, 118, 143, 147, 149, 273, 274, 289, 291, 306; *Spy Kids*, 281, 282-283, 284, 286, 291; *Spy Kids 2: Island of Lost Dreams*, 289, 290; and Texas Film Hall of Fame, 301

*Baghead* (2008), 312, 314
Baldwin, Craig, 93, 109
Banderas, Antonio, 137, 142, 275, 280-281, 283, 287, 288
Barbaro, Nick, 64-65, 67, 68-70, 182-186
*Barbarosa* (1982), 74, 78, 79, 185
Barker, Michael: background of, 7, 106; and Orion Pictures, 106, 111, 113, 114; *Slacker*, 106, 109, 111, 112, 113, 114; and Sony Pictures Classics, 135, 153, 199
Barnes, Danny, 209
Barnes, Dr. W. E., 23, 26, 30
Barrios, Greg, 8
Baumgarten, Marjorie, 7, 67, 69, 83
Bearden, Steve, 38, 66, 68, 309
*Beavis and Butt-head* (TV), 253-255, 257-258, 260
*Beavis and Butt-head Do America* (1996), 257, 261
*Bedhead* (1991), 117-121, 129, 130-131, 132, 273, 276, 285
*Before Sunrise* (1995), 188-190, 192-194, 195
Beiersdorf, Fred, 36, 38
Bell, Wayne, 19, 23, 33, 52, 54, 233
Benton, Robert, 1, 191, 299
Berg, Charles Ramírez: and Austin Film Society, 203, 292, 297, 303; and CinemaTexas, 8, 66; and Rodriguez, 141, 274
Berlin International Film Festival, 61, 102, 129, 195, 307
Berman, David, 8

Bernard, Tom, 106, 135, 153, 199
*Beverly Hills Cop* (1984), 222, 227
Bigley, Ivan, 10-11, 167, 208, 293-294
Black, Louis, 85, 129, 203, 211, 274, 305; and the *Austin Chronicle*, 69, 70; and the Austin Film Festival, 182-184, 186; background of, 67; and South by Southwest (SXSW), 182-185, 186; and Texas Film Hall of Fame, 1-2
*Blood Simple* (1984), 11, 63, 156
Bond, Gary, 294
*Bonnie and Clyde* (1967), 2, 191, 211, 251, 299
Boone, David, 71, 89-90
Borden, Bill, 141, 142, 144-145
*Boyz N the Hood* (1991), 116, 143
Bozman, Ron, 13, 18, 22, 24, 26-27, 31, 33, 37, 41
Bramhall, Doyle, 252, 256
*Brother from Another Planet, The* (1984), 83
Broyles, Bill, 15, 73, 184-185, 200, 220, 229
Bruckheimer, Jerry, 83
Bryanston Pictures, 36-38, 40-44. See also *The Texas Chainsaw Massacre*
Bullock, Sandra, 212, 217, 280
Burns, Marilyn, 18, 21, 24, 31-32, 38, 39
Burns, Michael, 232, 235, 242, 244, 246, 247
Burns, Robert (Bob), 22-23, 27, 28, 29, 33, 38, 40, 41, 77
Burnt Orange Productions, 312
Butthole Surfers, 98, 312

Calley, John, 235, 241-242
Cameron, John, 151, 157, 162, 163-164, 172
Campbell, Rebecca, 2, 291-292, 294-297, 299, 300, 302, 314
Candler, Kat, 311
Cannes Film Festival, 40, 130, 142, 147-148, 203, 312
Carpenter, John, 117, 143
Carroll, Larry, 9, 23, 26, 32-34

Carson, "Goat," 50
Carson, L. M. Kit, 5-6, 46, 50, 51
Cartwright, Gary, 7, 222, 303
*Cassidy Kids, The* (2006), 311, 312
Castle Rock, 196, 197, 199
Change the Reel Festival, 51, 181
*cicadas* (2000), 311
Cine Las Americas International Film
    Festival, 310
Cinema 40 Film Society, 8, 9, 20, 22, 38,
    66
Cinemaker Co-op, 309
CinemaTexas, 8-9, 40, 66-68, 309
CinemaTexas International Short Film
    Festival, 309, 311
Cine-Mex, 127
*Citizen's Band* (1977), 82, 244
Claerhout, Paul, 251, 338n12
Clayton, William, 279-280
Code and Ratings Administration, 33
Coen, Ethan, 11, 63, 156
Coen, Joel, 11, 63, 156
Coger, Lara, 310
Cokinos, Katie, 99, 102, 103, 104, 106,
    109, 111-112, 184, 202
Cole, Gary, 262-263, 266, 271
Columbia Pictures, 36, 185-186, 230,
    236; and *Desperado*, 140-148; and *El
    Mariachi*, 115, 116, 130-134, 136-
    137, 138, 139; and *Once Upon a Time
    in Mexico*, 287
*Comin' Back to Go*, 53. See also *The
    Whole Shootin' Match*
Cooper, Dawn, 309
Copeland, Tom, 3, 10, 85-86, 125-126,
    222, 232, 236-238
Coppola, Francis Ford, 2, 77, 291
*Country* (1984), 74, 78, 83
Coupland, Douglas, 111, 114
Crane, Cathy, 9, 294-296, 304
Craven, Don, 208
Cullum, Paul, 191

*Daily Texan, The*, 69, 70, 119, 148
Dal-Art, 36

Dallas: film production in, 5-6
*Dallas* (TV), 6, 49
*Dancer, Texas Pop. 81* (1998): box office
    and critical reception, 243-246; dis-
    tribution, 242, 244-245; financing,
    231-232, 235-236; home video and
    DVD release, 246; postproduction,
    240; preproduction, 221-222, 223-
    224, 232-233; production, 233-236,
    239-240; and Sony Pictures, 235-236,
    241-243, 244
Daniel, Bill, 109
Daniel, Frank, 82
Daniel, Lee, 199, 206; and Austin Film
    Society, 87, 91-94; background of, 9,
    47, 90; *Before Sunrise*, 180, 190, 193,
    195; *Dazed and Confused*, 152, 154,
    157, 164, 165, 167; and Linklater, 87,
    90, 91-92, 150, 154, 205; *Slacker*, 95,
    96-97, 99-100, 101, 104, 107, 108,
    112
Daniels, Greg, 258-259
Dano, Royal, 84, 85
Danziger, Allen, 25
Davis, Bob, 7
Davis, Sonny Carl, 79, 109; *A Hell of a
    Note*, 51-52, 53; *The Whole Shootin'
    Match*, 49, 56-58, 60, 62, 63
*Day Before Tomorrow (The Day After Yes-
    terday), The*. See *Slacker*
*Dazed and Confused* (1993): box office
    and critical reception, 173, 177-179;
    casting, 158-159; distribution, 169-
    170; marketing, 175-176; postproduc-
    tion, 167-172; preproduction, 155-
    157, 159-163; production, 150-151,
    163-167; soundtrack, 168, 170, 171,
    172-175, 179-180
*Dear Pillow* (2004), 311-312
Decker, Craig "Spike," 254
*Deep Throat* (1972), 18, 36, 40, 42, 43
DeForest, Kris, 309
Del Castillo, Anne, 292, 293, 298
Del Toro, Guillermo, 305-306
Delpy, Julie, 189, 193, 195

Demme, Jonathan, 65, 71, 82-83, 157, 220, 244

Dentler, Matt, 309, 310, 311, 314

*Desperado* (1995), 137, 141, 142-147, 148

Detour Filmproduction: *Before Sunrise*, 188, 192-194, 208; creation of, 89, 96; *Dazed and Confused*, 152; *The Newton Boys*, 191, 196, 201, 206, 209, 213, 294

*Dime Box*. See *Kid Blue*

Dimension Films, 148, 285, 286, 287, 290-291

Dinger, Scott, 87-88, 104-105, 107, 111, 129, 181

Dintenfass, Andrew, 223, 233, 239, 240

Dishner, Joe, 64-65, 66, 68-70

Dobie Theatre (Dobie 1 & 2), 87-88, 91-92, 95, 104-105, 106, 107, 111, 181

*Doc's Full Service* (1994), 49, 184, 307

Donner, Stanley, 6

D'Onofrio, Vincent, 210, 204, 207, 208, 212, 214

Draper, Robert, 185

Dugan, John, 30, 31, 318n30

Duplass, Jay, 312, 314

Duplass, Mark, 312, 314

Dütsch, Werner, 101

Earl Miller Productions, 10

Eastwood, Clint, 185, 307

*Easy Rider* (1969), 2, 12, 68, 310

Ebert, Roger, 49, 61, 135, 176, 195, 247, 286

*Eggshells* (1969), 10, 15, 19-20, 22-23, 25

Eisner, Michael, 74, 227, 228

*El Mariachi* (1992): box office and critical reception, 135, 138-140; distribution, 127-129, 133, 136; festivals, 134-135, 138-139; financing, 121; postproduction, 123-124, 134; preproduction, 121-122; production, 122-123

Embry, Ethan, 233, 239

English, Marc, 300

English, Paul, 81

Erwin, Frank, 68

*Escape From New York* (1981), 117

Esther's Follies, 8, 90

*Everlasting Secret Family, The* (1988), 181

*Excess Baggage* (1997), 186

*Exorcist, The* (1973), 35, 39, 43, 226

Facinelli, Peter, 233, 239

*Faculty, The* (1998), 250, 274-275, 276-280, 282, 286, 291, 293

Fairchild, Morgan, 79, 80, 81-82, 85

Falomir, Raoul, 122-123

Fantastic Fest, 311

Farmer, Ray, 90

*Fast Times at Ridgemont High* (1982), 49, 152, 156, 157, 159

Filmhouse, 9, 10, 11, 19, 34, 51

Film-Mex, 127

501 Studios, 71, 289

Fletcher, Keith, 156, 166, 190-191, 198, 205, 211

Fletcher, Melanie, 156

Foote, Horton, 82

*For All Mankind* (1989), 185

Ford, John, 50

Foster, Chase, 232, 238

Foster, David, 14, 36, 44

*Four Rooms* (1995), 145-146, 275-276

Fracasso, Michael, 180

Franklin, Jim, 70

Frick, John, 151, 155, 206

*Friday Night Lights* (2004), 216

*Friday Night Lights* (TV), 65, 216

*Friday Night Lights: A Town, a Team, and a Dream* (Bissinger), 215

Friedkin, William, 43

*From Dusk Till Dawn* (1996), 146-148, 219, 273, 277, 285

Funderburgh, Anson, 251, 252

Galán, Hector, 185

Gallardo, Carlos: background of, 116-117; *Desperado*, 127, 141-144; *El Mariachi*, 120-121, 122-123, 127-

129, 135, 138; *Once Upon a Time in Mexico*, 288; and Rodriguez, 116-117, 137, 144, 286
Gallegly, Dick, 78, 79
Galloway, Sheri, 167, 208
Gein, Ed, 25-26, 39
*Generation X*, 111, 114
*Getaway, The* (1972), 14, 36
Giant Records, 174-175
Gibson, Mel, 261, 311
Ginsel, Stan, 208, 293-296
Glass, Thomas, 37, 44
Godard, Jean-Luc, 3, 8, 66
*Godfather, The* (1972), 68, 148
Goldberg, Adam, 159, 160, 165, 166, 171, 178
*Good Will Hunting* (1997), 261-262
Goodin, Courtney, 9, 33
Gosling, Maureen, 51, 181
*Graduate, The* (1967), 2, 68, 310
Gramercy Pictures, 169, 170, 175-176
Gribble, Mike, 254
Grigson, Charles, 45
Grokenberger, Otto, 101, 102
Guber, Peter, 133
Gugino, Carla, 281-282, 283, 288, 289

Hall, Jerry, 12-14
Halle, David, 180
Haney, Richard, 34
Hansen, Brian, 71, 90
Hansen, Gunnar, 26, 28-32, 38
Harden, Marcia Gay, 300
Hardman, Cate, 78, 80, 82
Hardwicke, Catherine, 206-207
Hargrave, Doris, 49, 54, 55-57, 60, 62
Harrison, Ken, 185
Harrison, Tina, 172
Hawke, Ethan, 189, 193-194, 197, 212, 214, 305
Hayek, Salma, 142, 277, 287
Haynes, Todd, 139, 309
*Headcheese*, 19. See also *The Texas Chainsaw Massacre*
*Heart Full of Soul* (1990), 99, 307
Heart of Texas Film Festival, 182

Heart of Texas Filmmakers, 90
*Heisters, The* (1965), 10, 19, 51
*Hell of a Note, A*, 51-53
Henkel, Katherine, 21-22
Henkel, Kim: background of, 19; and Hooper, 19-20, 308; and Pennell, 53-54, 59, 62; *The Texas Chainsaw Massacre*, 22, 26, 27, 32, 43, 44; *The Texas Chainsaw Massacre: Next Generation*, 47, 184, 197
Henry, Kyle, 311
Henshaw, Eric, 54, 55, 56
Herman, Dave, 262, 266, 270
Holloway, Doug, 56
*Honeysuckle Rose* (1980), 74, 79
Hooper, Tobe, 3, 10, 11, 15, 53, 61, 182, 220, 225: background of, 19; early career of, 19; and Henkel, 19-20, 308; *Poltergeist*, 10, 308; *The Texas Chainsaw Massacre*, 22-23, 26, 27, 30, 31, 33, 43; *The Texas Chainsaw Massacre Part II*, 46
*Hope Floats* (1998), 200, 217
Hopper, Dennis, 11-12, 46, 307, 310
Houston: film production in, 5-6, 61, 126
Howard, Don, 5-6
Huberman, Brian, 50, 307
Huckabee, Tom, 71
Hugetz, Ed, 129
*Hunger* (Hamsun), 152-153, 155
Hurt, Sam, 70

*Idiocracy* (2006), 306-307
Ignite Entertainment, 232
Independent Feature Film Market (IFFM), 95, 100-101, 104, 113
Independent Images, 82-83, 87, 99
Independent Spirit Awards, 199, 262, 312
International Alliance of Theatrical Stage Employees (IATSE), 237-238
International Creative Management (ICM), 115, 126, 128-132, 138
International Producers Corporation (IPC), 35-36

*Invasion of the Aluminum People* (1980), 71, 89
*Iron Giant, The* (1999), 247

Jacks, Jim, 219; background of, 153, 158; *Dazed and Confused*, 151, 156, 157, 162, 166-170, 172-174, 177-180; and Linklater, 153, 163-164, 165, 177
Jackson, Jim, 92-93
Jackson, Peter, 311
*Jackyl*, 171, 172-173
Jacobson, Larry, 174-175, 179
James, Peter, 205-206, 217
Jarmusch, Jim, 88, 101
*Jaws* (1975), 39, 68, 121
Jernigan, Austin, 90
Jones, G. William, 5-6, 225. *See also* USA Film Festival
Joseph Brenner Associates, 44-45
Josephson, Barry, 185-186
Judge, Mike, 89, 274, 276, 289, 310; background and early career of, 251-253; *Beavis and Butt-head*, 253-255, 257-258, 260; *Idiocracy*, 306-307; *King of the Hill*, 257-259, 260, 266, 272; and Linklater, 252-253, 256, 268; and MTV, 254-256; *Office Space*, 249-250, 260-269, 270-272; and Rodriguez, 256, 261; and Twentieth Century Fox, 256, 261, 263, 267-269, 270-271
*Jumping off Bridges* (2006), 311

Kantor, Barna, 309
Katt, Nicky, 159, 166, 178
Katzenberg, Jeffrey, 74, 131, 227-228
*Kid Blue* (1973), 11-12, 83, 185, 225
Kidd, Richard, 9-10, 51
*King of the Hill* (TV), 257-259, 260, 266, 272
Kirkland, Cyndy, 309
KLRN (TV), 6, 10
KLRU (TV), 85, 90, 96
Knowles, Harry, 218-220, 273, 278-279, 308, 311

Kobrin, Rob, 241-242, 243
Kooris, Richard, 7, 8-10, 33, 71, 77, 79, 90, 96
Kristelis, Keith, 122, 123
Krizan, Kim, 99, 161, 171, 180, 189-190, 192-193, 195
Kuhn, Robert, 15-16, 21-22, 34, 42-47
Kuttruff, Alma, 156, 158, 162, 164

LaFave, Jimmy, 180, 185
Laney, James "Pete," 279-280
Lang, Fritz, 3
Las Colinas, 65
*Last Night at the Alamo* (1984), 62-63
League, Karrie, 47, 310
League, Tim, 47, 310-311
*Leatherface*, 15, 20, 23, 25, 26-27, 32-33. See also *The Texas Chainsaw Massacre*
*Legends of the Fall* (1994), 299, 307
Lellis, George, 66-68
Lewy, Eric, 208, 265, 267
Liatris Media, 182
Liberty Lunch, 91, 98
*Like Water for Chocolate* (1992), 118, 120, 122
Linklater, Richard, 10, 116, 121, 126, 140, 145, 181, 230, 236, 247, 264, 272, 274, 276, 289; and Austin Film Society, 87, 91-94, 109, 111; and Austin Studios, 294, 295-296; background of, 89-91; *Before Sunrise*, 188, 189-190, 192-193, 195; and Daniel, 87, 90, 91-92, 96, 104, 107, 205, 206; *Dazed and Confused*, 151-152, 153-156, 158-174, 175-176, 177, 179-180; *It's Impossible to Learn to Plow by Reading Books*, 93, 94; and Judge, 268; *The Newton Boys*, 191, 195, 196-197, 198, 200, 204-205, 208-212, 214, 216; and Pierson, 104-106, 109, 110; and Rodriguez, 132, 139; *School of Rock*, 304, 305; *Slacker*, 94-100, 101-103, 105-111, 113-114; *SubUrbia*, 198-199, 200; *Tape*, 305;

and Tarantino, 203, 204, 215; and Texas Film Hall of Fame, 1, 303; and Tina Harrison, 172; and Twentieth Century Fox, 196, 210; and Universal Pictures, 158, 160, 162-163, 165, 177; and UT-Austin RTF program, 216-217; *Waking Life*, 304-305

Liquid Television, 254-255

Livingston, Ron, 249-250, 262-265, 269, 270, 272

Logan, Richard, 34, 38

*Lone Star Kid, The* (1988), 86

*Lonesome Dove* (TV), 78, 155, 187, 307

Longley, Joe K., 34, 39, 45, 72

Lowrey, Amy, 107, 196

Lowry, Ed, 65-71, 83, 209

Lucas, George, 287, 290, 304

Lumet, Sidney, 14, 19, 24

MAB, 21-22, 35, 37, 40-44. See also *The Texas Chainsaw Massacre*

MacCambridge, Michael, 183, 185-186

"Made in Texas," 65, 71, 82

"Made in Texas, Part II," 82, 83

Majestic Theatre, 5. *See also* Paramount Theatre

Malick, Terrence, 93, 300, 303

Margulies, Julianna, 200, 212

Martin, Gary, 145-146, 147, 288, 306

Martinez, Lizzie, 201

Maverick Films, Inc., 54, 61

MCA Records, 75, 170, 173-175

McCall, John "Shampoo King," 276

McCanlies, Suzanne, 221, 233, 234, 235-236, 239, 240; and Tim McCanlies, 228-229, 230-231, 248

McCanlies, Tim, 250, 301; and Austin Film Festival, 186, 230; background of, 224-226; *Dancer, Texas Pop. 81*, 221-222, 223-224, 228-229, 231-236, 238-244, 246; early career of, 226-227; *The Iron Giant*, 231, 239-240, 247; and Linklater, 221, 230-231; and Rodriguez, 221, 230-231; as script doctor, 229-230; *Secondhand Lions*, 232, 247-248, 304, 305-306;

and Suzanne McCanlies, 228-229; *The Two Bobs*, 314; and Walt Disney Co., 227-228

McConaughey, Matthew, 197-198, 217; *Dazed and Confused*, 150-151, 164, 166-167; *The Newton Boys*, 198, 199-200, 201, 204, 207

McMinn, Teri, 28-29

McMurtry, Larry, 24, 78, 187

*Mean Streets* (1973), 68, 165, 191

Mechanic, Bill, 196, 211, 213, 218, 263, 268, 271

*Melvin and Howard* (1980), 63, 71, 157, 244

Meredith, Jack, 90, 91, 95

Mestres, Ricardo, 227-228, 229

Mex-American, 127-128, 129-130, 131

Meyer, Breckin, 233-234, 239

Middleton, David, 191, 208

Milam, Marsha, 180-185

Miller, Earl, 10-11

Miller, Fred, 10, 182

Mills, Eddie, 233-234, 239, 243

Mims, Steve, 119, 129, 141, 309

Miramax, 129, 130, 132-133, 145-146, 147-149, 275

*Miss Congeniality* (2000), 280

Montgomery, Denise (D.), 93, 96, 101, 114, 155, 176, 193, 209, 313

Moore, Michael, 100-101, 104, 113

Morgan, Barbara, 180-186

Morocco, Francesca, 251, 256

Morris, George, 4, 91-92, 93, 209

Moser, Margaret, 69

Motion Picture Association of America (MPAA), 14, 176

Motion Picture Productions of Texas, 9. *See also* Filmhouse

Mount, Thom, 59

MTV, 196, 250, 252, 254-256, 260

Mumblecore, 312

Museum of Light, 8

Nafus, Chale, 2, 90, 92, 203, 292, 303

Naidu, Ajay, 199, 249, 262

National Endowment for the Arts (NEA), 62, 202

Neal, Ed, 25, 27, 30, 41

*Ned Blessing: The True Story of My Life & Times* (1993), 187, 307

Nelson, Kathy, 170, 171, 172, 175, 331n59

Nelson, Lana, 80

Nelson, Willie, 51, 72, 75-76, 77-78, 79-82, 84-85

Netflix, 312

New Directors/New Films (Museum of Modern Art), 60, 109

New Hollywood, 2

New Line Cinema, 44-46, 58, 60, 248, 304

New Music Seminar, 182

New World Pictures, 36

New York Film Festival, 12, 63, 106

Newman, Robert, 115, 124, 126-132, 135

*Newton Boys, The* (1998): and Austin Film Society, 212; box office, 213; casting, 197-198, 199, 200-201; critical reception, 212-213, 219; post-production, 208-210; preproduction, 200, 204-206; production, 206-207; screenplay, 190-192, 194-195; sound-track, 206, 209; and SXSW, 211-212; and Twentieth Century Fox, 198

Nicolaou, Sally, 23, 30

Nicolaou, Ted, 9, 23, 26, 31, 33, 38

*Night in Old Mexico, A* (screenplay), 307

*Night of the Living Dead* (1968), 20, 39

*No Longer/Not Yet*, 95, 99. See also *Slacker*

Obst, Linda, 117, 217-218, 294

*Office Space* (1999), 276, 306; box office and critical reception, 269-270; cult status of, 271-272; development, 252, 260-261, 266; home video and DVD release, 271; postproduction, 264, 265, 267-268; preproduction, 261-263; production, 249-250, 263-266; and Twentieth Century Fox, 267-268

*Once Upon a Time in Mexico* (2003), 287, 290-291, 306

Orion Classics, 113-114

Other Cinema, 93

Ovitz, Michael, 74

Page, Jimmy, 171, 173, 174

Pahl Film, 61

Palotta, Tommy, 98

Panitch, Sanford, 270-271

Paragon Feature Film Company, 5

Paramount Pictures, 122, 131, 158, 227, 228, 237, 255, 260, 304

Paramount Theatre, 5, 212, 237, 243, 284

Parrington, Catherine, 313

Parsley, Bill, 3, 13-14, 15, 21-22, 26-27, 32-34, 40-44

Partain, Paul, 25

*Passion of the Christ, The* (2004), 311

Pastor, Deb, 96, 155

Pathe Freres, 4

Pearl, Daniel, 9, 18, 22, 23, 26-27, 30-33, 38, 47

Pearl, Dorothy (Dottie), 23, 24, 29, 31, 38, 308

Peckinpah, Sam, 13, 14, 76, 85, 91

Penn, Sean, 157, 198

Pennell, Eagle, 3, 75, 88, 98-99, 181, 184, 224; background of, 50-51; death of, 308; drug and alcohol abuse, 56, 59, 60, 308; *A Hell of a Note*, 51-53; and Henkel, 53-54, 59, 62; *The King of Texas*, 307, 308; *Last Night at the Alamo*, 62-63; and Sutherland, 53, 56-57, 58, 60-61; *The Whole Shootin' Match*, 48-49, 53-57, 58-59

Peraino, Anthony, 36

Peraino, Joseph C., 36-37

Peraino, Joseph S., 36, 43

Peraino, Louis "Butchie," 36-37, 40-41, 42-43, 44. See also Bryanston Pictures

*Perfect Storm, The* (2000), 299, 307

Perry, Rick (Governor), 313

Perryman, Lou, 30-31, 46, 48, 51-57, 60, 62

Perryman, Ron, 10

*Peter, Paul & Mary: Song is Love* (1970), 10, 182

Peters, Elizabeth, 202-203, 291-292

Pfeiffer, Carolyn, 312

Phillips, Don, 152, 156-157, 158-162, 197, 201, 210

Photo Processors, 48

Pickle, Gary, 9-10

Pickle, Jake, 92

Pie in the Sky (P.I.T.S.), 35, 38, 39, 41, 45. See also *The Texas Chainsaw Massacre*

Pierce, Jo Carol, 180

Pierson, Janet, 217

Pierson, John: background of, 103-104, 217; and Linklater, 146, 177, 215; *Slacker*, 103-104, 105-107, 108, 111, 112, 113-114

Pinnell, Chuck, 50, 52, 55, 57, 60, 63, 308

Pipkin, Turk, 301

Plant, Robert, 174

Poi Dog Pondering, 108, 205, 313

Policy, Ron, 7, 8, 66

*Political Touchdown, A* (1915), 5

Poyser, Brian, 311-312

Price, Gary, 90-91, 99, 106, 107, 112

*Puffy Chair, The* (2005), 312

*Pulp Fiction* (1994), 111, 146, 147, 189, 202-204, 212, 219

Purvis, Stephen, 84

Pyle, Charles C., 4-5

Quinn, Suzanne, 296-297, 310, 313

*Raggedy Man* (1981), 70-71, 73, 77, 300

Rapp, Anne, 1

Raul's, 69

Ray, Nicholas, 166, 192

*Rebel Without a Cause* (1955), 166, 178

Rector, Ken, 237

*Red Headed Stranger* (1986), 75, 156, 185, 187, 233, 279, 307; box office and critical reception, 84-85; financing, 72, 76; postproduction, 83-84; preproduction, 78-79; production, 79-82

Reddick, DeWitt, 6

Redford, Robert, 49, 58-59, 75, 195

Reel Women, 309, 311

Reinert, Al, 185, 200

Reinninger, Larry, 71

Remmert, Fred, 108

Rennie, Dave, 264-265, 267

Republic of Texas Film Festival, 182, 185. See also Austin Film Festival

Republic of Texas, 221, 222, 223, 239

*Reservoir Dogs* (1992), 50, 130, 135-136, 170, 219

*Return of El Mariachi, The*, 142. See also *Desperado*

*Return of the Texas Chainsaw Massacre* (1994), 184, 197. See also *The Texas Chainsaw Massacre: The Next Generation*

Rhodes, Scott, 100-101, 107, 112, 156

Rice, Peter, 210, 219

Richards, Ann, 2, 124-126, 232, 301

Richardson, Sallye, 34, 35

Ritz Theater, 51

*Rivethead: Tales From the Assembly Line* (Hamper), 215-216

Roach, Neil, 74, 78, 79-82

*Roadracers* (1994), 141-143

Roberts, Jack, 44-45

Roche, Jim, 95

Rochester, Art, 80

Rockwell, Alexander, 145-146

Rodriguez, Cecilio, 117

Rodriguez, Maricarmen, 119

Rodriguez, Rebel Antonio, 282

Rodriguez, Robert, 3, 65, 150, 188, 220, 221, 247, 250, 256, 297; and Avellán, 118, 147, 149, 273, 274, 291, 306; background of, 116-118; and Bob Weinstein, 276, 285; and Columbia Pictures, 115-116, 131, 132; conversion to digital filmmaking, 287, 290; *El Mariachi*, 120-124, 127-129, 132-136, 138-141; *The Faculty*, 276-278; and family, 147, 273, 282; *Four Rooms*, 145-146; *From Dusk Till Dawn*, 146-148; and Gallardo, 137,

143, 144; and Harvey Weinstein, 136; and Judge, 256, 261; and Link-later, 132, 139; and Los Hooligans, 148, 280; and Miramax, 129, 130, 132, 147-149, 275; and Pharmaco, 120-122; *Roadracers*, 141-142; *Sin City*, 291, 306; *Spy Kids*, 275-276, 278, 282-286, 287; and Tarantino, 137, 146; and UT-Austin RTF program, 117-118, 119-120, 132, 141, 216-217

Rodriguez Avellán, Racer Maximiliano, 273, 282

Rodriguez Avellán, Rocket Valentino, 147, 273, 282

*Roger & Me* (1989), 88, 100, 104, 107, 113

*Room* (2005), 311-312

Root, Stephen, 258-259, 262, 264, 266, 268, 270, 271

Ross, Katharine, 79-80

Rothman, Tom, 267, 269

Royal, Darrell, 72, 75, 76, 82

Rubin, Mark, 205, 209

Sabara, Daryl, 281, 282, 285, 288, 291

Sabiston, Bob, 305

Saenz, Richard, 22

San Antonio: film production in, 5

Saritzky, Marlene, 5, 125-126, 180, 182-185, 230, 232

Satex Film Company, 4-5

*Saturday Night*, 51. See also *A Hell of a Note*

Savisky, Luke, 312-313

Sayles, John, 65, 70, 82-83, 87-88, 198, 200, 295, 305-306

Schafer, Nancy, 184, 185

Schatz, Thomas (Tom), 7, 61, 66, 68, 129, 312

*School of Rock* (2003), 304-305

Schwartz, Russell, 169-170, 171, 175, 176, 177, 178

Scorsese, Martin, 2, 95, 295

Scott, Bill, 7, 187, 236-237, 276-278, 280, 282-283, 288-289

Scott, Jeanette, 213, 276, 277, 289

Scott, Tony, 12

*Scream* (1996), 201, 274, 278, 279

Screen Generation Film Festival, 5. *See also* USA Film Festival

*Secondhand Lions* (2003), 232, 247, 248, 304, 305-306, 307

Sedwick, Shannon, 8

*sex, lies, and videotape* (1989), 88, 129

*Shadow of the Virgin Gold* (c. 1913), 5

Shahan, James T. "Happy," 5

Shapiro, Chuck, 91

Shaye, Bob, 45. *See also* New Line Cinema

Shelton, Michael, 8

*She's Gotta Have It* (1985), 88, 95, 103, 105

Shootout Films, 9-11, 19, 22, 23, 33, 47

Shrake, Bud, 7, 11-12, 185, 220, 222-223, 225, 303, 310; *Red Headed Stranger*, 71-73, 76, 82-83

Siedow, Jim, 24-25, 30, 46

Simpson, Don, 83

Simpson, Mike, 12-13, 83, 126, 299-300, 302

*Simpsons, The* (TV), 231, 258, 259

Sims, Judith, 92, 129, 292, 297

*Sin City* (2005), 291, 306

Singleton, John, 116, 132

Siskel, Gene, 49, 61, 176, 255

Skaaren, Warren, 83; background of, 12-13; death of, 130; *The Texas Chainsaw Massacre*, 15-16, 21, 35-36, 42, 46; and Texas Film Commission, 13, 14-16; and Wittliff, 73-74, 87

*Slacker* (1991), 3-4, 49, 132, 140, 195, 216, 230, 313-314; and Austin Film Society, 111; book, 112, 114; box office, 112; critical reception, 103, 104-105, 109, 110, 111, 112; development, 94, 95-96; distribution, 104, 106, 111, 112; and festivals, 102-103, 108, 109; home video release, 113-114; marketing, 110-111; and New Directors/New Films, 109-110; and Orion Classics, 106-107, 108, 110-111, 112-114; postproduction,

100-102, 107; preproduction, 96-97; production, 97-100

Slate, John, 94, 97

Sloss, John, 157, 175

Smalley, Scott, 209

Smith, Artie, 83-84

Smith, Evan, 1-2, 200, 217, 297-301

Smith, Julia Null, 126, 218

Smith, Kevin, 275, 310

Smith, Liz, 299, 301

Smith, Lory, 58-59

Smith, Preston, 12-13

Soap Creek Saloon, 52

Soderbergh, Steven, 88-89, 105, 129

*Something Wild* (1986), 71

Sony Pictures Classics, 7, 113, 199

South by Southwest Film and Media Conference (SFMC), 184. *See also* South by Southwest Film Festival (SXSW)

South by Southwest Film Festival (SXSW), 1, 152, 182-186, 217, 220, 243, 296, 310

South by Southwest Music Festival (SXSW), 182

Southwest Alternate Media Project (SWAMP), 6, 61-62, 82, 98-99, 101, 202, 307

Spacek, Sissy, 1, 70, 300-301, 302-303

Spears, Bee, 81

*Speed of Light* (1980), 71, 90

Spielberg, Steven, 2, 14, 121, 201, 308

Spike and Mike's Sick and Twisted Festival of Animation, 253, 254

Spiro, Ellen, 217

*Spy Kids* (2001), 3-4, 148; box office and critical reception, 284, 285-286; casting, 280-282; development, 275-276; home video release, 288; marketing, 278-279, 284; postproduction, 283-284, 287; preproduction, 282; production, 279, 282-283

*Spy Kids 2: Island of Lost Dreams* (2002), 288-291

*Spy Kids 3-D: Game Over* (2003), 291

Stanush, Claude, 190-192, 194, 195, 204-205, 208, 212-214

Steinbomer, Robert, 147, 279

Stekler, Paul, 217

Stone, Oliver, 219, 280, 310

*Stranger Than Paradise* (1984), 88, 95

Student Association Film Program, 66. *See also* Cinema 40

*SubUrbia* (1996), 198-199, 200

Suhrstedt, Tim, 250, 261, 263-265, 267, 268, 272

Sundance Film Festival, 49, 88, 102, 108, 109, 129, 130, 137-139, 195, 199, 243, 312

Sundance Film Institute, 49, 59, 82

Sutherland, Lin: background of, 53; and Pennell, 53, 56-57, 58, 60-61; *The Whole Shootin' Match*, 48, 49, 53-54, 57-58, 61

Taggart, Patrick, 39, 105

Tanen, Ned, 43

*Tape* (2001), 304-305

Tarantino, Quentin, 1, 49-50, 111, 130, 189, 292, 310; and Austin Film Society, 203-204; and Knowles, 219; and Linklater, 203-204; and QT Fest, 203, 311; and Rodriguez, 137, 146, 291; and Texas Film Hall of Fame, 300, 302

Taylor, Teresa, 98, 110

*Territory, The* (TV), 129

*Texas Chainsaw Massacre Part II, The* (1986), 46, 308

*Texas Chainsaw Massacre, The* (1974), 3-4, 9, 11, 48, 51, 52, 58, 280; box office, 39, 40, 43-44, 45-46; casting, 24-26; critical reception, 39; cult status of, 18, 39, 46; distribution, 35-38, 45; financing, 21-22; postproduction, 32-35, 318n42; production, 17, 26-32, 318n30

*Texas Chainsaw Massacre, The* (2003), 47

*Texas Chainsaw Massacre: The Next Generation, The* (1997), 47. See also *Return of the Texas Chainsaw Massacre*

Texas Commission on the Arts, 92, 93

Texas Film Commission, 12-14, 15-16, 124, 125-126, 317n33

Texas Film Festival, 181–182
Texas Film Hall of Fame, 1–2, 297–303
Texas Filmmakers' Production Fund
  (TFPF), 202, 203. *See also* Austin Film
  Society
Texas Instruments (band), 90, 108
*Texas Monthly*, 1, 4, 15, 51, 73, 184, 185,
  217–218, 297–299
Texas Motion Picture Service (TMPS),
  10–11, 167, 208, 293
Texas Pacific Film, 9, 90
Texas Theater, 7
Texas Union film series, 309
*Their Lives By a Thread* (c. 1913), 5
Third Coast, 3, 64, 187, 220
Third Wave International Women's Film
  and Video Festival, 182
Thompson, Tommy, 78, 79, 80
*Ties That Bind*, 228, 229. See also *Dancer,*
  *Texas Pop. 81*
Tilley, Paul, 4–5
Tilley, W. Hope, 4–5
Todd, Connie, 78–79, 83
Torn, Rip, 1, 300, 302
Townsend, Tommy, 34
Trilogy Entertainment, 130, 131–132
TriStar Pictures, 130–132, 147, 236,
  238, 241–242, 244, 246
Troublemaker Studios, 279–280, 289–
  290, 291, 306, 314
Tsangari, Rachel, 309
Twentieth Century Fox, 12, 36, 146, 294,
  306; and *The Newton Boys*, 188, 196–
  198, 200–201, 205–206, 209–211,
  213–214, 217, 219; and *Office Space*,
  267–268
*Two Bobs, The* (2009), 314
2009 Texas film incentives program, 313

U.S. Film Festival, 49, 58–59, 129. *See*
  *also* Sundance Film Festival
Ulrich, Skeet, 201, 204, 212
Unions: growth in Texas, 236–238
Universal Pictures: and *Dazed and Con-*
  *fused*, 150–151, 153, 155–160, 162,
  165, 167, 168–171, 172–178, 180;

and Linklater, 158, 160, 162–163,
  165, 177; and Pennell, 49, 53, 59–60;
  and *The Texas Chainsaw Massacre*,
  18, 36, 43
University Film Program Committee
  (UFPC), 7–8
University of Texas at Austin, 7–8
University of Texas at Austin Dept. of
  Radio-Television-Film (RTF), 3, 19,
  50, 51, 64, 66–68, 77, 90, 103, 115,
  167, 202, 224, 309, 311; creation of,
  6–9, 11; in 1990s, 216–217
University of Texas Film Institute (UTFI),
  312
Uranium Savages, 51
USA Film Festival, 6, 57, 58, 63, 102,
  225, 244

Vail, Bill, 25, 27–28, 29
Valdes, David, 185–186, 307
Valenti, Jack, 14
Varsity Theater, 2, 7, 83, 95
Vaughn, Jacob, 311–312
Vega, Alexa, 281, 282–283, 284–285,
  288
Vortex, 22, 34–35, 37, 40–45. See also
  *The Texas Chainsaw Massacre*

Wade, Bob, 300
*Waking Life* (2001), 216, 304–305
Walker, Clark: and Austin Film Society,
  93; background of, 92–93; *Before Sun-*
  *rise*, 190, 193; *Dazed and Confused*,
  154, 155, 158; on Linklater, 88, 162,
  165; *The Newton Boys*, 190–192, 194–
  196, 197–198; *Slacker*, 95, 96, 100,
  101, 106, 107; and Walker-McBay, 96,
  194–195
Walker, Jim, 294
Walker-McBay, Anne, 314; *Before Sunrise*,
  180, 190, 193; and Clark Walker, 96,
  194–195; *Dazed and Confused*, 155–
  157, 160, 162–163, 167, 168, 171,
  173, 176, 179; *The Newton Boys*, 192,
  194, 196–201, 209–210, 215; *Slacker*,
  96–97, 104

Walt Disney Company, 130-131, 222, 223, 227-230, 247
Walters, Chris, 105, 114
Warhol, Andy, 8, 36
Warner Bros., 4-5, 36, 104, 158, 174, 224, 230-232, 247, 255, 307-308
Watson, Kirk, 293-295
WDR, 61, 101
Weinstein, Bob, 116, 219, 277-278, 283, 285
Weinstein, Harvey, 116, 133, 136, 142, 147, 148, 273, 283
Weinstein, Max, 129
Weinstein, Miriam, 129
Welles, Orson, 121
Whistler, Sarah, 70
Whitaker, Rod, 6-7
White, Cary, 76-78, 85, 88, 187, 276, 282, 288-289
Whitman, Charles, 6, 34
Whittington, Jeff, 70
*Whole Shootin' Match, The* (1978): critical reception, 57, 60, 61; development,

53-54; distribution, 58, 60, 61; and festivals, 49, 57, 58-59; production, 48-49, 55-56; soundtrack, 54-55, 57; and Sundance Institute, 49
Wiggins, Wiley, 155, 161, 163-164, 167-168
Williams, Anson, 85-86
Williams, Eric, 65, 84-85, 187, 278-279
Williamson, Kevin, 274-275, 278
Wittliff, Bill, 34, 89, 156, 220; and Austin Film Festival, 185, 187; background of, 72; early career of, 73-74; later career of, 187, 307; and Nelson, 72, 75-76; and *Red Headed Stranger,* 75-76, 77, 79, 80-81, 83-85; and Texas Film Hall of Fame, 1, 299-301, 303
*Woodshock* (1985), 91, 182
Writers Guild of America, West, 229

Yoakam, Dwight, 201, 205, 212

Zellweger, Renée, 47, 152, 159, 164